Basics of

Web Design

HTML5 & CSS3

Fourth Edition

Basics of

Web Design

HTML5 & CSS3

Fourth Edition

Terry Ann Felke-Morris, Ed.D.

Professor Emerita

Harper College

Pearson

330 Hudson Street, NY NY 10013

Senior Vice President, Portfolio Management, Engineering and Computer Science: Marcia Horton
Director, Portfolio Management: Julian Partridge
Executive Portfolio Manager: Matt Goldstein
Portfolio Management Assistant: Kristy Alaura
Product Marketing Manager: Yvonne Vannatta
Field Marketing Manager: Demetrius Hall
Marketing Assistant: Jon Bryant
Managing Producer: Scott Disanno
Content Producer: Erin Ault

Operations Specialist: Maura Zaldivar-Garcia
Manager, Rights and Permissions: Ben Ferrini
Cover Designer: Joyce Wells
Cover Art: Warut Prathaksithorn/123RF
Printer/Binder: LSC Communications
Cover Printer: Phoenix Color/Hagerstown
Full-Service Project Management: Prathiba Rajagopal, SPi Global
Composition: SPi Global
Text Font: ITC Franklin Gothic Std

The author has created a variety of fictitious names, company names, e-mail addresses, URLs, phone numbers, fax numbers, and other similar items for the purposes of illustrating the concepts and techniques described within this textbook. Any resemblance of these fictitious items to any person, company/organization, or location is unintentional and purely coincidental.

Credits and acknowledgments borrowed from other sources and reproduced, with permission, in this textbook appear on the appropriate page within text.

Library of Congress Cataloging-in-Publication Data

Names: Felke-Morris, Terry, author.
Title: Basics of web design : HTML5 & CSS3 / Terry Ann Felke-Morris, Ed.D., Professor Emerita, Harper College.
Description: Fourth edition. | Includes index.
Identifiers: LCCN 2016054602| ISBN 9780134444338 (alk. paper) | ISBN 0134444337 (alk. paper)
Subjects: LCSH: HTML (Document markup language) | Cascading style sheets. | Web site development—Computer programs. | Web sites—Design.
Classification: LCC QA76.76.H94 F455 2017 | DDC 006.7/4—dc23 LC record available at https://lccn.loc.gov/2016054602

 Pearson

2 17

ISBN 10: 0-13-444433-7
ISBN 13: 978-0-13-444433-8

Preface

Basics of Web Design: HTML5 & CSS3 is intended for use in a beginning web design or web development course. Topics are introduced in two-page sections that focus on key points and often include a hands-on practice exercise. The text covers the basics that web designers need to develop their skills:

- Introductory Internet and World Wide Web concepts
- Creating web pages with HTML5
- Configuring text, color, and page layout with Cascading Style Sheets
- Configuring images and multimedia on web pages
- Exploring new CSS3 properties
- Web design best practices
- Accessibility, usability, and search engine optimization considerations
- Obtaining a domain name and a web host
- Publishing to the Web

Student files are available for download from the companion website for this book at www.pearsonhighered.com/cs-resources. These files include solutions to the Hands-On Practice exercises, starter files for the Hands-On Practice exercises, and the starter files for the Case Study. See the access information on the inside front cover of this book for further instructions.

Building on this textbook's successful third edition, the fourth edition features:

- Additional Hands-On Practice exercises
- Updated code samples, case studies, and web resources
- Updates for HTML5.1 elements and attributes
- Expanded treatment of page layout design
- Expanded coverage of responsive web design techniques and CSS media queries
- Expanded coverage of responsive image techniques including the new HTML5 picture element
- Updated reference sections for HTML5 and CSS
- New Appendix introducing the CSS Flexible Layout Module: Flexbox

Features of the Text

Design for Today and Tomorrow. The textbook prepares students to design web pages that work today in addition to being ready to take advantage of new HTML5 coding techniques of the future.

Well-Rounded Selection of Topics. This text includes both "hard" skills such as HTML5 and Cascading Style Sheets (Chapters 1–2 and 4–11) and "soft" skills such as web design (Chapter 3) and publishing to the Web (Chapter 12). This well-rounded foundation will help students as they pursue careers as web professionals. Students and instructors will find classes more interesting because they can discuss, integrate, and apply both hard and soft skills as students create web pages and websites. The topics in each chapter are introduced on concise two-page sections that are intended to provide quick overviews and timely practice with the topic.

Two-Page Topic Sections. Most topics are introduced in a concise, two-page section. Many sections also include immediate hands-on practice of the new skill or concept. This approach is intended to appeal to your busy students—especially the millennial multitaskers—who need to drill down to the important concepts right away.

Hands-On Practice. Web design is a skill, and skills are best learned by hands-on practice. This text emphasizes hands-on practice through practice exercises within the chapters, end-of-chapter exercises, and the development of a website through ongoing real-world case studies. The variety of exercises provides instructors with a choice of assignments for a particular course or semester.

Website Case Study. There are case studies that continue throughout most of the text (beginning at Chapter 2). The case studies serve to reinforce skills discussed in each chapter. Sample solutions to the case study exercises are available on the Instructor Resource Center at http://www.pearsonhighered.com/irc.

Focus on Web Design. Every chapter offers an additional activity that explores web design topics related to the chapter. These activities can be used to reinforce, extend, and enhance the course topics.

FAQs. In her web design courses, the author is frequently asked similar questions by students. They are included in the book and are marked with the identifying FAQ icon.

Focus on Accessibility. Developing accessible websites is more important than ever, and this text is infused with accessibility techniques throughout. The special icon shown here makes accessibility information easy to find.

Focus on Ethics. Ethics issues as related to web development are highlighted throughout the text with the special ethics icon shown here.

Quick Tips. Quick tips, which provide useful background information, or help with productivity, are indicated with this Quick Tip icon.

Explore Further. The special icon identifies enrichment topics along with web resources useful for delving deeper into a concept introduced in book.

Reference Materials. The appendices offer reference material, including an HTML5 reference, a Cascading Style Sheets reference, a comparison of HTML5 and XHTML, a WCAG 2.0 Quick Reference, an overview of ARIA Landmark Roles, and a brief introduction to CSS Flexible Box Layout (Flexbox).

VideoNotes. VideoNotes are Pearson's new visual tool designed for teaching students key programming concepts and techniques. These short step-by-step videos demonstrate how to solve problems from design through coding. VideoNotes allow for self-placed instruction with easy navigation including the ability to select, play, rewind, fast-forward, and stop within each VideoNote exercise. Margin icons in your textbook let you know when a VideoNote video is available for a particular concept or hands-on practice.

Supplemental Materials

Student Resources. Student files for the case studies and the web page hands-on practice exercises, and access to the book's VideoNotes are available to all readers of this book at its companion website www.pearsonhighered.com/cs-resources. A complimentary access code for the companion website is available with a new copy of this book. Subscriptions may also be purchased online.

Instructor Resources. The following supplements are available to qualified instructors only. Visit the Pearson Instructor Resource Center (http://www.pearsonhighered.com/irc) for information on how to access them:

- Solutions to the end-of-chapter exercises
- Solutions for the case study assignments
- Test questions
- PowerPoint® presentations
- Sample syllabi

Author's Website. In addition to the publisher's companion website for this book, the author maintains a website at http://www.webdevbasics.net. This website contains additional resources, including a color chart, learning/review games, and a page for each chapter with examples, links, and updates. This website is not supported by the publisher.

Acknowledgments

Very special thanks go to the people at Pearson, including Matt Goldstein, Kristy Alaura, and Erin Ault.

A special thank you also goes to Enrique D'Amico at Harper College for taking time to provide additional feedback and sharing student comments about the book.

Most of all, I would like to thank my family for their patience and encouragement. My wonderful husband, Greg Morris, has been a constant source of love, understanding, support, and encouragement. Thank you, Greg! A big shout-out to my children, James and Karen, who grew up thinking that everyone's Mom had their own website. Thank you both for your understanding, patience, and timely suggestions. Finally, a very special dedication to the memory of my father who will be greatly missed.

About the Author

Dr. Terry Ann Felke-Morris is a Professor Emerita at Harper College in Palatine, Illinois. She holds a Doctor of Education degree, a Master of Science degree in information systems, and numerous certifications, including Adobe Certified Dreamweaver 8 Developer, WOW Certified Associate Webmaster, Microsoft Certified Professional, Master CIW Designer, and CIW Certified Instructor.

Dr. Felke-Morris received the Blackboard Greenhouse Exemplary Online Course Award in 2006 for use of Internet technology in the academic environment. She is the recipient of two international awards: the Instructional Technology Council's Outstanding e-Learning Faculty Award for Excellence and the MERLOT Award for Exemplary Online Learning Resources—MERLOT Business Classics.

With more than 25 years of information technology experience in business and industry, Dr. Felke-Morris published her first website in 1996 and has been working with the Web ever since. A long-time promoter of web standards, she was a member of the Web Standards Project Education Task Force. Dr. Felke-Morris is the author of the popular textbook *Web Development and Design Foundations with HTML5*, currently in its eighth edition. She was instrumental in developing the Web Development degree and certificate programs at Harper College. For more information about Dr. Terry Ann Felke-Morris, visit http://terrymorris.net.

CONTENTS

CHAPTER 11

Media and Interactivity Basics   355

CHAPTER 12

Web Publishing Basics   391

APPENDIX

VideoNotes

VideoNote

Locations of **VideoNotes**
www.pearsonhighered.com/cs-resources

Internet and Web Basics

The Internet and the Web are parts of our daily lives. How did they begin? What networking protocols and programming languages work behind the scenes to display a web page? This chapter provides an introduction to some of these topics and is a foundation for the information that web developers need to know. This chapter also gets you started with your very first web page. You'll be introduced to Hypertext Markup Language (HTML), the language used to create web pages.

You'll learn how to...

- Describe the evolution of the Internet and the Web
- Explain the need for web standards
- Describe universal design
- Identify benefits of accessible web design
- Identify reliable resources of information on the Web
- Identify ethical uses of the Web
- Describe the purpose of web browsers and web servers

- Identify Internet protocols
- Define URIs and domain names
- Describe HTML, XHTML, and HTML5
- Create your first web page
- Use the body, head, title, and meta elements
- Name, save, and test a web page

The Internet and the Web

The Internet

The **Internet**, the interconnected network of computer networks, seems to be everywhere today. You can't watch television or listen to the radio without being urged to visit a website. Even newspapers and magazines have their place on the Internet. It is possible that you may be reading an electronic copy of this book that you downloaded over the Internet. With the increased use of mobile devices such as tablets and smartphones, being connected to the Internet has become part of our daily lives.

The Birth of the Internet

The Internet began as a network to connect computers at research facilities and universities. Messages in this network would travel to their destinations by multiple routes or paths, allowing the network to function even if parts of it were broken or destroyed. The message would be rerouted through a functioning portion of the network while traveling to its destination. This network was developed by the Advanced Research Projects Agency (ARPA)—and the ARPAnet was born. Four computers (located at UCLA, Stanford Research Institute, University of California Santa Barbara, and the University of Utah) were connected by the end of 1969.

Growth of the Internet

As time went on, other networks, such as the National Science Foundation's NSFnet, were created and connected with the ARPAnet. Use of this interconnected network, or Internet, was originally limited to government, research, and educational purposes. The ban on commercial use of the Internet was lifted in 1991.

The growth of the Internet continues—Internet World Stats (http://www.internetworldstats .com/stats.htm) reported that over 3.6 billion users, about 49% of the world's population, were using the Internet by 2016.

When the restriction on commercial use of the Internet was lifted, the stage was set for future electronic commerce: businesses were now welcome on the Internet. However, while businesses were no longer banned, the Internet was still text based and not easy to use. The next developments addressed this issue.

The Birth of the Web

VideoNote
Evolution of the Web

While working at CERN, a research facility in Switzerland, Tim Berners-Lee envisioned a means of communication for scientists by which they could easily "hyperlink" to another research paper or article and immediately view it. Berners-Lee created the **World Wide Web** to fulfill this need. In 1991, Berners-Lee posted the code in a newsgroup and made it freely available. This version of the World Wide Web used **Hypertext Transfer Protocol (HTTP)** to communicate between the client computer and the web server, and it was text based, employing **Hypertext Markup Language (HTML)** to format the documents.

The First Graphical Browser

In 1993, Mosaic, the first graphical web browser, became available. Marc Andreessen and graduate students working at the National Center for Supercomputing Applications (NCSA) at the University of Illinois Urbana-Champaign developed Mosaic. Some individuals in this group later created another well-known web browser, Netscape Navigator, which is an ancestor of today's Mozilla Firefox browser.

Convergence of Technologies

By the early 1990s, personal computers with easy-to-use graphical operating systems (such as Microsoft's Windows, IBM's OS/2, and Apple's Macintosh OS) were increasingly available and affordable. Online service providers such as CompuServe, AOL, and Prodigy offered low-cost connections to the Internet. Figure 1.1 depicts this convergence of available computer hardware, easy-to-use operating systems, low-cost Internet connectivity, the HTTP protocol and HTML language, and a graphical browser that made information on the Internet much easier to access. The **World Wide Web**—the graphical user interface providing access to information stored on web servers connected to the Internet—had arrived!

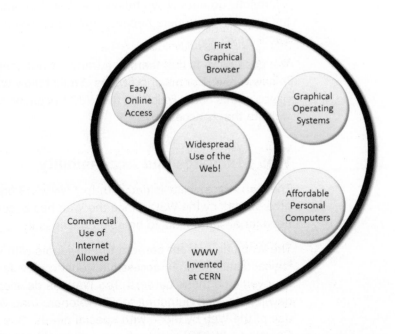

FIGURE 1.1 *Convergence of technologies.*

Web Standards and Accessibility

You are probably aware that no single person or group runs the World Wide Web. However, the **World Wide Web Consortium** (http://www.w3.org), commonly referred to as the **W3C**, takes a proactive role in developing recommendations and prototype technologies related to the Web. Topics that the W3C addresses include web architecture, standards for web design, and accessibility. In an effort to standardize web technologies, the W3C produces guidelines called recommendations.

W3C Recommendations

The W3C Recommendations are created in working groups with input from many major corporations involved in building web technologies. These recommendations are not rules; they are guidelines. Major software companies that build web browsers, such as Microsoft, do not always follow the W3C Recommendations. This makes life challenging for web developers because not all browsers will display a web page in exactly the same way.

The good news is that there is a trend toward conforming to the W3C Recommendations in new versions of major browsers. You'll follow W3C Recommendations as you code web pages in this book. Following the W3C Recommendations is the first step toward creating a website that is accessible.

Web Standards and Accessibility

The Web Accessibility Initiative (http://www.w3.org/WAI), referred to as the WAI, is a major area of work by the W3C. Since the Web has become an integral part of daily life, there is a need for all individuals to be able to access it.

The Web can present barriers to individuals with visual, auditory, physical, and neurological disabilities. An **accessible** website provides accommodations that help individuals overcome these barriers. The WAI has developed recommendations for web content developers, web authoring tool developers, and web browser developers to facilitate use of the Web by those with special needs. See the WAI's Web Content Accessibility Guidelines (WCAG) at http://www.w3.org/WAI/WCAG20/glance/WCAG2-at-a-Glance.pdf for a quick overview.

Accessibility and the Law

The **Americans with Disabilities Act (ADA)** of 1990 is a federal civil rights law that prohibits discrimination against people with disabilities. The ADA requires that business, federal, and state services are accessible to individuals with disabilities. A 1996 Department of Justice ruling (http://www.justice.gov/crt/foia/readingroom/frequent_requests/ada_coreletter/cltr204.txt) indicated that ADA accessibility requirements apply to Internet resources.

Section 508 of the Federal Rehabilitation Act was amended in 1998 to require that U.S. government agencies give individuals with disabilities access to information technology that is comparable to the access available to others. This law requires developers creating information technology (including web pages) for use by the federal government to provide for accessibility. The Federal IT Accessibility Initiative (http://www.section508.gov) provides accessibility requirement resources for information technology developers. As the Web and Internet technologies developed, it became necessary to revise the original Section 508 requirements. New proposed Section 508 requirements were aligned to WCAG 2.0 guidelines and released for comment in 2015. At the time this was written, the updates were still under review. This textbook focuses on WCAG 2.0 guidelines to provide for accessibility.

In recent years, state governments have also begun to encourage and promote web accessibility. The Illinois Information Technology Accessibility Act (IITAA) guidelines are an example of this trend (see http://www.dhs.state.il.us/IITAA/IITAAWebImplementationGuidelines.html).

Putting It All Together: Universal Design for the Web

The Center for Universal Design defines **universal design** as "the design of products and environments to be usable by all people, to the greatest extent possible, without the need for adaptation or specialized design." Examples of universal design are all around us. The cutouts in sidewalk curbs providing for wheelchair accessibility also benefit a person pushing a stroller or riding a Segway Personal Transporter (Figure 1.2). Doors that open automatically improve accessibility and also benefit people carrying packages. A ramp is useful for a person dragging a rolling backpack or carry-on bag, and so on.

FIGURE 1.2 *A smooth ride is a benefit of universal design.*

Awareness of universal design by web developers has been steadily increasing. Forward-thinking web developers design with accessibility in mind because it is the right thing to do. Providing access for visitors with visual, auditory, and other challenges should be an integral part of web design rather than an afterthought.

A person with visual difficulties may not be able to use graphical navigation buttons and may use a screen reader device to provide an audible description of the web page. By making a few simple changes, such as providing text descriptions for the images and perhaps providing a text navigation area at the bottom of the page, web developers can make the page accessible. Often, providing for accessibility increases the usability of the website for all visitors.

Accessible websites with alternate text for images, headings used in an organized manner, and captions or transcriptions for multimedia are more easily used not only by visitors with disabilities but also by visitors using a mobile browser. Finally, accessible websites may be more thoroughly indexed by search engines, which can be helpful in bringing new visitors to a site. As this book introduces web development and design techniques, corresponding web accessibility and usability issues are discussed.

Web Browsers and Web Servers

Network Overview

A **network** consists of two or more computers connected for the purpose of communicating and sharing resources. A diagram of a small network is shown in Figure 1.3. Common components of a network include the following:

- Server computer(s)
- Client workstation computer(s)
- Shared devices such as printers
- Networking devices (routers, hubs, and switches) and the media that connect them

FIGURE 1.3 *Common components of a network.*

The **clients** are the computer workstations used by individuals, such as a PC on a desk. The **server** receives requests from client computers for resources, such as a file. Computers used as servers are usually kept in a protected, secure area and are only accessed by network administrators. Networking devices such as hubs and switches provide network connections for computers, and routers direct information from one network to another. The **media** connecting the clients, servers, peripherals, and networking devices may consist of copper cables, fiber optic cables, or wireless technologies.

The Client/Server Model

The term **client/server** dates from the 1980s and refers to computers joined by a network. Client/server can also describe a relationship between two computer programs—the client and the server. The client requests some type of service (such as a file or database access) from the server. The server fulfills the request and transmits the results to the client over a network. While both the client and the server programs can reside on the same computer, typically they run on different computers (Figure 1.4). It is common for a server to handle requests from multiple clients.

The Internet is a great example of client/server architecture at work. Consider the following scenario: A person is at a computer using a web browser client to access the Internet. The person uses the web browser to visit a website, say http://www.yahoo.com. The server is the web server program running on the computer with an IP address that corresponds to yahoo.com. The web server is contacted, it locates the web page and related resources that

Browser Request

Server Response

Web Client　　　　　　　　　　　**Web Server**

FIGURE 1.4 *Web client and web server.*

were requested, and it responds by sending them. Here's how to distinguish between web clients and web servers:

Web Client

- ▶ Connected to the Internet when needed
- ▶ Usually runs web browser (client) software such as Edge or Firefox
- ▶ Uses HTTP
- ▶ Requests web pages from a web server
- ▶ Receives web pages and associated files from a web server

Web Server

- ▶ Continually connected to the Internet
- ▶ Runs web server software (such as Apache or Microsoft Internet Information Server)
- ▶ Uses HTTP
- ▶ Receives a request for the web page
- ▶ Responds to the request and transmits the status code, web page, and associated files

When clients and servers exchange files, they often need to indicate the type of file that is being transferred; this is done through the use of a MIME type. **Multi-Purpose Internet Mail Extensions (MIME)** are rules that allow multimedia documents to be exchanged among many different computer systems. MIME was initially intended to extend the original Internet e-mail protocol, but it is also used by HTTP. MIME provides for the exchange of seven different media types on the Internet: audio, video, image, application, message, multipart, and text. MIME also uses subtypes to further describe the data. The MIME type of a web page is text/html. MIME types of gif and jpeg images are image/gif and image/jpeg, respectively.

A web server determines the MIME type of a file before it is transmitted to the web browser. The MIME type is sent along with the document. The web browser uses the MIME type to determine how to display the document.

How does information get transferred from the web server to the web browser? Clients (such as web browsers) and servers (such as a web server) exchange information through the use of communication protocols such as HTTP, TCP, and IP, which are introduced in the next section.

Internet Protocols

Protocols are rules that describe how clients and servers communicate with each other over a network. There is no single protocol that makes the Internet and the Web work—a number of protocols with specific functions are needed.

E-Mail Protocols

Most of us take e-mail for granted, but there are two servers involved in its smooth functioning—an incoming mail server and an outgoing mail server. When you send e-mail to others, **Simple Mail Transfer Protocol (SMTP)** is used. When you receive e-mail, **Post Office Protocol** (POP; currently **POP3**) and **Internet Message Access Protocol (IMAP)** can be used.

Hypertext Transfer Protocol

Hypertext Transfer Protocol (HTTP) is a set of rules for exchanging files such as text, graphic images, sound, video, and other multimedia files on the Web. Web browsers and web servers usually use this protocol. When the user of a web browser requests a file by typing a website address or clicking a hyperlink, the browser builds an HTTP request and sends it to the server. The web server in the destination machine receives the request, does any necessary processing, and responds with the requested file and any associated media files.

File Transfer Protocol

File Transfer Protocol (FTP) is a set of rules that allow files to be exchanged between computers on the Internet. Unlike HTTP, which is used by web browsers to request web pages and their associated files in order to display a web page, FTP is used simply to move files from one computer to another. Web developers commonly use FTP to transfer web page files from their computers to web servers.

Transmission Control Protocol/Internet Protocol

Transmission Control Protocol/Internet Protocol (TCP/IP) has been adopted as the official communication protocol of the Internet. TCP and IP have different functions that work together to ensure reliable communication over the Internet.

TCP. The purpose of TCP is to ensure the integrity of network communication. TCP starts by breaking files and messages into individual units called **packets**. These packets (see Figure 1.5) contain information such as the destination, source, sequence number, and checksum values used to verify the integrity of the data.

FIGURE 1.5 *TCP packet.*

TCP is used together with IP to transmit files efficiently over the Internet. IP takes over after TCP creates the packets, using IP addressing to send each packet over the Internet using the best path at the particular time. When the destination address is reached, TCP verifies the integrity of each packet using the checksum, requests a resend if a packet is damaged, and reassembles the file or message from the multiple packets.

IP. Working in harmony with TCP, IP is a set of rules that controls how data are sent between computers on the Internet. IP routes a packet to the correct destination address. Once sent, the packet gets successively forwarded to the next closest router (a hardware device designed to move network traffic) until it reaches its destination.

IP Addresses

Each device connected to the Internet has a unique numeric **IP address.** These addresses consist of a set of four groups of numbers, called octets. The current widely used version of IP, IPv4, uses 32-bit (binary digit) addressing. This results in a decimal number in the format of xxx.xxx.xxx.xxx, where each xxx is a value from 0 to 255. The IP address may correspond to a domain name. The **Domain Name System (DNS)** associates these IP addresses with the text-based URLs and domain names you type into a web browser address box (more on this later). For example, at the time this was written an IP address for Google was 216.58.194.46.

You can enter this number in the address text box in a web browser (as shown in Figure 1.6), press Enter, and the Google home page will display. Of course, it's much easier to type "google.com," which is why domain names such as google.com were created in the first place! Since long strings of numbers are difficult for humans to remember, the Domain Name System was introduced as a way to associate text-based names with numeric IP addresses.

FIGURE 1.6 *Entering an IP address in a web browser.*

What Is IPv6?

IPv6, Internet Protocol Version 6, intended to replace IPv4, was designed as an evolutionary set of improvements and is backwardly compatible with IPv4. Service providers and Internet users can update to IPv6 independently without having to coordinate with each other. IPv6 provides for more Internet addresses because the IP address is lengthened from 32 bits to 128 bits. This means that there are potentially 2^{128} unique IP addresses possible, or 340,282,366,920,938,463,463,347,607,431,768,211,456.

HTTP/2 will be the first major update to HTTP, which was first developed in 1999. As websites have become more image and media intensive, the number of requests needed to display a web page and its related files have increased. A major benefit of HTTP/2 will be quicker loading of web pages by processing multiple concurrent HTTP requests. Visit https://http2.github.io for more information about HTTP/2.

Uniform Resource Identifiers and Domain Names

URIs and URLs

A Uniform Resource Identifier (URI) identifies a resource on the Internet. A **Uniform Resource Locator (URL)** is a type of URI that represents the network location of a resource such as a web page, a graphic file, or an MP3 file. The URL consists of the protocol, the domain name, and the hierarchical location of the file on the web server.

The URL http://www.webdevbasics.net/4e/index.html, as shown in Figure 1.7, denotes the use of HTTP protocol and the web server named www at the domain name of webdevbasics.net. In this case, the root file (which is usually index.html or index.htm) of the 4e directory will be displayed.

FIGURE 1.7
URL describing a file within a folder.

Domain Names

A **domain name** locates an organization or other entity on the Internet. The purpose of the **Domain Name System (DNS)** is to divide the Internet into logical groups and understandable names by identifying the exact address and type of the organization. The DNS associates the text-based domain names with the unique numeric IP address assigned to a device.

Let's consider the domain name www.google.com. The .com is the top-level domain name. The portion google.com is the domain name that is registered to Google and is considered a second-level domain name. The www is the name of the web server (sometimes called a host) at the google.com domain.

A **subdomain** can be configured to house a separate website located at the same domain. For example, Google's Gmail can be accessed by using the subdomain "gmail" in the domain name (gmail.google.com). Google Maps can be accessed at maps.google.com and Google News Search is available at news.google.com. The combination of host/subdomain, second-level domain, and top-level domain name (such as www.google.com or gmail.google.com) is called a **Fully Qualified Domain Name (FQDN)**.

Top-Level Domain Names

A **top-level domain (TLD)** identifies the rightmost part of the domain name. A TLD is either a **generic top-level domain (gTLD)**, such as com for commercial, or a country-code top-level domain, such as fr for France. The Internet Assigned Numbers Authority (IANA) website has a complete list of TLDs (http://www.iana.org/domains/root/db).

Generic Top-Level Domain Names (gTLDs)

The Internet Corporation for Assigned Names and Numbers (ICANN) administers gTLDs (http://www.icann.org). Table 1.1 shows a collection of gTLDs and their intended use.

TABLE 1.1 *Generic Top-Level Domains*

gTLD	Intended for Use By
.aero	Air-transport industry
.asia	Pan-Asia and Asia Pacific community
.biz	Businesses
.cat	Catalan linguistic and cultural community
.com	Commercial entities
.coop	Cooperative
.edu	Restricted to accredited degree-granting institutions of higher education
.gov	Restricted to government use
.info	Unrestricted use
.int	International organization (rarely used)
.jobs	Human resource management community
.mil	Restricted to military use
.mobi	Corresponds to a .com website—designed for easy access by mobile devices
.museum	Museums
.name	Individuals
.net	Entities associated with network support of the Internet, usually Internet service providers or telecommunication companies
.org	Nonprofit entities
.post	Generic TLD for the Universal Postal Union, an agency of the United Nations
.pro	Accountants, physicians, and lawyers
.tel	Contact information for individuals and businesses
.travel	Travel industry

The .com, .org, and .net gTLD designations are currently used on the honor system, which means that an individual who owns a shoe store (not related to networking) can register shoes.net.

Expect the number and variety of gTLDs to increase. ICANN accepted proposals for almost 2000 new gTLDs in 2012. A wide variety of new gTLDs were proposed including place names (.quebec, .vegas, and .moscow), retail terms (.blackfriday), financial terms (.cash, .trade, and .loans), technology terms (.systems, .technology, and .app) and whimsical, fun terms (.ninja, .buzz, and .cool). Some of the first new gTLDs to become available included .bike, .guru, .holdings, .clothing, .singles, .ventures, and .plumbing. ICANN has set a schedule to periodically launch new gTLDs. Visit http://newgtlds.icann.org/en/program-status/delegated-strings for a list of new gTLDs.

Country-Code Top-Level Domain Names

Two-character country codes have also been assigned as TLD names. The country-code TLD names were originally intended to designate the geographical location of the individual or organization that registered the name. Table 1.2 lists some popular country codes used on the Web.

TABLE 1.2 *Country-Code TLDs*

Country-Code TLD	Country
.au	Australia
.es	Spain
.eu	European Union (a group of countries rather than a single country)
.jp	Japan
.ly	Libya
.nl	Netherlands
.us	United States
.ws	Samoa

The IANA website at http://www.iana.org/domains/root/db has a complete list of country-code TLDs. Domain names with country codes are often used for municipalities, schools, and community colleges in the United States. For example, the domain name www.harper.cc.il.us denotes, from right to left, the United States, Illinois, community college, Harper, and the web server named "www" as the website for Harper College in Illinois.

Although country-code TLD names were intended to designate geographical location, it is fairly easy to obtain a domain name with a country-code TLD that is not local to the registrant. Examples of non geographical use of country-code TLDs include domain names such as mediaqueri.es, webteacher.ws, and bit.ly. Visit http://register.com, http://godaddy.com, and many other domain name registration companies for examples of readily available country-code TLDs.

Domain Name System (DNS)

The DNS associates domain names with IP addresses. As shown in Figure 1.8, the following happens each time a new URL is typed into a web browser:

1. The DNS is accessed.
2. The corresponding IP address is obtained and returned to the web browser.
3. The web browser sends an HTTP request to the destination computer with the corresponding IP address.
4. The HTTP request is received by the web server.
5. The necessary files are located and sent by HTTP responses to the web browser.
6. The web browser renders and displays the web page and associated files.

We all get impatient sometimes when we need to view a web page. The next time you wonder why it's taking so long to display a web page, consider all of the processing that goes on behind the scenes before the browser receives the files needed to display the web page.

FIGURE 1.8 *Accessing a web page.*

Information on the Web

FIGURE 1.9 *Who really updated that web page you are viewing?*

These days anyone can publish just about anything on the Web. In this section, we'll explore how you can tell if the information you've found is reliable and also how you can use that information. There are many websites—but which ones are reliable sources of information? When visiting websites to find information it is important not to take everything at face value (Figure 1.9).

▶ **Is the organization credible?**

Anyone can post anything on the Web! Choose your information sources wisely.

First, evaluate the credibility of the website itself. Does it have its own domain name, such as http://mywebsite.com, or is it a free website consisting of just a folder of files hosted on a free web hosting site (such as weebly.com, awardspace.com, or 000webhost.com)?

The URL of a site hosted on a free web server usually includes part of the free web host's domain name. Information obtained from a website that has its own domain name will usually (but not always) be more reliable than information obtained from a free website.

Evaluate the type of domain name—is it a nonprofit organization (.org), a business (.com or .biz), an educational institution (.edu)? Businesses may provide information in a way that gives them an advantage, so be careful. Nonprofit organizations or schools will sometimes treat a subject more objectively.

▶ **How recent is the information?**

Another item to look at is the date the web page was created or last updated. Although some information is timeless, very often a web page that has not been updated for several years is outdated and may not be the best source of information.

▶ **Are there links to additional resources?**

Hyperlinks indicate websites with supporting or additional information that can be helpful to you in your research as you explore a topic. Look for these types of hyperlinks to aid you in your studies.

▶ **Is it Wikipedia?**

Wikipedia (http://wikipedia.org) is a good place to begin research, but don't accept what you read there for fact, and avoid using Wikipedia as a resource for academic assignments. Why? Well, except for a few protected topics, anyone can update Wikipedia with anything!

Usually it all gets sorted out eventually—but be aware that the information you read may not be valid.

Feel free to use Wikipedia to begin exploring a topic, but scroll down to the bottom of the Wikipedia web page and look for "References"—and explore those websites and others that you may find. As you gather information on these sites, also consider the other criteria: credibility, domain name, timeliness, and links to additional resources.

Ethical Use of Information on the Web

The wonderful technology called the World Wide Web provides us with information, graphics, music, and video—all virtually free (after you pay your Internet service provider, of course). Let's consider the following issues relating to the ethical use of this information:

> Is it acceptable to copy someone's graphic to use on your website?
> Is it acceptable to copy someone's music or video to use on your website?
> Is it acceptable to copy someone's website design to use on your site or on a client's site?
> Is it acceptable to copy an essay that appears on a web page and use it or parts of it as your writing?
> Is it acceptable to insult someone on your website or link to another website in a derogatory manner?

The answer to all these questions is no. Using someone's graphic, music, or video without permission is the same as stealing it. In fact, if you link to it you are actually using up some of their bandwidth and may be costing them money. Copying the website design of another person or company is also a form of stealing. Any text or graphic on a website is automatically copyrighted in the United States whether or not a copyright symbol appears on the site. Insulting a person or company on your website or linking to them in a derogatory manner could be considered a form of defamation.

Issues related to intellectual property, copyright, and freedom of speech are regularly discussed and decided in courts of law. Good web etiquette requires that you ask permission before using others' work, give credit for what you use as a student ("fair use" in the U.S. copyright law), and exercise your freedom of speech in a manner that is not harmful to others. The **World Intellectual Property Organization (WIPO)** is dedicated to protecting intellectual property rights internationally (see http://wipo.int).

What if you'd like to retain ownership but make it easy for others to use or adapt your work? Creative Commons (http://creativecommons.org) is a nonprofit organization that provides free services that allow authors and artists to register a type of a copyright license called a Creative Commons license. There are several licenses to choose from, depending on the rights you wish to grant. The Creative Commons license informs others exactly what they can and cannot do with your creative work. See http://meyerweb.com/eric/tools/color-blend/ for a web page licensed under a Creative Commons Attribution-ShareAlike 1.0 License.

HTML Overview

Markup languages consist of sets of directions that tell the browser software (and other user agent software that retrieves and renders web content) how to display and manage a web document. These directions are usually called tags and perform functions such as displaying graphics, formatting text, and referencing hyperlinks.

The World Wide Web is composed of files containing Hypertext Markup Language (HTML) and other markup languages that describe web pages. Tim Berners-Lee developed HTML using Standard Generalized Markup Language (SGML). SGML prescribes a standard format for embedding descriptive markup within a document and for describing the structure of a document. SGML is not in itself a document language, but rather a description of how to specify one and create a document type definition (DTD). The W3C (http://www.w3c.org) sets the standards for HTML and its related languages. HTML (like the Web itself) is in a constant state of change.

What Is HTML?

HTML (Hypertext Markup Language) is the set of markup symbols or codes placed in a file that is intended for display on a web page. These markup symbols and codes identify structural elements such as paragraphs, headings, and lists. HTML can also be used to place media (such as graphics, video, and audio) on a web page and describe fill-in forms. The browser interprets the markup code and renders the page. HTML permits the platform-independent display of information across a network. No matter what type of computer a web page was created on, any browser running on any operating system can display the page.

Each individual markup code is referred to as an **element** or **tag**. Each tag has a purpose. Tags are enclosed in angle brackets, the < and > symbols. Most tags come in pairs: an opening tag and a closing tag. These tags act as containers and are sometimes referred to as container tags. For example, when an HTML document is displayed by a web browser, the text that appears between the <title> and </title> tags would be displayed in the title bar on the browser window.

Some tags are used alone and are not part of a pair. For example, a <hr> tag that displays a horizontal line on a web page is a stand-alone or self-contained tag and does not have a closing tag. You will become familiar with these as you use them. Most tags can be modified with **attributes** that further describe their purpose.

What Is XML?

XML (eXtensible Markup Language) was developed by the W3C to create common information formats and share the format and the information on the Web. It is a text-based syntax designed to describe, deliver, and exchange structured information, such as RSS feeds. XML is not intended to replace HTML, but to extend the power of HTML by separating data from presentation. Using XML, developers can create any tags they need to describe their information.

What Is XHTML?

eXtensible HyperText Markup Language (XHTML) uses the tags and attributes of HTML4 along with the more rigorous syntax of XML. XHTML has been used on the Web for over a decade and you'll find many web pages coded with this markup language. At one point the W3C was working on a new version of XHTML, called XHTML 2.0. However, the W3C stopped development of XHTML 2.0 because it was not backward compatible with HTML4. Instead, the W3C decided to move forward with HTML5.

HTML5—The Newest Version of HTML

HTML5 is the successor to HTML and replaces XHTML. HTML5 incorporates features of both HTML and XHTML, adds new elements, provides new functionality such as form edits and native video, and is designed to be backward compatible.

The W3C approved HTML5 for Candidate Recommendation status in late 2012. HTML5 reached final Recommendation status in late 2014. The W3C continued its development of HTML and added more new elements, attributes, and features in an udpate to HTML5 called HTML 5.1. At the time this was written, HTML5.1 was in Candidate Recommendation status and work had already begun on HTML5.2.

Recent versions of popular browsers, such as Microsoft Edge, Internet Explorer 11, Firefox, Safari, Google Chrome, and Opera already support many of the new features of HTML5 and HTML5.1. You'll learn to use HTML5.1 syntax as you work through this textbook. W3C HTML5 documentation is available at http://www.w3.org/TR/html.

Under the Hood of a Web Page

FIGURE 1.10 *It's what is under the hood that matters.*

You already know that the HTML markup language tells browsers how to display information on a web page. Let's take a closer look at what's "under the hood" (Figure 1.10) of every web page you create.

Document Type Definition

Because multiple versions and types of HTML and XHTML exist, the W3C recommends identifying the markup language used in a web page document with a **Document Type Definition (DTD).** The DTD identifies the version of HTML contained in the document. Browsers and HTML code validators use the information in the DTD when processing the web page. The DTD statement, commonly called a **DOCTYPE** statement, is the first line of a web page document. The DTD for HTML5 is:

```
<!DOCTYPE html>
```

Web Page Template

Every single web page you create will include the html, head, title, meta, and body elements. We will follow the coding style to use lowercase letters and place quotes around attribute values. A basic HTML5 web page template (found in the student files at chapter1/template.html) is

```
<!DOCTYPE html>
<html lang="en">
<head>
<title>Page Title Goes Here</title>
<meta charset="utf-8">
</head>
<body>
. . . body text and more HTML tags go here . . .
</body>
</html>
```

With the exception of the specific page title, the first seven lines will usually be the same on every web page that you create. Review the code above and notice the DTD statement has its own formatting, but that the HTML tags all use lowercase letters. Next, let's explore the purpose of the html, head, title, meta, and body elements.

HTML Element

The purpose of the **html element** is to indicate that the document is HTML formatted. The html element tells the browser how to interpret the document. The opening `<html>` tag is placed on a line below the DTD. The closing `</html>` tag indicates the end of the web page and is placed after all other HTML elements in the document.

The html element also needs to indicate the spoken language, such as English, of the text in the document. This additional information is added to the `<html>` tag in the form of an **attribute**, which modifies or further describes the function of an element. The **lang attribute** specifies the spoken language of the document. For example, `lang="en"` indicates the English language. Search engines and screen readers may access this attribute.

The html element contains the two sections of a web page: the head and the body. The **head section** contains information that describes the web page document. The **body section** contains the actual tags, text, images, and other objects that are displayed by the browser as a web page.

Head Section

Elements that are located in the head section include the title of the web page, meta tags that describe the document (such as the character encoding used and information that may be accessed by search engines), and references to scripts and styles. Many of these do not show directly on the web page.

Head Element. The **head element** contains the head section, which begins with the `<head>` tag and ends with the `</head>` tag. You'll always code at least two other elements in the head section: a title element and a meta element.

Title Element. The first element in the head section, the **title element**, configures the text that will appear in the title bar of the browser window. The text between the `<title>` and `</title>` tags is called the title of the web page. This title text is accessed when web pages are bookmarked and printed. Popular search engines, such as Google, use the title text to help determine keyword relevance and even display the title text on the results page of a search. A descriptive title that includes the website or organization name is a crucial component for establishing a brand or presence on the Web.

Meta Element. The **meta element** describes a characteristic of a web page, such as the character encoding. **Character encoding** is the internal representation of letters, numbers, and symbols in a file, such as a web page or other file, that is stored on a computer and may be transmitted over the Internet. There are many different character-encoding sets. Web pages typically use utf-8 character encoding, which is a form of Unicode (http://www.unicode.org). The meta tag is not used as a pair of opening and closing tags. It is a stand-alone self-contained tag (referred to as a **void** element in HTML5). The meta tag uses the **charset attribute** to indicate the character encoding. An example meta tag is:

```
<meta charset="utf-8">
```

Body Section

The body section contains text and elements that display directly on the web page within the browser window, also referred to as the browser viewport. The purpose of the body section is to configure the contents of the web page.

Body Element. The **body element** contains the body section, which begins with the `<body>` tag and ends with the `</body>` tag. You will spend most of your time writing code in the body of a web page. Text and elements typed between the opening and closing body tags will display on the web page in the browser viewport.

Your First Web Page

VideoNote

*Your First
Web Page*

No special software is needed to create a web page document—all you need is a text editor. The Notepad text editor is included with Microsoft Windows. TextEdit is distributed with the Mac OS X operating system. An alternative to using a simple text editor or word processor is to use a commercial web-authoring tool, such as Adobe Dreamweaver. There are also many free or shareware editors available, including Notepad++, TextPad, and TextWrangler. Regardless of the tool you use, having a solid foundation in HTML will be useful. The examples in this book use Notepad.

 Hands-On Practice 1.1

Now that you're familiar with the basic elements used on every web page, it's your turn to create your first web page, shown in Figure 1.11.

FIGURE 1.11
Your first web page.

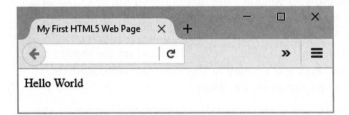

Create a Folder

You'll find it helpful to create folders to organize your files as you develop web pages and create your own websites. Use your operating system to create a new folder named chapter1 on your hard drive or on a portable flash drive.

To create a new folder on a Mac:

1. In the Finder, go to the location where you'd like to create the new folder.
2. Choose File > New Folder. An untitled folder is created.
3. To rename the folder with a new name: select the folder and click on the current name. Type a name for the folder and press the Return key.

To create a new folder with Windows:

1. Right-click on the Start Button and select File Explorer. Then, navigate to the location where you'd like to create the new folder, such as Documents, your C: drive, or an external USB drive.

2. Select the Home tab. Select New folder.

3. To rename the new folder: right-click on it, select Rename from the context-sensitive menu, type the new name, and press the Enter key.

Now you are ready to create your first web page. Launch Notepad or another text editor. Type in the following code.

```
<!DOCTYPE html>
<html lang="en">
<head>
<title>My First HTML5 Web Page</title>
<meta charset="utf-8">
</head>
<body>
Hello World
</body>
</html>
```

Notice that the first line in the file contains the DTD. The HTML code begins with an opening `<html>` tag and ends with a closing `</html>` tag. The purpose of these tags is to indicate that the content between the tags makes up a web page.

The head section is delimited by `<head>` and `</head>` tags and contains a pair of title tags with the words "My First HTML5 Web Page" in between along with a `<meta>` tag to indicate the character encoding.

The body section is delimited by `<body>` and `</body>` tags. The words "Hello World" are typed on a line between the body tags. See Figure 1.12 for a screenshot of the code as it would appear in Notepad. You have just created the source code for a web page document.

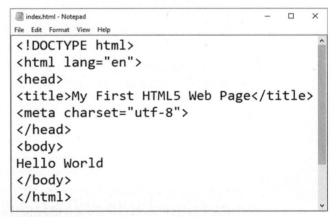

FIGURE 1.12 *Your web page source code displayed in Notepad.*

Do I have to start each tag on its own line?

No, you are not required to start each tag on a separate line. A browser can display a page even if all the tags follow each other on one line with no spaces. Humans, however, find it easier to write and read web page code if line breaks and indentation are used.

Save Your File

Web pages use either an .htm or .html file extension. A common file name for the home page of a website is index.html or index.htm. The web pages in this book use the .html file extension.

You will save your file with the name of index.html.

1. Display your file in Notepad or another text editor.
2. Select File from the menu bar, and then select Save As.
3. The Save As dialog box appears. Using Figure 1.13 as an example, type the file name.
4. Click the Save button.

FIGURE 1.13 *Save and name your file.*

Sample solutions for Hands-On Practice exercises are available in the student files. If you would like, compare your work with the solution (chapter1/index.html) before you test your page.

 Why does my file have a .txt file extension?

In some older versions of Windows, Notepad will automatically append a .txt file extension. If this happens, rename your file index.html.

Why should I create a folder, why not just use the desktop?

Folders will help you to organize your work. If you just used the desktop, it would quickly become cluttered and disorganized. It's also important to know that websites are organized on web servers within folders. By starting to use folders right away to organize related web pages, you are on your way to becoming a successful web designer.

Test Your Page

There are two ways to test your page:

1. In Windows Explorer (Windows) or the Finder (Mac), navigate to your index.html file. Double-click index.html. The default browser will launch and will display your index.html page.

2. Launch a web browser. Select File > Open, and navigate to your index.html file. Double-click index.html and click OK. The browser will display your index.html page.

If you are using Microsoft Edge, your page should look similar to the one shown in Figure 1.14. A display of the page using Firefox is shown in Figure 1.11. Notice how the title text, "My First HTML5 Web Page" displays in the tab and the title bar of the browser window. Some search engines use the text surrounded by the `<title>` and `</title>` tags to help determine relevance of keyword searches, so make certain that your pages contain descriptive titles. The `<title>` tag is also used when viewers bookmark your page or add it to their Favorites. An engaging and descriptive page title may entice a visitor to revisit your page. If your web page is for a company or an organization, it's a good idea to include the name of the company or organization in the title.

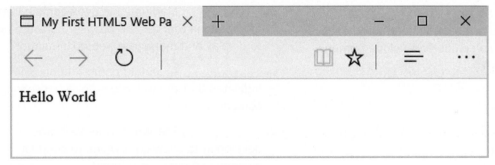

FIGURE 1.14 *Web page displayed by Microsoft Edge.*

?FAQ When I viewed my page in a browser, the file name was index.html.html—why did this happen?

This usually happens when your operating system is configured to hide file extension names. You will correct the file name, using one of the following two methods:

▶ Use the operating system to rename the file from "index.html.html" to "index.html".

OR

▶ Open the index.html.html file in your text editor and save it with the name "index.html".

It's a good idea to change the settings in your operating system to show file extension names. Follow the steps at the resources below to show file extension names:

▶ *Windows:* http://www.file-extensions.org/article/show-and-hide-file-extensions-in-windows-10
▶ *Mac:* http://www.fileinfo.com/help/mac_show_extensions

Review and Apply

Review Questions

Multiple Choice. Choose the best answer for each question.

1. Select the item below that indicates the top-level domain name for the URL http://www.mozilla.com.
   a. http
   b. com
   c. mozilla
   d. www

2. What is a unique text-based Internet address corresponding to a computer's unique numeric IP address called?
   a. IP address
   b. domain name
   c. URL
   d. user name

3. The purpose of _____ is to ensure the integrity of the communication.
   a. IP
   b. TCP
   c. HTTP
   d. FTP

4. Choose the true statement:
   a. The title of the web page is displayed by the meta element.
   b. Information about the web page is contained in the body section.
   c. The content that displays in the browser viewport is contained in the head section.
   d. The content that displays in the browser viewport is contained in the body section.

True or False. Choose the best answer, true or false, for each question.

5. _____ Markup languages contain sets of directions that tell the browser software how to display and manage a web document.

6. _____ A domain name that ends in .net indicates that the website is for a networking company.

7. _____ The World Wide Web was developed to allow companies to conduct e-commerce over the Internet.

Fill in the Blank. Fill in the missing term.

8. _html_____ is the set of markup symbols or codes placed in a file intended for display on a web browser.

9. Web page documents typically use the .html____ or _____ file extension.

10. The home page of a website is typically named index.html or _____.

Hands-On Exercises

1. A **blog**, or web log, is a journal that is available on the Web—it's a frequently updated page with a chronological list of ideas and links. Blog topics range from political journals to technical information to personal diaries. It's up to the person, called a blogger, who creates and maintains the blog.

Create a blog to document your learning experiences as you study web design. Visit one of the many sites that offer free blogs, such as http://blogger.com, http://tumblr.com, or http://www.wordpress.com. Follow their instructions to establish your blog. Your blog could be a place to note websites that you find useful or interesting. You might report on websites that contain useful web design resources. You might describe sites that have interesting features, such as compelling graphics or easy-to-use navigation. Write a few sentences about the site that you find intriguing. After you begin to develop your sites, you could include the URLs and reasons for your design decisions. Share this blog with your fellow students and friends.

2. Twitter (http://www.twitter.com) is a social networking website for **microblogging**, or frequently communicating with a brief message (140 characters or less) called a **tweet**. Twitter users (referred to as twitterers) tweet to update a network of friends and followers about their daily activities, observations, and information related to topics of interest. A **hashtag** (the # symbol) can be placed in front of a word or term within a tweet to categorize the topic, such as typing the hashtag #SXSWi in all tweets about the SXSW Interactive Conference for the web design industry. The use of a hashtag makes it easy to search for tweets about a category or event in Twitter.

If you don't already use Twitter, sign up for a free account at http://www.twitter.com. Use your Twitter account to share information about websites that you find useful or interesting. Post at least three tweets. You might tweet about websites that contain useful web design resources. You might describe sites that have interesting features, such as compelling graphics or easy-to-use navigation. After you begin to develop your own websites, you can tweet about them, too!

Your instructor may direct you to include a distinctive hashtag (for example, something like #CIS110) in your tweets that are related to your web design studies. Searching Twitter for the specified hashtag will make it easy to collect all the tweets posted by the students in your class.

Web Research

1. The World Wide Web Consortium creates standards for the Web. Visit its site at http://www.w3c.org and then answer the following questions:
   a. How did the W3C get started?
   b. Who can join the W3C? What does it cost to join?
   c. The W3C home page lists a number of technologies. Choose one that interests you, click its link, and read several of the associated pages. List three facts or issues you discover.

2. HTTP/2 is the first major update to HTTP, which was first developed in the late 1990s. As websites have become more image and media intensive, the number of requests needed to display a web page and its related files have increased. A major benefit of HTTP/2 will be quicker loading of web pages.

   HTTP/2 Resources:

   • http://readwrite.com/2015/02/18/http-update-http2-what-you-need-to-know
   • https://http2.github.io

- http://www.engadget.com/2015/02/24/what-you-need-to-know-about-http-2
- https://tools.ietf.org/html/rfc7540

Use the resources listed above as a starting point as you research HTTP/2 and answer the following questions.

a. Who developed HTTP/2?

b. When was the HTTP/2 proposed standard published?

c. Describe three methods used by HTTP/2 intended to decrease latency and provide for quicker loading of web pages in browsers.

Focus on Web Design

Visit a website referenced in this chapter that interests you. Print the home page or one other pertinent page from the site. Write a one-page summary and your reaction to the site. Address the following topics:

a. What is the purpose of the site?

b. Who is the intended audience?

c. Do you think that the site reaches its intended audience? Why or why not?

d. Is the site useful to you? Why or why not?

e. List one interesting fact or issue that this site addresses.

f. Would you encourage others to visit this site?

g. How could this site be improved?

CHAPTER 2

HTML Basics

In the previous chapter, you created your first web page using HTML5. You coded a web page and tested it in a browser. You used a Document Type Definition to identify the version of HTML being used along with the `<html>`, `<head>`, `<title>`, `<meta>`, and `<body>` tags. In this chapter, you will continue your study of HTML and configure the structure and formatting of text on a web page using HTML elements, including the new HTML5 header, nav, and footer elements. You're also ready to explore hyperlinks, which make the World Wide Web into a web of interconnected information. In this chapter, you will configure the anchor element to connect web pages to each other with hyperlinks. As you read this chapter, be sure to work through the examples. Coding a web page is a skill, and every skill improves with practice.

You'll learn how to...

- Configure the body of a web page with headings, paragraphs, divs, lists, and blockquotes
- Configure special entity characters, line breaks, and horizontal rules
- Configure text with phrase elements
- Test a web page for valid syntax

- Configure a web page using new HTML5 header, nav, main, and footer elements
- Use the anchor element to link from page to page
- Configure absolute, relative, and e-mail hyperlinks

Heading Element

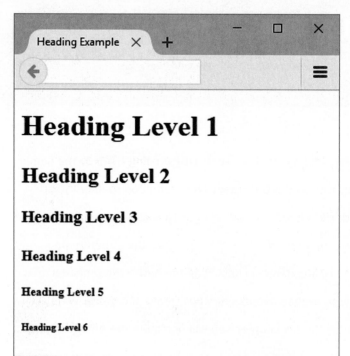

FIGURE 2.1 *Sample heading.html.*

Heading elements are organized into six levels: h1 through h6. The text contained within a heading element is rendered as a "block" of text by the browser (referred to as block display) and appears with empty space (sometimes called "white space" or "negative space") above and below. The size of the text is largest for `<h1>` (called the heading 1 tag) and smallest for `<h6>` (called the heading 6 tag). Depending on the font being used, the text contained within `<h4>`, `<h5>`, and `<h6>` tags may be displayed smaller than the default text size. All text contained within heading tags is displayed with bold font weight.

Figure 2.1 shows a web page document with six levels of headings.

 Hands-On Practice 2.1

To create the web page shown in Figure 2.1, launch a text editor, and open the template.html file from the chapter1 folder in the student files. Modify the title element and add heading tags to the body section as indicated by the following highlighted code:

```
<!DOCTYPE html>
<html lang="en">
<head>
<title>Heading Example</title>
<meta charset="utf-8">
</head>
<body>
<h1>Heading Level 1</h1>
<h2>Heading Level 2</h2>
<h3>Heading Level 3</h3>
<h4>Heading Level 4</h4>
<h5>Heading Level 5</h5>
<h6>Heading Level 6</h6>
</body>
</html>
```

Save the document as heading.html on your hard drive or flash drive. Launch a browser such as Edge or Firefox to test your page. It should look similar to the page shown in Figure 2.1. You can compare your work with the solution found in the student files (chapter2/heading.html).

Accessibility and Headings

Heading tags can help to make your pages more accessible and usable. It is good coding practice to use heading tags to outline the structure of your web page content. To indicate areas within a page hierarchically, code heading tags numerically as appropriate (h1, h2, h3, and so on), and include page content in block display elements such as paragraphs and lists. In Figure 2.2, the <h1> tag contains the name of the website in the logo header area at the top of the web page, the <h2> tag contains the topic or name of the page in the content area, and other heading elements are coded in the content area as needed to identify major topics and subtopics.

Visually challenged visitors who are using a screen reader can configure the software to display a list of the headings used on a page in order to focus on the topics that interest them. Your well-organized page will be more usable for every visitor to your site, including those who are visually challenged.

FIGURE 2.2 *Heading tags outline the page.*

More Heading Options in HTML5

You may have heard about the new HTML5 header element. The header element offers additional options for configuring headings and typically contains an h1 element. We'll introduce the header element later in this chapter.

Paragraph Element

Paragraph elements group sentences and sections of text together. Text that is contained by `<p>` and `</p>` tags is rendered as block display with empty space above and below.

Figure 2.3 shows a web page document containing a paragraph after the first heading.

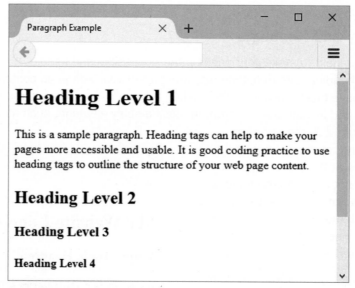

FIGURE 2.3 *Web page using headings and a paragraph.*

 Hands-On Practice 2.2

To create the web page shown in Figure 2.3, launch a text editor, and open the heading.html file from the chapter2 folder in the student files. Modify the page title and add a paragraph of text to your page below the line with the `<h1>` tags and above the line with the `<h2>` tags.

```
<!DOCTYPE html>
<html lang="en">
<head>
<title>Paragraph Example</title>
<meta charset="utf-8">
</head>
<body>
<h1>Heading Level 1</h1>
<p>This is a sample paragraph. Heading tags can help to make your
pages more accessible and usable. It is good coding practice to use
heading tags to outline the structure of your web page content.
</p>
<h2>Heading Level 2</h2>
<h3>Heading Level 3</h3>
<h4>Heading Level 4</h4>
<h5>Heading Level 5</h5>
<h6>Heading Level 6</h6>
</body>
</html>
```

Save the document as paragraph.html on your hard drive or flash drive. Launch a browser to test your page. It should look similar to the page shown in Figure 2.3. You can compare your work with the solution found in the student files (chapter2/paragraph.html). Notice how the text in the paragraph wraps automatically as you resize your browser window.

Alignment

As you test your web pages, you may notice that the headings and text begin near the left margin. This is called **left alignment**, and it is the default alignment for web pages. There are times when you want a paragraph or heading to be centered or right aligned (justified). In previous versions of HTML, the align attribute can be used for this. However, the align attribute is **obsolete** in HTML5, which means that the attribute has been removed from the W3C HTML5 draft specification. You'll learn techniques to configure alignment with Cascading Style Sheets (CSS) in Chapters 6, 7, and 8.

When writing for the Web, avoid long paragraphs. People tend to skim web pages rather than reading them word for word. Use heading tags to outline the page content along with short paragraphs (about three to five sentences each) and lists (which you'll learn about later in this chapter).

Line Break and Horizontal Rule

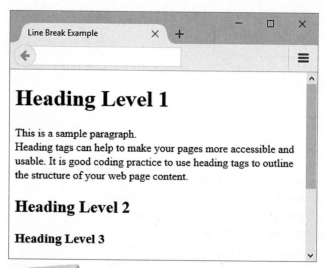

FIGURE 2.4 *Notice the line break after the first sentence.*

The Line Break Element

The **line break element** causes the browser to advance to the next line before displaying the next element or text on a web page. The line break tag is not coded as a pair of opening and closing tags. It is a void element and is coded as **
**. Figure 2.4 shows a web page document with a line break after the first sentence in the paragraph.

 Hands-On Practice 2.3

To create the web page shown in Figure 2.4, launch a text editor, and open the paragraph.html file from the chapter2 folder in the student files. Modify the text contained between the title tags to be "Line Break Example." Place your cursor after the first sentence in the paragraph (after "This is a sample paragraph."). Press the Enter key. Save your file. Test your page in a browser and notice that even though your source code displayed the "This is a sample paragraph." sentence on its own line, the browser did not render it that way. A line break tag is needed to configure the browser to display the second sentence on a new line. Edit the file in a text editor and add a <br> tag after the first sentence in the paragraph as shown in the following code snippet.

```
<body>
<h1>Heading Level 1</h1>
<p>This is a sample paragraph. <br> Heading tags can help to make your
pages more accessible and usable. It is good coding practice to use
heading tags to outline the structure of your web page content.
</p>
<h2>Heading Level 2</h2>
<h3>Heading Level 3</h3>
<h4>Heading Level 4</h4>
<h5>Heading Level 5</h5>
<h6>Heading Level 6</h6>
</body>
```

Save your file as linebreak.html. Launch a browser to test your page. It should look similar to the page shown in Figure 2.4. You can compare your work with the solution found in the student files (chapter2/linebreak.html).

The Horizontal Rule Element

Web designers often use visual elements such as lines and borders to separate or define areas on web pages. The **horizontal rule** element, **<hr>**, configures a horizontal line across a web page. Since the horizontal rule element does not contain any text, it is coded as a void element and not in a pair of opening and closing tags. The horizontal rule element has an additional purpose in HTML5, it can be used to indicate a thematic break or change in the content. Figure 2.5 shows a web page document (also found in the student files at chapter2/hr.html) with a horizontal rule after the paragraph. In Chapter 6, you'll learn how to configure lines and borders on web page elements with Cascading Style Sheets (CSS).

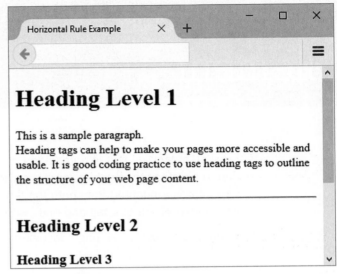

FIGURE 2.5 *The horizontal line is below the paragraph.*

 Hands-On Practice 2.4

To create the web page shown in Figure 2.5, launch a text editor, and open the linebreak.html file from the chapter2 folder in the student files. Modify the text contained between the title tags to be: Horizontal Rule Example. Place your cursor on a new line after the </p> tag. Code the <hr> tag on the new line as shown in the following code snippet.

```
<body>
<h1>Heading Level 1</h1>
<p>This is a sample paragraph. <br> Heading tags can help to make your
pages more accessible and usable. It is good coding practice to use
heading tags to outline the structure of your web page content.
</p>
<hr>
<h2>Heading Level 2</h2>
<h3>Heading Level 3</h3>
<h4>Heading Level 4</h4>
<h5>Heading Level 5</h5>
<h6>Heading Level 6</h6>
</body>
```

Save your file as hr.html. Launch a browser to test your page. It should look similar to the page shown in Figure 2.5. You can compare your work with the solution found in the student files (chapter2/hr.html).

> **Quick TIP** When you are tempted to use a horizontal rule on a web page, consider whether it is really needed. Usually, just leaving extra blank space (referred to as "white space" or "negative space") on the page will serve to separate the content. *Note:* The term white space is borrowed from the print industry—since paper is generally white, extra blank space is known as white space.

Blockquote Element

Besides organizing text in paragraphs and headings, sometimes you need to add a quotation to a web page. The **blockquote element** is used to display a block of quoted text in a special way—indented from both the left and right margins. A block of indented text begins with a **<blockquote>** tag and ends with a **</blockquote>** tag.

Figure 2.6 shows a web page document with a heading, a paragraph, and a blockquote.

FIGURE 2.6 *The text within the blockquote element is indented.*

Quick TIP You've probably noticed how convenient the <blockquote> tag could be if you needed to indent an area of text on a web page. You may have wondered whether it would be OK to use <blockquote> anytime you'd like to indent text or whether the blockquote element is reserved only for long quotations. The semantically correct use of the <blockquote> tag is to use it only when displaying large blocks of quoted text within a web page. Why should you be concerned about semantics? Consider the future of the Semantic Web, described in *Scientific American* as "A new form of Web content that is meaningful to computers [that] will unleash a revolution of new possibilities." Using HTML in a semantic, structural manner is one step toward the Semantic Web. So, avoid using a <blockquote> just to indent text. You'll learn modern techniques to configure margins and padding on elements later in this book.

Hands-On Practice 2.5

To create the web page shown in Figure 2.6, launch a text editor, and open the template.html file from the chapter1 folder in the student files. Modify the text in the title element. Add a heading tag, a paragraph tag, and a blockquote tag to the body section as indicated by the following highlighted code.

```
<!DOCTYPE html>
<html lang="en">
<head>
<title>Blockquote Example</title>
<meta charset="utf-8">
</head>
<body>
<h1>The Power of the Web</h1>
<p>According to Tim Berners-Lee, the inventor of the World Wide Web,
at http://www.w3.org/WAI/:
</p>
<blockquote>
The power of the Web is in its universality. Access by everyone
regardless of disability is an essential aspect.
</blockquote>
</body>
</html>
```

Save the document as blockquote.html on your hard drive or flash drive. Launch a browser such as Edge or Firefox to test your page. It should look similar to the page shown in Figure 2.6. You can compare your work with the solution found in the student files (chapter2/blockquote.html).

 Why does my web page still look the same?

Often, students make changes to a web page but get frustrated because their browser shows an older version of the page. The following troubleshooting tips are helpful when you know you modified your web page, but the changes do not show up in the browser:

1. Be sure that you save your web page file after you make changes.

2. Verify the location to which you save your file—the hard drive, a particular folder.

3. Verify the location from which your browser is requesting the file—the hard drive, a particular folder.

4. Be sure to click your browser's Refresh or Reload button.

Phrase Elements

Phrase elements indicate the context and meaning of the text between the container tags. It is up to each browser to interpret that style. Phrase elements are displayed directly in line with the text (referred to as inline display) and can apply to either a section of text or even a single character of text. For example, the **<strong>** element indicates that the text associated with it has strong importance and should be displayed in a "strong" manner in relation to normal text on the page.

Table 2.1 lists common phrase elements and examples of their use. Notice that some tags, such as <cite> and <dfn>, result in the same type of display (italics) as the <em> tag in today's browsers. These tags semantically describe the text as a citation or definition, but the physical display is usually italics in both cases.

TABLE 2.1   *Phrase Elements*

Element	Example	Usage
<abbr>	WIPO	Identifies text as an abbreviation
<b>	**bold** text	Text that has no extra importance but is styled in bold font
<cite>	*cite* text	Identifies a citation or reference; usually displayed in italics
<code>	code text	Identifies program code samples; usually a fixed-space font
<dfn>	*dfn* text	Identifies a definition of a word or term; usually displayed in italics
<em>	*emphasized* text	Causes text to be emphasized; usually displayed in italics
<i>	*italicized* text	Text that has no extra importance but is styled in italics
<kbd>	kbd text	Identifies user text to be typed; usually a fixed-space font
<mark>	mark text	Text that is highlighted in order to be easily referenced (HTML5 only)
<samp>	samp text	Shows program sample output; usually a fixed-space font
<small>	small text	Legal disclaimers and notices (fine print) displayed in small font size
<strong>	**strong** text	Strong importance; usually displayed in bold
<sub>	$_{sub}$text	Displays a subscript as small text below the baseline
<sup>	^{sup}text	Displays a superscript as small text above the baseline
<var>	*var* text	Identifies and displays a variable output; usually displayed in italics

Note that all phrase elements are container tags—both an opening and a closing tag is used. As shown in Table 2.1, the `<strong>` element indicates that the text associated with it has "strong" importance. Usually the browser (or other user agent) will display `<strong>` text in bold type. A screen reader, such as JAWS or Window-Eyes, might interpret `<strong>` text to indicate that the text should be more strongly spoken. In the following line the phone number is displayed with strong importance:

Call for a free quote for your web development needs: **888.555.5555**

The code is

```
<p>Call for a free quote for your web development needs:
<strong>888.555.5555</strong></p>
```

Notice that the opening `<strong>` and closing `<strong>` tags are contained within the paragraph tags (`<p>` and `</p>`). This code is properly nested and is considered to be **well formed**. When improperly nested, the `<p>` and `<strong>` tag pairs overlap each other instead of being nested within each other. Improperly nested code will not pass validation testing (see the HTML Syntax Validation section later in this chapter) and may cause display issues.

Figure 2.7 shows a web page document (also found in the student files at chapter2/em.html) that uses the `<em>` tag to display the emphasized phrase, "Access by everyone," in italics.

FIGURE 2.7 *The `<em>` tag in action.*

The code snippet is

```
<blockquote>
The power of the Web is in its universality.
<em>Access by everyone</em> regardless of disability is an essential
aspect.
</blockquote>
```

Ordered List

Lists are used on web pages to organize information. When writing for the Web, headings, short paragraphs, and lists can make your page more clear and easy to read. HTML can be used to create three types of lists—description lists, ordered lists, and unordered lists. All lists are rendered as block display with empty space above and below. This section focuses on the **ordered list**, which displays a numbering or lettering system to sequence the information contained in the list. An ordered list can be organized using numerals (the default), uppercase letters, lowercase letters, uppercase Roman numerals, and lowercase Roman numerals. See Figure 2.8 for a sample ordered list.

My Favorite Colors

1. Blue
2. Teal
3. Red

FIGURE 2.8 *Sample ordered list.*

Ordered lists begin with an **\<ol\>** tag and end with an **\</ol\>** tag. Each list item begins with an **\<li\>** tag and ends with an **\</li\>** tag. The code to configure the heading and ordered list shown in Figure 2.8 follows:

```
<h1>My Favorite Colors</h1>
<ol>
  <li>Blue</li>
  <li>Teal</li>
  <li>Red</li>
</ol>
```

The `type`, `start`, and `reversed` Attributes

The **type attribute** configures the symbol used for ordering the list. For example, to create an ordered list organized by uppercase letters, use `<ol type="A">`. Table 2.2 documents the type attribute and its values for ordered lists.

TABLE 2.2 *The type Attribute for Ordered Lists*

Value	Symbol
1	Numerals (the default)
A	Uppercase letters
a	Lowercase letters
I	Roman numerals
i	Lowercase Roman numerals

Another handy attribute that can be used with ordered lists is the **start attribute**, with which you can specify the start value for the list (for example, `start="10"`). In addition, HTML5 introduces the new **reversed attribute** (`reversed="reversed"`) to indicate that a list is in descending order.

Hands-On Practice 2.6

In this Hands-On Practice you will use a heading and an ordered list on the same page. To create the web page shown in Figure 2.9, launch a text editor, and open the template.html file from the chapter1 folder in the student files. Modify the title element and add h1, h2, ol, and li tags to the body section, as indicated by the following highlighted code:

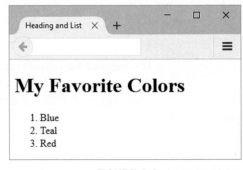

FIGURE 2.9 *An ordered list.*

```
<!DOCTYPE html>
<html lang="en">
<head>
<title>Heading and List</title>
<meta charset="utf-8">
</head>
<body>
<h1>My Favorite Colors</h1>
<ol>
  <li>Blue</li>
  <li>Teal</li>
  <li>Red</li>
</ol>
</body>
</html>
```

Save your file as ol.html. Launch a browser and test your page. It should look similar to the page shown in Figure 2.9. You can compare your work with the solution in the student files (chapter2/ol.html).

Take a few minutes to experiment with the `type` attribute. Configure the ordered list to use uppercase letters instead of numerals. Save your file as ola.html. Test your page in a browser. You can compare your work with the solution in the student files (chapter2/ola.html).

FAQ **Why is the web page code in the examples indented?**

Actually, it doesn't matter to the browser if web page code is indented, but humans find it easier to read and maintain code when it is logically indented. This makes it easier for you or another web developer to understand the source code in the future. For example, it's common practice to indent `<li>` tags a few spaces in from the left margin because it makes it easier to "see" the list with a quick glance at the source code. There is no "rule" as to how many spaces to indent, although your instructor or the organization you work for may have a standard. Consistent indentation helps to create more easily maintainable web pages.

Unordered List

Unordered lists display a bullet, or list marker, before each list entry. The default list marker is determined by the browser but is typically a disc, which is a filled-in circle. See Figure 2.10 for a sample unordered list.

My Favorite Colors

- Blue
- Teal
- Red

FIGURE 2.10 *Sample unordered list.*

Unordered lists begin with a **<ul>** tag and end with a **</ul>** tag. The ul element is a block display element and is rendered with empty space above and below. Each list item begins with an <li> tag and ends with an </li> tag. The code to configure the heading and unordered list shown in Figure 2.10 is

```
<h1>My Favorite Colors</h1>
<ul>
  <li>Blue</li>
  <li>Teal</li>
  <li>Red</li>
</ul>
```

? **FAQ** **Can I change the "bullet" in an unordered list?**

Back in the day before HTML5, the type attribute could be included with a <ul> tag to change the default list marker to a square (type="square") or open circle (type="circle"). However, be aware that using the type attribute on an unordered list is considered obsolete in HTML5 because it is decorative and does not convey meaning. No worries, though—there are CSS techniques to configure list markers (bullets) to display images and shapes.

Hands-On Practice 2.7

In this Hands-On Practice you will use a heading and an unordered list on the same page. To create the web page shown in Figure 2.11, launch a text editor, and open the template.html file from the chapter1 folder in the student files. Modify the title element and add h1, ul, and li tags to the body section as indicated by the following highlighted code:

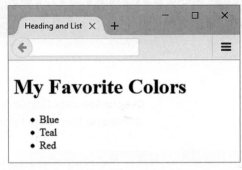

FIGURE 2.11 *An unordered list.*

```
<!DOCTYPE html>
<html lang="en">
<head>
<title>Heading and List</title>
<meta charset="utf-8">
</head>
<body>
<h1>My Favorite Colors</h1>
<ul>
  <li>Blue</li>
  <li>Teal</li>
  <li>Red</li>
</ul>
</body>
</html>
```

Save your file as ul.html. Launch a browser and test your page. It should look similar to the page shown in Figure 2.11. You can compare your work with the solution in the student files (chapter2/ul.html).

Description List

Description lists (formerly called **definition lists** in XHTML and HTML4) help to organize terms and their descriptions. The terms stand out, and their descriptions can be as long as needed to convey your message. Each term begins on its own line at the margin. Each description begins on its own line and is indented. Description lists are also handy for organizing Frequently Asked Questions (FAQs) and their answers. The questions and answers are offset with indentation. Any type of information that consists of a number of corresponding terms and associated descriptions is well suited to being organized in a description list. See Figure 2.12 for an example of a web page that uses a description list.

Description lists begin with the **<dl>** tag and end with the **</dl>** tag. Each term or name in the list begins with the **<dt>** tag and ends with the **</dt>** tag. Each term description begins with the **<dd>** tag and ends with the **</dd>** tag.

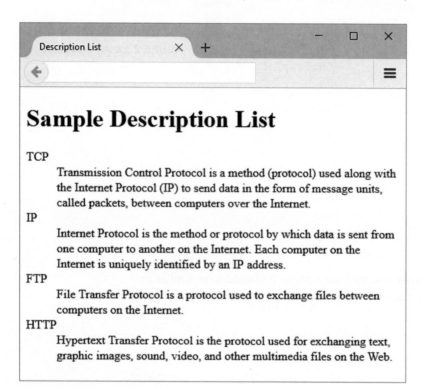

FIGURE 2.12 *A description list.*

 Hands-On Practice 2.8

In this Hands-On Practice you will use a heading and a description list on the same page. To create the web page shown in Figure 2.12, launch a text editor, and open the template.html file from the chapter1 folder in the student files. Modify the title element and add h1, dl, dd, and dt tags to the body section as indicated by the following highlighted code:

```
<!DOCTYPE html>
<html lang="en">
<head>
<title>Description List</title>
<meta charset="utf-8">
</head>
<body>
<h1>Sample Description List</h1>
<dl>
  <dt>TCP</dt>
    <dd>Transmission Control Protocol is a method (protocol) used along
with the Internet Protocol (IP) to send data in the form of message
units, called packets, between computers over the Internet.</dd>
  <dt>IP</dt>
    <dd>Internet Protocol is the method or protocol by which data is
sent from one computer to another on the Internet. Each computer on
the Internet is uniquely identified by an IP address.</dd>
  <dt>FTP</dt>
    <dd>File Transfer Protocol is a protocol used to exchange files
between computers on the Internet.</dd>
  <dt>HTTP</dt>
    <dd>Hypertext Transfer Protocol is the protocol used for exchanging
text, graphic images, sound, video, and other multimedia files on the
Web.</dd>
</dl>
</body>
</html>
```

Save your file as description.html. Launch a browser and test your page. It should look similar to the page shown in Figure 2.12. Don't worry if the word wrap is a little different—the important formatting is that each `<dt>` term should be on its own line and the corresponding `<dd>` description should be indented under it. Try resizing your browser window and notice how the word wrap on the description text changes. You can compare your work with the solution in the student files (chapter2/description.html).

? FAQ   **Why does the text in my web page wrap differently than the examples?**

The text may wrap a little differently because your screen resolution or browser viewport size may not be the same as those on the computer used for the screen captures. That's part of the nature of working with the Web—expect your web pages to look slightly different in the multitude of screen resolutions, browser viewport sizes, and devices that people will use to view your designs.

Special Entity Characters

In order to use special characters such as quotation marks, the greater-than sign (>), the less-than sign (<), and the copyright symbol (©) in your web page document, you need to use special characters, sometimes called entity characters. For example, if you want to include a copyright line on your page as follows:

© Copyright 2018 My Company. All rights reserved.

you need to use the special character **©** to display the copyright symbol, as shown in here:

```
&copy; Copyright 2018 My Company. All rights reserved.
```

Another useful special character is ** **, which stands for nonbreaking space. You may have noticed that web browsers treat multiple spaces as a single space. If you want to display in your text, you can use   multiple times to indicate multiple blank spaces. This is acceptable if you simply need to tweak the position of an element a little. If you find that your web pages contain many   special characters in a row, you should use a different method to align elements, such as configuring the margin or padding with Cascading Style Sheets (see Chapter 6).

See Table 2.3 and http://dev.w3.org/html5/html-author/charref for a description of more special characters and their codes.

TABLE 2.3 *Common Special Characters*

Character	Entity Name	Code
"	Quotation mark	"
©	Copyright symbol	©
&	Ampersand	&
Empty space	Nonbreaking space	
'	Right single quote	’
—	Long dash	—
|	Vertical bar	|
<	Less than sign	<
>	Greater than sign	>

Figure 2.13 shows the web page you will create in this Hands-On Practice. Launch a text editor, and open the template.html file from the chapter1 folder in the student files.

Change the title of the web page to "Web Design Steps" by modifying the text between the `<title>` and `</title>` tags.

The sample page shown in Figure 2.13 contains a heading, an unordered list, and copyright information. You will add these elements to your file next.

Configure the phrase, "Web Design Steps", as a level 1 heading (`<h1>`) as follows:

`<h1>Web Design Steps</h1>`

Now create the unordered list. The first line of each bulleted item is the title of the web design step. In the sample, each step title should be strong or stand out from the rest of the text. The code for the beginning of the unordered list is

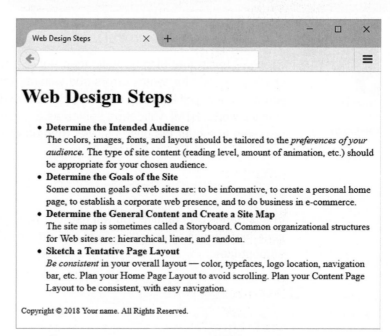

FIGURE 2.13 *Sample design.html.*

```
<ul>
  <li><strong>Determine the
  Intended Audience</strong>
  <br> The colors, images, fonts, and layout should be tailored to
  the <em> preferences of your audience.</em> The type of site content
  (reading level, amount of animation, etc.) should be appropriate for
  your chosen audience.</li>
```

Edit your design.html file and code the entire ordered list shown in Figure 2.13. Remember to code the closing `</ul>` tag at the end of the list. Finally, configure the copyright information in a paragraph and apply the small element. Use the special character `&copy;` for the copyright symbol. The code for the copyright line is

```
<p><small>Copyright &copy; 2018 Your name. All Rights
Reserved.</small></p>
```

Save your file as design.html. Launch a browser and test your page. How did you do? Compare your work to the sample in the student files (chapter2/design.html).

HTML Syntax Validation

VideoNote

HTML Validation

The W3C has a free Markup Validation Service available at http://validator.w3.org that will check your code for syntax errors and validate your web pages. **HTML validation** provides you with quick self-assessment—you can prove that your code uses correct syntax. In the working world, HTML validation serves as a quality assurance tool. Invalid code may cause browsers to render the pages slower than otherwise.

 Hands-On Practice 2.10

In this Hands-On Practice you will use the W3C Markup Validation Service to validate a web page file. Launch a text editor, and open the design.html file from the chapter2 folder in the student files.

FIGURE 2.14 *Validate your page.*

1. We will add an error to the design.html page. Delete the first closing `</strong>` tag. This modification should generate several error messages.

2. Next, attempt to validate the design.html file. Launch a browser and visit the W3C Markup Validation Service file upload page at http://validator.w3.org and select the "Validate by File Upload" tab. Click the Browse button and select the chapter2/design.html file from your computer. Click the Check button to upload the file to the W3C site (Figure 2.14).

3. A results page will display. Scroll down the page to view the errors, as shown in Figure 2.15.

4. Notice that the message indicates line 12, which is the first line after the missing closing `</strong>` tag. HTML error messages often point to a line that follows the error. The text of the message "End tag for li seen, but there were open elements" lets you know that something is wrong. It's up to you to figure out what it is. A good place to start is to check your container tags and make sure they are in pairs. In this case, that is the problem. You can scroll down to view the other errors. However, since multiple error messages are often displayed after a single error occurs, it's a good idea to fix one item at a time and then revalidate.

5. Edit the design.html file in a text editor and add the missing `</strong>` tag. Save the file. Launch a browser and visit http://validator.w3.org and select the "Validate by File Upload" tab. Click the Browse button and select your file. Click the Check button.

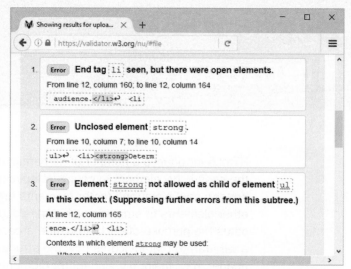

FIGURE 2.15 *The error indicates line 12.*

6. Your display should be similar to that shown in Figure 2.16. Notice the "Document checking completed. No errors or warnings to show." message. This means that your page passed the validation test. Congratulations, your web page is valid! You may also notice a message that indicates the HTML5 conformance checker is in experimental status.

FIGURE 2.16 *The page has passed the validation test.*

 It's a good practice to validate your web pages. However, when validating code, use common sense. Since web browsers still do not completely follow W3C recommendations, there will be situations, such as when adding multimedia to a web page, when HTML code configured to work reliably across a variety of browsers and platforms will not pass validation.

In addition to the W3C validation service, there are other tools that you can use to check the syntax of your code. Explore the HTML5 validator at http://html5.validator.nu and the HTML & CSS Validation Service at http://www.onlinewebcheck.com.

Structural
Elements

HTML5 introduces a number of semantic structural elements that can be used along with the generic div element to configure specific areas on a web page. These new HTML5 header, nav, main, and footer elements are intended to be used in conjunction with div and other elements to structure web page documents in a more meaningful manner that indicates the purpose of each structural area. Figure 2.17 shows a diagram of a page (called a **wireframe**) that indicates how the structure of a web page could be configured with the header, nav, main, div, and footer elements.

| header |
| nav |
| main |
| div div div |
| footer |

FIGURE 2.17 *Structural elements.*

The Div Element

The **div element** has been used for many years to configure a generic structural area or "division" on a web page as a block display with empty space above and below. A div element begins with a `<div>` tag and ends with a `</div>` tag. Use a div element when you need to format an area of a web page that may contain other block display elements such as headings, paragraphs, unordered lists, and even other div elements. You'll use Cascading Style Sheets (CSS) later in this book to style and configure the color, font, and layout of HTML elements.

The Header Element

The purpose of the HTML5 **header element** is to contain the headings of either a web page document or an area within the document such as a section or article (more on the section element and article element in Chapter 8). The header element begins with the `<header>` tag and ends with the `</header>` tag. The header element is block display and typically contains one or more heading level elements (h1 through h6).

The Nav Element

The purpose of the HTML5 **nav element** is to contain a section of navigation links. The block display nav element begins with the `<nav>` tag and ends with the `</nav>` tag.

The Main Element

The purpose of the HTML5 **main** element is to contain the main content of a web page document. There should be only one main element per web page. The block display main element begins with the `<main>` tag and ends with the `</main>` tag.

The Footer Element

The purpose of the HTML5 **footer element** is to contain the footer content of a web page or section of a web page. The block display footer element begins with the `<footer>` tag and ends with the `</footer>` tag.

 Hands-On Practice 2.11

In this Hands-On Practice you will practice using structural elements as you create the Trillium Media Design home page, shown in Figure 2.18. Launch a text editor, and open the template.html file from the chapter1 folder in the student files. Edit the code as follows:

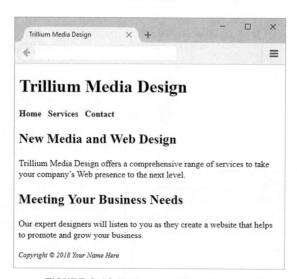

FIGURE 2.18 *Trillium home page.*

1. Modify the title of the web page by changing the text between the `<title>` and `</title>` tags to Trillium Media Design.

2. Position your cursor in the body section and code the header element with the text, "Trillium Media Design" contained in an h1 element:

   ```
   <header>
     <h1>Trillium Media Design</h1>
   </header>
   ```

3. Code a nav element to contain text that will indicate the main navigation for the website. Configure bold text (use the b element) and use the ` ` special character to add extra blank space:

   ```
   <nav>
     <b>Home   Services   Contact</b>
   </nav>
   ```

4. Code the content within a main element that contains the h2 and paragraph elements:

   ```
   <main>
     <h2>New Media and Web Design</h2>
     <p>Trillium Media Design offers a comprehensive range of
   services to take your company&rsquo;s Web presence to the next
   level.</p>
     <h2>Meeting Your Business Needs</h2>
     <p>Our expert designers will listen to you as they create a website
   that helps to promote and grow your business.</p>
   </main>
   ```

5. Configure the footer element to contain a copyright notice displayed in small font size (use the small element) and italic font (use the i element). Be careful to properly nest the elements as shown here:

   ```
   <footer>
     <small><i>Copyright &copy; 2018 Your Name Here</i></small>
   </footer>
   ```

Save your page as structure.html. Test your page in a browser. It should look similar to Figure 2.18. You can compare your work to the sample in the student files (chapter2/structure.html).

Practice with Structural Elements

Coding HTML is a skill and skills are best learned by practice. You'll get more practice coding a web page using structural elements in this section.

 Hands-On Practice 2.12

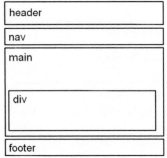

FIGURE 2.19 *Wireframe for Casita Sedona.*

In this Hands-On Practice you will use the wireframe shown in Figure 2.19 as a guide as you create the Casita Sedona Bed & Breakfast web page, shown in Figure 2.20.

Launch a text editor, and open the template.html file from the chapter1 folder in the student files. Edit the code as follows:

1. Modify the title of the web page by changing the text between the `<title>` and `</title>` tags to Casita Sedona.

2. Position your cursor in the body section and code the header element with the text, "Casita Sedona Bed & Breakfast" contained in an h1 element. Be sure to use the special character `&amp;` for the ampersand.

```
<header>
  <h1>
  Casita Sedona Bed &amp; Breakfast
  </h1>
</header>
```

3. Code a nav element to contain text that will indicate the main navigation for the website. Configure bold text (use the b element) and use the ` ` special character to add extra blank space:

```
<nav>
  <b>
    Home  
    Rooms  
    Events  
    Contact
  </b>
</nav>
```

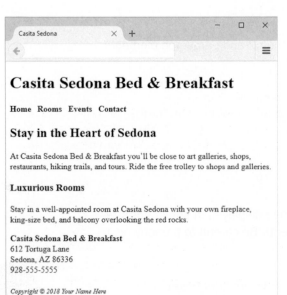

FIGURE 2.20 *Casita Sedona web page.*

4. Code the content within a main element. Start with the h2 and paragraph elements:

```
<main>
<h2>Stay in the Heart of Sedona</h2>
   <p>At Casita Sedona Bed &amp; Breakfast you&rsquo;ll be close to
art galleries, shops, restaurants, hiking trails, and tours. Ride
the free trolley to shops and galleries.</p>
      <h3>Luxurious Rooms</h3>
      <p>Stay in a well-appointed room at Casita Sedona with your own
fireplace, king-size bed, and balcony overlooking the red rocks.</p>
</main>
```

5. Configure the company name, address, and phone number within a div element. Code the div element *within* the main element before the closing main tag. Use line break tags to display the name, address, and phone information on separate lines and to create extra empty space before the footer.

```
<div>
      <strong>Casita Sedona Bed &amp; Breakfast</strong><br>
      612 Tortuga Lane<br>
      Sedona, AZ 86336<br>
      928-555-5555<br>
</div>
```

6. Configure the footer element to contain a copyright notice displayed in small font size (use the small element) and italic font (use the i element). Be careful to properly nest the elements as shown here:

```
<footer>
      <small><i>Copyright &copy; 2018 Your Name Here</i></small>
</footer>
```

Save your page as casita.html. Test your page in a browser. It should look similar to Figure 2.20. You can compare your work to the sample in the student files (chapter2/casita.html).

Older browsers (such as Internet Explorer 8 and earlier) do not support the new HTML5 elements. In Chapter 8, we'll explore coding techniques that will force older browsers to correctly display HTML5 structural tags. For now, be sure to use a current version of any popular browser to test your pages.

Are there more new structural elements in HTML5?

Yes, one of the characteristics of HTML5 is an emphasis on semantics. While the div element is useful, it is also generic. HTML5 offers a variety of special-purpose structural elements, including section, article, header, nav, main, aside, and footer. You'll explore the section, article, and aside elements in Chapter 8.

Anchor Element

Use the **anchor element** to specify a **hyperlink,** often referred to as a *link*, to another web page or file that you want to display. Each anchor element begins with an **<a>** tag and ends with an **</a>** tag. The opening and closing anchor tags surround the text that the user can click to perform the hyperlink. Use the **href attribute** to configure the hyperlink reference, which identifies the name and location of the file to access.

Figure 2.21 shows a web page document with an anchor tag that configures a hyperlink to this book's website, http://webdevbasics.net.

The code for the anchor tag in Figure 2.21 is

```
<a href="http://webdevbasics.net">Basics of Web Design Textbook
Companion</a>
```

Notice that the href value is the URL for the website and will display the home page. The text that is typed between the two anchor tags displays on the web page as a hyperlink and is underlined by most browsers. When you move the mouse over a hyperlink, the cursor changes to a pointing hand, as shown in Figure 2.21.

 Hands-On Practice 2.13

To create the web page shown in Figure 2.21, launch a text editor, and open the template.html file from the chapter1 folder in the student files. Modify the title element and add an anchor tag to the body section as indicated by the following highlighted code:

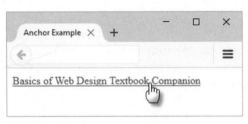

FIGURE 2.21 *Sample hyperlink.*

```
<!DOCTYPE html>
<html lang="en">
<head>
<title>Anchor Example</title>
<meta charset="utf-8">
</head>
<body>
<a href="http://webdevbasics.net">Basics of Web
Design Textbook Companion</a>
</body>
</html>
```

Save the document as anchor.html on your hard drive or flash drive. Launch a browser and test your page. It should look similar to the page shown in Figure 2.21. You can compare your work with the solution found in the student files (chapter2/anchor.html).

Can images be hyperlinks?

Yes. Although we'll concentrate on text hyperlinks in this chapter, it is also possible to configure an image as a hyperlink. You'll get practice with image links in Chapter 5.

Targeting Hyperlinks

You may have noticed in Hands-On Practice 2.13 that when a visitor clicks a hyperlink, the new web page automatically opens in the same browser window. You can configure the **target attribute** on an anchor tag with `target="_blank"` to open a hyperlink in a *new* browser window or browser tab. Note that you cannot control whether the web page opens in a new window or opens in a new tab—that is dependent on your visitor's browser configuration. To see the target attribute in action, try the example in the student files at chapter2/target.html.

Absolute Hyperlinks

An **absolute hyperlink** indicates the absolute location of a resource on the Web. The hyperlink in Hands-On Practice 2.13 is an absolute hyperlink. Use absolute hyperlinks when you need to link to resources on other websites. The href value for an absolute hyperlink to the home page of a website includes the http://protocol and the domain name. The following hyperlink is an absolute hyperlink to the home page of this book's website:

```
<a href="http://webdevbasics.net">Basics of Web Design</a>
```

Note that if we want to access a web page other than the home page on the book's website, we can also include a specific folder name and file name. For example, the following anchor tag configures an absolute hyperlink for a file named chapter1.html located in a folder named 4e on this book's website:

```
<a href="http://webdevbasics.net/4e/chapter1.html">Chapter 1</a>
```

Relative Hyperlink

When you need to link to web pages within your site, use a **relative hyperlink**. The href value for a relative hyperlink does not begin with http:// and does not include a domain name. For a relative hyperlink, the href value will contain only the file name (or folder and file name) of the web page you want to display. The hyperlink location is relative to the page currently being displayed. For example, if you are coding a home page (index.html) for a website and want to link to a page named contact.html located in the same folder as index.html, you can configure a relative hyperlink as shown in the following code sample:

```
<a href="contact.html">Contact Us</a>
```

Block Anchor

It's typical to use anchor tags to configure phrases or even just a single word as a hyperlink. HTML5 provides a new function for the anchor tag—the block anchor. A block anchor can configure one or more entire elements (even those that display as a block, such as a div, h1, or paragraph) as a hyperlink. See an example in the student files (chapter2/block.html).

Accessibility and Hyperlinks

Visually challenged visitors who are using a screen reader can configure the software to display a list of the hyperlinks in the document. However, a list of hyperlinks is only useful if the text describing each hyperlink is actually helpful and descriptive. For example, on your college website, a "Search the course schedule" link would be more useful than a hyperlink that simply says "More information" or "click here." Keep this in mind as you are coding hyperlinks in your web pages.

Practice with Hyperlinks

The best way to learn how to code web pages is by actually doing it! In this section, you'll create three pages in a small website so that you can practice using the anchor tag to configure hyperlinks.

Site Map

Figure 2.22 displays the site map for your new website—a Home page with two content pages: a Services page and a Contact page.

FIGURE 2.22 *Site map.*

A **site map** represents the structure, or organization, of pages in a website in a visual manner. Each page in the website is represented by a box on the site map. Review Figure 2.22 and notice that the Home page is at the top of the site map. The second level in a site map shows the other main pages of the website. In this very small three-page website, the other two pages (Services and Contact) are included on the second level. The main navigation of a website usually includes hyperlinks to the pages shown on the first two levels of the site map.

 Hands-On Practice 2.14

Figure 2.22 displays the site map for your new website—a home page (index.html) with two content pages: services page (services.html) and contact page (contact.html).

1. **Create a Folder.**   If you had printed papers to organize you would probably store them in a paper folder. Web designers store and organize their computer files by creating a folder on a hard drive (or portable storage such as an SD card or Flash drive) for each website. This helps them to be efficient as they work with many different websites.

? **FAQ**   **How do I create a new folder?**

Before you begin to learn how to code web pages, it's a good idea to be comfortable using your computer for basic tasks such as creating a new folder. If you don't remember how to create a folder, review Hands-On Practice 1.1 for instructions. You may also benefit from a brush-up course on either the Windows or Mac operating systems before you continue. For a quick review on how to use your operating system, check out the following resources:

▶ *Mac:* https://www.apple.com/support/macbasics/

▶ *Windows:* https://support.microsoft.com/en-us/products/windows?os=windows-10

You will organize your own web design work by creating a new folder for each website and storing your files for that website in the new folder. Use your operating system to create a new folder named mypractice for your new website.

2. **Create the Home Page.** Use the Trillium Media Design web page (Figure 2.18) from Hands-On Practice 2.11 as a starting point for your new home page (shown in Figure 2.23). Copy the sample file for Hands-On Practice 2.11 (chapter2/structure.html) into your mypractice folder. Change the file name of structure.html to index.html. It's common practice to use the file name index.html for the home page of a website.

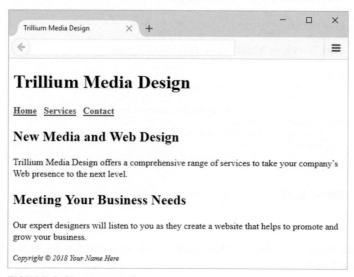

FIGURE 2.23 *New index.html web page.*

Launch a text editor, and open the index.html file.

a. The navigation hyperlinks will be located within the nav element. You will edit the code within the nav element to configure three hyperlinks:

  ▶ The text "Home" will hyperlink to index.html

  ▶ The text "Services" will hyperlink to services.html

  ▶ The text "Contact" will hyperlink to contact.html

Modify the code within the nav element as follows:

```
<nav>
  <b>
    <a href="index.html">Home</a>  
    <a href="services.html">Services</a>  
    <a href="contact.html">Contact</a>
  </b>
</nav>
```

b. Save the index.html file in your mypractice folder. Test your page in a browser. It should look similar to Figure 2.21. You can compare your work to the sample in the student files (chapter2/2.14/index.html).

3. **Create the Services Page.** It is common practice to create a new web page based on an existing page. You will use the index.html file as a starting point for the new services page, as shown in Figure 2.24.

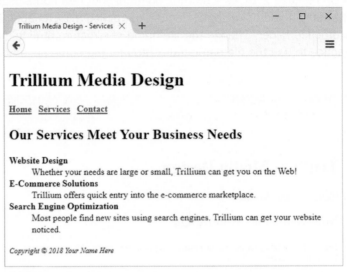

FIGURE 2.24 *The services.html web page.*

Open your index.html file in a text editor and save the file as services.html. Edit the code as follows:

a. Modify the title of the web page by changing the text between the `<title>` and `</title>` tags to "Trillium Media Design - Services". In order to create a consistent header, navigation, and footer for the web pages in this website, do not change the code within the header, nav, or footer elements.

b. Position your cursor in the body section and delete the code and text between the opening and closing main tags. Code the main page content (heading 2 and description list) for the services page between the main tags as follows:

```
<h2> Our Services Meet Your Business Needs</h2>
  <dl>
    <dt><strong>Website Design</strong></dt>
      <dd>Whether your needs are large or small, Trillium can get
      you on the Web!</dd>
    <dt><strong>E-Commerce Solutions</strong></dt>
      <dd>Trillium offers quick entry into the e-commerce
      marketplace.</dd>
    <dt><strong>Search Engine Optimization</strong></dt>
      <dd>Most people find new sites using search engines.
      Trillium can get your website noticed.</dd>
  </dl>
```

c. Save the services.html file in your mypractice folder. Test your page in a browser. It should look similar to Figure 2.24. You can compare your work to the sample in the student files (chapter2/2.14/services.html).

4. **Create the Contact Page.** Use the index.html file as a starting point for the Contact page, as shown in Figure 2.25. Launch a text editor, open index.html, and save the file as contact.html. Edit the code as follows:

a. Modify the title of the web page by changing the text between the `<title>` and `</title>` tags to "Trillium Media Design - Contact". In order to create a consistent header, navigation, and footer for the web pages in this website, do not change the code within the header, nav, or footer elements.

FIGURE 2.25 *The contact.html web page.*

b. Position your cursor in the body section and delete the code and text contained between the opening main tag and the closing main tag. Code the main page content for the contact page between the main tags:

```
<h2>Contact Trillium Media Design Today</h2>
   <ul>
     <li>E-mail: contact@trilliummediadesign.com</li>
     <li>Phone: 555-555-5555</li>
   </ul>
```

c. Save the contact.html file in your mypractice folder. Test your page in a browser. It should look similar to Figure 2.25. Test your page by clicking each link. When you click the "Home" hyperlink, the index.html page should display. When you click the "Services" hyperlink, the services.html page should display. When you click the "Contact" hyperlink, the contact.html page will display. You can compare your work to the sample in the student files (chapter2/2.14/contact.html).

What if my relative hyperlink doesn't work?

Check the following:

▶ Did you save files in the specified folder?

▶ Did you save the files with the names as requested? Use Windows Explorer or Finder (Mac users) to verify the actual names of the files you saved.

▶ Did you type the file names correctly in the anchor tag's href property? Check for typographical errors.

▶ When you place your mouse over a link, the file name of a relative link will display in the status bar in the lower edge of the browser window. Verify that this is the correct file name. On many operating systems, such as UNIX or Linux, the use of uppercase and lowercase letters in file names matters—make sure that the file name and the reference to it are in the same case. It's a good practice to always use lowercase for file names used on the Web.

E-Mail Hyperlinks

The anchor tag can also be used to create e-mail hyperlinks. An e-mail hyperlink will automatically launch the default mail program configured for the browser. It is similar to an external hyperlink with the following two exceptions:

▶ It uses `mailto:` instead of `http://`.

▶ It launches the default e-mail application for the visitor's browser with your e-mail address as the recipient.

For example, to create an e-mail hyperlink to the e-mail address help@webdevbasics.net, code the following:

```
<a href="mailto:help@webdevbasics.net">help@webdevbasics.net</a>
```

It is good practice to place the e-mail address both on the web page and within the anchor tag. Not everyone has an e-mail program configured with his or her browser. By placing the e-mail address in both places, you increase usability for all of your visitors.

 Hands-On Practice 2.15 ─────────────────────────

In this Hands-On Practice you will modify the contact page (contact.html) of the website you created in Hands-On Practice 2.14 and configure an e-mail link in the page content area. Launch a text editor, and open the contact.html file from your mypractice folder. This example uses the contact.html file found in the student files in the chapter2/2.14 folder.

FIGURE 2.26 *An e-mail hyperlink has been configured on the contact page.*

Configure the e-mail address in the content area as an e-mail hyperlink as follows:

```
<li>E-mail:
<a href="mailto:contact@trilliummediadesign.com">contact@trilliummediadesign.com</a>
</li>
```

Save and test the page in a browser. The browser display should look similar to the page shown in Figure 2.26. Compare your work with the sample in the student files (chapter2/2.15/contact.html).

Free web-based e-mail is offered by many providers, such as Yahoo!, Google, Hotmail, and so on. You can create one or more free e-mail accounts to use when communicating with new websites or signing up for free services, such as newsletters. This will help to organize your e-mail into those you need to access and respond to right away (such as school, work, or personal messages) and those you can get to at your convenience.

Won't displaying my actual e-mail address on a web page increase spam?

Yes and no. While it's possible that some unethical spammers may harvest web pages for e-mail addresses, the chances are that your e-mail application's built-in spam filter will prevent your inbox from being flooded with messages. When you configure an easily readable e-mail hyperlink you increase the usability of your website for your visitors in the following situations:

▶ The visitor may be at a public computer with no e-mail application configured. In this case, when the e-mail hyperlink is clicked, an error message may display, and the visitor will have difficulty contacting you using the e-mail link.

▶ The visitor may be at a private computer but may prefer not to use the e-mail application (and address) that is configured by default to work with the browser. Perhaps he or she shares the computer with others, or perhaps he or she wishes to preserve the privacy of the default e-mail address

If you prominently displayed your actual e-mail address, in both of these situations the visitor can still access your e-mail address and use it to contact you (in either their e-mail application or via a web-based e-mail system such as Google's Gmail). The result is a more usable website for your visitors.

CHAPTER 2

Review and Apply

Review Questions

1. Which tag is used to hyperlink web pages to each other?

   a. `<br>`
   b. `<hyperlink>`
   c. `<a>`
   d. `<link>`

2. Which tag pair configures the largest heading?

   a. `<h1> </h1>`
   b. `<h9> </h9>`
   c. `<h type="largest"> </h>`
   d. `<h6> </h6>`

3. Which tag configures the following text or element to display on a new line?

   a. `<new line>`
   b. `<nl>`
   c. `<br>`
   d. `<line>`

4. Which tag pair configures a paragraph?

   a. `<para> </para>`
   b. `<paragraph> </paragraph>`
   c. `<p> </p>`
   d. `<body> </body>`

5. Which of the following is an HTML5 element used to indicate navigational content?

   a. nav
   b. header
   c. footer
   d. a

6. When should you code an absolute hyperlink?

   a. when linking to a web page that is internal to your website

   b. when linking to a web page that is external to your website

   c. always; the W3C prefers absolute hyperlinks

   d. never; absolute hyperlinks are obsolete

7. Which tag pair is the best choice to emphasize text with italic font on a web page?

   a. `<b> </b>`
   b. `<strong> </strong>`
   c. `<em> </em>`
   d. `<bold> </bold>`

8. Which tag configures a horizontal line on a web page?

   a. `<br>`
   b. `<hr>`
   c. `<line>`
   d. `<h1>`

9. Which type of HTML list will automatically number the items for you?

   a. numbered list
   b. ordered list
   c. unordered list
   d. description list

10. Which statement is true?

    a. The W3C Markup Validation Service describes how to fix the errors in your web page.

    b. The W3C Markup Validation Service lists syntax errors in a web page.

    c. The W3C Markup Validation Service is only available to W3C members.

    d. None of the above statements are true.

Hands-On Exercises

1. Write the markup language code to display your name in the largest-size heading element.

2. Write the markup language code for an unordered list to display the days of the week.

3. Write the markup language code for an ordered list that uses uppercase letters to order the items. This ordered list will display the following: Spring, Summer, Fall, and Winter.

4. Think of a favorite quote by someone you admire. Write the HTML code to display the person's name in a heading and the quote in a blockquote.

5. Modify the following code snippet to indicate that the bolded text has strong importance.

```
<p>A diagram of the organization of a website is called a <b>site
map</b> or <b>storyboard</b>. Creating the <b>site map</b> is one
of the initial steps in developing a website.</p>
```

6. Write the code to create an absolute hyperlink to your school's website.

7. Write the code to create a relative hyperlink to a web page named clients.html.

8. Create a web page about your favorite musical group. Include the name of the group, the members of the group, a hyperlink to the group's website, your favorite three (or fewer if the group is new) album releases, and a brief review of each album. Be sure to use the following elements: html, head, title, meta, body, header, footer, main, h1, h2, p, ul, li, and a. Configure your name in an e-mail link in the page footer area. Save the page as band.html. Open your file in a text editor and print the source code for the page. Display your page in a browser and print the page. Hand in both printouts to your instructor.

Focus on Web Design

Markup language code alone does not make a web page—design is very important. Access the Web and find two web pages—one that is appealing to you and one that is unappealing to you. Print each page. Create a web page that answers the following questions for each of your examples.

a. What is the URL of the website?

b. Is the page appealing or unappealing? List three reasons for your answer.

c. If the page is unappealing, what would you do to improve it?

d. Would you encourage others to visit this site? Why or why not?

Case Study

The following case studies continue throughout most of the text. This chapter introduces each website scenario, presents the site map, and directs you to create two pages for the site.

Pacific Trails Resort Case Study

Melanie Bowie is the owner of Pacific Trails Resort, located right on the California North Coast. The resort offers a quiet getaway with luxury camping in yurts along with an upscale lodge for dining and visiting with fellow guests. The target audience for Pacific Trails Resort is couples who enjoy nature and hiking. Melanie would like a website that emphasizes the uniqueness of the location and accommodations. She would like the website to include a

FIGURE 2.27 *Pacific Trails Resort site map.*

FIGURE 2.28 *Pacific Trails Resort wireframe page layout.*

home page, a page about the special yurt accommodations, a reservations page with a contact form, and a page to describe the activities available at the resort.

A site map for the Pacific Trails Resort website is shown in Figure 2.27. The site map describes the architecture of the website—a Home page with three main content pages: Yurts, Activities, and Reservations.

Figure 2.28 displays a wireframe sketch of the page layout for the Pacific Trails Resort website. The wireframe contains a header area, a navigation area, a main content area, and a footer area for copyright information.

You have three tasks in this case study:

1. Create a folder for the Pacific Trails Resort website.
2. Create the Home page: index.html.
3. Create the Yurts page: yurts.html.

Task 1: Create a folder on your hard drive or portable storage device (thumb drive or SD card) called pacific to contain your Pacific Trails Resort website files.

Task 2: **The Home Page.** You will use a text editor to create the Home page for the Pacific Trails Resort website. The Home page is shown in Figure 2.29.

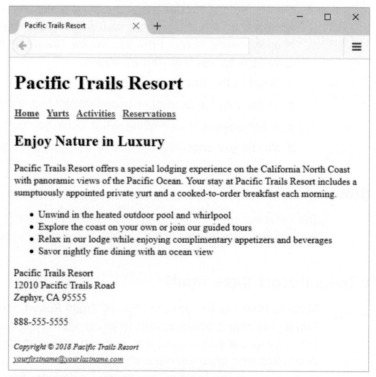

FIGURE 2.29 *Pacific Trails Resort index.html.*

Launch a text editor, and create a web page document with the following specifications:

1. **Web Page Title:** Use a descriptive page title—the company name is a good choice for a business website.

2. **Wireframe Header Area:** Code the header element with the text, "Pacific Trails Resort" contained within an h1 heading element.

3. **Wireframe Navigation Area:** Place the following text within a nav element with bold text (use the `<b>` element):

   Home   Yurts   Activities   Reservations

   Code anchor tags so that "Home" links to index.html, "Yurts" links to yurts.html, "Activities" links to activities.html, and "Reservations" links to reservations.html. Add extra blank spaces between the hyperlinks with the ` ` special character as needed.

4. **Wireframe Main Content Area:** Code the page content within a main element. Use Hands-On Practices 2.11 and 2.12 as a guide.

   a. Place the following within an h2 element: Enjoy Nature in Luxury

   b. Place the following content in a paragraph:

   Pacific Trails Resort offers a special lodging experience on the California North Coast with panoramic views of the Pacific Ocean. Your stay at Pacific Trails Resort includes a sumptuously appointed private yurt and a cooked-to-order breakfast each morning.

   c. Place the following content in an unordered list:

   Unwind in the heated outdoor pool and whirlpool
   Explore the coast on your own or join our guided tours
   Relax in our lodge while enjoying complimentary appetizers and beverages
   Savor nightly fine dining with an ocean view

   d. Contact information:

   Place the address and phone number information within a div below the unordered list. Use line break tags to help you configure this area and add extra space between the phone number and the footer area.

   Pacific Trails Resort
   12010 Pacific Trails Road
   Zephyr, CA 95555
   888-555-5555

5. **Wireframe Footer Area:** Configure the copyright and e-mail address information within a footer element. Also configure small text size (use the `<small>` element) and italics font style (use the `<i>` phrase element). The copyright information is

   Copyright © 2018 Pacific Trails Resort

   Place your name in an e-mail link on the line under the copyright.

The web page in Figure 2.29 may seem a little sparse, but don't worry. As you gain experience and learn to use more advanced techniques, your pages will look more professional. White space (blank space) on the page can be added with `<br>` tags where needed. Your page does not need to look exactly the same as the sample. Your goal at this point should be to practice and get comfortable using HTML. Save your file in the pacific folder and name it index.html.

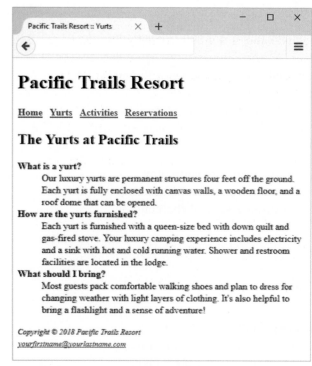

FIGURE 2.30 *The new Yurts page.*

Task 3: The Yurts Page. Create the Yurts page shown in Figure 2.30. A productivity technique is to create new pages based on existing pages so you can benefit from your previous work. Your new Yurts page will use the index.html page as a starting point. Open the index.html page for the Pacific Trails Resort website in a text editor. Select File > Save As and save the file with the new name of yurts.html in the pacific folder.

Now you are ready to edit the page.

1. **Web Page Title:** Modify the page title. Change the text contained between the `<title>` and `</title>` tags to Pacific Trails Resort :: Yurts.

2. **Wireframe Main Content Area:**

   a. Replace the text contained within the `<h2>` tags with The Yurts at Pacific Trails.

   b. Delete the Home page paragraph, unordered list, and the contact information.

   c. The Yurts page contains a list with questions and answers. Add this content to the page using a description list. Use the `<dt>` element to contain each question. Configure the question to display in bold text (use the `<strong>` element). Use the `<dd>` element to contain the answer to the question. The questions and answers are as follows:

   What is a yurt?

   Our luxury yurts are permanent structures four feet off the ground. Each yurt is fully enclosed with canvas walls, a wooden floor, and a roof dome that can be opened.

   How are the yurts furnished?

   Each yurt is furnished with a queen-size bed with down quilt and gas-fired stove. Your luxury camping experience includes electricity and a sink with hot and cold running water. Shower and restroom facilities are located in the lodge.

   What should I bring?

   Most guests pack comfortable walking shoes and plan to dress for changing weather with light layers of clothing. It's also helpful to bring a flashlight and a sense of adventure!

Save your page and test it in a browser. Test the hyperlink from the yurts.html page to index.html. Test the hyperlink from the index.html page to yurts.html. If your links do not work, review your work with close attention to these details:

- Verify that you have saved the pages with the correct names in the correct folder.
- Verify your spelling of the page names in the anchor tags.
- After you make changes, test again.

Path of Light Yoga Studio Case Study

Path of Light Yoga Studio is a small, recently opened yoga studio. The owner, Ariana Starrweaver, would like a website to showcase her yoga studio and provide information for both new and current students. Ariana would like a home page, a classes page that contains information about the types of yoga classes offered, a schedule page, and a contact page. A site map for the Path of Light Yoga Studio website is shown in Figure 2.31.

FIGURE 2.31 *Path of Light site map.*

The site map describes the architecture of the website, which consists of Home page with three main content pages: Classes, Schedule, and Contact.

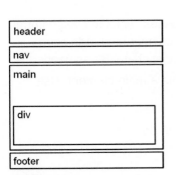

Figure 2.32 displays a wireframe sketch of the page layout for the website. It contains a site logo, a navigation area, a main content area, and a footer area for copyright information. You have three tasks in this case study:

1. Create a folder for the Path of Light Yoga Studio website.
2. Create the Home page: index.html.
3. Create the Classes page: classes.html.

FIGURE 2.32 *Path of Light wireframe.*

Hands-On Practice Case Study

Task 1: Create a folder on your hard drive or portable storage device (thumb drive or SD card) called yoga to contain your Path of Light Yoga Studio website files.

Task 2: The Home Page. You will use a text editor to create the Home page for the Path of Light Yoga Studio website. The Home page is shown in Figure 2.33.

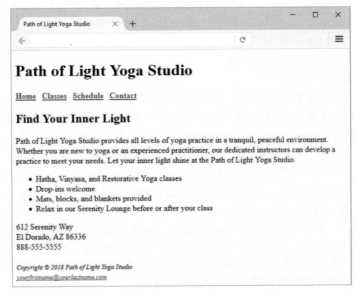

FIGURE 2.33 *Path of Light Yoga Studio index.html.*

Launch a text editor, and create a web page with the following specifications:

1. **Web Page Title:** Use a descriptive page title. The company name is a good choice for a business website.

2. **Wireframe Header Area:** Code the header element with the text, "Path of Light Yoga Studio" contained within an h1 heading element.

3. **Wireframe Navigation Area:** Place the following text within a nav element with bold text (use the `<b>` element):

   Home   Classes   Schedule   Contact

   Code anchor tags so that "Home" links to index.html, "Classes" links to classes.html, "Schedule" links to schedule.html, and "Contact" links to contact.html. Add extra blank spaces between the hyperlinks with the ` ` special character as needed.

4. **Wireframe Main Content Area:** Code the page content within a main element. Use Hands-On Practices 2.11 and 2.12 as a guide.

   a. Code the following text within an h2 element:

      Find Your Inner Light

   b. Configure the following sentences in a paragraph:

      Path of Light Yoga Studio provides all levels of yoga practice in a tranquil, peaceful environment. Whether you are new to yoga or an experienced practitioner, our dedicated instructors can develop a practice to meet your needs. Let your inner light shine at the Path of Light Yoga Studio.

   c. Configure the following content in an unordered list:

      Hatha, Vinyasa, and Restorative Yoga classes
      Drop-ins welcome
      Mats, blocks, and blankets provided
      Relax in our Serenity Lounge before or after your class

   d. Code the following address and phone number contact information within a div element. Use line break tags to help you configure this area and add extra space between the phone number and the footer area.

      612 Serenity Way
      El Dorado, AZ 86336
      888-555-5555

5. **Wireframe Footer Area:** Configure the following copyright and e-mail link information within a footer element. Format it with small text size (use the `<small>` tag) and italics font style (use the `<i>` tag).

   Copyright © 2018 Path of Light Yoga Studio
   Place your name in an e-mail link on the line under the copyright.

   The page in Figure 2.33 may seem a little sparse, but don't worry; as you gain experience and learn to use more advanced techniques, your pages will look more professional. White space (blank space) on the page can be added with `<br>` tags where needed. Your page does not need to look exactly the same as the sample. Your goal at this point should be to practice and get comfortable using HTML. Save your page in the yoga folder, and name it index.html.

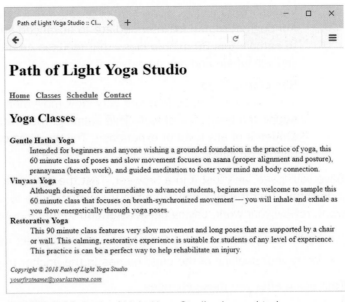

FIGURE 2.34 *Path of Light Yoga Studio classes.html.*

Task 3: **The Classes Page.** Create the Classes page shown in Figure 2.34. A technique that improves productivity is to create new pages based on existing pages so that you can benefit from your previous work. Your new Classes page will use the index.html page as a starting point.

Open the index.html page for the Path of Light Yoga Studio website in a text editor. Select File > Save As, and save the file with the new name of classes.html in the yoga folder. Now you are ready to edit the page.

1. **Web Page Title:** Modify the page title. Change the text contained between the `<title>` and `</title>` tags to the following:

   Path of Light Yoga Studio :: Classes

2. **Wireframe Main Content Area:**

   a. Delete the Home page content paragraph, unordered list, and contact information.

   b. Configure the following text in the heading 2 element:
   Yoga Classes

   c. Use a description list to configure information about the yoga classes. Configure the name of each class to have strong importance and bold font weight (use the `<strong>` tag) within a `<dt>` tag. Configure `<dd>` tags to contain the class descriptions. The information follows:

   Gentle Hatha Yoga
   Intended for beginners and anyone wishing a grounded foundation in the practice of yoga, this 60 minute class of poses and slow movement focuses on asana (proper alignment and posture), pranayama (breath work), and guided meditation to foster your mind and body connection.

Vinyasa Yoga

Although designed for intermediate to advanced students, beginners are welcome to sample this 60 minute class that focuses on breath-synchronized movement—you will inhale and exhale as you flow energetically through yoga poses.

Restorative Yoga

This 90 minute class features very slow movement and long poses that are supported by a chair or wall. This calming, restorative experience is suitable for students of any level of experience. This practice can be a perfect way to help rehabilitate an injury.

Save your page, and test it in a browser. Test the hyperlink from the classes.html page to index.html. Test the hyperlink from the index.html page to classes.html. If your links do not work, review your work, paying close attention to these details:

- Verify that you have saved the pages with the correct names in the correct folder.
- Verify your spelling of the page names in the anchor tags.

Test again after you make changes.

CHAPTER 3

Web Design Basics

As a website visitor, you have probably found that some websites are appealing and easy to use, while others seem awkward or just plain annoying. What separates the good from the bad? This chapter discusses recommended website design practices. The topics include site organization, site navigation, page design, choosing a color scheme, text design, graphic design, and accessibility considerations.

You'll learn how to...

▶ Describe the most common types of website organization

▶ Describe principles of visual design

▶ Design for your target audience

▶ Create clear, easy-to-use navigation

▶ Improve the readability of the text on your web pages

▶ Use graphics appropriately on web pages

▶ Choose a color scheme for your website

▶ Apply the concept of universal design to web pages

▶ Describe web page layout design techniques

▶ Describe the concept of responsive web design

▶ Apply best practices of web design

Your Target Audience

Whatever your personal preferences, your website should appeal to your **target audience**—the people who will use your site. Your intended target audience may be specific, such as kids, college students, young couples, or seniors, or you may intend your site to appeal to everyone. The purpose and goals of your visitors will vary—they may be casually seeking information, performing research for school or work, comparison shopping, job hunting, and so on. The design of a website should appeal to and meet the needs of the target audience.

For example, the web page shown in Figure 3.1 features compelling graphics and has a different look and feel from the text and link intensive web page displayed in Figure 3.2.

The first site engages you, draws you in, and invites exploration. The second site provides you with text-based information so that you can quickly get down to work. Keep your target audience in mind as you explore the web design practices in this chapter.

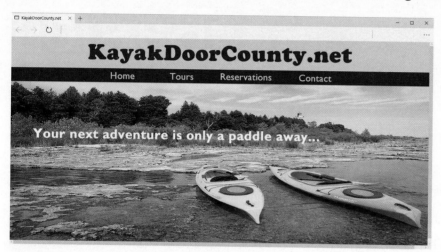

FIGURE 3.1 *The compelling graphic draws you in.*

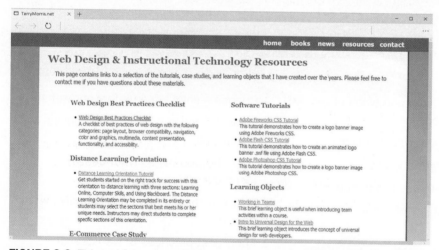

FIGURE 3.2 *This text-intensive website immediately offers numerous choices.*

Browsers

Just because your web page looks great in your favorite browser doesn't automatically mean that all browsers will render it well. Net Market Share (http://marketshare.hitslink.com) reported the market share of the top four desktop browsers in a recent month as Chrome (44.9%), Internet Explorer (34.46%), Firefox (9.52%), and Edge (4.59%). The market share of the top four mobile/tablet browsers was reported by Net Market Share: Chrome (54.3%), Safari (25.66%), Android Browser (9.06%), and Opera Mini (6.53%).

Apply the principle of **progressive enhancement**: Design a website so that it looks good in commonly used browsers and then add enhancements with CSS3 and/or HTML5 for display in the most recent versions of browsers.

Always try to test your pages with the most popular versions of browsers on both PC and Mac operating systems. Many web page components, including default text size and default margin size, are different among browsers, browser versions, and operating systems. Also try to test your website on other types of devices, such as tablets and smartphones.

Screen Resolution

Your website visitors will use a variety of screen resolutions. A recent survey by Net Market Share (http://marketshare.hitslink.com/report.aspx?qprid=17) reported the use of more than 90 different screen resolutions, with the top four being 1366×768 (with 13.9%), 360×640 (10.46%), 1920×1080 (9.74%), and 768×1024 (6.9%). Mobile use will vary with the purpose of the website, but it is expected to grow as the use of smartphones and tablets increases. Be aware that some smartphones have low screen resolution, such as 240×320, 320×480, or 480×800. Popular tablet devices offer a higher screen resolution: Apple iPad mini (1024×768), Apple iPad Air (2048×1536), Samsung Galaxy Tab (1280×800), and Kindle Fire (1024×600). In Chapter 8, you'll explore CSS media queries, which is a technique for configuring a web page to display well on various screen resolutions.

? FAQ How can I create web pages that look exactly the same on all browsers?

You can't. Design with the most popular browsers and screen resolutions in mind, but expect your web pages to look slightly different when displayed by different browsers and on monitors with different screen resolutions. Expect web pages to look even more different when displayed on mobile devices. You'll learn about responsive web design techniques later in this chapter.

Website Organization

How will visitors move around your site? How will they find what they need? This is largely determined by the website's organization or architecture. There are three common types of website organization:

▶ Hierarchical

▶ Linear

▶ Random (sometimes called web organization)

A diagram of the organization of a website is called a **site map**. Creating the site map is one of the initial steps in developing a website.

FIGURE 3.3 *Hierarchical site organization.*

Hierarchical Organization

Most websites use **hierarchical organization**. A site map for hierarchical organization, such as the one shown in Figure 3.3, is characterized by a clearly defined home page with links to major site sections. Web pages within sections are placed as needed. The home page plus the first level of pages in a hierarchical site map typically indicate the hyperlinks that will be displayed on the main navigation bar of each web page within the website.

FIGURE 3.4 *This site design uses a shallow hierarchy.*

It is important to be aware of pitfalls of hierarchical organization. Figure 3.4 shows a site design that is too shallow—there could be too many major site sections. This site design needs to be organized into fewer, easily managed topics or units of information, a process called **chunking**. In the case of web page design, each unit of information is a page. Nelson Cowan, a research psychologist at the University of Missouri, found that adults are typically able to keep about four items or chunks of items (such as the three parts of a phone number 888-555-5555) in their short-term memory (http://web.missouri.edu/~cowann/research.html). Following this principle, be aware of the number of major navigation links and try to group them into visually separate sections on the page, with each group having no more than about four links.

Another potential design pitfall of hierarchical website design is creating a site whose structure is too deep. Figure 3.5 shows an example of this. The interface design "three-click rule" says that a web page visitor should be able to get to any page on your site with a maximum of three hyperlinks. In other words, a visitor who cannot get what he or she wants in three mouse clicks will begin to feel frustrated and may leave your site. This rule may be very difficult to satisfy on a large site, but in general, the goal is to organize your site so that your visitors can easily navigate from page to page within the site structure.

FIGURE 3.5 *This site design uses a deep hierarchy.*

Linear Organization

Linear organization, shown in Figure 3.6, is useful when the purpose of a website or series of pages within a site is to provide a tutorial, tour, or presentation that needs to be viewed sequentially.

FIGURE 3.6 *Linear site organization.*

In linear organization, the pages are viewed one after another. Some websites use hierarchical organization in general but with linear organization in a few small areas.

Random Organization

Random organization (sometimes called web organization) offers no clear path through the site, as shown in Figure 3.7. There is often no clear home page and no discernible structure. Random organization is not as common as hierarchical or linear organization and is usually found only on artistic sites or sites that strive to be especially different and original. This type of organization is typically not used for commercial websites.

FIGURE 3.7 *Random site organization.*

What's a good way to organize my site map?

Sometimes it is difficult to begin creating a site map for a website. Some design teams meet in a room with a blank wall and a package of large Post-it Notes. They write the titles of topics and subtopics needed on the site on the Post-it Notes. They arrange the notes on the wall and discuss until a site structure evolves and there is consensus within the group. If you are not working in a group, you can try this on your own and then discuss the way you have chosen to organize the website with a friend or fellow student.

Principles of Visual Design

VideoNote
Principles of Visual Design

There are four visual design principles that you can apply to the design of just about anything: repetition, contrast, proximity, and alignment. Whether you are designing a web page, a button, a logo, a DVD cover, a brochure, or a software interface, the design principles of repetition, contrast, proximity, and alignment will help to create the "look" (visual aesthetic), of your project and will determine whether your message is effectively communicated.

Repetition: Repeat Visual Components Throughout the Design

When applying the principle of **repetition**, the web designer repeats one or more components throughout the page. The repeating aspect ties the work together. Figure 3.8 displays the home page for a bed and breakfast business. The page design demonstrates the use of repetition in a variety of design components, including color, shape, font, and images.

- The photographs displayed on the web page use similar colors (brown, tan, dark green, and off-white) which are repeated in other areas on the web page. Browns are used for background color of the navigation area, call-to-action "Search" and "Subscribe" buttons, and the color of text in the center and right columns. An off-white color is used for the logo text, navigation text, and center column background. The dark green is used as the background color of the navigation area and also as the topic headings in the center column.
- The call-to-action "Reservations" and "Newsletter" areas have a similar shape and format with heading, content, and button.
- The use of only two font typefaces on the page also demonstrates repetition and helps to create a cohesive look. The website name and page topic headings are configured with Trebuchet font. Other page content uses Arial font.

Whether it is color, shape, font, or image, repetition helps to unify a design.

Contrast: Add Visual Excitement and Draw Attention

To apply the principle of **contrast**, emphasize the differences between page elements in order to make the design interesting and direct attention. There should be good contrast between the background color and the text color on a web page. If there is too little contrast, the text will be difficult to read. Notice how the upper right navigation area in Figure 3.8 uses a text color that has good contrast with the dark background color. The left column features a medium dark background that has good contrast with the light off-white text. The middle column features dark text on a medium-light background to provide good visual contrast and easy reading. The dark text in the footer area contrasts well with the medium-light background color.

FIGURE 3.8 *The design principles of repetition, contrast, proximity, and alignment are well used on this web page.*

Proximity: Group Related Items

When designers apply the principle of **proximity**, related items are placed physically close together. Unrelated items should have space separating them. The placing of "Reservations" form controls close together gives visual clues to the logical organization of the information or functionality. In Figure 3.8, the horizontal navigation links are all placed in close proximity to each other. This creates a visual group on the page and makes the navigation easier to use. Proximity is used well on this page to group related elements.

Alignment: Align Elements to Create Visual Unity

Another principle that helps to create a cohesive web page is **alignment**. When applying this principle, the designer organizes the page so that each element placed has some alignment (vertical or horizontal) with another element on the page. The page shown in Figure 3.8 also applies this principle. Notice how the page components are vertically aligned in columns of equal height.

Repetition, contrast, proximity, and alignment are four visual design principles that can greatly improve your web page designs. If you apply these principles effectively, your web pages will look more professional and you will communicate your message more clearly. Keep these principles in mind as you design and build web pages.

Design to Provide for Accessibility

In Chapter 1, you were introduced to the concept of **universal design**. The Center for Universal Design defines universal design as "the design of products and environments to be usable by all people, to the greatest extent possible, without the need for adaptation or specialized design."

Who Benefits from Universal Design and Increased Accessibility?

Consider the following scenarios:

▶ Maria is a young woman in her twenties with physical challenges who cannot manipulate a mouse and who uses a keyboard with much effort. Accessible web pages designed to function without a mouse will help Maria access content.

▶ Leotis is a college student who is deaf and wants to be a web developer. Captions for audio/video content and transcripts will provide Leotis access to content.

▶ Jim is a middle-aged man who has a dial-up Internet connection and is using the Web for personal enjoyment. Alternate text for images and transcripts for multimedia will provide Jim improved access to content.

▶ Nadine is a mature woman with age-related macular degeneration who has difficulty reading small print. Web pages designed so that text can be enlarged in the browser will make it easier for Nadine to read.

▶ Karen is a college student using a smartphone to access the Web. Accessible content organized with headings and lists will make it easier for Karen to surf the Web on a mobile device.

▶ Prakesh is a man in his thirties who is legally blind and needs access to the Web to do his job. Web pages designed to be accessible (which are organized with headings and lists, display descriptive text for hyperlinks, provide alternate text descriptions for images, and are usable without a mouse) will help Prakesh access content when using a screen reader application such as JAWS or Window-Eyes.

All of these individuals benefit from web pages designed with accessibility in mind. A web page that is designed to be accessible is typically more usable for all—even a person who has no physical challenges and is using a broadband connection benefits from the improved presentation and organization of a well-designed web page.

Accessible Design Can Benefit Search Engine Listing

Search engine programs (commonly referred to as bots or spiders) walk the Web and follow hyperlinks on websites. An accessible website with descriptive page titles that is well organized with headings, lists, descriptive text for hyperlinks, and alternate text for images is more visible to search engine robots and may result in better ranking.

Legal Requirements

The Internet and World Wide Web are such a pervasive part of our culture that accessibility is mandated by laws in the United States. Section 508 of the Rehabilitation Act requires electronic and information technology, including web pages, used by federal agencies to be accessible to people with disabilities. The accessibility recommendations presented in this text are intended to satisfy the Section 508 standards and the W3C Web Accessibility Initiative guidelines. At the time this was written, the Section 508 standards were undergoing revision. New proposed Section 508 requirements have been aligned to WCAG 2.0 guidelines and were still under review in late 2016. Visit http://www.access-board.gov for current information.

Accessibility Is the Right Thing to Do

The federal government is promoting accessibility by law, and the private sector is following its lead. The W3C is quite active in this cause and has created the Web Accessibility Initiative (WAI) to create guidelines and standards applicable to web content developers, authoring-tool developers, and browser developers. The following four content accessibility principles are essential to conformance with WCAG 2.0—**P**erceivable, **O**perable, **U**nderstandable, and **R**obust—referred to by the acronym **POUR**.

1. Content must be **Perceivable**. Perceivable content is easy to see or hear. Any graphic or multimedia content should be available in a text format, such as text descriptions for images, closed captions for videos, and transcripts for audio.

2. Interface components in the content must be **Operable**. Operable content has interactive features, such as navigation forms, that can be used or operated with either a mouse or keyboard. Multimedia content should be designed to avoid flashing, which may cause a seizure.

3. Content and controls must be **Understandable**. Understandable content is easy to read, organized in a consistent manner, and provides helpful error messages when appropriate.

4. Content should be **Robust** enough to work with current and future user agents, including assistive technologies. Robust content is written to follow W3C Recommendations and should be compatible with multiple operating systems, browsers, and assistive technologies such as screen reader applications.

The WCAG 2.0 Quick Reference in the Appendix contains a brief list of guidelines for designing accessible web pages. You can access WAI's Web Content Accessibility Guidelines 2.0 (WCAG 2.0) at http://www.w3.org/TR/WCAG20/Overview.

As you work through this book you'll learn to include accessibility features as you create practice pages. You've already discovered the importance of configuring the title tag, heading tags, and descriptive text for hyperlinks in Chapters 1 and 2. You're already well on your way to creating accessible web pages!

Use of Text

Writing for the Web

Long-winded sentences and explanations are often found in academic textbooks and romance novels, but they really are not appropriate on a web page. Long blocks of text and long paragraphs are difficult to read on the Web. The following suggestions will help to increase the readability of your web pages.

- ▶ Be concise. Use the text equivalent of sound bytes—short sentences and phrases.
- ▶ Organize the page content with headings and subheadings.
- ▶ Use lists to help text stand out and make content easier to read.

The web page shown in Figure 3.9 provides an example of using headings and brief paragraphs to organize web page content so that it is easy to read and visitors can quickly find what they need.

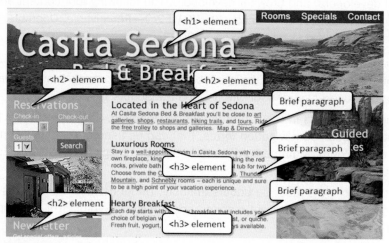

FIGURE 3.9 *The web page content is well organized with headings.*

Text Design Considerations

You may be wondering how to know whether a web page is easy to read. Readable text is crucial to providing content of value for your web page visitors. Carefully consider the typeface, size, weight, and color when you select fonts for your web pages. The following are some suggestions that will help increase the readability of your pages:

- ▶ **Use Common Fonts**

  Use common fonts such as Arial, Verdana, or Times New Roman. Remember that the web page visitor must have the font installed on his or her computer in order for that particular font to appear. Your page may look great with Gill Sans Ultra Bold Condensed, but if your visitor doesn't have this typeface, the browser's default font will be displayed. Explore the list of "web-safe" fonts at http://www.ampsoft.net/webdesign-l/WindowsMacFonts.html.

▶ **Carefully Choose Fonts**

Serif fonts, such as Times New Roman, were originally developed for printing text on paper, not for displaying text on a computer monitor. Research shows that sans-serif fonts, such as Arial and Verdana, are easier to read than serif fonts when displayed on a computer screen (see http://alexpoole.info/blog/which-are-more-legible-serif-or-sans-serif-typefaces/ or http://www.webdesignerdepot.com/2013/03/serif-vs-sans-the-final-battle/).

▶ **Check Font Size**

Be aware that fonts display smaller on a Mac than on a PC. Even within the PC platform, the default font size displayed by browsers may not be the same. Consider creating prototype pages of your font size settings to test on a variety of browsers and screen resolution settings.

▶ **Check Font Weight**

Bold or *emphasize* important text (use the `<strong>` element for bold and the `<em>` element to configure italics). However, be careful not to bold everything—that has the same effect as bolding nothing.

▶ **Check Font Color for Contrast**

Use appropriate color combinations. Newbie web designers sometimes choose color combinations for web pages that they would never dream of using in their wardrobe. An easy way to choose colors that contrast well and look good together is to select colors from an image or logo that you will use for your site. Visit http://webdevbasics.net/4e/chapter3.html for links to online tools that can help you verify that your page background color properly contrasts with your text and hyperlink colors.

▶ **Check Line Length**

Be aware of line length—use white space and multiple columns if possible. Christian Holst at the Baymard Institute (http://baymard.com/blog/line-length-readability) recommends using between 50 and 60 characters per line for readability. Look ahead to Figure 3.37 for examples of text placement on a web page.

▶ **Check Alignment**

A paragraph of centered text is more difficult to read than left-aligned text.

▶ **Carefully Choose Text in Hyperlinks**

Use hyperlinks for keywords and descriptive phrases. Do not hyperlink entire sentences. Also avoid the use of the words "click here" in hyperlinks—users know what to do by now.

▶ **Check Spelling and Grammar**

Unfortunately, many websites contain misspelled words. Most web-authoring tools have built-in spell checkers; consider using this feature.

Finally, be sure that you proofread and test your site thoroughly. It's very helpful if you can find web developer buddies—you check their sites, and they check yours. It's always easier to see someone else's mistake than your own.

Web Color Palette

Red: #FF0000

Green: #00FF00

Blue: #0000FF

Black: #000000

White: #FFFFFF

Grey: #CCCCCC

FIGURE 3.10
Sample colors.

Computer monitors display color as a combination of different intensities of red, green, and blue, also known as **RGB color**. RGB intensity values are numeric from 0 to 255.

Each RGB color has three values, one each for red, green, and blue. These are always listed in the same order (red, green, and blue) and specify the numerical value of each color (see examples in Figure 3.10). You will usually use hexadecimal color values to specify RGB color on web pages.

Hexadecimal Color Values

Hexadecimal is the name for the base 16 numbering system, which uses the characters 0, 1, 2, 3, 4, 5, 6, 7, 8, 9, A, B, C, D, E, and F to specify numeric values.

Hexadecimal color values specify RGB color with numeric value pairs ranging from 00 to FF (0 to 255 in base 10). Each pair is associated with the amount of red, green, and blue displayed. Using this notation, one would specify the color red as #FF0000 and the color blue as #0000FF. The # symbol signifies that the value is hexadecimal. You can use either uppercase or lowercase letters in hexadecimal color values; #FF0000 and #ff0000 both configure the color red.

Don't worry—you won't need to do calculations to work with web colors. Just become familiar with the numbering scheme. See Figure 3.11 for an excerpt from the textbook companion website at http://webdevbasics.net/color.

#FFFFFF	#FFFFCC	#FFFF99	#FFFF66	#FFFF33	#FFFF00
#FFCCFF	#FFCCCC	#FFCC99	#FFCC66	#FFCC33	#FFCC00
#FF99FF	#FF99CC	#FF9999	#FF9966	#FF9933	#FF9900
#FF66FF	#FF66CC	#FF6699	#FF6666	#FF6633	#FF6600
#FF33FF	#FF33CC	#FF3399	#FF3366	#FF3333	#FF3300
#FF00FF	#FF00CC	#FF0099	#FF0066	#FF0033	#FF0000

FIGURE 3.11 *Partial color chart.*

Web-Safe Colors

It is easy to tell whether a color is a web-safe color—check the hexadecimal color values.

Web-Safe Hexadecimal Values

00, 33, 66, 99, CC, FF

Look at the color chart at the end of the book (also shown at http://webdevbasics.net/color). Note that all the colors listed follow this numbering scheme—they comprise the Web-Safe Color Palette.

Accessibility and Color

While color can help you create a compelling web page, keep in mind that not all of your visitors will see or be able to distinguish between colors. Some visitors will use a screen reader and will not experience your colors, so your information must be clearly conveyed even if the colors cannot be viewed. According to Color Blindness Awareness (http://www. colourblindawareness.org/), 1 in 12 men and 1 in 200 women experience some type of color perception deficiency.

Color choices can be crucial. For example, red text on a blue background, as shown in Figure 3.12, is usually difficult for everyone to read. Also avoid using red, green, brown, gray, or purple next to each other. Visit http://colorfilter.wickline.org to simulate how a person with a color deficiency experiences the colors on a web page. White, black, and shades of blue and yellow are easier for most people to discern.

Can you read this easily?

FIGURE 3.12 *Some color combinations are difficult to read.*

Choose text and background colors with enough contrast so the text can be easily read. The WCAG 2.0 guidelines recommend a contrast ratio of 4.5:1 for standard text. If the text has a large font, the contrast ratio can be as low as 3:1. Jonathan Snook's online Colour Contrast Check at http://snook.ca/technical/colour_contrast/colour.html can help you to verify the contrast level of your text and background colors.

Check out the following websites for some color ideas. Then continue with the next section for more tips on choosing colors for your web pages.

▌ http://paletton.com
▌ http://0to255.com
▌ http://www.colorsontheweb.com/Color-Tools/Color-Wizard

Design for Your Target Audience

The first section in this chapter introduced the importance of designing for your target audience. In this section, we consider how to use color, graphics, and text to appeal to a target audience.

FIGURE 3.13 *A web page intended to appeal to children.*

Appealing to Children and Preteens

Younger audiences, such as children and preteens, prefer bright, lively colors. The web page shown in Figure 3.13, features bright graphics, lots of color, and interactivity. Examples of websites designed to appeal to children:

▶ http://www.sesamestreet.org/games

▶ http://www.nick.com

▶ http://www.usmint.gov/kids

FIGURE 3.14 *Many teens and young adults find dark sites appealing.*

Appealing to Young Adults

Individuals in their late teens and early twenties generally prefer dark background colors with occasional use of bright contrast, music, and dynamic navigation. Figure 3.14 shows a web page designed for this age group. Note how it has a completely different look and feel from the site designed for young children. Examples of websites designed to appeal to young adults:

▶ http://us.battle.net/wow

▶ http://www.twentyonepilots.com

▶ http://www.thresholdrpg.com

Appealing to Everybody

If your goal is to appeal to everyone, follow the example of the popular Amazon.com and eBay.com websites in their use of color. These sites display a neutral white background with splashes of color to add interest and highlight page areas. Use of white as a background color was found to be quite popular by Jakob Nielsen and Marie Tahir in *Homepage Usability: 50 Websites Deconstructed*, a book that analyzed 50 top websites. According to this study, 84% of the sites used white as the background color and 72% used black as the text color. This maximized the contrast between text and background—providing maximum ease of reading.

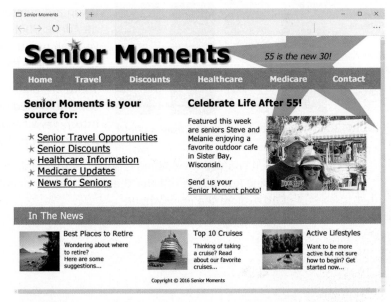

FIGURE 3.15 *A compelling graphic along with white background for the content area.*

You'll also notice that websites targeting "everyone" often include compelling visual graphics. The web page shown in Figure 3.15, provides the text content on a white background for maximum contrast while engaging the visitor with a large graphic, called a **hero**, intended to grab attention and entice the visitor to want to explore the website.

Appealing to Older Adults

For an older target audience, light backgrounds, well-defined images, and large text are appropriate. The web page shown in Figure 3.16 is an example of a web page intended for the 55-and-older age group. Examples of websites designed to appeal to older adults:

- ▶ http://www.aarp.org
- ▶ http://www.theseniornews.com
- ▶ http://senior.org

FIGURE 3.16 *A site designed specifically for the 55-and-older age group.*

Choosing a Color Scheme

A compelling color scheme can attract and engage your website visitors while a garish color scheme can drive them away. This section introduces several methods for choosing a color scheme.

Color
Scheme A:

Color
Scheme B:

FIGURE 3.17 *A color scheme selected from a photo.*

Color Scheme Based on an Image

One of the easiest ways to select a color scheme for your website is to start with an existing graphic image, such as a logo or a photograph of nature. If the organization already has a logo, select colors from the logo for use as the basis of your color scheme.

Another option is to use a photograph that captures the mood of the website—you can create a color scheme using colors found in the image. Figure 3.17 shows a photograph along with two potential color schemes created by selecting colors from the image.

If you are comfortable using a graphic application (such as Adobe Photoshop, GIMP, or http://pixlr.com/editor), you can use the color picker tool within the application to determine the colors used in an image.

There are also websites that will generate a color scheme based on a photograph, including http://www.cssdrive.com/imagepalette and http://www.pictaculous.com.

Even if you use an existing graphic as the basis for a color scheme, it's helpful to have a working knowledge of **color theory**, the study of color and its use in design. A starting point is to explore the color wheel.

Color Wheel

A **color wheel** (see Figure 3.18) is a circle of color depicting the primary colors (red, yellow, and blue), the secondary colors (orange, violet, and green), and the tertiary colors (yellow-orange, red-orange, red-violet, violet-blue, blue-green, and yellow-green).

FIGURE 3.18 *Color wheel.*

Shades, Tints, and Tones

There is no need to restrict your choices to the web-safe color palette. Modern monitors can display millions of colors. You are free to choose a shade, tint, or tone of a color. Figure 3.19 shows four swatches: yellow, a shade of yellow, a tint of yellow, and a tone of yellow.

Yellow Shade Tint Tone

FIGURE 3.19 *Yellow with a shade, tint, and tone.*

- A **shade** of a color is darker than the original color and is created by mixing the color with black.
- A **tint** of a color is lighter than the original color and is created by mixing color with white.
- A **tone** of a color has less saturation than the original color and is created by mixing the color with gray.

Next, let's explore the six commonly used types of color schemes: monochromatic, analogous, complementary, split complementary, triadic, and tetradic.

Monochromatic Color Scheme

FIGURE 3.20 *Monochromatic color scheme.*

Figure 3.20 shows a **monochromatic color scheme** which consists of shades, tints, or tones of the same color. You can determine these values yourself, or use an online tool provided by one of the following resources:

- http://meyerweb.com/eric/tools/color-blend
- http://www.colorsontheweb.com/Color-Tools/Color-Wizard (choose a color and select monochromatic)
- http://paletton.com (choose a color and select monochromatic).

Analogous Color Scheme

FIGURE 3.21 *Analogous color scheme.*

To create an analogous color scheme, select a main color and the two colors that are adjacent to it on the color wheel. Figure 3.21 displays an analogous color scheme with orange, red-orange, and yellow-orange.

When you design a web page with an analogous color scheme, the main color is the most dominant on the web page. The adjacent colors are typically configured as accents. Be sure that the main content of the page is easy to read and use neutrals white, off-white, gray, black, or brown along with the analogous color scheme.

Complementary Color Scheme

FIGURE 3.22 *Complementary color scheme.*

A **complementary color scheme** consists of two colors that are opposite each other on the color wheel. Figure 3.22 displays a complementary color scheme with yellow and violet.

When you design a web page with a complementary color scheme, choose one color to be the main or dominant color. The other color is considered to be the **complement**. Configure the complement along with colors adjacent to the dominant color as accents. Use neutrals white, off-white, gray, black, or brown as part of a complementary color scheme.

Split Complementary Color Scheme

A **split complementary color scheme** is comprised of a main color, the color opposite it on the color wheel (the complement) and two colors adjacent to the complement. Figure 3.23 shows a split complementary color scheme with yellow (main), violet (complementary), red-violet, and blue violet.

FIGURE 3.23 *Split complementary color scheme.*

Triadic Color Scheme

Choose three colors that are equidistant on the color wheel to create a **triadic color scheme**. Figure 3.24 displays a triadic color scheme with blue-green (teal), yellow-orange, and red-violet.

FIGURE 3.24 *Triadic color scheme.*

Tetradic Color Scheme

Figure 3.25 shows a **tetradic color scheme** which consists of four colors which are two complementary pairs. For example, the complementary pair yellow and violet along with the complementary pair yellow-green and red-violet make up a tetradic color scheme.

FIGURE 3.25 *Tetradic color scheme.*

Implementing a Color Scheme

When designing a web page with a color scheme, one color is typically dominant. The other colors are configured as accents such as colors for headings, subheadings, borders, list markers, and backgrounds.

No matter what your color scheme, you will typically also use neutral colors such as white, off-white, gray, black, or brown. Selecting the best color scheme for your website often takes some trial and error.

Feel free to use tints, shades, or tones of the primary, secondary, and tertiary colors.

There are so many colors to choose from! The following resources can help you choose a color scheme for your website:

- http://paletton.com
- http://www.colorsontheweb.com/Color-Tools/Color-Wizard
- http://color.adobe.com
- http://www.colorspire.com

Use of Graphics and Multimedia

As shown in Figure 3.15, a compelling graphic can be an engaging element on a web page. However, be aware that you should avoid relying on images to convey meaning. Some individuals may not be able to see your images and multimedia—they may be accessing your site with a mobile device or using an assistive technology such as a screen reader to visit your page. You may need to include text descriptions of important concepts or key points that a graphic image or multimedia file conveys. In this section, you'll explore recommended techniques for use of graphics and multimedia on web pages.

File Size and Dimensions Matter

Image optimization is the process of creating an image with the lowest file size that still renders a good-quality image—balancing image quality and file size. The dimensions of the image should be as close to possible as the actual display size to enable speedy browser rendering of the image. Other approaches to image optimization are to crop an image or create a thumbnail image that links to a larger version of the image. Adobe Photoshop and Adobe Fireworks are often used by web professionals to optimize images for the Web. A free online tool for image editing and optimization is Pixlr Editor at http://www.pixlr.com/editor.

Antialiased

FIGURE 3.26 *Antialiased text.*

FIGURE 3.27 *This graphic has a jagged look and was not saved using antialiasing.*

Antialiased/Aliased Text Considerations

Refer back to Figure 3.13 and notice how easy it is to read the text in the navigation buttons—the text in each button is antialiased text. **Antialiasing** introduces intermediate colors to smooth jagged edges in digital images. Graphic applications such as Adobe Photoshop and Adobe Fireworks can be used to create antialiased text images. The graphic shown in Figure 3.26 was created using antialiasing. Figure 3.27 displays an image created without antialiasing; note the jagged edges.

Use Only Necessary Multimedia

Use animation and multimedia only if it will add value to your site. Limit the use of animated items. Only use animation if it makes the page more effective. Consider limiting how long an animation plays. Don't include an animated GIF or a Flash animation just because you happen to have one.

In general, younger audiences find animation more appealing than older audiences. The web page shown in Figure 3.13 is geared to children and uses lots of animation. This would be too much animation for a website targeted to adult shoppers. However, a well-done navigation animation or an animation that describes a product or service could be appealing to almost any target group, as shown in Figure 3.28. You'll work with new CSS3 properties to add animation and interactivity to web pages in Chapters 7 and 11.

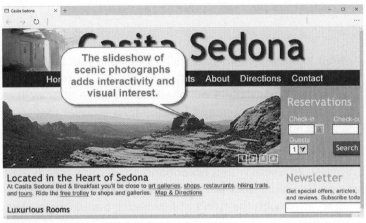

FIGURE 3.28 *The slideshow adds visual interest and interactivity.*

Provide Alternate Text

Each image on your web page should be configured with alternate text. (See Chapter 5 for a discussion of configuring images on web pages.) Alternate text may be displayed instead of the image when the page is displayed by mobile devices, while the image is loading (when the image is slow to load), and when a browser is configured to not show images. Alternate text is also read aloud when a person with a disability uses a screen reader to access your website.

To satisfy accessibility requirements, also provide alternate text equivalents for multimedia, such as video and audio. A text transcript of an audio recording can be useful not only to those with hearing challenges but also to individuals who prefer to read when accessing new information. In addition, the text transcript may be accessed by a search engine and used when your site is categorized and indexed. Captions help to provide accessibility for video files. See Chapter 11 for more on accessibility and multimedia.

More Design Considerations

Load Time

The last thing you want to happen is for your visitors to leave your page before it has even finished loading! Make sure your pages load as quickly as possible. Web usability expert Jakob Nielsen reports that visitors will often leave a page after waiting more than 10 seconds. It takes less than 9 seconds at 56Kbps for a browser to display a web page and associated files of 60KB.

According to a recent study by the PEW Internet and American Life Project, the percentage of U.S. Internet users with a broadband connection (cable, DSL, and so on) at home or at work is rising. Sixty-seven percent of adult Americans have access to broadband at home. Even with the trend of increasing bandwidth available to your visitors, keep in mind that 33% of households do not have broadband Internet access. Visit http://www.pewinternet.org for the most up-to-date statistics. The chart shown in Figure 3.29 compares file sizes and connection speed download times.

FIGURE 3.29 *File size download times and internet connection speeds.*

One method to help determine whether the load time of your page is acceptable is to view the size of your website files in Windows Explorer or MacOS Finder. Calculate the total file size of your web page plus all of its associated images and media. If the total file size for a single page and of its associated files is greater than 90KB and it is likely that your target audience may not be using broadband access, take a closer look at your design. Consider whether you really need to use all the images to convey your message. Perhaps the images can be better optimized for the Web or the content of the page should be divided into multiple pages. This is a time for some decision making! Popular web-authoring tools such as Adobe Dreamweaver will calculate load time at various transmission speeds.

Perceived Load Time

Perceived load time is the amount of time a web page visitor is aware of waiting while your page is loading. Since visitors often leave a website if a page takes too long to load, it is important to shorten their perception of waiting. In addition to optimizing all images, another common technique for shortening perceived load time is to utilize image sprites (see Chapter 7), which combine multiple small images into a single file.

Above the Fold

Placing important information **above the fold** is a technique borrowed from the newspaper industry. When newspapers are sitting on a counter or in a vending machine waiting to be sold, you can see the portion of the page that is "above the fold." Publishers noticed that more papers were sold when the most important, attention-getting information was placed in this location. You may use this technique to attract visitors and to keep visitors on your web pages. Arrange interesting content above the fold. On web pages, this is the area the visitor sees without scrolling down the page. At one of the most popular screen resolutions of 1024×768, the amount of screen viewable above the fold (after accounting for browser menus and controls) is about 600 pixels. Avoid placing important information and navigation on the far right side because this area may not be initially displayed by browsers at some screen resolutions.

Adequate White Space

The term **white space** is also borrowed from the publishing industry. Placing blank or white space (because paper is usually white) in areas around blocks of text increases the readability of the page. Placing white space around graphics helps them to stand out. Allow for some blank space between blocks of text and images. How much is adequate? It depends—experiment until the page is likely to look appealing to your target audience.

Horizontal Scrolling

In order to make it easy for visitors to view and use your web pages, avoid creating pages that are too wide to be displayed in the browser window. These pages require the user to scroll horizontally. Cameron Moll (http://www.cameronmoll.com/archives/001220.html) suggests that the optimal web page width for display at 1024×768 screen resolution is 960 pixels. Be mindful that many of your web page visitors will not maximize their browser viewport.

Navigation Design

Ease of Navigation

Sometimes web developers are so close to their sites that they can't see the forest for the trees. A new visitor will wander onto the site and not know what to click or how to find the information he or she seeks. Clearly labeled navigation on each page is helpful and should be in the same location on each page for maximum usability.

FIGURE 3.30 *Horizontal text-based navigation.*

Navigation Bars

Clear **navigation bars,** either graphic or text based, make it obvious to website users where they are and where they can go next. It's quite common for site-wide navigation to be located in either a horizontal navigation bar placed under the header (see Figure 3.30) or in a vertical navigation bar on the left side of the page (see Figure 3.31). Less common is a vertical navigation bar on the right side of the page—this area can be cut off at lower screen resolutions.

Breadcrumb Navigation

Jakob Nielsen, a well-known usability and web design professional, favors what he calls a **breadcrumb trail** for larger sites, which indicates the path of web pages a visitor has viewed during the current session. Figure 3.31 shows a page with a vertical navigation area in addition to the breadcrumb trail navigation above the main content area that indicates the pages the visitor has viewed during this visit: Home > Tours > Half-Day Tours > Europe Lake Tour. Visitors can easily retrace their steps or jump back to a previously viewed page.

FIGURE 3.31 *Visitors can follow the "breadcrumbs" to retrace their steps.*

Using Graphics for Navigation

Sometimes graphics are used to provide navigation, as in the pink navigation buttons on the web page shown in Figure 3.13. The "text" for the navigation is actually stored in image files. Be aware that using graphics for navigation is an outdated design technique. A website with text navigation is more accessible and more easily indexed by search engines.

Even when image hyperlinks instead of text hyperlinks provide the main navigation of the site, you can use two techniques that provide for accessibility:

▶ Configure each image with an alternate text description (see Chapter 5).

▶ Configure text hyperlinks in the footer area.

Dynamic Navigation

In your experiences visiting websites you've probably encountered navigation menus that display additional options when your mouse cursor moves over an item. This is dynamic navigation, which provides a way to offer many choices to visitors while at the same time avoid overwhelming them. Instead of showing all the navigation links all the time, menu items are dynamically displayed (typically using a combination of HTML and CSS) as appropriate. The additional items are made available when a related top-level menu item is selected by the cursor. In Figure 3.32, "Tours" has been selected, causing the vertical menu to appear.

FIGURE 3.32 *Dynamic navigation with HTML, CSS, and JavaScript.*

Site Map

Even with clear and consistent navigation, visitors sometimes may lose their way on large websites. A site map, also referred to as a site index, provides an outline of the organization of the website with hyperlinks to each major page. This can help visitors find another route to get to the information they seek, as shown in Figure 3.33.

Site Search Feature

Note the search feature on the right side of the web page in Figure 3.33. The site search feature helps visitors find information that is not apparent from the navigation or the site map.

FIGURE 3.33 *This large site offers a site search and a site map to visitors.*

Wireframes and Page Layout

A **wireframe** is a sketch or diagram of a web page that shows the structure (but not the detailed design) of basic page elements such as the header, navigation, content area, and footer. Wireframes are used as part of the design process to experiment with various page layouts, develop the structure and navigation of the site, and provide a basis for communication among project members. Note that the exact content (text, images, logo, and navigation) does not need to be placed in the wireframe diagram—the wireframe depicts the overall structure of the page.

Figures 3.34, 3.35, and 3.36 show wireframe diagrams of three possible page designs with horizontal navigation. The wireframe in Figure 3.34 is adequate and may be appropriate for when the emphasis is on text information content, but it's not very engaging.

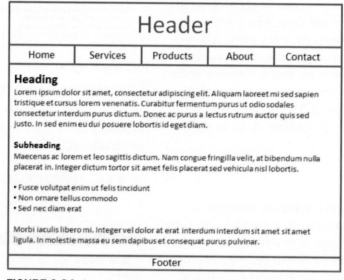

FIGURE 3.34 *An adequate page layout.*

Figure 3.35 shows a diagram of a web page containing similar content formatted in three columns along with an image. This is an improvement, but something is still missing.

Figure 3.36 shows a diagram of the same content but formatted in three columns of varying width with a header area, navigation area, content area (with headings, subheadings, paragraphs, and unordered lists), and a footer area. This is the most appealing layout of the three. Notice how the use of columns and images in Figures 3.35 and 3.36 increase the appeal of the page.

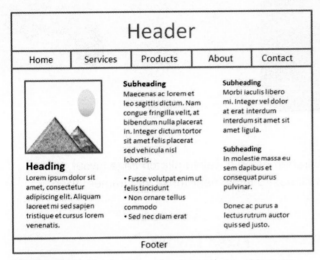

FIGURE 3.35 *The image and columns make this page layout more interesting.*

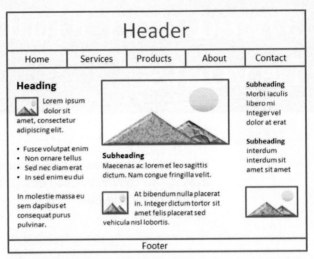

FIGURE 3.36 *This wireframe page layout uses images and columns of various widths.*

The wireframe in Figure 3.37 displays a web page with a header, vertical navigation area, content area (with headings, subheadings, images, paragraphs, and unordered lists), and a footer area.

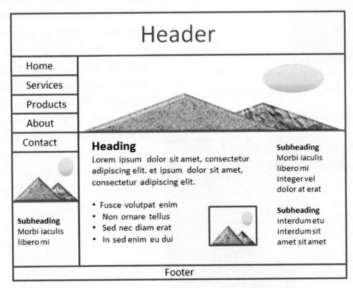

FIGURE 3.37 *Wireframe with vertical navigation.*

Often the page layout for the home page is different from the page layout used for the content pages. Even in this situation, a consistent logo header, navigation, and color scheme will produce a more cohesive website. You'll learn to use Cascading Style Sheets (CSS) along with HTML to configure color, text, and layout as you work through this book. In the next section, you will explore two commonly used layout design techniques: fixed layout and fluid layout.

Fixed and Fluid Layouts

Now that you have been introduced to wireframes as a way to sketch page layout, let's explore two commonly used design techniques to implement those wireframes: fixed layout and fluid layout.

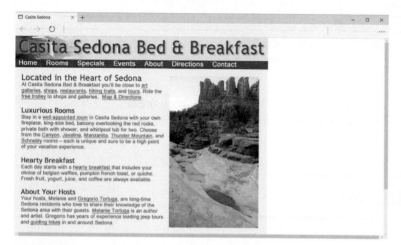

FIGURE 3.38 *This page is configured with a fixed layout design.*

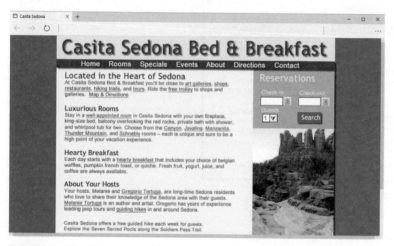

FIGURE 3.39 *This fixed width centered content is balanced on the page by left and right margins.*

Fixed Layout

The **fixed layout** technique is sometimes referred to as a solid or "ice" design. The web page content has a fixed width and may hug the left margin as shown in Figure 3.38.

Notice the empty space in the right side of the browser viewport in Figure 3.38. To avoid this unbalanced look, a popular method to create a fixed layout design is to configure the content with a specific width in pixels (such as 960px) and center it in the browser viewport as shown in Figure 3.39. As the browser is resized, it will expand or contract the left and right margin areas to center the content in the viewport. In Chapter 6, you'll learn how to use Cascading Style Sheets (CSS) to configure width and center content.

Fluid Layout

The **fluid layout** technique, sometimes referred to as a "liquid" layout, results in a fluid web page with content typically configured with percentage values for widths—often taking up 100% of the browser viewport. The content will flow to fill whatever size browser window is used to display it, as shown in Figure 3.40. One disadvantage of liquid layout is that when displayed in maximized browser viewports using high screen resolutions the lines of text may be quite wide and become difficult to scan and read.

Figure 3.41 shows an adaptation of liquid layout that utilizes a 100% width for the header and navigation area along with an 80% width for the centered page content. Compare this to Figure 3.40, the centered content area grows and shrinks as the browser viewport is resized. Readability can be ensured by using CSS to configure a maximum width value for this area.

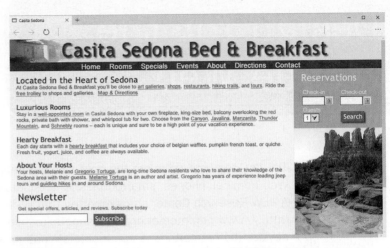

FIGURE 3.40 *This fluid layout expands to fill 100% of the browser viewport.*

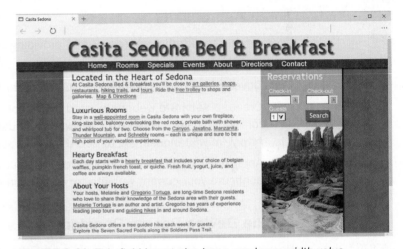

FIGURE 3.41 *This fluid layout also has a maximum width value configured for the centered content area.*

Websites designed using fixed and fluid layout techniques can be found throughout the Web. Fixed-width layouts provide the web developer with the most control over the page configuration but can result in pages with large empty areas when viewed at higher screen resolutions. Fluid designs may become less readable when viewed at high screen resolutions due to the page stretching to fill a wider area than originally intended by the developer. Configuring a maximum width on text content areas can alleviate the text readability issues. Even when using an overall fluid layout, portions of the design can be configured with a fixed width (such as the "Reservations" column on the right side of the web page in Figures 3.40 and 3.41). Whether employing a fixed or fluid layout, web pages with centered content are typically pleasing to view on a variety of desktop screen resolutions.

Design for the Mobile Web

The desktop browser is not the only way that people access websites. Access to the Web from cell phones, smartphones, and tablets makes it possible to always be online. A PEW Research Center study reported that 63% of American adults own a smartphone (http://www.pewinternet.org/fact-sheets/mobile-technology-fact-sheet). Usage of mobile devices (both smartphones and tablets) continues to grow. With this in mind, it's becoming more important to design web pages that are appealing and usable for your mobile visitors.

Three Approaches

There are three different approaches to providing a satisfactory mobile experience for your website visitor:

1. Develop a separate mobile site with a .mobi TLD (see Chapter 1 to review TLDs).
2. Create a separate website hosted within your current domain that is targeted for mobile users. Visit http://www.whitehouse.gov and the mobile version at http://m.whitehouse.gov to see this approach in action.
3. Apply techniques of responsive web design (see the next section) by using CSS to configure your current website for display on mobile devices.

Mobile Device Design Considerations

No matter which approach you choose to use, here are some considerations to keep in mind when designing a mobile website.

▶ **Small screen size.** Common mobile phone screen sizes include 320×480, 480×800, 640×960, 1136×640, and 750×1334. Even on one of the large phones, that's not a lot of pixels to work with!

▶ **Low bandwidth (slow connection speed).** Although the use of faster 4G networks is becoming more widespread, many mobile users experience slow connection speeds. Images usually take up quite a bit of bandwidth on a typical website. Depending on the service plan, some mobile web visitors may be paying per kilobyte. Be aware of this and eliminate unnecessary images.

▶ **Font, color, and media issues.** Mobile devices may have very limited font support. Configure font size using ems or percentages and configure generic font family names (see Chapter 5). Mobile devices may have very limited color support. Choose colors carefully to maximize contrast. Many mobile devices do not support Adobe Flash media.

- **Awkward controls; limited processor and memory.** While smartphones with touch controls are becoming more popular, many mobile users will not have access to mouselike controls. Provide keyboard access to assist these users. Although mobile device processing speed and available memory are improving, they still cannot compare to the resources of a desktop computer. While this won't be an issue for the websites you create for the exercises in this text, be mindful of this issue in the future as you continue to develop your skills and create web applications.

- **Functionality.** Provide easy access to your website's features with prominent hyperlinks or a prominent search button.

Example Desktop Website and Mobile Website

The website shown in Figures 3.42 and 3.43 utilizes the second approach—separate websites within the same domain for desktop display and mobile display.

The desktop site shown in Figure 3.42 features a large graphic and interactive slideshow.

The mobile site shown in Figure 3.43 features a prominent navigation area, phone number, and small background image.

FIGURE 3.42 *The website in a desktop browser.*

Mobile Design Quick Checklist

- Be aware of the small screen size and bandwidth issues.
- Configure nonessential content, such as sidebar content, to not display.
- Consider replacing desktop background images with graphics optimized for small screen display.
- Provide descriptive alternate text for images.
- Use a single-column layout for mobile display.
- Choose colors to maximize contrast.

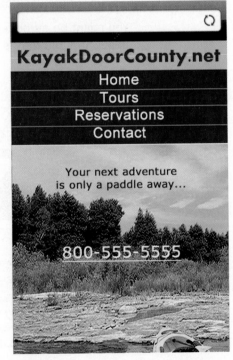

FIGURE 3.43 *A mobile version of the website.*

Responsive Web Design

As mentioned earlier in this chapter, a recent survey by Net Market Share reported the use of more than 90 different screen resolutions and that websites are expected to display and function well on desktop browsers, tablets, and smartphones. While you can develop separate desktop and mobile websites, a more streamlined approach is to utilize the same website for all devices. The W3C's **One Web** initiative refers to the concept of providing a single resource that is configured for optimal display on multiple types of devices.

Responsive web design is a term coined by noted web developer Ethan Marcotte (http://alistapart.com/article/responsive-web-design) to describe progressively enhancing a web page for different viewing contexts (such as smartphones and tablets) through the use of coding techniques, including fluid layouts, flexible images, and media queries. In Chapter 8, you'll learn to configure flexible images and code CSS **media queries,** which is a technique for configuring a web page to display well at various screen resolutions.

Visit the Media Queries website (http://mediaqueri.es) to view a gallery of sites that demonstrate this method for responsive web design. The screen captures in the Media Queries gallery show web pages at the following screen widths: 320px (smartphone display), 768px (tablet portrait display), 1024px (netbook display and landscape tablet display), and 1600px (large desktop display).

You might be surprised to discover that Figures 3.44–3.47 are actually the same web page .html file that is configured with CSS to display differently, depending on the

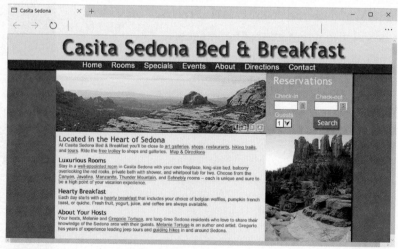

FIGURE 3.44 *Desktop display of the web page.*

viewport size detected by media queries. Figure 3.44 shows the standard desktop browser display.

Display for netbooks and tablets using landscape orientation is depicted in Figure 3.45. Figure 3.46 demonstrates how the page would render on a tablet using portrait orientation. Figure 3.47 shows the web page displayed on a mobile device such as a smartphone—note the reduction of the logo area, removal of images, and prominent phone number.

You'll explore how to configure web pages with CSS media queries in Chapter 8.

FIGURE 3.45 *Netbook display of the web page.*

FIGURE 3.46 *Portrait orientation tablet display of the web page.*

FIGURE 3.47 *Smartphone display of the web page.*

Web Design Best Practices Checklist

Use Table 3.1 as a guide to help you create easy-to-read, usable, and accessible web pages.

TABLE 3.1 *Web Design Best Practices Checklist*

Page Layout Criteria

- ☐ 1. Consistent site header/logo
- ☐ 2. Consistent navigation area
- ☐ 3. Informative page title that includes the company/organization/site name
- ☐ 4. Page footer area—copyright, last update, contact e-mail address
- ☐ 5. Good use of basic design principles: repetition, contrast, proximity, and alignment
- ☐ 6. Displays without horizontal scrolling at 1024×768 and higher resolutions
- ☐ 7. Balance of text/graphics/white space on page
- ☐ 8. Repetitive information (header/logo and navigation) takes up no more than one-fourth to one-third of the browser window at 1024×768 resolution
- ☐ 9. Home page has compelling information before scrolling at 1024×768 resolution
- ☐ 10. Home page downloads within 10 seconds on dial-up connection
- ☐ 11. Viewport meta tag is used to enhance display on smartphone
- ☐ 12. Media queries configure responsive page layout for smartphone and tablet display

Navigation Criteria

- ☐ 1. Main navigation links are clearly and consistently labeled
- ☐ 2. Navigation is structured within an unordered list
- ☐ 3. When the main navigation consists of images and/or multimedia, the page footer area contains plain text hyperlinks (accessibility)
- ☐ 4. Navigational aids, such as site map, skip to content link, or breadcrumbs, are used

Color and Graphics Criteria

- ☐ 1. Use of different colors is limited to a maximum of three or four plus neutrals
- ☐ 2. Color is used consistently
- ☐ 3. Background and text colors have good contrast
- ☐ 4. Color is not used alone to convey meaning (accessibility)
- ☐ 5. Use of color and graphics enhances rather than distracts from the site
- ☐ 6. Graphics are optimized and do not slow download significantly

- [ ] 7. Each graphic used serves a clear purpose
- [ ] 8. Image tags use the alt attribute to configure alternate text (accessibility)
- [ ] 9. Animated images do not distract from the site and do not loop endlessly

Multimedia Criteria

- [ ] 1. Each audio/video/flash file used serves a clear purpose
- [ ] 2. The audio/video/flash files used enhance rather than distract from the site
- [ ] 3. Captions or transcripts are provided for each audio or video file used (accessibility)
- [ ] 4. Download times for audio or video files are indicated

Content Presentation Criteria

- [ ] 1. Common fonts such as Arial or Times New Roman are used
- [ ] 2. Techniques of writing for the Web are applied: headings, subheadings, bulleted lists, short sentences in brief paragraphs, use of white space
- [ ] 3. Fonts, font sizes, and font colors are consistently used
- [ ] 4. Content provides meaningful, useful information
- [ ] 5. Content is organized in a consistent manner
- [ ] 6. Information is easy to find (minimal clicks)
- [ ] 7. Timeliness: The date of the last revision and/or copyright date is accurate
- [ ] 8. Content is free of typographical and grammatical errors
- [ ] 9. Avoids the use of "Click here" when writing text for hyperlinks
- [ ] 10. Hyperlinks use a consistent set of colors to indicate visited/nonvisited status
- [ ] 11. Alternate text equivalent of content is provided for graphics and media (accessibility)

Functionality Criteria

- [ ] 1. All internal hyperlinks work
- [ ] 2. All external hyperlinks work
- [ ] 3. All forms function as expected
- [ ] 4. No error messages are generated by the pages

Additional Accessibility Criteria

- [ ] 1. Use attributes designed to improve accessibility such as alt and title where appropriate
- [ ] 2. The html element's lang attribute indicates the spoken language of the page

Browser Compatibility Criteria

- [ ] 1. Displays on current versions of Edge, Internet Explorer, Firefox, Safari, Chrome, and Opera
- [ ] 2. Displays on popular mobile devices (including tablets and smartphones)

Review and Apply

Review Questions

1. Which of the following is a sketch or diagram of a web page that shows the structure (but not the detailed design) of basic page elements?

   a. drawing

   b. HTML code

   c. site map

   d. wireframe

2. Which of the following are the three most common methods of organizing websites?

   a. horizontal, vertical, and diagonal

   b. hierarchical, linear, and random

   c. accessible, readable, and maintainable

   d. none of the above

3. Which of the following is not a web design recommended practice?

   a. design your site to be easy to navigate

   b. colorful pages appeal to everyone

   c. design your pages to load quickly

   d. limit the use of animated items

4. Which are the four principles of the Web Content Accessibility Guidelines?

   a. contrast, repetition, alignment, and proximity

   b. perceivable, operable, understandable, and robust

   c. accessible, readable, maintainable, and reliable

   d. hierarchical, linear, random, and sequential

5. Which of the following would a consistent website design *not* have?

   a. a similar navigation area on each content page

   b. the same fonts on each content page

   c. a different background color on each page

   d. the same logo in the same location on each content page

6. Which of the following is the design technique used to create pages that stretch to fill the browser window?

   a. fixed

   b. fluid

   c. wireframe

   d. sprites

7. Which of the following recommended design practices applies to a website that uses images for its main site navigation?

   a. provide alternative text for the images

   b. place text links at the bottom of the page

   c. both a and b

   d. no special considerations are needed

8. Which of the following is a mobile web design best practice?

   a. configure a single-column page layout

   b. configure a multiple-column page layout

   c. avoid using lists to organize information

   d. embed text in images wherever possible

9. Which of the following should you do when creating text hyperlinks?

   a. create the entire sentence as a hyperlink

   b. include the words "click here" in your text

   c. use a key phrase as a hyperlink

   d. none of the above

10. Which of the following is a color scheme that consists of two colors opposite each other on the color wheel?

    a. contrasting

    b. analogous

    c. split complementary

    d. complementary

Hands-On Exercise

1. **Website Design Evaluation.** In this chapter you've explored web page design, including navigation design techniques and the design principles of contrast, repetition, alignment, and proximity. In this Hands-On Exercise, you'll review and evaluate the design of a website. Your instructor may provide you with the URL of a website to evaluate. If not, choose a website to evaluate from the following list of URLs:

   http://www.arm.gov

   http://www.telework.gov

   http://www.dcmm.org

   http://www.sedonalibrary.org

   http://bostonglobe.com

   http://www.alistapart.com

   Visit the website you are evaluating. Write a paper that includes the following information:
   a. URL of the website
   b. Name of the website
   c. Target audience
   d. Screen shot of the home page
   e. Indicate the type(s) of navigation evident.
   f. Describe how the design principles of contrast, repetition, alignment, and proximity are applied. Be specific.
   g. Complete the Web Design Best Practices Checklist (see Table 3.1).
   h. Recommend three improvements for the website.

2. **Responsive Web Design.** Visit the Media Queries website at http://mediaqueri.es to view a gallery of sites that demonstrate responsive web design. Choose one of the example responsive websites to explore. Write a paper that includes the following:
   a. URL of the website
   b. Name of the website
   c. Target audience
   d. Three screen shots of the website (desktop display, tablet display, and smartphone display).
   e. Describe the similarities and differences between the three screen shots.
   f. Describe two ways in which the display has been modified for smartphones.
   g. Does the website meet the needs of its target audience in all three display modes? Why or why not? Justify your answer.

Focus on Web Design

1. Choose two sites that are similar in nature or have a similar target audience, such as the following:

   • http://amazon.com and http://bn.com

   • http://chicagobears.com and http://greenbaypackers.com

   • http://cnn.com and http://msnbc.com

a. Describe how the two sites that you chose to review exhibit the design principles of repetition, contrast, alignment, and proximity.

b. Describe how the two sites that you chose to review exhibit web design best practices. How would you improve these sites? Recommend three improvements for each site.

2. Explore the trend of flat web design, which is a minimalistic design style that avoids the use of 3D effects such as drop shadows and gradients, and, instead, features blocks of color and distinctive typography. Visit the resources listed below to get started:

- http://designmodo.com/flat-design-principles
- http://designmodo.com/flat-design-examples
- http://psd.fanextra.com/articles/flat-design-trend
- http://smashinghub.com/flat-designs-color-trends.htm
- http://www.designyourway.net/drb/the-new-hot-trent-of-flat-web-design-with-examples

If these resources are no longer available, search the Web for information on "flat web design". Read one or more articles and visit the example websites listed in the articles. Search the Web and locate a website that uses flat design. Write a paragraph that includes the URL of the website and describes how the website demonstrates the use of flat web design.

Web Project Case Study

The purpose of this Web Project Case Study is to design a website using recommended design practices. Your website might be about a favorite hobby or subject, your family, a church or club you belong to, a company that a friend owns, the company you work for, and so on. Your website will contain a home page and at least six (but no more than ten) content pages. The Web Project Case Study provides an outline for a semester-long project in which you design, create, and publish an original website.

Project Milestones

- Web Project Topic Approval (must be approved before moving on to other milestones)
- Web Project Planning Analysis Sheet
- Web Project Site Map
- Web Project Page Layout Design
- Web Project Update 1
- Web Project Update 2
- Publish and Present Project

1. **Web Project Topic Approval.** The topic of your website must be approved by your instructor. Write a one-page paper with a discussion of the following items:

- What is the name and purpose of the site?

  List the website name and the reasons you are creating the site.

- What do you want the site to accomplish?

  Explain the goal you have for the site. Describe what needs to happen for you to consider your site a success.

- Who is your target audience?

  Describe your target audience by age, gender, socioeconomic characteristics, and so on.

- What opportunity or issue is your site addressing?

  Note: Your site might be addressing the opportunity of providing information about a topic to others, creating an initial web presence for a company, and so on.

- What type of content might be included in your site?

  Describe the type of text, graphics, and media you will need for the site.

- List at least two related or similar sites found on the Web.

2. **Web Project Planning Analysis Sheet.** Write a one-page paper with a discussion of the following items. Include the following headings:

   Website Goal

   List the website name and describe the goal of your site in one or two sentences.

   What results do I want to see?

   List the working title of each page on your site. A suggested project scope is seven to eleven pages.

   What information do I need?

   List the sources of the content (facts, text, graphics, sounds, video) for the web pages you listed. While you should write the text content yourself, you may use outside sources for royalty-free images and multimedia. Review copyright considerations (see Chapter 1).

3. **Web Project Site Map.** Use the drawing features of a word processing program, a graphic application, or paper and pencil to create a site map of your website that shows the hierarchy of pages and relationships between pages. Unless otherwise directed by your instructor, use the style for a site map shown in Figure 3.3.

4. **Web Project Page Layout Design.** Use the drawing features of a word processing program, a graphic application, or paper and pencil to create wireframe page layouts for the home page and content pages of your site. Unless otherwise directed by your instructor, use the style for page layout composition shown in Figures 3.34–3.37. Indicate where the logo, navigation, text, and images will be located. Do not worry about exact wording or exact images.

5. **Project Update Meeting 1.** You should have at least three pages of your website completed by this time. If you have not done so already, your instructor will help you to publish your pages to the Web (see Chapter 12 for information about selecting a web host). Unless prior arrangements to meet are made, the Project Update Meeting will be held during class lab time. Bring the following items to discuss with your instructor:

   - The URL of your website
   - Source files of your web pages and images
   - Site map (revise as needed)

6. **Project Update Meeting 2.** You should have at least six pages of your website completed by this time. They should be published to the Web. Unless prior arrangements to

meet are made, the Project Update Meeting will be held during class lab time. Prepare the following items to discuss with your instructor:

- The URL of your website
- Source files of your web pages and images
- Site map (revise as needed)

7. **Publish and Present Project.** Finish publishing your project to your website. Be prepared to show your website to the class, explaining project goal, target audience, use of color, and any challenges you faced (and how you overcame them) while you completed the project.

CHAPTER 4

Cascading Style Sheets Basics

Now that you have experience with configuring the structure and information on a web page with HTML, let's explore **Cascading Style Sheets (CSS)**. Web designers use CSS to separate the presentation style of a web page from the information on the web page. CSS is used to configure text, color, and page layout.

CSS first became a W3C Recommendation in 1996. Additional properties for positioning web page elements were introduced to the language with CSS level 2 (CSS2) in 1998, but did not reach official Recommendation status until 2011. CSS level 3 (CSS3) properties are well-supported in modern browsers and include features such as embedding fonts, rounded corners, and transparency. The W3C continues to evolve CSS, with proposals for CSS level 4 (CSS4) currently in draft form. This chapter introduces you to the use of CSS on the Web as you explore configuring color on web pages.

You'll learn how to...

▸ Describe the purpose of Cascading Style Sheets

▸ List advantages of using Cascading Style Sheets

▸ Configure color on web pages with Cascading Style Sheets

▸ Configure inline styles

▸ Configure embedded style sheets

▸ Configure external style sheets

▸ Configure web page areas with element name, class, id, and descendant selectors

▸ Describe the order of precedence in CSS

▸ Test your Cascading Style Sheets for valid syntax

Cascading Style Sheets Overview

For years, style sheets have been used in desktop publishing to apply typographical styles and spacing instructions to printed media. CSS provides this functionality (and much more) for web designers. CSS allows web designers to apply typographical styles (typeface, font size, and so on), color, and page layout instructions to a web page.

The CSS Zen Garden (http://www.csszengarden.com) exemplifies the power and flexibility of CSS. Visit this site for an example of CSS in action. Notice how the content looks dramatically different depending on the design (configured with CSS style rules) that you select. Although the designs on CSS Zen Garden are created by CSS masters, at some point these designers were just like you—starting out with CSS basics.

CSS is a flexible, cross-platform, standards-based language developed by the W3C (see http://www.w3.org/Style). Be aware that even though CSS has been in use for many years, it is still considered an emerging technology, and different browsers do not support it in exactly the same way. We concentrate on aspects of CSS that are well supported by popular browsers.

Advantages of Cascading Style Sheets

There are several advantages to using CSS (see Figure 4.1):

- **Typography and page layout can be better controlled.**   These features include font size, line spacing, letter spacing, indents, margins, and element positioning.
- **Style is separate from structure.**   The format of the text and colors used on the page can be configured and stored separately from the body section of the web page document.
- **Styles can be stored.**   You can store styles in a separate document and associate them with the web page. When the styles are modified, the web page code remains intact. This means that if your client decides to change the background color from red to white, you only need to change one file that contains the styles, instead of each web page document.
- **Documents are potentially smaller.**   The formatting is separate from the document; therefore, the actual documents should be smaller.
- **Site maintenance is easier.**   Again, if the styles need to be changed, it's possible to complete the modifications by changing only the style sheet file.

An issue to be aware of when using CSS is that CSS technology is still not uniformly supported by browsers. We focus on features of CSS that are well supported by modern browsers in this book.

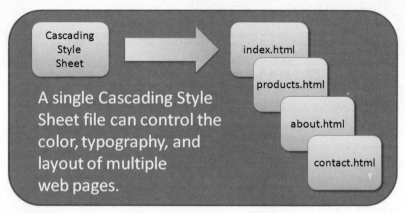

FIGURE 4.1 *The power of a single CSS file.*

Methods of Configuring Cascading Style Sheets

Web designers use four methods to incorporate CSS technology in a website: inline, embedded, external, and imported.

- ▶ **Inline styles** are coded in the body of the web page as an attribute of an HTML tag. The style only applies to the specific element that contains it as an attribute.

- ▶ **Embedded styles** are defined in the head section of a web page. These style instructions apply to the entire web page document.

- ▶ **External styles** are coded in a separate text file, called an external style sheet. This text file is associated with a web page by coding a link element in the head section.

- ▶ **Imported styles** are similar to external styles in that they can connect styles coded in a separate text file with a web page document. An external style sheet can be imported into embedded styles or into another external style sheet by using the `@import` directive.

The "Cascade" in Cascading Style Sheets

Figure 4.2 shows the "cascade" (**order of precedence**) that applies the styles in order from outermost (external styles) to innermost (inline styles). This allows the site-wide styles to be configured with an external style sheet file but overridden when needed by more granular, page-specific styles (such as embedded or inline styles). The order the styles are coded in the web page matters. If styles are conflicting or apply to the same element, the last style rendered by the browser overrides earlier styles.

You'll learn to configure inline styles, embedded styles, and external styles in this chapter.

FIGURE 4.2 *The "cascade" of Cascading Style Sheets.*

CSS Selectors and Declarations

Style Rule Basics

Style sheets are composed of **rules** that describe the styling to be applied. Each **rule** has two parts: a **selector** and a **declaration**.

▶ **CSS Style Rule Selector**

There are several different types of selectors. The selector can be an HTML element name, a class name, or an id name. In this section, we'll focus on applying styles to element name selectors. You'll work with class selectors and id selectors later in this chapter.

▶ **CSS Style Rule Declaration**

The declaration indicates the CSS property you are setting (such as color) and the value you are assigning to the property.

FIGURE 4.3 *Using CSS to set the text color to blue.*

For example, the CSS rule shown in Figure 4.3 would set the color of the text used on a web page to blue. The selector represents the body element, and the declaration sets the color property to the value of blue.

The `background-color` Property

The CSS property to configure the background color of an element is `background-color`. The following style rule will configure the background color of a web page to be yellow:

```
body { background-color: yellow }
```

Notice how the declaration is enclosed within braces and how the colon symbol (:) separates the declaration property and the declaration value.

The `color` Property

The CSS property to configure the text color of an element is `color`. The following CSS style rule will configure the text color of a web page to be blue:

```
body { color: blue }
```

Configure Background and Text Color

To configure more than one property for a selector, use a semicolon (;) to separate the declarations. The following CSS style rule configures the web page in Figure 4.4 with white text and an orchid background:

```
body { color: white; background-color: orchid; }
```

FIGURE 4.4 *A web page with orchid background color and white text color.*

You might be asking how you would know what properties and values are allowed to be used. See the CSS Cheat Sheet in the Appendix for a detailed list of CSS properties. This chapter introduces you to the CSS properties commonly used to configure color, shown in Table 4.1.

TABLE 4.1 *CSS Properties Used in This Chapter*

Property	Description	Value
`background-color`	Background color of an element	Any valid color value
`color`	Foreground (text) color of an element	Any valid color value

CSS Syntax for Color Values

The previous section used color names to configure color with CSS. You can find a list of color names and numerical color values on the textbook's companion website at

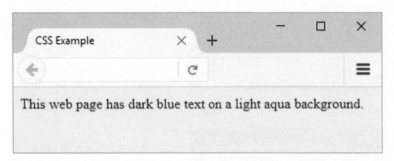

This web page has dark blue text on a light aqua background.

FIGURE 4.5 *The color was configured using hexadecimal color values.*

http://webdevbasics.net/color. However, there are a limited number of color names, and all the names may not be supported by all browsers.

For more flexibility and control, use a numerical color value, such as the hexadecimal color values introduced in Chapter 3 (in the Web Color Palette section). The Web Safe Color Palette, located at the end of the book provides examples of colors created with hexadecimal values (also see http://webdevbasics.net/color).

A style rule to configure the web page displayed in Figure 4.5 with dark blue text (#000066) on a light aqua background (#CCFFFF) is

```
body { color: #000066; background-color: #CCFFFF; }
```

The spaces in these declarations are optional. The ending semicolon (;) is also optional but useful in case you need to add additional style rules at a later time. The following alternative versions of the code above are also valid:

EXAMPLE 1:
```
body {color:#000066;background-color:#CCFFFF}
```

EXAMPLE 2:
```
body { background-color:#000066; color:#CCFFFF; }
```

EXAMPLE 3:
```
body {
color: #000066;
background-color: #CCFFFF;
}
```

EXAMPLE 4:
```
body { color: #000066;
       background-color: #CCFFFF;
}
```

CSS syntax allows you to configure colors in a variety of ways:

- ▶ color name
- ▶ hexadecimal color value
- ▶ hexadecimal shorthand color value
- ▶ decimal color value (RGB triplet)
- ▶ HSL (hue, saturation, and lightness) color value notation new to CSS3 (introduced in Chapter 6)

Visit http://meyerweb.com/eric/css/colors/ to view a chart with examples of configuring color values using different notations. We'll typically use hexadecimal color values in this book. Table 4.2 shows a variety of CSS syntax examples that configure a paragraph with red text.

TABLE 4.2 *Syntax to Configure a Paragraph with Red Text*

CSS Syntax	Color Type
`p { color: red }`	Color name
`p { color: #FF0000 }`	Hexadecimal color value
`p { color: #F00 }`	Shorthand hexadecimal (one character for each hexadecimal pair—only used with web-safe colors)
`p { color: rgb(255,0,0) }`	Decimal color value (RGB triplet)
`p { color: hsl(0, 100%, 50%) }`	HSL color values

Although hexadecimal color notation is commonly used on most web pages, the W3C developed a new color notation called HSL (hue, saturation, and lightness) as part of CSS3 to provide a more intuitive way to describe color on web pages. The hue is the actual color which is represented by numeric values ranging from 0 to 360 (like the 360 degrees in a circle). For example, red is represented by both the values 0 and 360, green is represented by 120, and blue is represented by 240. Saturation is indicated by a percentage value (full color saturation = 100%, gray = 0%). A percentage value is also used to configure lightness (normal color = 50%, white = 100%, black = 0%). Table 4.2 includes the HSL representation for the color red. A dark blue color could be represented by `hsl(240, 100%, 25%)`. Explore the color tools at http://www.colorhexa.com and http://www.workwithcolor.com/color-converter-01.htm. For more information about HSL color visit http://www.w3.org/TR/css3-color/#hsl-color.

Are there other methods to configure color with CSS?

Yes, the CSS3 Color Module provides a way for web designers to configure not only color, but also the transparency of the color with RGBA (Red, Green, Blue, Alpha) color and HSLA (Hue, Saturation, Lightness, Alpha) color. Also new to CSS3 is the opacity property, and CSS gradient backgrounds. You'll explore these techniques in Chapter 6.

Configure Inline CSS

There are four methods for configuring CSS: inline, embedded, external, and imported. In this section we focus on inline CSS.

The `style` Attribute

Inline styles are coded as an attribute on an HTML tag using the **`style` attribute**. The value of the `style` attribute is set to the style rule declaration that you need to configure. Recall that a declaration consists of a property and a value. Each property is separated from its value with a colon (:). The following code will set the text color of an `<h1>` tag to a shade of red:

```
<h1 style="color:#cc0000">This is displayed as a red heading</h1>
```

If there is more than one property, each is separated by a semicolon (;). The following code configures the heading with a red text color and a gray background color:

```
<h1 style="color:#cc0000;background-color:#cccccc;">
This is displayed as a red heading on a gray background</h1>
```

 Hands-On Practice 4.1

In this Hands-On Practice you will configure a web page with inline styles. The inline styles will specify the following:

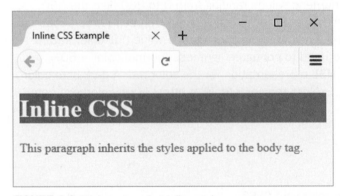

FIGURE 4.6 *Web page using inline styles.*

▶ Global body tag styles for an off-white background with teal text. These styles will be inherited by other elements within the body of the web page by default.

▶ Styles for an h1 element with a teal background with off-white text. This will override the global styles configured on the body element.

A sample is shown in Figure 4.6. Launch a text editor, and open the template.html file from the chapter1 folder in the student files.

Modify the title element and add heading tag, paragraph tags, style attributes, and text to the body section as indicated by the following highlighted code:

```html
<!DOCTYPE html>
<html lang="en">
<head>
<title>Inline CSS Example</title>
<meta charset="utf-8">
</head>
<body style="background-color:#F5F5F5;color:#008080;">
  <h1 style="background-color:#008080;color:#F5F5F5;">Inline CSS</h1>
  <p>This paragraph inherits the styles applied to the body tag.</p>
</body>
</html>
```

Save the document as inline.html on your hard drive or flash drive. Launch a browser to test your page. It should look similar to the page shown in Figure 4.6. Note that the inline styles applied to the body tag are inherited by other elements on the page (such as the paragraph) unless more-specific styles are specified (such as those coded on the `<h1>` tag. You can compare your work with the solution found in the student files (chapter4/4.1/inline.html).

Let's continue and add another paragraph with the text color configured to be dark gray.

```html
<p style="color:#333333"> This paragraph overrides the text color style applied to the body tag.</p>
```

Save the document as inline2.html. It should look similar to the page shown in Figure 4.7. You can compare your work with the solution at chapter4/4.1/inline2.html in the student files.

Note that the inline styles applied to the second paragraph override the global styles applied to the body of the web page. What if you had ten paragraphs that needed to be configured in this manner? You'd have to code an inline style on *each* of the ten paragraph tags. This would add quite a bit of redundant code to the page. For this reason, inline styles are not the most efficient way to use CSS. In the next section you'll learn how to configure embedded styles, which can apply to the entire web page document.

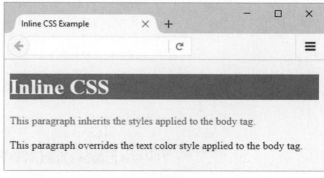

FIGURE 4.7 *The second paragraph's inline styles override the global styles configured on the body tag.*

While inline styles can sometimes be useful, you'll find that you won't use this technique much in practice—it's inefficient, adds extra code to the web page document, and is inconvenient to maintain. However, inline styles can be quite handy in some circumstances, such as when you post an article to a content management system or blog and need to tweak the site-wide styles a bit to help get your point across.

Configure Embedded CSS

The Style Element

Embedded styles apply to the entire document and are placed within a **style element** located in the head section of a web page. The opening `<style>` tag begins the area with embedded style rules, and the closing `</style>` tag ends the area containing embedded style rules. When using XHTML syntax, the `<style>` tag requires a `type` attribute that should have the value of `"text/css"` to indicate the CSS MIME type. HTML5 syntax does not require the type attribute.

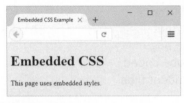

FIGURE 4.8 *Web page using embedded styles.*

The web page in Figure 4.8 uses embedded styles to set the text color and background color of the web page document with the body element selector. See the example in the student files at chapter4/embed.html.

```
<!DOCTYPE html>
<html lang="en">
<head>
<title>Embedded CSS Example</title>
<meta charset="utf-8">
<style>
body { background-color: #E6E6FA;
       color: #191970;
}
</style>
</head>
<body>
  <h1>Embedded CSS</h1>
  <p>This page uses embedded styles.</p>
</body>
</html>
```

Notice the way the style rules were coded with each rule on its own line. This makes the styles more readable and easier to maintain than one long row of text. The styles are in effect for the entire web page document because they were applied to the `<body>` tag using the body element selector.

 Hands-On Practice 4.2

Launch a text editor and open the starter.html file from the chapter4 folder in the student files. Save your page as embedded.html and test it in a browser. Your page should look similar to the one shown in Figure 4.9.

In this Hands-On Practice you'll code embedded styles to configure selected background and text colors. You'll use the body element selector to configure the default background color (#E6E6FA) and default text color (#191970) for the entire page. You'll also use the h1 and h2 element selectors to configure different background and text colors for the heading areas.

Edit the embedded.html file in a text editor and add the following code in the head section above the closing `</head>` tag:

```
<style>
body { background-color: #E6E6FA;
       color: #191970; }
h1 { background-color: #191970;
     color: #E6E6FA; }
h2 { background-color: #AEAED4;
     color: #191970; }
</style>
```

Save and test your file in a browser. Figure 4.10 displays the web page along with color swatches. A monochromatic color scheme was chosen. Notice how the repetition of a limited number of colors adds interest and unifies the design of the web page.

View the source code for your page and review the CSS and HTML code. See chapter4/4.2/embedded.html in the student files for an example of this web page. Note that all the styles are in a single location on the web page. Since embedded styles are coded in a specific location, they are easier to maintain over time than inline styles. Also notice that you only needed to code the styles for the h2 element selector once (in the head section) and *both* of the `<h2>` tags applied the h2 style. This is more efficient than coding the same inline style on each `<h2>` tag.

However, it's uncommon for a website to have only one page. Repeating the CSS in the head section of each web page file is inefficient and difficult to maintain. In the next section, you'll use a more efficient approach—configuring an external style sheet.

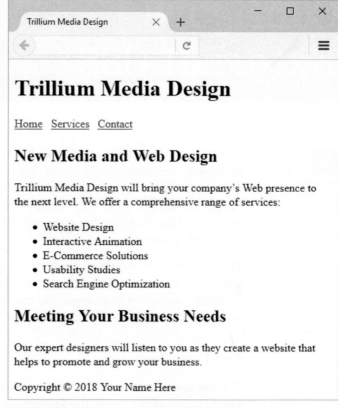

FIGURE 4.9 *The web page without any styles.*

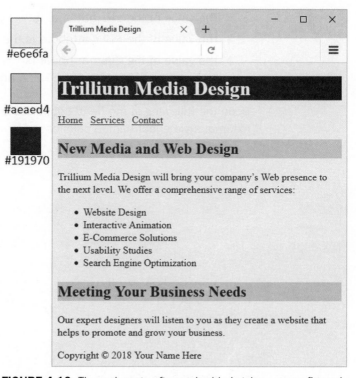

FIGURE 4.10 *The web page after embedded styles are configured.*

Configure External CSS

VideoNote

External Style Sheets

The flexibility and power of CSS are best utilized when the CSS is external to the web page document. An external style sheet is a text file with a .css file extension that contains CSS style rules. The external style sheet file is associated with a web page using the link element. This provides a way for multiple web pages to be associated with the same external style sheet file. The external style sheet file does not contain any HTML tags—it only contains CSS style rules.

The advantage of external CSS is that styles are configured in a single file. This means that when styles need to be modified, only one file needs to be changed, instead of multiple web pages. On large sites this can save a web developer much time and increase productivity. Let's get some practice with this useful technique.

The Link Element

The **link element** associates an external style sheet with a web page. It is placed in the head section of the page. The link element is a stand-alone, void tag. Three attributes are used with the link element: `rel`, `href`, and `type`.

- The value of the `rel` attribute is `"stylesheet"`.
- The value of the `href` attribute is the name of the style sheet file.
- The value of the `type` attribute is `"text/css"`, which is the MIME type for CSS. The type attribute is optional in HTML5 and required in XHTML.

Code the following in the head section of a web page to associate the document with the external style sheet named color.css:

```
<link rel="stylesheet" href="color.css">
```

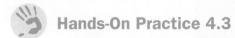
Let's practice using external styles. First, you'll create an external style sheet. Then you'll configure a web page to be associated with the external style sheet.

Create an External Style Sheet. Launch a text editor and type style rules to set the background color of a page to blue and the text color to white. Save the file as color.css. The code is as follows:

```
body { background-color: #0000FF;
       color: #FFFFFF; }
```

Figure 4.11 shows the external color.css style sheet displayed in Notepad. Notice that there is no HTML in this file. HTML tags are not coded within an external style sheet. Only CSS rules (selectors, properties, and values) are coded in an external style sheet.

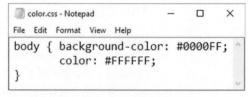

FIGURE 4.11 *The external style sheet color.css.*

Configure the Web Page. To create the web page shown in Figure 4.12, launch a text editor and open the template.html file from the chapter1 folder in the student files. Modify the title element, add a link tag to the head section, and add a paragraph to the body section as indicated by the following highlighted code:

```
<!DOCTYPE html>
<html lang="en">
<head>
<title>External Styles</title>
<meta charset="utf-8">
<link rel="stylesheet" href="color.css">
</head>
<body>
<p>This web page uses an external style sheet.</p>
</body>
</html>
```

Save your file as external.html in the same folder as your color.css file. Launch a browser and test your page. It should look similar to the page shown in Figure 4.12. You can compare your work with the solution in the student files (chapter4/4.3/external.html).

The color.css style sheet can be associated with any number of web pages. If you ever need to change the style of formatting, you only need to change a single file (color.css) instead of multiple

FIGURE 4.12 *This page is associated with an external style sheet.*

files (all of the web pages). As mentioned earlier, this technique can boost productivity on a large site. This is a simple example, but the advantage of having only a single file to update is significant for both small and large websites.

CSS Selectors: Class, Id, and Descendant

The Class Selector

Use a CSS **class selector** to apply a CSS declaration to one or more areas on a web page. When setting a style for a class, configure the class name as the selector. Place a dot or period (.) in front of the class name in the style sheet. A class name must begin with a letter and may contain numbers, hyphens, and underscores. Class names may not contain spaces. The following code configures a class called `feature` in a style sheet with a foreground (text) color set to red: `.feature { color: #FF0000; }`

The styles set in the new class can be applied to any element you wish. You do this by using the class attribute, such as `class="feature"`. The following code will apply the feature class styles to a `<li>` element: `<li class="feature">Usability Studies</li>`

The Id Selector

Use an **id selector** to identify and apply a CSS rule uniquely to a *single area* on a web page. Unlike a class selector which can be applied multiple times on a web page, an id may only be applied once per web page. When setting a style for an id, place a hash mark (#) in front of the id name in the style sheet. An id name may contain letters, numbers, hyphens, and underscores. Id names may not contain spaces. The following code will configure an id called `content` in a style sheet:

`#content { color: #333333; }`

The styles set in the `content` id can be applied to the element you wish by using the id attribute, `id="content"`. The following code will apply the content id styles to a div tag:

`<div id="content">This sentence will be displayed using styles configured in the content id.</div>`

The Descendant Selector

Use a **descendant selector** to specify an element within the context of its container (parent) elements. Using descendant selectors can help you to reduce the number of different classes and ids but still allow you to configure CSS for specific areas on the web page. To configure a descendant selector, list the container selector (which can be an element selector, class, or id) followed by the specific selector you are styling. For example, to specify a green text color for paragraphs located *within* the `main` element, code the following style rule:

`main p { color: #00ff00; }`

Hands-On Practice 4.4

In this Hands-On Practice you will modify the Trillium Media Design page while you practice configuring a class and an id. Launch a text editor and open the embedded.html file from the chapter4/4.2 folder in the student files. Save the file as classid.html.

Configure the CSS. Edit the embedded CSS in the head section of the web page as you configure a class named `feature` and an id named `new`.

1. Create a class named `feature` that configures red (#FF0000) text. Add the following code to the embedded styles in the head section of the web page:

   `.feature { color: #FF0000; }`

2. Create an id named `new` that configures a bright pink text color. Add the following code to the embedded styles in the head section of the web page:

   `#new { color: #FF00CC; }`

Configure the HTML. Associate HTML elements with the class and id you just created.

1. Modify the last two `<li>` tags in the unordered list. Add a class attribute that associates the `<li>` with the `feature` class as follows:

   `<li class="feature">Usability Studies</li>`
   `<li class="feature">Search Engine Optimization</li>`

2. Modify the second opening paragraph tag. Add an id attribute that associates the paragraph with the id named `new`:

   `<p id="new">`

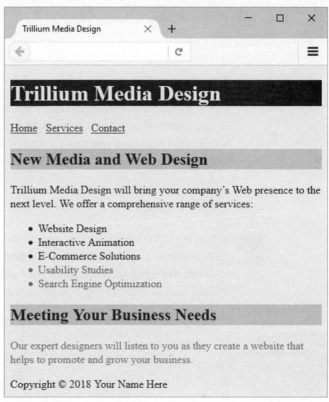

FIGURE 4.13 *CSS class and id selectors are used on this page.*

Save your classid.html file, and test it in a browser. Your page should look similar to the image shown in Figure 4.13. Notice how the class and id styles are applied. The student files contain a sample solution at chapter4/4.4/classid.html.

 For maximum compatibility, choose your class and id names carefully. Always begin with a letter. Do not use any blank spaces. Feel free to use numerals, the dash character, and the underscore character in addition to letters. For a list of commonly used class names visit http://code.google.com/webstats/2005-12/classes.html.

Span Element

The Span Element

The inline **span element** defines a section on a web page that is displayed inline without empty space above and below. A span element begins with a `<span>` tag and ends with a `</span>` tag. Use the span element when you need to format an area that is contained within another, such as within a `<p>`, `<blockquote>`, or `<div>` element.

 Hands-On Practice 4.5 ————————————————————

In this Hands-On Practice you will experiment with span elements in the Trillium Media Design home page. Launch a text editor and open the starter.html file from the chapter4 folder in the student files. Save your page as span.html and test it in a browser. Your page should look similar to the one shown in Figure 4.9.

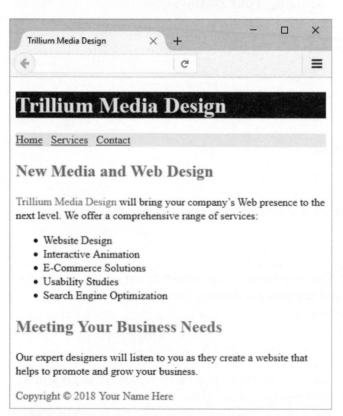

FIGURE 4.14 *This page uses the span element.*

Open span.html in a text editor and view the source code. In this Hands-On Practice you'll code embedded styles to configure selected background and text colors. You'll also add `<span>` tags to the web page. When you are finished with the first part of this Hands-On Practice, your web page will be similar to Figure 4.14.

Part 1

Configure the Embedded Styles. Edit span2.html in a text editor and add embedded styles in the head section above the closing `</head>` tag. You will configure styles for a class named `companyname` and for the body, h1, h2, nav, and footer element selectors. The code is

```
<style>
body { background-color: #FFFFFF;
      color: #191970; }
h1 { background-color: #191970;
    color: #E6E6FA; }
h2 { color: #6A6AA7; }
nav { background-color: #E2E2EF; }
footer { color: #666666; }
.companyname { color: #6A6AA7; }
</style>
```

Configure the Company Name. View Figure 4.14 and notice that the company name, Trillium Media Design, is displayed in a different color than the other text within the first paragraph. You've already created a class named `companyname` in the CSS. You'll use a span to apply this formatting. Find the text "Trillium Medium Design" in the first paragraph. Configure a span element to contain this text. Assign the span to the class named `companyname`. A sample code excerpt is

```
<p><span class="companyname">Trillium Media Design</span> will bring
```

Save your file and test in a browser. Your page should look similar to the one shown in Figure 4.14. The student files contain a sample solution at chapter4/4.5/span.html.

Part 2

As you review your web page and Figure 4.14, notice the empty space between the h1 element and the navigation area—the empty space is the default bottom margin of the h1 element. The margin is one of the components of the CSS box model with which you'll work in Chapter 6. One technique that will cause the browser to collapse this empty space is to configure the margin between the elements. Add the following style to the h1 element selector in the embedded CSS: `margin-bottom: 0;`

Save the file and launch in a browser. Your web page should now be similar to Figure 4.15. Notice how the display of the h1 and navigation area has changed. The student files contain a sample solution at chapter4/4.5/rework.html.

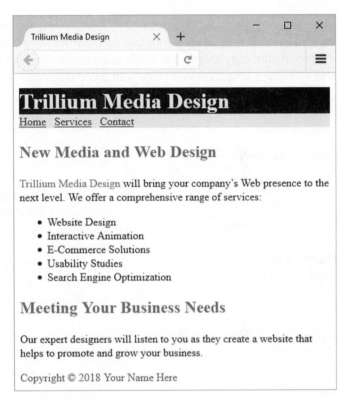

FIGURE 4.15 *The new header area.*

How do I know when to use an id, a class, or a descendant selector?

The most efficient way to configure CSS is to use HTML elements as selectors. However, sometimes you need to be more specific—that's when other types of selectors are useful. Create a class when you need to configure one or more specific objects on a web page in the same way. A class can be applied more than once per web page. An id is similar to a class, but be mindful that it is not valid to apply an id more than once on a web page. To repeat: an id can be used once and only once on each web page. Use an id for a unique item, such as the navigation hyperlink that indicates the current page. As you become more comfortable with CSS, you'll begin to see the power and efficiency of descendant selectors, which allow you to target elements within a specific context (such as all paragraphs in the footer area) without the need to code additional classes or ids within the HTML code.

Practice with CSS

 Hands-On Practice 4.6

In this Hands-On Practice you'll continue to gain experience using external style sheets as you modify the Trillium Media Design website to use an external style sheet. You'll create the external style sheet file named trillium.css, modify the home page (index.html) to use external styles instead of embedded styles, and associate a second web page with the trillium.css style sheet.

You'll use the span.html file from Hands-On Practice 4.5 shown in Figure 4.14 as a starting point.

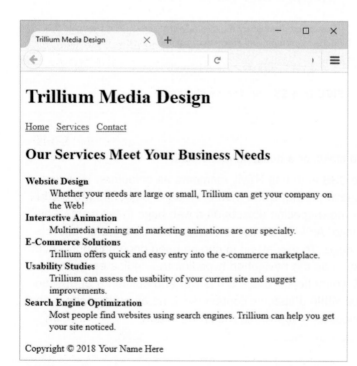

FIGURE 4.16 *The external style sheet named trillium.css.*

Launch a text editor and open the span.html file from the chapter4/4.5 folder in the student files. Save the file as index.html in a folder named trillium.

Convert the Embedded CSS to External CSS Edit the index.html file and select the CSS rules (all the lines of code between, but not including, the `<style>` and `</style>` tags). Select Edit > Copy to copy the CSS code to the clipboard. You will place the CSS in a new file. Launch a text editor, select File > New to create a new file, paste the CSS style rules by selecting Edit > Paste, and save the file as trillium.css in the trillium folder. See Figure 4.16 for a screenshot of the new trillium.css file in the Notepad text editor. Notice that there are no HTML elements in trillium.css—not even the `<style>` element. The file contains CSS rules only.

Associate the Web Page with the External CSS File Next, edit the index.html file in a text editor. Delete the CSS code you just copied. Delete the closing `</style>` tag. Replace the opening `<style>` tag with a `<link>` element to associate the style sheet named trillium.css. The `<link>` element code follows:

```
<link href="trillium.css"
rel="stylesheet">
```

Save the file, and test it in a browser. Your web page should look just like the one shown in Figure 4.14. Although it looks the same, the difference is in the code—the page now uses external instead of embedded CSS.

FIGURE 4.17 *The services.html page is not yet associated with a style sheet.*

Now, for the fun part—you'll associate a second page with the style sheet. The student files contain a services.html page for Trillium at chapter4/services.html. When you display this page in a browser it should look similar to the one shown in Figure 4.17. Notice that although the structure of the page is similar to the home page, the styling of the text and colors is absent.

Launch a text editor to edit the services.html file. Code a `<link>` element to associate the services.html web page with the trillium.css external style sheet. Place the following code in the head section above the closing `</head>` tag:

```
<link href="trillium.css"
rel="stylesheet">
```

Save your file in the trillium folder and test in a browser. Your page should look similar to Figure 4.18—the CSS rules have been applied!

If you click the "Home" and "Services" hyperlinks, you can move back and forth between the index.html and services.html pages in the browser. The student files contain a sample solution in the chapter4/4.6 folder.

FIGURE 4.18 *The services.html page has been associated with trillium.css.*

Notice that when using an external style sheet, if the style rule declarations need to be changed in the future, you'll typically only have to modify *one* file—the external style sheet. Think about how this can improve productivity on a site with many pages. Instead of modifying potentially hundreds of pages to make a color or font change, only a single file—the CSS external style sheet—needs to be updated. Becoming comfortable with CSS will be important as you develop your skills and increase your technical expertise.

(?) FAQ   **My CSS doesn't work; what can I do?**

Coding CSS is a detail-oriented process. There are several common errors that can cause the browser not to apply CSS correctly to a web page. With a careful review of your code and the following tips, you should get your CSS working:

▶ Verify that you are using the colon " : " and semicolon " ; " symbols in the right spots—they are easy to confuse. The : symbol should separate the properties from their values. The ; symbol should be placed between each property : value configuration.

▶ Check that you are not using = signs instead of : between each property and its value.

▶ Verify that the { and } symbols are properly placed around the style rules for each selector.

▶ Check the syntax of your selectors, their properties, and property values for correct usage.

▶ If part of your CSS works and part doesn't, read through the CSS and check to determine the first rule that is not applied. Often the error is in the rule *above* the rule that is not applied.

▶ Use the W3C's CSS validator at http://jigsaw.w3.org/css-validator to help you find syntax errors. See the next section for an overview of how to use this tool to validate your CSS.

The Cascade

FIGURE 4.19 *The cascade.*

Figure 4.19 shows the "cascade" (**order of precedence**) that applies the styles from outermost (external styles) to innermost (inline styles).

This set of rules allows the site-wide styles to be configured, but overridden when needed by more granular page-specific styles (such as embedded or inline styles).

External styles can apply to multiple pages. The order the styles are coded in the web page matters. When using both external and embedded styles, it is typical practice to code the link element (for external styles) before the style element (for embedded styles). So, when a web page contains both an association with an external style sheet and embedded styles, the external styles will be applied first, and then the embedded styles will be applied. This approach allows a web developer to override global external styles on selected pages.

If a web page also contains inline styles, any external and embedded styles are applied first as just described, and then the inline styles are applied. This approach allows a web developer to override page-wide styles for particular HTML tags or classes.

Note that an HTML tag or attribute will override styles. For example, a `<strong>` tag will override corresponding font-related styles configured for an element. If no attribute or style is applied to an element, the browser's default is applied. However, the appearance of the browser's default may vary by browser, and you might be disappointed with the result. Use CSS to specify the properties of your text and web page elements. Avoid depending on the browser's default.

In addition to the general cascade of CSS types described previously, the style rules themselves follow an order of precedence. Style rules applied to more local elements (such as a paragraph) take precedence over those applied to more global elements (such as a `<div>` that contains the paragraph).

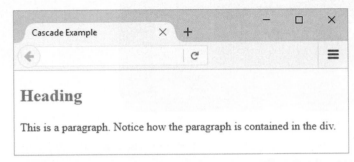

FIGURE 4.20 *Inheritance in action.*

Let's look at the code for the page shown in Figure 4.20 (also found in the student files at chapter4/cascade1.html). Consider the following CSS code:

```
.special { color: red; }
p { color: blue; }
```

The CSS has two style rules: a rule creating a class named `special` that configures red text and a rule configuring all paragraphs to display blue text.

The HTML on the page contains a `<div>` with multiple elements, such as headings and paragraphs, as shown in the following code:

```
<div class="special">
<h2>Heading</h2>
<p>This is a paragraph. Notice how the paragraph is contained in the div.</p>
</div>
```

As shown in Figure 4.20, here is how the browser would render the code:

1. The text contained in the heading is displayed using the color red because it is part of the `<div>` assigned to the special class. It inherits the properties from its parent (`<div>`) class. This is an example of **inheritance,** in which certain CSS properties are passed down to elements nested within a container element, such as a `<div>` or `<body>` element.

2. The text contained in the paragraph is displayed using the color blue because the browser applies the styles associated with the most local element (the paragraph). Even though the paragraph is contained in (and is considered a child of) the `special` class, the local paragraph style rules takes precedence and are applied by the browser.

Don't worry if inheritance and order of precedence seem a bit overwhelming at this point. CSS definitely becomes easier with practice. You will get a chance to practice with the "cascade" as you complete the next Hands-On Practice.

Practice with the Cascade

 Hands-On Practice 4.7

You will experiment with the "cascade" in this Hands-On Practice as you work with a web page that uses external, embedded, and inline styles.

1. Create a new folder named mycascade.

2. Launch a text editor. Open a new file. Save the file as site.css in the mycascade folder. You will create an external style sheet that sets the background color of the web page to a shade of yellow (#FFFFCC) and the text color to black (#000000). The code follows:

   ```
   body { background-color: #FFFFCC; color: #000000; }
   ```

   Save and close the site.css file.

3. Open a new file in the text editor, and save it as index.html in the mycascade folder. The web page will be associated with the external style sheet site.css, use embedded styles to set the global text color to blue, and use inline styles to configure the text color of the second paragraph. The file index.html will contain two paragraphs of text. The code for index.html follows:

   ```
   <!DOCTYPE html>
   <html lang="en">
   <head>
   <title>The Cascade in Action</title>
   <meta charset="utf-8">
   <link rel="stylesheet" href="site.css">
   <style>
   body { color: #0000FF; }
   </style>
   </head>
   <body>
   <p>This paragraph applies the external and embedded styles &mdash;
   note how the blue text color that is configured in the embedded
   styles takes precedence over the black text color configured in
   the external stylesheet.</p>
   <p style="color: #FF0000">Inline styles configure this paragraph
   to have red text and take precedence over the embedded and external
   styles.</p>
   </body>
   </html>
   ```

4. Save index.html, and display it in a browser. Your page should look similar to the sample shown in Figure 4.21. The student files contain a sample solution at chapter4/4.7/index.html.

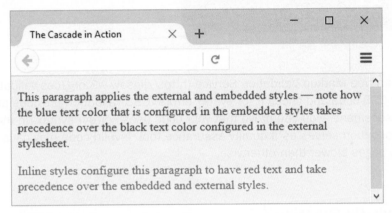

FIGURE 4.21 *The cascade in action.*

Take a moment to examine the index.html web page and compare it with its source code. The web page picked up the yellow background from the external style sheet. The embedded style configured the text to be the color blue, which overrides the black text color in the external style sheet. The first paragraph in the web page does not contain any inline styles, so it inherits the style rules in the external and embedded style sheets. The second paragraph contains an inline style of red text color; this setting overrides the corresponding external and embedded styles.

Is it always better to use external CSS?

FAQ The answer is it depends. If you are creating a stand-alone web page (like some of the practice pages in this chapter), it is easier to work with a single file and code embedded CSS in the head section than to work with two files (the web page and the external CSS file). However, if you are creating a website, the best approach is to place all the CSS in an external CSS file. Later on if you need to change the styles, you'll only need to edit the CSS file!

CSS Syntax Validation

VideoNote

CSS Validation

The W3C has a free Markup Validation Service (http://jigsaw.w3.org/css-validator) that will validate your CSS code and check it for syntax errors. CSS validation provides students with quick self-assessment—you can prove that your code uses correct syntax. In the working world, CSS validation serves as a quality assurance tool. Invalid code may cause browsers to render the pages slower than otherwise.

 Hands-On Practice 4.8

In this Hands-On Practice you will use the W3C CSS Validation Service to validate an external CSS style sheet. This example uses the color.css file completed in Hands-On Practice 4.3 (student files chapter4/4.3/color.css). Locate color.css and open it in a text editor. We will add an error to the color.css file. Find the body element selector style rule and delete the first "r" in the `background-color` property. Remove the # from the `color` property value. Save the file.

Next, attempt to validate the color.css file. Visit the W3C CSS Validation Service page at http://jigsaw.w3.org/css-validator, and select the "By file upload" tab. Click the "Browse" button, and select the color.css file from your computer. Click the "Check" button. Your display should be similar to that shown in Figure 4.22. Notice that two errors were found. The selector is listed, followed by the reason an error was noted.

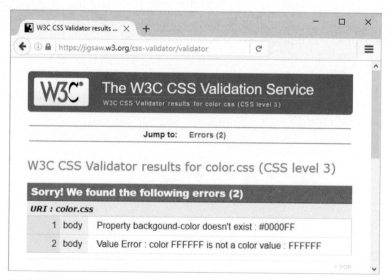

FIGURE 4.22 *The validation results indicate errors.*

Notice that the first message in Figure 4.22 indicates that the "backgound-color" property does not exist. This is a clue to check the syntax of the property name. Edit color.css and correct the error. Test and revalidate your page. Your browser should now look similar to the one shown in Figure 4.23 and report only one error.

FIGURE 4.23 *The valid CSS is displayed below the errors (and warnings, if any).*

The error reminds you that FFFFFF is not a color value—the validator expects you to already know that you need to add a "#" character to code a valid color value, #FFFFFF. Notice how any valid CSS rules are displayed below the error messages. Correct the color value, save the file, and test again.

Your results should look similar to those shown in Figure 4.24. There are no errors listed. This means that your file passed the CSS validation test. Congratulations, your color.css file contains valid CSS syntax! It's a good practice to validate your CSS style rules. The CSS validator can help you to identify code that needs to be corrected quickly and indicate which style rules a browser is likely to consider valid. Validating CSS is one of the many productivity techniques that web developers commonly use.

FIGURE 4.24 *The CSS is valid!*

Review and Apply

Review Questions

1. Which type of CSS is coded in the body of the web page as an attribute of an HTML tag?
   a. embedded   b. inline
   c. external   d. imported

2. Which of the following can be a CSS selector?
   a. an HTML element name
   b. a class name
   c. an id name
   d. all of the above

3. Which of the following is the CSS property used to set the background color?
   a. bgcolor   b. color
   c. bcolor   d. background-color

4. Which of the following describes two components of CSS rules?
   a. selectors and declarations
   b. properties and declarations
   c. selectors and attributes
   d. none of the above

5. Which of the following associates a web page with an external style sheet?
   a. `<style rel="external" href="style.css">`
   b. `<style src="style.css">`
   c. `<link rel="stylesheet" href="style.css">`
   d. `<link rel="stylesheet" src="style.css">`

6. Which of the following configures a CSS class called news with red text (#FF0000) and light gray background (#EAEAEA)?

   a. `news { color: #FF0000; background-color: #EAEAEA; }`
   b. `.news { color: #FF0000; background-color: #EAEAEA; }`
   c. `.news { text: #FF0000; background-color: #EAEAEA; }`
   d. `#news {color: #FF0000; background-color: #EAEAEA; }`

7. An External Style Sheet uses the _____ file extension.
   a. ess
   b. css
   c. htm
   d. No file extension is necessary

8. Where do you place the code to associate a web page with an external style sheet?
   a. in the external style sheet
   b. in the DOCTYPE of the web page document
   c. in the body section of the web page document
   d. in the head section of the web page document

9. Which of the following configures a background color of #FFF8DC for a web page using CSS?
   a. `body { background-color: #FFF8DC; }`
   b. `document { background: #FFF8DC; }`
   c. `body {bgcolor: #FFF8DC;}`
   d. `body { color: #FFF8DC; }`

10. Which of the following do you configure to apply a style to more than one area on a web page?
    a. id   b. class
    c. group   d. link

Hands-On Exercise

Practice with External Style Sheets. In this exercise you will create two external style sheet files and a web page. You will experiment with linking the web page to the external style sheets and note how the display of the page is changed.

a. Create an external style sheet (call it format1.css) to format as follows: document background color of white, document text color of #000099.

b. Create an external style sheet (call it format2.css) to format as follows: document background color of yellow, document text color of green.

c. Create a web page about your favorite movie that displays the movie name in an `<h1>` tag, a description of the movie in a paragraph, and an unordered (bulleted) list of the main actors and actresses in the movie. The page should also include a hyperlink to a website about the movie and an e-mail link to yourself. This page should be associated with the format1.css file. Save the page as moviecss1.html. Be sure to test your page in more than one browser.

d. Modify the moviecss1.html page to be associated with the format2.css external style sheet instead of the format1.css file. Save the page as moviecss2.html and test it in a browser. Notice how different the page looks!

Focus on Web Design

In this chapter you learned how to configure color with CSS. In this activity you will design a color scheme, code an external CSS file for the color scheme, and code an example web page that applies the styles you configured. Use any of the following sites to help you get started with color and web design ideas:

Psychology of Color

- http://www.infoplease.com/spot/colors1.html
- http://www.empower-yourself-with-color-psychology.com/meaning-of-colors.html
- http://www.designzzz.com/infographic-psychology-color-web-designers

Color Scheme Generators

- http://meyerweb.com/eric/tools/color-blend
- http://www.colr.org
- http://colorsontheweb.com/colorwizard.asp
- https://color.adobe.com/create/color-wheel
- http://paletton.com

You have the following tasks:

a. Design a color scheme. List three hexadecimal color values in addition to white (#FFFFFF) or black (#000000) in your design.

b. Describe the process you went through as you selected the colors. Describe why you chose these colors. What type of website would they be appropriate for? List the URLs of any resources you used.

c. Create an external CSS file name color1.css that configures text color and background color selections for the document, h1 element selector, p element selector, and footer element selector using the colors you have chosen.

d. Create a web page named color1.html that shows examples of the CSS style rules.

Pacific Trails Resort Case Study

In this chapter's case study you will use the existing Pacific Trails (Chapter 2) website as a starting point while you create a new version of the website that uses an external style sheet to configure color (see Figure 4.25).

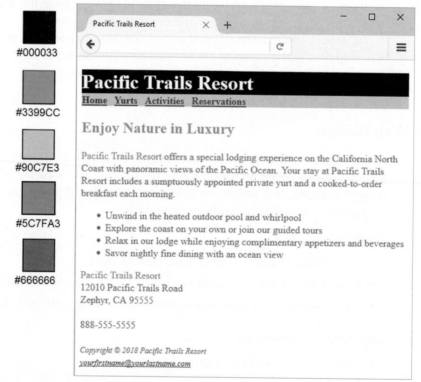

FIGURE 4.25 *New Pacific Trails Resort home page with color swatches.*

You have five tasks in this case study:

1. Create a new folder for the Pacific Trails Resort website.

2. Create an external style sheet named pacific.css.

3. Update the Home page: index.html.

4. Update the Yurts page: yurts.html.

5. Update the pacific.css style sheet.

Task 1: Create a folder called ch4pacific to contain your Pacific Trails Resort website files. Copy the index.html and yurts.html files from the Chapter 2 Case Study pacific folder.

Task 2: The External Style Sheet. Launch a text editor. You will create an external style sheet named pacific.css. A sample wireframe is shown in Figure 4.26.

Code CSS to configure the following:

- Global styles for the document (use the body element selector) with background color white (#FFFFFF) and text color dark gray (#666666).
- Style rules for the header element selector that configure background color (#000033) and text color (#FFFFFF).
- Styles for the nav element selector that configure sky blue background color (#90C7E3).
- Styles for the h2 element selector that configure medium blue text color (#3399CC).
- Styles for the dt element selector that configure dark blue text color (#000033).
- Styles for a class named `resort` that configure medium dark blue text color (#5C7FA3).

Save the file as pacific.css in the ch4pacific folder. Check your syntax with the CSS validator at http://jigsaw.w3.org/css-validator. Correct and retest if necessary.

Task 3: The Home Page. Launch a text editor and open the home page, index.html.

a. Associate the pacific.css external style sheet. Add a `<link>` element in the head section to associate the web page with the pacific.css external style sheet file.

b. Find the company name (Pacific Trails Resort) in the first paragraph below the `h2`. Configure a span that contains this text. Assign the span tag to the `resort` class.

c. Look for the company name (Pacific Trails Resort) directly above the street address. Configure a span that contains this text. Assign the span tag to the `resort` class.

d. Assign the div that contains the address and phone information to an id named `contact`. We'll configure CSS for this id in a future case study.

Save and test your index.html page in a browser. It should be similar to the page shown in Figure 4.27, and you'll notice that the styles you configured in the external CSS file are applied!

FIGURE 4.26 *The wireframe for the Pacific Trails Resort home page.*

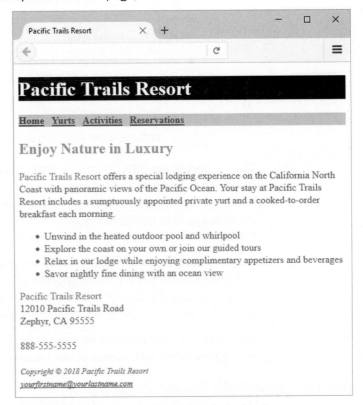

FIGURE 4.27 *First version of the new index.html page.*

Task 4: The Yurts Page. Launch a text editor and open the yurts.html file. An example of the new version of the web page is shown in Figure 4.28.

  a. Add a `<link>` element in the head section to associate the web page with the pacific.css external style sheet file.

Save and test your new yurts.html page. It should look similar to the one shown in Figure 4.28.

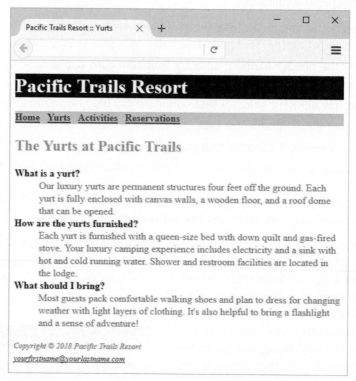

FIGURE 4.28 *First version of the new yurts.html page.*

Task 5: Update the CSS. You may notice an empty space between the header area and the navigation area. The empty space is the default bottom margin of the h1 element. Refer back to Hands-On Practice 4.5 (Part 2), and recall that a technique to cause the browser to collapse this empty space is to configure the margin. To set the bottom margin of the h1 element to 0, code the following style for the h1 element selector in the pacific.css file: `margin-bottom: 0;`

Save the pacific.css file. Launch a browser and test your index.html and yurts.html pages. The gap between the h1 element and the navigation area should be gone. Your home page should now display similar to Figure 4.25. Click the navigation link to display the yurts.html page it should also render with the new styling from the pacific.css external style sheet.

This case study demonstrated the power of CSS. Just a few lines of code have transformed the display of the web pages in the browser.

Path of Light Yoga Studio Case Study

In this chapter's case study you will use the existing Path of Light Yoga Studio (Chapter 2) website as a starting point while you create a new version of the website that uses an external style sheet to configure color (see Figure 4.29).

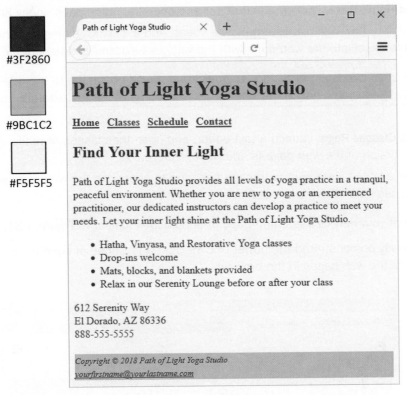

FIGURE 4.29 *New Path of Light Yoga Studio home page with color swatches.*

You have four tasks in this case study:

1. Create a new folder for the Path of Light Yoga Studio website.

2. Create an external style sheet named yoga.css.

3. Update the Home page: index.html.

4. Update the Classes page: classes.html.

Task 1: Create a folder called ch4yoga to contain your Path of Light Yoga Studio website files. Copy the index.html and classes.html files from the Chapter 2 Case Study yoga folder.

Task 2: The External Style Sheet. Launch a text editor. You will create an external style sheet named yoga.css. A sample wireframe is shown in Figure 4.30.

Code CSS to configure the following:

- Global styles for the document (use the body element selector) with an off-white background color (#F5F5F5) and violet text color (#3F2860).
- Styles for the header element selector that configure a background color (#9BC1C2).
- Styles for the footer element selector that configure a background color (#9BC1C2).

Save the file as yoga.css in the ch4yoga folder. Check your syntax with the CSS validator at http://jigsaw.w3.org/css-validator. Correct and retest if necessary.

FIGURE 4.30 *The wireframe for the Path of Light Yoga Studio home page.*

Task 3: The Home Page. Launch a text editor and open the home page, index.html.

    a. Associate the yoga.css external style sheet. Add a `<link>` element in the head section to associate the web page with the yoga.css external style sheet file.

Save and test your index.html page in a browser. It should be similar to the page shown in Figure 4.29, and you'll notice that the styles you configured in the external CSS file are applied!

Task 4: The Classes Page. Launch a text editor, and open the classes.html file. An example of the new version of the web page is shown in Figure 4.31.

    a. Code a `<link>` element in the head section to associate the web page with the yoga.css external style sheet file.

Save and test your new classes.html page. It should look similar to Figure 4.31.

This case study demonstrated the power of CSS. Just a few lines of code have transformed the display of the web pages in the browser.

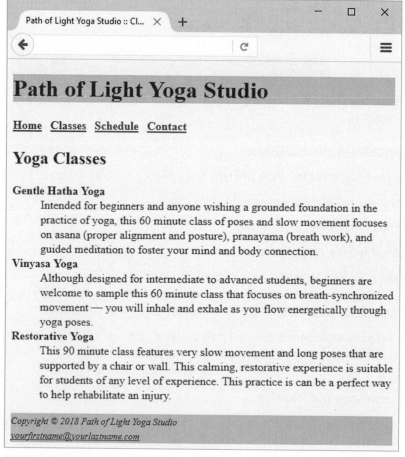

FIGURE 4.31 *The new classes.html page.*

CHAPTER 5

Graphics & Text Styling Basics

A key component of a compelling website is the use of interesting and appropriate graphics. This chapter introduces configuring text with CSS as you work with visual elements on web pages. When you include images on your website, it is important to remember that not all web users are able to view them. Some users may have vision problems and need assistive technology such as a screen reader application that reads the web page to them. In addition, search engines send out spiders and robots to walk the web and catalog pages for their indexes and databases; such programs do not access your images. Some of your visitors may be using a mobile device that may not display your images. As a web designer, strive to create pages that are enhanced by graphical elements but that are usable without them.

You'll learn how to...

▶ Describe types of graphics used on the Web

▶ Apply the image element to add graphics to web pages

▶ Configure images as backgrounds on web pages

▶ Configure images as hyperlinks

▶ Configure image maps

▶ Configure bullets in unordered lists with images

▶ Configure multiple background images with CSS3

▶ Configure text typeface, size, weight, and style with CSS

▶ Align and indent text with CSS

Web Graphics

Graphics can make web pages compelling and engaging. This section discusses types and features of graphic files used on the Web: **GIF**, **JPEG**, and **PNG**. Table 5.1 lists these graphic file types and their characteristics.

Graphic Interchange Format (GIF) Images

FIGURE 5.1 *This logo is a GIF.*

GIF images are best used for flat line drawings containing mostly solid tones and simple images such as clip art. The maximum number of colors in a GIF file is 256. GIF images have a .gif file extension. Figure 5.1 shows a logo image created in GIF format. **Lossless compression** is used when a GIF is saved. This means that nothing in the original image is lost and that the compressed image, when rendered by a browser, will contain the same pixels as the original. An **animated GIF** consists of several images or frames, each of which is slightly different. When the frames flash on the screen in order, the image appears animated.

The format GIF89A used by GIF images supports image **transparency**. In a graphics application, such as the open-source GIMP, one color (typically the background color) of the image can be set to be transparent. The background color (or background image) of the web page shows through the transparent area in the image. Figure 5.2 displays two GIF images on a blue texture background.

GIF saved with Transparency GIF saved without Transparency

FIGURE 5.2 *Comparison of transparent and nontransparent GIFs.*

To avoid slow-loading web pages, graphic files should be optimized for the Web. Image **optimization** is the process of creating an image with the lowest file size that still renders a good-quality image—balancing image quality and file size. GIF images are typically optimized by reducing the number of colors in the image using a graphics application, such as Adobe Photoshop.

Joint Photographic Experts Group (JPEG) Images

JPEG images are best used for photographs. In contrast to a GIF image, a JPEG image can contain 16.7 million colors. However, JPEG images cannot be made transparent and they cannot be animated. JPEG images usually have a .jpg or .jpeg file extension. JPEG images are saved using **lossy compression**. This means that some pixels in the original image are lost or removed from the compressed file. When a browser renders the compressed image, the display is similar to but not exactly the same as the original image.

There are trade-offs between the quality of the image and the amount of compression. An image with less compression will have higher quality and result in a larger file size. An image with more compression will have lower quality and result in a smaller file size.

When you take a photo with a digital camera, the file size is too large for optimal display on a web page. Figure 5.3 shows an optimized version of a digital photo with an original file size of 250KB. The image was optimized using a graphics application set to 80% quality, is now only 55KB, and displays well on a web page.

FIGURE 5.3 *JPEG saved at 80% quality (55KB file size) displays well on a web page.*

Figure 5.4 was saved with 20% quality and is only 19KB, but its quality is unacceptable. The quality of the image degrades as the file size decreases. The square blockiness you see in Figure 5.4 is called **pixelation** and should be avoided.

Adobe Photoshop and Adobe Fireworks are often used by web professionals to optimize images for the Web. GIMP (http://www.gimp.org) is a popular open-source image editor that supports multiple platforms. Pixlr offers a free, easy-to-use, online photo editor at http://pixlr.com/editor.

Another technique used with web graphics is to display a small version of the image, called a **thumbnail image**. Often the thumbnail is configured as an image hyperlink to display the larger image. Figure 5.5 shows a thumbnail image.

FIGURE 5.4 *JPEG saved at 20% quality (19KB file size).*

Portable Network Graphic (PNG) Images

PNG images combine the best of GIF and JPEG images and will be a replacement for GIF in the future. PNG graphics can support millions of colors, support variable transparency levels, and use lossless compression.

FIGURE 5.5
This small thumbnail image is only 5KB.

TABLE 5.1   *Overview of Image File Types*

Image Type	Extension	Compression	Transparency	Animation	Colors
GIF	.gif	Lossless	Yes	Yes	256
JPEG	.jpg or .jpeg	Lossy	No	No	Millions
PNG	.png	Lossless	Yes	No	Millions

Google's new WebP image format offers improved compression and smaller image file sizes, but it's not yet ready for use in commercial websites. WebP (pronounced "weppy") graphics are currently supported only by the Google Chrome Browser. More information about this new image format is available at http://developers.google.com/speed/webp.

Image Element

The **image element** configures graphics on a web page. These graphics can be photographs, banners, company logos, navigation buttons—you are limited only by your creativity and imagination. The image element is a void element and is not coded as a pair of opening and closing tags. The following code example configures an image named logo.gif, which is located in the same folder as the web page:

```
<img src="logo.gif" height="200" width="500" alt="My Company Name">
```

The **src attribute** specifies the file name of the image. The **alt attribute** provides a text replacement, typically a text description, of the image. The browser reserves the correct amount of space for your image if you use the height and width attributes with values either equal to or approximately the size of the image. Table 5.2 lists `<img>` tag attributes and their values. Commonly used attributes are shown in bold.

Review Table 5.2 and notice that several attributes are marked as obsolete. Although obsolete in HTML5, they are still valid in XHTML, so you'll see them coded in existing web pages. As you work through this book, you'll learn to use CSS to recreate the functions of these now-obsolete attributes.

TABLE 5.2 *Attributes of the <img> Tag*

Attribute	Value
align	right, left (default) top, middle, bottom; (obsolete)
alt	Text phrase that describes the image; required
height	Height of image in pixels
hspace	Number in pixels of empty space to the left and right of the image; (obsolete)
id	Text name, alphanumeric, beginning with a letter, no spaces—the value must be unique and not used for other id values on the same web page document
longdesc	URL of a resource that contains an accessible description of a complex image
name	Text name, alphanumeric, beginning with a letter, no spaces—this attribute names the image so that it can be easily accessed by client-side scripting languages such as JavaScript; (obsolete)
src	The URL or file name of the image; required
srcset	New HTML 5.1 attribute that supports the browser display of responsive images (see Chapter 7)
title	A text phrase containing advisory information about the image—typically more descriptive than the alt text
vspace	Number in pixels of empty space above and below the image; (obsolete)
width	Width of image in pixels

Hands-On Practice 5.1

In this Hands-On Practice you will place a logo graphic and a photograph on a web page. Create a new folder called kayakch5. The images used in this Hands-On Practice are located in the student files chapter5/starters folder. Copy the kayakdc.gif and hero.jpg files into your kayakch5 folder. A starter version of the KayakDoorCounty.net Home page is ready for you in the student files. Copy the chapter5/starter.html file into your kayakch5 folder. When you complete this Hands-On Practice, your page will look similar to the one shown in Figure 5.6—with two images. Launch a text editor and open the file.

1. Delete the text contained between the h1 opening and closing tags. Code an `<img>` tag for kayakdc.gif in this area. Remember to include the `src`, `alt`, `height`, and `width` attributes. Sample code follows:

```
<img src="kayakdc.gif"
alt="KayakDoorCounty.net"
width="500" height="60">
```

2. Code an image tag to display the hero.jpg image below the h2 element. The image is 500 pixels wide and 350 pixels high. Configure appropriate alt text for the image.

3. Save your page as index.html in the kayakch5 folder. Launch a browser and test your page. It should look similar to the one shown in Figure 5.6.

Note: If the images did not display on your web page, verify that you have saved the files inside the kayakch5 folder and that you have spelled the file names correctly in the `<img>` tags. The student files contain a sample solution in the chapter5/5.1 folder. Isn't it interesting how images can add visual interest to a web page?

FIGURE 5.6 *A web page with images.*

Accessibility and the alt Attribute

Use the `alt` attribute to provide accessibility. Section 508 of the Rehabilitation Act requires the use of accessibility features for information technology (including websites) associated with the federal government. The alt attribute configures an alternative text description of the image. This alt text may be used by the browser in two ways: The browser will show the alt text in the image area before the graphic is downloaded and displayed. Some browsers will also show the alt text as a tool tip whenever the web page visitor places a mouse over the image area.

Standard browsers such as Internet Explorer and Mozilla Firefox are not the only type of application or user agent that can access your website. Major search engines run programs called spiders or robots; these programs index and categorize websites. They cannot process images, but some process the value of the alt attributes in image tags. Applications such as screen readers will read the text in the alt attribute out loud. A mobile browser may display the alt text instead of the image.

Writing the code to make an image function as a hyperlink is very easy. To create an **image link** all you need to do is surround your `<img>` tag with anchor tags. For example, to place a link around an image called home.gif, use the following code:

```
<a href="index.html"><img src="home.gif" height="19" width="85"
alt="Home"></a>
```

A **thumbnail image link** is a small image configured as an image link with an href attribute value that points to another image file instead of to a web page. For example,

```
<a href="sunset.jpg"><img src="thumb.jpg" height="100" width="100"
alt="view a larger sunset"></a>
```

To see this in action, launch a browser and view chapter5/thumb.html in the student files.

Hands-On Practice 5.2

You will add image links to the KayakDoorCounty.net Home page in this Hands-On Practice. You should already have the index.html, kayakdc.gif, and hero.jpg files in your kayakch5 folder. The new graphics used in this Hands-On Practice are located in the student files in the chapter5/starters folder. Copy the home.gif, tours.gif, reservations.gif, and contact.gif files into your kayakch5 folder. View Figure 5.7 to see how your page should look after you are done with this Hands-On Practice.

Let's get started. Launch a text editor and open index.html. Notice that the anchor tags are already coded—you'll just need to convert the text links to image links!

1. Whenever the main navigation consists of media, such as an image, some individuals may not be able to see the images (or may have images turned off in their browser). To provide navigation that is accessible to all, configure a set of plain text navigation links in the page footer area. Copy the `<nav>` element containing the navigation area to the lower portion of the page and paste it within the footer element, above the copyright line.

2. Locate the style tags in the head section and code the following style rule to configure a green background color for an id named bar:

   ```
   #bar { background-color: #152420; }
   ```

3. Now, focus on the top navigation area. Code `id="bar"` on the opening nav tag. Next, replace the text contained between each pair of anchor tags with an image element. Use home.gif for the link to index.html, tours.gif for the link to tours.html, reservations.gif for the link to reservations.html, and contact.gif for the link to contact.html. Be careful not to leave any extra spaces between the img tag and the opening and closing anchor tags. A sample follows:

```
<a href="index.html"><img src="home.gif"
alt="Home" width="90" height="35"></a>
```

As you code the img tags be mindful of the width of each image: home.gif (90 pixels), tours.gif (90 pixels), reservations.gif (190 pixels), and contact.gif (130 pixels).

4. Save your page as index.html. Launch a browser and test your page. It should look similar to the one shown in Figure 5.7.

The student files contain a sample solution in the chapter5/5.2 folder.

FIGURE 5.7 *The new Home page navigation with image links.*

Accessibility and Image Hyperlinks

When using an image for main navigation, there are two methods to provide for accessibility:

1. Add a row of plain text navigation hyperlinks in the page footer. These won't be noticed by most people but could be helpful to a person using a screen reader to visit your web page.

2. Configure the `alt` attribute for each image to contain the exact text that displays in the image. For example, code `alt="Home"` in the `<img>` tag for the Home button.

What if my images don't display?

The following are common reasons for an image to not display on a web page:

▶ Is your image *really* in the website folder? Use Windows Explorer or the Mac Finder to double check.

▶ Did you code the HTML and CSS correctly? Perform W3C CSS and HTML validation testing to find syntax errors that could prevent the image from displaying.

▶ Does your image have the exact file name that you have used in the CSS or HTML code? Attention to detail and consistency will be very helpful here.

Configure Background Images

Back in Chapter 4, you learned how to configure background color with the CSS `background-color` property. In addition to a background color, you can also choose to use an image for the background of an element.

The `background-image` Property

Use the CSS **background-image** property to configure a background image. For example, the following CSS code configures the HTML body selector with a background using the graphic texture1.png, located in the same folder as the web page file:

```
body { background-image: url(texture1.png); }
```

Using Both Background Color and a Background Image

You can configure both a background color and a background image. The background color (specified by the `background-color` property) will display first. Next, the image specified as the background will be displayed as it is loaded by the browser.

By coding both a background color and a background image you provide your visitor with a more pleasing visual experience. If the background image does not load for some reason, the background color will still have the expected contrast with your text color. If the background image is smaller than the web browser window and the web page is configured with CSS to not automatically tile (repeat), the page background color will display in areas not covered by the background image. The CSS for a page with both a background color and a background image is as follows:

```
body { background-color: #99cccc;
       background-image: url(background.jpg); }
```

Browser Display of a Background Image

You may think that a graphic created to be the background of a web page would always be about the size of the browser window viewport. However, the dimensions of the background image are often much smaller than the typical viewport. The shape of a background image is typically either a long thin rectangle or a small rectangular block. Unless otherwise specified in a style rule, browsers repeat, or tile, these images to cover the page background, as shown in Figures 5.8 and 5.9. The images have small file sizes so that they download quickly.

Background Image

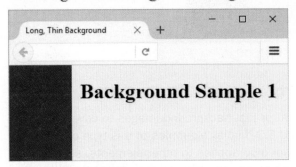

Web Page with Background Image

FIGURE 5.8 *A long, thin background image tiles down the page.*

Background Image

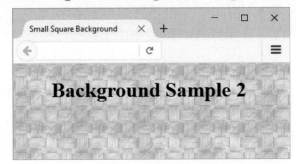

Web Page with Background Image

FIGURE 5.9 *A small square background is repeated to fill the web page window.*

The `background-attachment` Property

Use the **background-attachment property** to configure whether the background image remains fixed in place or scrolls along with the page in the browser viewport. Valid values for the `background-attachment` property include `fixed` and `scroll` (the default).

FAQ

What if my images are in their own folder?

It's a good idea to organize your website by placing all your images in a folder separate from your web pages. Notice that the CircleSoft website shown in Figure 5.10 has a folder called images, which contains GIF and JPEG files. To refer to these files in code, you also need to refer to the images folder. The following are some examples:

▶ The CSS code to configure the background.gif file from the images folder as the page background is as follows:

```
body { background-image: url(images/background.gif); }
```

▶ To configure a web page to display the logo.jpg file from the images folder, use the following code:

```
<img src="images/logo.jpg" alt="CircleSoft" width="588"
height="120">
```

FIGURE 5.10 *A folder named "images."*

Position Background Images

VideoNote
Background Images

The `background-repeat` Property

The default behavior of a browser is to repeat, or tile, background images to cover the entire element's background. Figures 5.8 and 5.9 display examples of this type of tiling for a web page background. This tiling behavior also applies to other elements, such as backgrounds for headings, paragraphs, and so on. You can change automatic tiling of a background image with the CSS **background-repeat** property. The values for the `background-repeat` property include `repeat` (default), `repeat-y` (vertical repeat), `repeat-x` (horizontal repeat), and `no-repeat` (image does not repeat). Configure `background-repeat: no-repeat;` to display the background image only once. Figure 5.11 provides examples of the actual background image and the result of applying various `background-repeat` property values. CSS3 provides for additional values for the `background-repeat` property that are not yet well supported by browsers:

FIGURE 5.11 *Examples of the CSS* `background-repeat` *property.*

- `background-repeat: space;` Repeats the image in the background without clipping (or cutting off) parts of the image by adjusting empty space around the repeated images.
- `background-repeat: round;` Repeats the image in the background and scales (adjusts) the dimensions of the image to avoid clipping.

Positioning the Background Image

You can specify other locations for the background image besides the default top left location using the `background-position` property. Valid values for the `background-position` property include percentages; pixel values; or `left`, `top`, `center`, `bottom`, and `right`. The first value indicates horizontal position. The second value indicates vertical position. If only one value is provided, the second value defaults to center. In Figure 5.12, the flower image has been placed on the right side of the element using the style rule

FIGURE 5.12 *The flower background image was configured to display on the right side with CSS.*

```
h2 { background-image: url(flower.gif);
     background-position: right;
     background-repeat: no-repeat; }
```

Hands-On Practice 5.3

Let's practice using a background image. You will update the index.html file from Hands-On Practice 5.2 (shown in Figure 5.7). In this Hands-On Practice you will configure the main element selector with a background image that does not repeat. Obtain the heroback.jpg image from the student files chapter5/starters folder. Copy the image into your kayakch5 folder. When you have completed this exercise, your page should look similar to the one shown in Figure 5.13. Launch a text editor and open index.html.

1. Locate the style tags in the head section. Code a new style rule for the main element selector to configure the `background-image` and `background-repeat` properties. Set the background image to be heroback.jpg. Set the background not to repeat. The main element selector style rules follow:

```
main { background-image: url(heroback.jpg);
       background-repeat: no-repeat; }
```

2. Remove the img tag that displays the hero.jpg image from the body of the web page.

3. Save your page as index.html. Launch a Firefox or Chrome browser, and test your page. You may notice that the text within the main element is displayed over the background image. In this case, the page would look more appealing if the paragraph did not extend across the background image. Open index.html in a text editor and code a line break tag before the word "explore".

4. Save and test your page again in Firefox or Chrome. It should look similar to the page shown in Figure 5.13. The student files contain a sample solution in the chapter5/5.3 folder. At the time this was written, Internet Explorer did not support default styles for the HTML5 main element. You may need to nudge this browser to comply by adding the `display: block;` declaration (see Chapter 7) to the styles for the main element selector. An example solution is in the student files (chapter5/5.3/iefix.html).

FIGURE 5.13 *The background image in the* `<main>` *area is configured with* `background-repeat: no-repeat.`

CSS3 Multiple Background Images

Now that you are familiar with background images, let's explore applying multiple background images to a web page. Although the CSS3 Backgrounds and Borders Module is in candidate recommendation status, current versions of most popular web browsers support the use of multiple background images.

Figure 5.14 shows a web page with two background images configured on the body selector: a green gradient image that repeats across the entire browser viewport and a flower image that displays once in the right footer area. Use the CSS3 **background property** to configure multiple background images. Each image declaration is separated by a comma. You can optionally add property values to indicate the image's position and whether the image repeats. The `background` property uses a shorthand notation—just list the values that are needed for relevant properties such as `background-position` and `background-repeat`.

FIGURE 5.14 *The browser displays multiple background images.*

Progressive Enhancement

Multiple background images are currently supported by recent versions of Firefox, Chrome, Safari, and Opera. Although support for multiple background images began in Internet Explorer 9, multiple background images are not supported by earlier versions of Internet Explorer. You'll use the technique of **progressive enhancement**, which is defined by web developer and HTML5 evangelist, Christian Heilmann, as "Starting with a baseline of usable functionality, then increasing the richness of the user experience step by step by testing for support for enhancements before applying them." In other words, start with a web page that displays well in most browsers and then add new design techniques, such as multiple background images, in a way that enhances the display for visitors using browsers that support the new technique.

To provide for progressive enhancement when using multiple background images, first configure a separate `background-image` property with a single image (rendered by browsers that do not support multiple background images) prior to the `background` property configured for multiple images (to be rendered by supporting browsers and ignored by nonsupporting browsers).

Let's practice configuring multiple background images. In this Hands-On Practice you will configure the body element selector to display multiple background images on the web page. Create a new folder named trilliumch5. Copy all the files from the student files chapter5/trillstarters folder into your trilliumch5 folder. You'll update the index.html file. Launch a text editor and open index.html.

1. Modify the style rule for the body element selector. Configure the `background-image` property to display trilliumgradient.png. This style rule will be applied by browsers that do not support multiple background images. Configure a `background` property to display both the trilliumfoot.gif image and the trilliumgradient.png image. The trilliumfoot.gif image should not repeat and should be displayed in the lower right corner. The body selector style rules are as follows:

```
body { background-color: #f4ffe4; color: #333333;
       background-image: url(trilliumgradient.png);
       background: url(trilliumfoot.gif) no-repeat right bottom,
                   url(trilliumgradient.png); }
```

2. Save your page as index.html. Launch a browser and test your page in Firefox, Chrome, or Internet Explorer version 9 or later. Your display should be similar to Figure 5.14.

3. There is usually more than one way to design a web page. Let's consider the placement of the flower image in the footer area of the web page. Why not configure the gradient image as the body element selector background and the flower image as the footer element selector background? This will provide for a similar display on all currently popular browsers. Let's try this out. Edit the index.html file. Remove the `background` property from the body element selector. A code sample is

```
body { background-color: #f4ffe4; color: #333333;
       background-image: url(trilliumgradient.png); }
```

Next, configure the trilliumfoot.gif image as the background for the footer element selector. Configure a height value that will be large enough to display the image. The code is

```
footer { background-image: url(trilliumfoot.gif);
         background-repeat: no-repeat;
         background-position: right top;
         height: 75px; }
```

4. Save your page as index2.html. Launch a browser and test your page. It should look similar to Figure 5.14 on all popular modern browsers. See the chapter5/5.4 folder in the student files for solutions to this Hands-On Practice.

Fonts with CSS

The `font-family` Property

The **`font-family` property** configures font typefaces. A web browser displays text with the fonts that have been installed on the user's computer. When a font that is not installed on your web visitor's computer is specified, the default font is substituted. Times New Roman is the default font displayed by most web browsers. Figure 5.15 shows font family categories and some common font typefaces.

Font Family Category	Font Family Description	Font Typeface Examples
serif	Serif fonts have small embellishments on the end of letter strokes; often used for headings.	Times New Roman, Georgia, Palatino
sans-serif	Sans-serif fonts do not have serifs; often used for web page text.	Arial, Tahoma, Helvetica, Verdana
monospace	Fixed-width font; often used for code samples.	Courier New, Lucida Console
cursive	Hand-written style; use with caution; may be difficult to read on a web page.	Lucida Handwriting, Brush Script, Comic Sans MS
fantasy	Exaggerated style; use with caution; sometimes used for headings; may be difficult to read on a web page.	Jokerman, Impact, Papyrus

FIGURE 5.15 *Common fonts.*

The Verdana, Tahoma, and Georgia font typefaces were specifically designed to display well on computer monitors. A common practice is to use a serif font (such as Georgia or Times New Roman) for headings and a sans-serif font (such as Verdana or Arial) for detailed text content. Not every computer has the same fonts installed. See http://www.ampsoft.net/webdesign-l/WindowsMacFonts.html for a list of "web-safe" fonts. Create a built-in backup plan by listing multiple fonts and categories for the value of the `font-family` property. The browser will attempt to use the fonts in the order listed. The following CSS configures the p element selector to display text in Verdana (if installed) or Arial (if installed) or the default installed sans-serif font.

```
p { font-family: Verdana, Arial, sans-serif; }
```

Hands-On Practice 5.5

In this Hands-On Practice you will configure the `font-family` property. In this exercise you will use your files from Hands-On Practice 5.3 (see the student files chapter5/5.3 folder) as a starting point. Launch a browser to display the index.html web page—notice that the text displays in the default browser font (typically Times New Roman). When you are finished with this Hands-On Practice, your page will look similar to the one shown in Figure 5.16.

Launch a text editor and open the index.html file. Configure the embedded CSS as follows:

1. Configure the body element selector to set global styles to use a sans-serif font typeface, such as Verdana or Arial. An example is

```
body { font-family: Verdana, Arial, sans-serif; }
```

2. Configure h2 and h3 element selectors to use a serif font typeface, such as Georgia or Times New Roman. You can configure more than one selector in a style rule by placing a comma before each new selector. Notice that "Times New Roman" is enclosed within quotation marks because the font name is more than a single word. Code the following style rule:

```
h2, h3 { font-family: Georgia,
         "Times New Roman", serif; }
```

Save your page as index.html in the kayakch5 folder. Launch a browser and test your page. It should look similar to the one shown in Figure 5.16. A sample solution is in the chapter5/5.5 folder.

FIGURE 5.16 *The new home page.*

For many years, web designers have been limited to a set of common fonts for text on web pages. CSS3 introduced @font-face, which can be used to "embed" other fonts within web pages although you actually provide the location of the font and the browser downloads it. For example, if you own the rights to freely distribute the font named MyAwesomeFont and it is stored in a file myawesomefont.woff in the same folder as your web page, the following CSS will make it available to your web page visitors:

```
@font-face { font-family: MyAwesomeFont;
            src: url(myawesomefont.woff) format("woff"); }
```

After you code the @font-face rule, you can apply that font to a selector in the usual way, such as in the following example that configures h1 elements:

```
h1 { font-family: MyAwesomeFont, Georgia, serif; }
```

Current browsers support @font-face but there can be copyright issues. When you purchase a font for use on your own computer you do not necessarily purchase the right to freely distribute it. Visit http://www.fontsquirrel.com to browse a selection of commercial-use free fonts available for download and use.

Google Web Fonts provides a collection of free hosted embeddable web fonts. Explore the fonts available at http://www.google.com/webfonts. Once you choose a font, all you need to do is:

1. Copy and paste the link tag provided by Google in your web page document. (The link tag associates your web page with a CSS file that contains the appropriate @font-face rule.)

2. Configure your CSS font-family property with the Google web font name.

See the Getting Started guide at https://developers.google.com/webfonts/docs/getting_started for more information. Use web fonts judiciously to conserve bandwidth and avoid applying multiple web fonts to a web page. It's a good idea to use just one web font on a web page along with your typical fonts. This can provide you a way to use an uncommon font typeface in page headings and/or navigation without the need to create graphics for these page areas.

CSS Text Properties

CSS provides you with lots of options for configuring the text on your web pages. In this section, you'll explore the `font-size`, `font-weight`, `font-style`, `line-height`, `text-align`, `text-decoration`, `text-indent`, `text-transform`, and `letter-spacing` properties.

The `font-size` Property

The **`font-size` property** sets the size of the font. Table 5.3 lists several categories of font size values, characteristics, and recommended usage.

TABLE 5.3 *Configuring Font Size*

Value Category	Values	Notes
Text Value	`xx-small`, `x-small`, `small`, `medium` (default), `large`, `x-large`, `xx-large`	Scales well when text is resized; limited options for text size
Pixel Unit (px)	Numeric value with unit, such as `10px`	Pixel-perfect display depends on screen resolution; may not scale in every browser when text is resized
Point Unit (pt)	Numeric value with unit, such as `10pt`	Use to configure print version of web page (see Chapter 8); may not scale in every browser when text is resized
Em Unit (em)	Numeric value with unit, such as `.75em`	Recommended by W3C; scales well when text is resized in browser; many options for text size
Percentage Value	Numeric value with percentage, such as `75%`	Recommended by W3C; scales well when text is resized in browser; many options for text size

The **em unit** is a relative font unit that has its roots in the print industry back in the day when printers set type manually with blocks of characters. An em unit is the width of a square block of type (typically the uppercase M) for a particular font and type size. On web pages, an em unit corresponds to the width of the font and size used in the parent element (typically the body element). With this in mind, the size of an em unit is relative to the font typeface and default size. Percentage values work in a manner similar to em units. For example, `font-size: 100%;` and `font-size: 1em;` should render the same in a browser. To compare font sizes on your computer, launch a browser and view chapter5/fonts.html in the student files.

The `font-weight` Property

The **`font-weight`** property configures the boldness of the text. The CSS `font-weight: bold;` declaration has an effect similar to the `<b>` or `<strong>` HTML element. CSS to configure bold text in the nav:

```
nav { font-weight: bold; }
```

The `font-style` Property

The **font-style** property typically is used to configure text displayed in italics. Va[lues are] (the default), `italic`, and `oblique`. The CSS `font-style: italic;` declaratio[n] effect in the browser as an `<i>` or `<em>` HTML element. CSS to configure italic te[xt:]

```
footer { font-style: italic; }
```

The `line-height` Property

The **line-height** property modifies the default height of a line of text and is often configured using a percentage value. CSS to configure a paragraph with double-spaced lines:

```
p { line-height: 200%; }
```

The `text-align` Property

HTML elements are left-aligned by default—they begin at the left margin. The CSS **text-align** property configures the alignment of text and inline elements within block elements such as headings, paragraphs, and divs. The `left` (default), `center`, `right`, and `justify` values are valid. CSS to configure centered text within an h1 element:

```
h1 { text-align: center; }
```

The `text-decoration` Property

The purpose of the CSS **text-decoration property** is to modify the display of text. Commonly used values include `none`, `underline`, `overline`, and `line-through`. Although hyperlinks are underlined by default, you can remove the underline with the text-decoration property. CSS to remove the underline on a hyperlink:

```
a { text-decoration: none; }
```

The `text-indent` Property

The CSS **text-indent** property configures the indentation of the first line of text within an element. The value can be numeric (with a px, pt, or em unit) or a percentage. CSS to configure a 5em indent for the first line of paragraphs:

```
p { text-indent: 5em; }
```

The `text-transform` Property

The **text-transform** property configures the capitalization of text. Valid values are `none` (default), `capitalize`, `uppercase`, or `lowercase`. CSS to configure uppercase text within an h3 element:

```
h3 { text-transform: uppercase; }
```

The `letter-spacing` Property

The **letter-spacing** property configures the space between text characters. Valid values are `normal` (default) and a numeric pixel or em unit. CSS to configure extra spacing within an h3 element:

```
h3 { letter-spacing: 3px; }
```

You'll get some practice using many of these new properties in the next section.

ctice with

raphics and Text

Hands-On Practice 5.6

In this Hands-On Practice you will apply your new skills with configuring images and text while you create the web page shown in Figure 5.17.

Create a folder named ch5practice.

Copy the starter.html file from the chapter5 folder in the student files into your ch5practice folder.

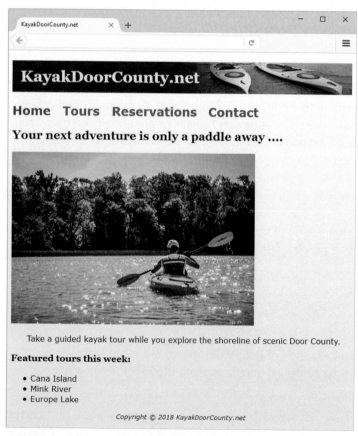

FIGURE 5.17 *The new Home page.*

Copy the following files from the chapter5/starters folder into your ch5practice folder: hero.jpg, background.jpg, and headerbackblue.jpg.

Launch a text editor, open the starter.html file, and save the file as index.html. Edit the code as follows:

1. Locate the style tags in the head section and code embedded CSS to style the following:

    a. Configure the body element selector to display background.jpg as the page background and set Verdana, Arial or the default sans-serif font as the global font typeface.

    ```
    body { background-image:
        url(background.jpg);
        font-family: Verdana,
        Arial, sans-serif; }
    ```

    b. Configure the header element selector with a #000033 background color and to display the headerbackblue.jpg image in the background. Configure this image to display on the right and to not repeat. Also configure #FFFF99 text color, 400% line height, and a 1em text indent.

```
header { background-color: #000033;
         background-image: url(headerbackblue.jpg);
         background-position: right;
         background-repeat: no-repeat;
         color: #FFFF99;
         line-height: 400%;
         text-indent: 1em; }
```

c. Configure the h1, h2, and h3 element selectors with Georgia, Times New Roman, or the default serif font.

```
h1, h2, h3 { font-family: Georgia, "Times New Roman", serif; }
```

d. Configure the nav element selector with bold font that is 1.5em in size.

```
nav { font-weight: bold;
      font-size: 1.5em; }
```

e. Configure navigation anchor elements to not display an underline. Use a descendant selector.

```
nav a { text-decoration: none; }
```

f. Configure paragraph elements to be indented 2em units.

```
p { text-indent: 2em; }
```

g. Configure the footer element selector to be centered with italic font that is .80em in size.

```
footer { text-align: center;
         font-style: italic;
         font-size: .80em; }
```

2. Remove the small and i tags from the page footer area.

3. Code an image element after the h2 element to display the hero.jpg image. Set appropriate values for the alt, width, and height attributes.

```
<img src="hero.jpg" alt="tour guide paddling a kayak" width="500" height="350">
```

Save your file. Test your page in a browser. It should look similar to Figure 5.17. You can compare your work to the sample in the student files (chapter5/5.6).

We used line-height and text-indent properties to configure empty space in this Hands-On Practice. However, there are other CSS properties which would be more appropriate to use for this purpose. You'll explore the box model in Chapter 6 and learn about how to configure empty space with the margin and padding properties.

Is there a way to place a comment within CSS?

Comments are ignored by browsers and can be helpful to document or annotate (in human terms) the purpose of the code. An easy way to add a comment to CSS is to type "/*" before your comment and "*/" after your comment. For example,

```
/* Configure Footer */
footer { font-size: .80em; font-style: italic; text-align: center; }
```

Configure List Markers with CSS

The default display for an unordered list is to show a disc marker (often referred to as a bullet) in front of each list item. The default display for an ordered list is to show a decimal number in front of each list item. Use the **list-style-type** property to configure the marker for an unordered or ordered list. See Table 5.4 for common property values.

TABLE 5.4 *CSS Properties for Ordered and Unordered List Markers*

Property	Description	Value	List Marker Display
list-style-type	Configures the style of the list marker	none	No list markers display
		disc	Circle ("bullet")
		circle	Open circle
		square	Square
		decimal	Decimal numbers
		upper-alpha	Uppercase letters
		lower-alpha	Lowercase letters
		lower-roman	Lowercase Roman numerals
list-style-image	Image replacement for the list marker	The url keyword with parentheses surrounding the file name or path for the image	The image displays in front of each list item
list-style-position	Configures placement of markers	inside	Markers are indented, text wraps under the markers
		outside (default)	Markers have default placement

The property list-style-type: none prevents the browser from displaying the list markers (you'll see a use for this when configuring navigation hyperlinks in Chapter 7). Figure 5.18 shows an unordered list configured with square markers using the following CSS:

```
ul { list-style-type: square; }
```

FIGURE 5.18
The unordered list markers are square.

- Website Design
- Interactive Animation
- E-Commerce Solutions
- Usability Studies
- Search Engine Optimization

Figure 5.19 shows an ordered list configured with uppercase letter markers using the following CSS:

```
ol { list-style-type: upper-alpha; }
```

Configure an Image as a List Marker

Use the `list-style-image` property to configure an image as the marker in an unordered or ordered list. In Figure 5.20 an image named trillium.gif was configured to replace the list markers using the following CSS:

```
ul {list-style-image: url(trillium.gif); }
```

 Hands-On Practice 5.7

In this Hands-On Practice you'll replace the list markers on the Trillium Media Design home page with an image file named trillium.gif. In this exercise you will use your files from Hands-On Practice 5.4 (see the student files chapter5/5.4 folder) as a starting point.

1. Launch a text editor and open index.html. Add the following style rule to the embedded CSS in the head section to configure the ul element selector with the `list-style-image` property:

   ```
   ul { list-style-image: url(trillium.gif); }
   ```

2. Save your page as index.html. Launch in a browser and test your page. You should see the small trillium flower before each item in the unordered list as shown in Figure 5.20. The student files contain a sample solution in the chapter5/5.7 folder.

The Favorites Icon

Ever wonder about the small icon you sometimes see in the address bar or tab of a browser? That's a **favorites icon**, often referred to as a **favicon**, which is a square image (either 16 × 16 pixels or 32 × 32 pixels) associated with a web page. The favicon shown in Figure 5.21 may display in the browser address bar, tab, or the favorites/bookmarks list.

FIGURE 5.21 *The favorites icon displays in the browser tab.*

Configuring a Favorites Icon

Recall that in Chapter 4 you coded the `<link>` tag in the head section of a web page to associate an external style sheet file with a web page file. You can also use the `<link>` tag to associate a favorites icon with a web page. Three attributes are used to associate a web page with a favorites icon: `rel`, `href`, and `type`. The value of the `rel` attribute is `icon`. The value of the href attribute is the name of the image file. The value of the `type` attribute describes the MIME type of the image—which defaults to `image/x-icon` for .ico files. The code to associate a favorites icon named favicon.ico to a web page is as follows:

```
<link rel="icon" href="favicon.ico" type="image/x-icon">
```

You may need to publish your files to the Web (see Chapter 12) in order for the favorites icon to display in Microsoft Edge and Internet Explorer. Other browsers, such as Firefox, display favicons more reliably and also support GIF, JPG, and PNG image formats. Be aware that if you use a .gif, .png, or .jpg file as a favorites icon, the MIME type should be image/ico. For example:

```
<link rel="icon" href="favicon.gif" type="image/ico">
```

Hands-On Practice 5.8

Let's practice using a favorites icon. In this exercise you will use your files from Hands-On Practice 5.7 (see the student files chapter5/5.7 folder) as a starting point and configure the favico.ico file as a favorites icon.

1. Launch a text editor and open index.html. Add the following link tag to the head section of the web page:

```
<link rel="icon" href="favicon.ico" type="image/x-icon">
```

2. Save your page as index.html. Launch a browser and test your page. You may notice the small trillium flower in the browser tab as shown in Figure 5.22. The student files contain a sample solution in the chapter5/5.8 folder.

FIGURE 5.22 *The favorites icon displays in the Firefox browser tab.*

 How can I create my own favorites icon?

You can create your own favicon with a graphics application, such as Adobe Fireworks, or with one of the following online tools:

▶ http://favicon.cc
▶ http://tools.dynamicdrive.com/favicon/
▶ http://www.freefavicon.com
▶ http://www.xiconeditor.com

Image Maps

An **image map** is an image configured with multiple clickable or selectable areas that link to another web page or website. The selectable areas are called **hotspots**. Image maps can configure clickable areas in three shapes: rectangles, circles, and polygons. An image map requires the use of the image element, map element, and one or more area elements.

Map Element

The map **element** is a container tag that indicates the beginning and ending of the image map description. The **name attribute** is coded to associate the `<map>` tag with its corresponding image. The `id` attribute must have the same value as the `name` attribute. To associate a map element with an image, configure the image tag with the **usemap attribute** to indicate which `<map>` to use.

Area Element

The **area element** defines the coordinates or edges of the clickable area. It is a void tag that uses the `href`, `alt`, `title`, `shape`, and `coords` attributes. The `href` attribute identifies the web page to display when the area is clicked. The `alt` attribute provides a text description for screen readers. Use the **title attribute** to specify text that some browsers may display as a tooltip when the mouse is placed over the area. The **coords attribute** indicates the coordinate position of the clickable area. Table 5.5 describes the type of coordinates needed for each `shape` attribute value.

TABLE 5.5 *Shape Coordinates*

Shape	Coordinates	Meaning
rect	"x1,y1,x2,y2"	The coordinates at point (x1,y1) represent the upper-left corner of the rectangle. The coordinates at point (x2,y2) represent the lower-right corner of the rectangle
circle	"x,y,r"	The coordinates at point (x,y) indicate the center of the circle. The value of r is the radius of the circle, in pixels
polygon	"x1,y1,x2,y2,x3,y3", etc.	The values of each (x,y) pair represent the coordinates of a corner point of the polygon

Exploring a Rectangular Image Map

We'll focus on a rectangular image map. For a rectangular image map, the value of the `shape` attribute is `rect`, and the coordinates indicate the pixel positions as follows:

- distance of the upper-left corner from the left side of the image
- distance of the upper-left corner from the top of the image
- distance of the lower-right corner from the left edge of the image
- distance to the lower-right corner from the top of the image.

Figure 5.23 shows an image of a fishing boat. This example is in the student files at chapter5/map.html.

- The dotted rectangle around the fishing boat indicates the location of the hotspot.
- The coordinates shown (24, 188) indicate that the top-left corner is 24 pixels from the left edge of the image and 188 pixels from the top of the image.
- The pair of coordinates in the lower-right corner (339, 283) indicates that this corner is 339 pixels from the left edge of the image and 283 pixels from the top of the image.

FIGURE 5.23 *A sample image map.*

The HTML code to create this image map follows:

```
<map name="boat" id="boat">
<area href="http://www.fishingdoorcounty.com"
  shape="rect" coords="24,188,339,283"
  alt="Door County Fishing Charter"
  title="Door County Fishing Charter">
</map>
<img src="fishingboat.jpg" usemap="#boat"
  alt="Door County" width="416" height="350">
```

Note the use of the `alt` attribute on the area element in the previous code sample. Configure a descriptive `alt` attribute for each area element associated with an image map to provide for accessibility.

Most web developers do not hand-code image maps. Web authoring tools, such as Adobe Dreamweaver, have features that help you to generate image maps. There are also free online image map generators available at:

- http://www.maschek.hu/imagemap/imgmap
- http://image-maps.com
- http://mobilefish.com/services/image_map/image_map.php

Review and Apply

Review Questions

1. Which attribute specifies text that is available to browsers and other user agents that do not support graphics?

   a. `alt`

   b. `text`

   c. `src`

   d. `accessibility`

2. Which of the following creates an image link to the index.html page when the home.gif graphic is clicked?

   a. `<a href="index.html" src="home.gif" alt="Home"></a>`

   b. `<a href="index.html"><img src="home.gif" alt="Home"></a>`

   c. `<img src="home.gif" href="index.html" alt="Home">`

   d. `<a src="home.gif"><img src="home.gif" alt="Home"></a>`

3. Why should you include `height` and `width` attributes on an `<img>` tag?

   a. They are required attributes and must always be included.

   b. They help the browser reserve the appropriate space for the image.

   c. They help the browser display the image in its own window.

   d. None of the above.

4. Which declaration configures an unordered list item with a square list marker?

   a. `list-bullet: none;`

   b. `list-style-type: square;`

   c. `list-style-image: square;`

   d. `list-marker: square;`

5. Which CSS property will configure the font typeface?

   a. `font-face`

   b. `font-style`

   c. `font-family`

   d. `typeface`

6. Which configures a class called news with red text, large font, and Arial or a sans-serif font using CSS?

   a. `news { text: red;`
   `        font-size: large;`
   `        font-family: Arial,`
   `        sans-serif; }`

   b. `.news { text: red;`
   `        font-size: large;`
   `        font-family: Arial,`
   `        sans-serif; }`

   c. `#news { color: red;`
   `        font-size: large;`
   `        font-family: Arial,`
   `        sans-serif; }`

   d. `.news { color: red;`
   `        font-size: large;`
   `        font-family: Arial,`
   `        sans-serif; }`

7. Which of the following configures a graphic to repeat vertically down the side of a web page?

   a. `background-repeat: repeat-x;`

   b. `background-repeat: repeat;`

   c. `valign="left"`

   d. `background-repeat: repeat-y;`

8. Which CSS property configures the background image of an element?

   a. `background-color`

   b. `bgimage`

   c. `favicon`

   d. `background-image`

9. What is the process of creating an image with the lowest file size that still renders a good-quality image—balancing image quality and file size?

a. progressive enhancement

b. optimization

c. usability

d. image validation

10. What is the process of ensuring that web pages that are coded with new or advanced techniques are still usable in browsers that do not support the new techniques?

a. validation

b. progressive enhancement

c. valid enhancement

d. optimization

Hands-On Exercises

1. Write the CSS code for an external style sheet file named mystyle.css that configures the text to be brown, 1.2em in size, and in Arial, Verdana, or a sans-serif font.

2. Write the HTML and CSS code for an embedded style sheet that configures a class called priority, which has bold and italic text.

3. Write the code to place an image called primelogo.gif on a web page. The image is 100 pixels high by 650 pixels wide.

4. Write the code to create an image hyperlink. The image is called schaumburgthumb.jpg. It is 100 pixels high by 150 pixels wide. The image should link to a larger image called schaumburg.jpg. There should be no border on the image.

5. Write the code to create a `nav` element containing three images used as navigation links. Table 5.6 provides information about the images and their associated links.

TABLE 5.6

Image Name	Link Page Name	Image Height	Image Width
homebtn.gif	index.html	50	200
productsbtn.gif	products.html	50	200
orderbtn.gif	order.html	50	200

6. Experiment with background images.

a. Locate the twocolor.gif file in the student files chapter5/starters folder. Design a web page that uses this file as a background image that repeats down the left side of the browser window. Save your file as bg1.html.

b. Locate the twocolor1.gif file in the student files chapter5/starters folder. Design a web page that uses this file as a background image that repeats across the top of the browser window. Save your file as bg2.html.

7. Design a new web page about your favorite movie. Name the web page movie5.html. Configure a background color for the page and either background images or background colors for at least two sections of the page. Search the Web for a photo of a scene from the movie, an actress in the movie, or an actor in the movie. Include the following information on your web page:

- Title of the movie

- Director or producer

- Leading actor
- Leading actress
- Rating (R, PG-13, PG, G, NR)
- A brief description of the movie
- An absolute link to a review about the movie

It is unethical to steal an image from another website. Some websites have a link to their copyright policy. Most websites will give permission for you to use an image in a school assignment. If there is no available policy, e-mail the site's contact person and request permission to use the photo. If you are unable to obtain permission, you may substitute with clip art or an image from a free site instead.

Focus on Web Design

Providing access to the Web for all people is an important issue. Visit the W3C's Web Accessibility Initiative and explore their WCAG 2.0 Quick Reference at http://w3.org/WAI/WCAG20/quickref. View additional pages at the W3C's site as necessary. Explore the checkpoints that are related to the use of color and images on web pages. Create a web page that uses color, uses images, and includes the information that you discovered.

Pacific Trails Resort Case Study

In this chapter's case study you will use the existing Pacific Trails (Chapter 4) website as a starting point to create a new version of the website that incorporates images.

You have five tasks in this case study:

1. Create a new folder for the Pacific Trails Resort website.
2. Update the pacific.css external style sheet file.
3. Update the Home page: index.html.
4. Update the Yurts page: yurts.html.
5. Create a new Activities page: activities.html.

Task 1: Create a folder called ch5pacific to contain your Pacific Trails Resort website files. Copy the index.html, yurts.html, and pacific.css files from the Chapter 4 Case Study ch4pacific folder. Copy the following files from the chapter5/casestudystarters/pacific folder in the student files and place them in your ch5pacific folder: coast.jpg, marker.gif, sunset.jpg, trail.jpg, and yurt.jpg.

Task 2: **The External Style Sheet.** Launch a text editor and open the pacific.css external style sheet file.

1. **The body element selector.** Add a declaration that configures Arial, Helvetica, or sans-serif font typeface.

2. **The header element selector.** Add declarations to display the background image named sunset.jpg on the right without any repeats. Also configure declarations to set 400% line-height and 1em text-indent.

3. **The nav element selector.** Add a declaration to configure bold text.

4. **The nav a element selector.** Code styles to eliminate the display of the underline for hyperlinks (hint: use the `nav a` descendant selector with text-decoration: none;)

5. **The h1 element selector.** Add a declaration to display text in Georgia, Times New Roman, or serif font typeface.

6. **The h2 element selector.** Add a declaration to display text in Georgia, Times New Roman, or serif font typeface.

7. **The h3 element selector.** Code styles to display text in Georgia, Times New Roman, or serif font typeface. Also configure #000033 text color for the h3 element selector.

8. **The ul element selector.** Code styles to display the marker.gif as the list marker (bullet).

9. **The footer element selector.** Code styles to configure 75% font size, italic font style, centered text, and Georgia, Times New Roman, or serif font typeface.

10. **The resort class selector.** Add a declaration to display bold text.

11. **The contact id selector.** Code styles to display text with 90% font size.

Save your pacific.css file. Check your syntax with the CSS validator (http://jigsaw.w3.org/css-validator). Correct and retest if necessary.

Task 3: **The Home Page.** Launch a text editor and open the home page, index.html. Remove the b, small, and i tags from the page. Code an `<img>` tag below the h2 element. Configure the `<img>` tag to display the coast.jpg image. Configure the `alt`, `height`, and `width` attributes for the image. Save and test your page in a browser. It should look similar to Figure 5.24.

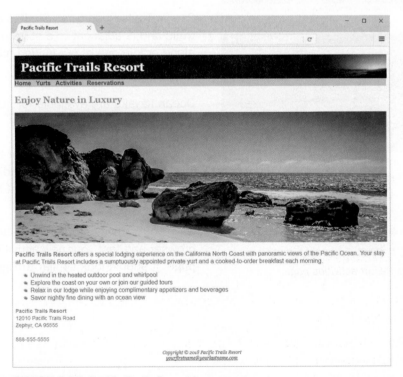

FIGURE 5.24 *Pacific Trails Resort home page.*

FIGURE 5.25 *Pacific Trails Resort yurts page.*

FIGURE 5.26 *New Pacific Trails Resort activities page.*

Task 4: The Yurts Page. Launch a text editor and open the yurts.html file. Remove the b, small, and i tags from the page. Next, you will modify this file to display the yurt.jpg image below the h2 element and configure it in a similar manner as you configured the coast.jpg image on the home page. Save and test your new yurts.html page. It should look similar to the one shown in Figure 5.25.

Task 5: The Activities Page. Launch a text editor, open the yurts.html document, and save the file as activities.html—this is the start of your new activities page.

1. Modify the page title area as appropriate.

2. Change the h2 text to be Activities at Pacific Trails.

3. Modify the `<img>` tag to display the trail.jpg image.

4. Delete the description list.

5. Configure the following text using h3 tags for the headings and paragraph tags for the sentences.

   "**Hiking**

   Pacific Trails Resort has 5 miles of hiking trails and is adjacent to a state park. Go it alone or join one of our guided hikes.

   Kayaking

   Ocean kayaks are available for guest use.

   Bird Watching

   While anytime is a good time for bird watching at Pacific Trails, we offer guided bird-watching trips at sunrise several times a week."

Save your activities.html file. Launch a browser and test your new activities.html page. It should look similar to Figure 5.26.

What if I don't know the height and width of an image?

FAQ Most graphics applications can display the height and width of an image. If you have a graphics application such as Adobe Photoshop or Adobe Fireworks handy, launch the application and open the image. These applications include options that will display the properties of the image, such as height and width.

If you don't have a graphics application available, you can determine the dimensions of an image using the Firefox browser. Display the image on a web page. Right-click on the image to display the context-sensitive menu. Select "View Image Info" and view the dimensions (height and width) of the image. (*Warning*: if the height and width are specified on the web page, those values will be displayed even if the image's actual height and width are different.)

Path of Light Yoga Studio Case Study

In this chapter's case study you will use the existing Path of Light Yoga Studio (Chapter 4) website as a starting point while you create a new version of the website that incorporates images.

You have five tasks in this case study:

1. Create a new folder for the Path of Light Yoga Studio website.

2. Update the yoga.css external style sheet.

3. Update the Home page: index.html.

4. Update the Classes page: classes.html.

5. Create a new Schedule page: schedule.html.

Task 1: Create a folder called ch5yoga to contain your Path of Light Yoga Studio website files. Copy the files from the Chapter 4 Case Study ch4yoga folder and place them in your ch5yoga folder. Locate the chapter5/casestudystarters/yoga folder in the student files. Copy the following files to your ch5yoga folder: lilyheader.jpg, yogadoor.jpg, yogalounge.jpg, and yogamat.jpg.

Task 2: **The External Style Sheet.** Launch a text editor and open the yoga.css external style sheet file.

1. **The body element selector.** Add a declaration that configures Verdana, Arial, or sans-serif font typeface.

2. **The header element selector.** Add declarations to configure lilyheader.jpg as a background image that displays on the right without repeating.

3. **The nav element selector.** Code styles to configure centered, bold text.

4. **The nav a element selector.** Code styles to eliminate the display of the underline for hyperlinks (hint: use the `nav a` descendant selector with text-decoration: none;).

5. **The h1 element selector.** Code styles to display 400% line height and 1em text-indent.

6. **The footer selector.** Add declarations to configure small, italic, and centered text.

7. **The li element selector.** Code styles to configure 90% font size.

FIGURE 5.27 *Path of Light Yoga Studio home page.*

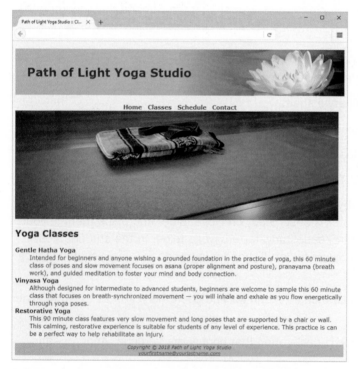

FIGURE 5.28 *New Path of Light Yoga Studio wireframe.*

Save your file. Use the CSS Validator (http://jigsaw.w3.org/css-validator) to check your syntax. Correct and retest if necessary.

Task 3: The Home Page. Launch a text editor and open the home page, index.html. Remove the b, small, and i tags from the page. Add an `<img>` tag above the h2 element. Configure the `<img>` tag to display the yogadoor.jpg image. Configure the `alt`, `height`, and `width` attributes for the image. Also configure the image to appear to the right of the text by coding the `align="right"` attribute on the `<img>` tag. Note: The W3C HTML validator will indicate that the align attribute is invalid. We'll overlook the error for this case study. In Chapter 7, you'll learn to use the CSS float property (instead of the align attribute) to configure this type of layout. Save and test your page in a browser. It should look similar to Figure 5.27.

Task 4: The Classes Page. Launch a text editor and open the classes page, classes.html. Remove the b, small, and i tags from the page. Add an `<img>` tag above the h2 element. Configure the `<img>` tag to display the yogamat.jpg image. Configure the alt, height, and width attributes for the image. Save and test your page in a browser. It should look similar to Figure 5.28.

Task 5: The Schedule Page. Use the Classes page as the starting point for the Schedule page. Launch a text editor and open the classes.html file in the ch5yoga folder. Save the file as schedule.html.

Modify the schedule.html file to look similar to the Schedule page, as shown in Figure 5.29:

1. Change the page title to an appropriate phrase.

2. Replace the text contained within the h2 element with the following: Yoga Schedule.

3. Modify the `<img>` tag to display the yogalounge.jpg image.

4. Delete the description list from the page.

5. Configure a paragraph below the h2 element. The text of the paragraph follows:

   Mats, blocks, and blankets provided. Please arrive 10 minutes before your class begins. Relax in our Serenity Lounge before or after your class.

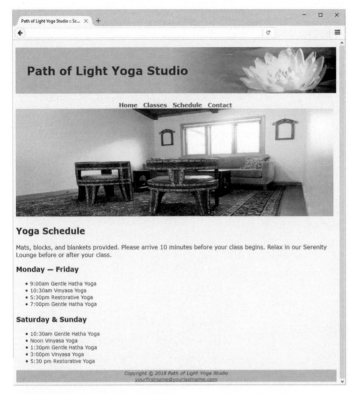

FIGURE 5.29 *Path of Light Yoga Studio schedule page.*

6. Configure an h3 element with the following text: Monday—Friday.

7. Configure an unordered list with the following text:

   9:00am Gentle Hatha Yoga

   10:30am Vinyasa Yoga

   5:30pm Restorative Yoga

   7:00pm Gentle Hatha Yoga

8. Configure an h3 element with the following text: Saturday & Sunday.

9. Configure an unordered list with the following text:

   10:30am Gentle Hatha Yoga

   Noon Vinyasa Yoga

   1:30pm Gentle Hatha Yoga

   3:00pm Vinyasa Yoga

   5:30 pm Restorative Yoga

Save the schedule.html file. When you test your page in a browser, it should look similar to Figure 5.29.

CHAPTER 6

More CSS Basics

You'll add to your CSS skill set in this chapter. You will begin to work with the CSS box model and configure margin, border, and padding. You'll also explore new CSS3 properties to round corners, apply shadow, adjust display of background images, and configure color and opacity.

You'll learn how to...

- Describe and apply the CSS box model
- Configure width and height with CSS
- Configure margin, border, and padding with CSS
- Center web page content with CSS
- Apply shadows with CSS3
- Configure rounded corners with CSS3
- Apply CSS3 properties to background images
- Configure opacity, RGBA color, HSLA color, and gradients with CSS3

Width and Height with CSS

The `width` Property

The **width property** configures the width of an element's content in the browser viewport with either a numeric value unit (such as `100px` or `20em`) or percentage (such as `80%`, as shown in Figure 6.1) of the parent element. The actual width of an element displayed in the browser viewport includes the width of the element's content, padding, border, and margin—it is not the same as the value of the `width` property, which only configures the width of the element's *content*.

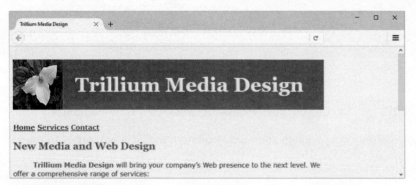

FIGURE 6.1 *The web page is set to 80% width.*

The `min-width` Property

The **min-width property** sets the minimum width of an element's content in the browser viewport with either a numeric value unit (such as `700px` or `20em`) or percentage (such as `75%`) of the parent element. This minimum width value can prevent content from jumping around when a browser is resized. Scrollbars appear if the browser viewport is resized below the minimum width (see Figures 6.2 and 6.3).

FIGURE 6.2 *As the browser is resized, the "Trillium Media Design" text wraps.*

FIGURE 6.3 *The* `min-width` *property avoids display issues.*

The `max-width` Property

The **max-width** property sets the maximum width of an element's content in the browser viewport with either a numeric value unit (such as `960px`) or percentage (such as `90%`) of the parent element. This maximum width value can reduce the possibility of text stretching across large expanses of the screen by a high-resolution monitor.

The `height` Property

The **height property** configures the height of an element's content in the browser viewport with either a numeric value unit (such as `900px`) or percentage (such as `60%`) of the parent element. Figure 6.4 shows a web page with an h1 area without a `height` or `line-height` property configured. Notice how part of the background image is truncated, or cut off. In Figure 6.5, the h1 area is configured with the `height` property. Notice the improved display of the background image.

FIGURE 6.4 *The background image is truncated.*

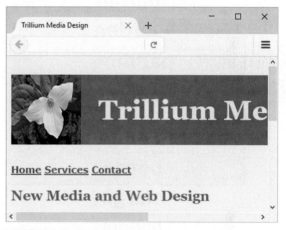

FIGURE 6.5 *The* `height` *property value corresponds to the height of the background image.*

Hands-On Practice 6.1

You'll work with the `height` and `width` properties in this Hands-On Practice.

Create a new folder called trilliumch6. Copy the trilliumlogo.jpg file from the chapter6/starters folder into your trilliumch6 folder. Copy the chapter6/starter1.html file into your trilliumch6 folder. Launch a text editor and open the file.

1. Edit the embedded CSS to configure the document to take up 80% of the browser window but with a minimum width of 750px. Add the following style rules to the body element selector:

   ```
   width: 80%; min-width: 750px;
   ```

2. Add style declarations to the h1 element selector to configure height as 120px (the height of the background image) and line height as 250%.

   ```
   height: 120px; line-height: 250%;
   ```

Save your file as index.html. Launch a browser and test your page. Your web page should look similar to Figure 6.1. A sample solution is in the chapter6/6.1 folder.

Each element in a document is considered to be a rectangular box. As shown in Figure 6.6, this box consists of a content area surrounded by padding, a border, and margins. This is known as the box model.

FIGURE 6.6 *The CSS box model.*

Content

The content area can consist of a combination of text and web page elements such as images, paragraphs, headings, lists, and so on. The visible width of the element on a web page is the total of the content width, the padding width, and the border width. However, the `width` property only configures the actual width of the content—not including any padding, border, or margin.

Padding

The padding area is between the content and the border. The default padding value is zero. When the background of an element is configured, the background is applied to both the padding and the content areas.

Border

The border area is between the padding and the margin. The default border has a value of 0 and does not display.

Margin

The margin determines the empty space between the element and any adjacent elements. The margin is always transparent—the background color of the web page or container element (such as a div) shows in this area. The solid line in Figure 6.6 that contains the margin area does not display on a web page. Browsers often have default margin values set for the web page document and for certain elements such as paragraphs, headings, forms, and so on. Use the margin property to override the default browser values.

The Box Model in Action

The web page shown in Figure 6.7 (student files chapter6/box.html) depicts the box model in action with an h1 and a div element.

- The h1 element is configured to have a light blue background, 20 pixels of padding (the space between the content and the border), and a black 1-pixel border.
- The empty space where the white web page background shows through is the margin. When two vertical margins meet (such as between the h1 element and the div element), the browser collapses the margin size to be the larger of the two margin values instead of applying both margins.
- The div element has a medium-blue background, the browser default padding (which is no padding), and a black 5-pixel border.

You will get more practice using the box model in this chapter. Feel free to experiment with the box model and the chapter6/box.html file.

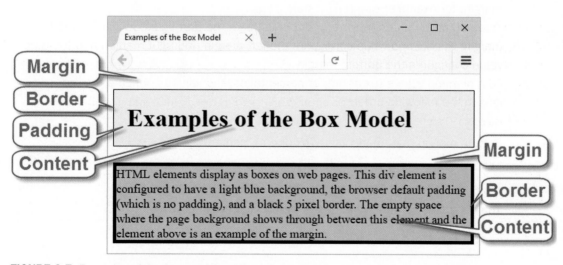

FIGURE 6.7 *Examples of the box model.*

Margin and Padding with CSS

The `margin` Property

Use the **`margin` property** to configure margins on all sides of an element. The margin determines the empty space between the element and any adjacent elements. The margin is always transparent—the background color of the web page or parent element shows in this area.

To configure the size of the margin, use a numeric value (px or em). To eliminate the margin, configure it to 0 (with no unit). Use the value `auto` to indicate that the browser should calculate the margin (more on this later in the chapter). You can also configure individual settings for `margin-top`, `margin-right`, `margin-bottom`, and `margin-left`. Table 6.1 shows CSS properties that configure margin.

TABLE 6.1   *Configuring* `margin` *with CSS*

Property	Description and Common Values
`margin`	Shorthand notation to configure the margin surrounding an element
	A numeric value (px or em) or percentage; for example: `margin: 10px;` if you set a value to 0, omit the unit
	The value `auto` is used to cause the browser to automatically calculate the margin for the element
	Two numeric values (px or em) or percentages; the first value configures the top margin and bottom margin, the second value configures the left margin and right margin; for example: `margin: 20px 10px;`
	Three numeric values (px or em) or percentage; the first value configures the top margin, the second value configures the left margin and right margin, and the third value configures the bottom margin
	Four numeric values (px or em) or percentages; the values configure the margins in the following order: `margin-top`, `margin-right`, `margin-bottom`, `margin-left`
`margin-bottom`	Bottom margin; a numeric value (px or em), percentage, or `auto`
`margin-left`	Left margin; a numeric value (px or em), percentage, or `auto`
`margin-right`	Right margin; a numeric value (px or em), percentage, or `auto`
`margin-top`	Top margin; a numeric value (px or em), percentage, or `auto`

The `padding` Property

The **padding property** configures empty space between the content of the HTML element (such as text) and the border. By default, the padding is set to 0. If you configure a background color or background image for an element, it is applied to both the padding and the content areas. See Table 6.2 for CSS properties that configure padding.

TABLE 6.2   *Configuring* `padding` *with CSS*

Property	Description and Common Values
`padding`	Shorthand notation to configure the amount of padding—the empty space between the element's content and border A numeric value (px or em) or percentage; for example: `padding: 10px`; if you set a value to 0, omit the unit Two numeric values (px or em) or percentages; the first value configures the top padding and bottom padding, the second value configures the left padding and right padding; for example: `padding: 20px 10px;` Three numeric values (px or em) or percentage; the first value configures the top padding, the second value configures the left padding and right padding, and the third value configures the bottom padding Four numeric values (px or em) or percentages; the values configure the padding in the following order: `padding-top`, `padding-right`, `padding-bottom`, `padding-left`
`padding-bottom`	Empty space between the content and bottom border; a numeric value (px or em) or percentage
`padding-left`	Empty space between the content and left border; a numeric value (px or em) or percentage
`padding-right`	Empty space between the content and right border; a numeric value (px or em) or percentage
`padding-top`	Empty space between the content and top border; a numeric value (px or em) or percentage

The web page shown in Figure 6.8 demonstrates use of the margin and padding properties. The example is in the student files at chapter6/box2.html.

The CSS is shown below:

```
body { background-color: #FFFFFF; }
h1   { background-color: #D1ECFF;
       padding-left: 60px; }
#box { background-color: #74C0FF;
       margin-left: 60px;
       padding: 5px 10px; }
```

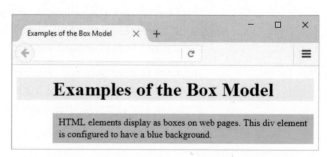

FIGURE 6.8 *Margin and padding have been configured.*

Borders with CSS

The **border property** configures the border, or boundary, around an element. By default, the border has a width set to 0 and does not display. See Table 6.3 for commonly used CSS properties that configure border.

TABLE 6.3 *Configuring* border *with CSS*

Property	Description and Common Values
border	Shorthand notation to configure the border-width, border-style, and border-color of an element; the values for border-width, border-style, and border-color separated by spaces; for example, border: 1px solid #000000;
border-bottom	Bottom border; the values for border-width, border-style, and border-color separated by spaces
border-left	Left border; the values for border-width, border-style, and border-color separated by spaces
border-right	Right border; the values for border-width, border-style, and border-color separated by spaces
border-top	Top border; the values for border-width, border-style, and border-color separated by spaces
border-width	Width of the border; a numeric pixel value (such as 1px) or the values thin, medium, thick
border-style	Style of the border; none, inset, outset, double, groove, ridge, solid, dashed, dotted
border-color	Color of the border; a valid color value

The **border-style property** offers a variety of formatting options. Be aware that these property values are not all uniformly applied by browsers. Figure 6.9 shows how a recent version of Firefox renders various border-style values.

The CSS to configure the borders shown in Figure 6.9 uses a border-width of 3 pixels, border-color of #000033, and the value indicated for the border-style property. For example, the style rule to configure the dashed border is

```
.dashedborder { border-width: 3px;
                border-style: dashed;
                border-color: #000033; }
```

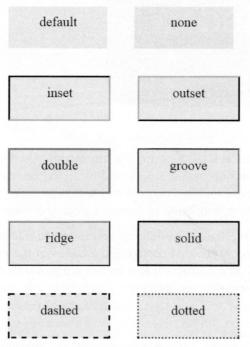

FIGURE 6.9 *Examples of the various* `border-style` *values displayed in Firefox.*

A shorthand notation allows you to configure all the border properties in one style rule by listing the values of `border-width`, `border-style`, and `border-color`. An example is

`.dashedborder { border: 3px dashed #000033; }`

 Hands-On Practice 6.2

You'll work with the `border` property in this Hands-On Practice. When complete, your web page will look similar to the one shown in Figure 6.10. You will use the box2.html file in the chapter6 folder of the student files as a starter file.

Launch a text editor and open the box2.html file. Configure the embedded CSS as follows:

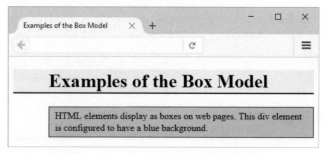

1. Configure the h1 to display a 3-pixel ridged bottom border in a dark gray color. Add the following style rule to the h1 element selector:

   `border-bottom: 3px ridge #330000;`

2. Configure the `box` id to display a 1-pixel solid black border. Add the following style rule to the `#box` selector:

   `border: 1px solid #000000;`

FIGURE 6.10 *The* `border` *property has been configured.*

3. Save your page as boxborder.html. Launch a browser and test your page. Compare your work with the sample solution at chapter6/6.2/index.html.

CSS3 Rounded Corners

VideoNote
CSS Rounded Corners

Now that you have worked with borders and the box model, you may have begun to notice a lot of rectangles on your web pages! CSS3 introduced the **border-radius property**, which can be used to create rounded corners and soften up those rectangles. The `border-radius` property is supported by current versions of major browsers.

Valid values for the `border-radius` property include one to four numeric values (using pixel or em units) or percentages that configure the radius of the corner. If a single value is provided, it configures all four corners. If four values are provided, the corners are configured in order of top left, top right, bottom right, and bottom left. You can configure corners individually with the `border-bottom-left-radius`, `border-bottom-right-radius`, `border-top-left-radius`, and `border-top-right-radius` properties.

CSS declarations to set a border with rounded corners are shown below. If you would like a visible border to display, configure the border property. Then set the value of the `border-radius` property to a value below 20px for best results.

```
border: 1px solid #000000;
border-radius: 15px;
```

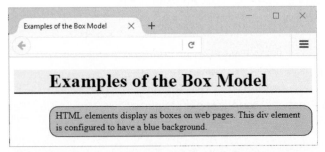

FIGURE 6.11 *Rounded corners were configured with CSS.*

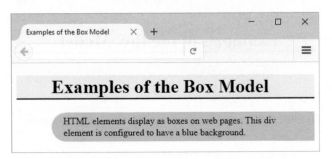

FIGURE 6.12 *Top and bottom left corners are rounded.*

See Figure 6.11 (chapter6/box3.html in the student files) for an example of this code in action.

Figure 6.12 (see chapter6/box4.html) shows a div element with only the top and bottom left corners rounded. The `border-top-left-radius` and `border-bottom-left-radius` properties were used. The code follows.

```
#box { background-color: #74C0FF;
       margin-left: 60px;
       padding: 5px 20px;
       border-top-left-radius: 90px;
       border-bottom-left-radius: 90px; }
```

You can use your creativity to configure one, two, three, or four corners of an element when using `border-radius`. With progressive enhancement in mind, note that visitors to your site that are using older versions of Internet Explorer (versions 8 and earlier) will see only right-angle rather than rounded corners. However, the functionality and usability of the web page will not be affected. Keep in mind that another approach to getting a rounded look is to create a rounded rectangle background image with a graphics application.

Hands-On Practice 6.3

You'll configure a logo header area that uses a background image and rounded borders in this Hands-On Practice.

1. Create a new folder called borderch6. Copy the lighthouselogo.jpg and background.jpg files in the chapter6/starters folder to your borderch6 folder. A starter file is ready for you in the student files. Copy the chapter6/starter2.html file into your borderch6 folder. Launch a browser to display the starter2.html web page shown in Figure 6.13.

2. Launch a text editor and open the starter2.html file. Save the file as index.html. Edit the embedded CSS and code an h1 element selector with style declarations that will configure the lighthouselogo.jpg image as a background image that does not repeat: height of 100px, width of 700px, font size of 3em, 150px of left padding, 30px of top padding, and a border radius of 15px. The style declarations are as follows:

FIGURE 6.13 *The starter2.html file.*

```
h1 { background-image: url(lighthouselogo.jpg);
     background-repeat: no-repeat;
     height: 100px; width: 700px; font-size: 3em;
     padding-left: 150px; padding-top: 30px;
     border-radius: 15px; }
```

3. Save the file. When you test your index.html file in a browser, it should look similar to the one shown in Figure 6.14 if you are using a browser that supports rounded corners. Otherwise the logo will have right-angle corners, but the web page will still be usable. Compare your work with the solution in the student files (chapter6/6.3/index.html).

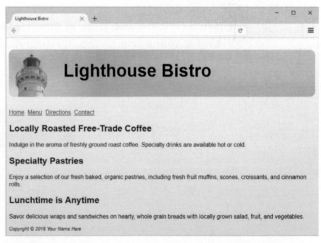

FIGURE 6.14 *The web page with the logo area configured.*

Center Page Content with CSS

You learned how to center text within a div or other block display element in Chapter 5—but what about centering the entire web page itself within the browser viewport? A popular page layout design that is easy to accomplish with just a few lines of CSS is to center the entire content of a web page within a browser viewport. The key is to configure a div element that contains or "wraps" the entire page content. The HTML is

```
<body>
<div id="wrapper">
... page content goes here ...
</div>
</body>
```

Next, configure CSS style rules for this container. Set the `width` property to an appropriate value. Set the `margin-left` and `margin-right` CSS properties to the value `auto`. This tells the browser to automatically divide the amount of space available for the left and right margins. The CSS is

```
#wrapper { width: 750px;
          margin-left: auto;
          margin-right: auto; }
```

You'll practice this technique in the next Hands-On Practice.

 Hands-On Practice 6.4

You'll center a web page in this Hands-On Practice. When complete, your web page will look similar to the one shown in Figure 6.15.

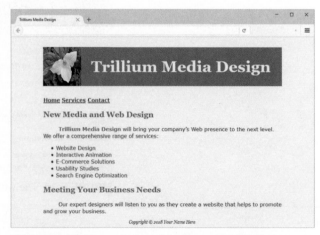

FIGURE 6.15 *The web page is centered with CSS.*

You should already have the index.html and trilliumlogo.jpg files in your trilliumch6 folder. If not, obtain these files from the chapter6/6.1 folder.

Launch a text editor and open the index.html file.

1. Edit the embedded CSS, and remove the `width` and `min-width` style declarations from the body selector.

2. Edit the embedded CSS, and configure a new selector, an id named `container`. Add style declarations for the `width`, `min-width`, `margin-left`, and `margin-right` properties as follows:

```
#container { margin-left: auto;
             margin-right: auto;
             width: 80%;
             min-width: 750px; }
```

3. Edit the HTML. Configure a div element assigned to the id `container` that "wraps" or contains the code within the body section. Code an opening div tag on a new line after the opening body tag. Assign the div to the id named `container`. Code the closing div tag on a new line before the closing body tag. Save the file. When you test your index.html file in a browser, it should look similar to the one shown in Figure 6.15. The student files contain a sample solution in the chapter6/6.4 folder.

A common design practice is to configure the background color of the wrapper or container to be a light, neutral color that provides good contrast with text. Figure 6.16 (found in the student files, chapter6/lighthouse/lcenter.html) shows a web page with a background image along with centered page content (in a div assigned to the `container` id) with a neutral background. The example uses shorthand notation to set all margins for #container to the value `auto`. The padding is configured with three values setting 0 top padding, 20px left and right padding, and 10px bottom padding. The CSS is as follows:

```
#container { margin: auto;
             background-color: #ffffff;
             width: 850px;
             padding: 0 20px 10px; }
```

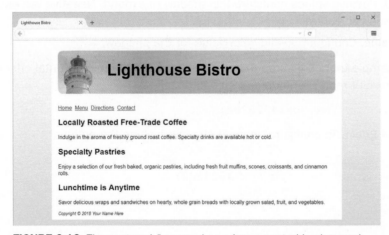

FIGURE 6.16 *The centered* #container *has a neutral background.*

CSS3 Box Shadow and Text Shadow

The CSS3 shadow properties **box-shadow** and **text-shadow** add depth and dimension to the visual display of a web page, as shown in Figure 6.17.

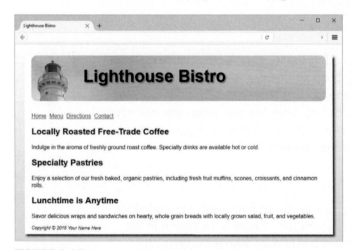

FIGURE 6.17 *Shadow properties add dimension.*

CSS3 `box-shadow` Property

CSS3 introduced the **box-shadow property**, which can be used to create a shadow effect on the box model. The `box-shadow` property is supported by current versions of major browsers. Configure a box shadow by coding values for the shadow's horizontal offset, vertical offset, blur radius (optional), spread distance (optional), and color:

▶ **Horizontal offset.** Use a numeric pixel value. Positive value configures a shadow on the right. Negative value configures a shadow on the left.

▶ **Vertical offset.** Use a numeric pixel value. Positive value configures a shadow below. Negative value configures a shadow above.

▶ **Blur radius (optional).** Configure a numeric pixel value. If omitted, defaults to the value 0 which configures a sharp shadow. Higher values configure more blur.

▶ **Spread distance (optional).** Configure a numeric pixel value. If omitted, defaults to the value 0. Positive values configure the shadow to expand. Negative values configure the shadow to contract.

▶ **Color value.** Configure a valid color value for the shadow.

Here's an example that configures a dark gray shadow with 5px horizontal offset, 5px vertical offset, 5px blur radius, and default spread distance:

```
box-shadow: 5px 5px 5px #828282;
```

Inner Shadow Effect. To configure an inner shadow, include the optional `inset` value. For example:

```
box-shadow: inset 5px 5px 5px #828282;
```

CSS3 `text-shadow` Property

The CSS3 **text-shadow property** is supported by current versions of modern browsers. Configure a text shadow by coding values for the shadow's horizontal offset, vertical offset, blur radius (optional), and color:

- **Horizontal offset.** Use a numeric pixel value. Positive value configures a shadow on the right. Negative value configures a shadow on the left.
- **Vertical offset.** Use a numeric pixel value. Positive value configures a shadow below. Negative value configures a shadow above.
- **Blur radius (optional).** Configure a numeric pixel value. If omitted, defaults to the value 0 which configures a sharp shadow. Higher values configure more blur.
- **Color value.** Configure a valid color value for the shadow.

Here's an example that configures a dark gray shadow with 3px horizontal offset, 3px vertical offset, and 5px blur radius:

```
text-shadow: 3px 3px 5px #666;
```

Hands-On Practice 6.5

You'll configure `text-shadow` and `box-shadow` in this Hands-On Practice. When complete, your web page will look similar to the one shown in Figure 6.17. Create a new folder called shadowch6. Copy the lighthouselogo.jpg and the background.jpg files from the chapter6/ starters folder to your shadowch6 folder. Open the chapter6/lighthouse/lcenter.html file (shown in Figure 6.16) in a text editor. Save the file in your shadowch6 folder with the name index.html.

1. Edit the embedded CSS and add the following style declarations to the `#container` selector to configure a box shadow:

   ```
   box-shadow: 5px 5px 5px #1e1e1e;
   ```

2. Add the following style declaration to the h1 element selector to configure a dark gray text shadow:

   ```
   text-shadow: 3px 3px 3px #666;
   ```

3. Add the following style declaration to the h2 element selector to configure a light gray text shadow with no blur: `text-shadow: 1px 1px 0 #ccc;`

4. Save the file. When you test your index.html file in a browser, it should look similar to the one shown in Figure 6.17 if you are using a browser that supports the `box-shadow` and `text-shadow` properties. Otherwise the shadows will not display, but the web page will still be usable. See the student files for a solution (chapter6/6.5/index.html).

Browser support changes with each new browser version. There is no substitute for thoroughly testing your web pages. However, several resources are available with support lists: http://fmbip.com/litmus, http://css3clickchart.com, and http://caniuse.com.

CSS3 Background Clip and Origin

You're already familiar with how to configure a background image on a web page. This section introduces two CSS3 properties related to background images that provide you with options for clipping and sizing background images: `background-clip` and `background-origin`. As you work with these properties, keep in mind that block display elements such as div, header, and paragraph elements are rendered by the browser using the box model (refer to Figure 6.6), which surrounds the content of an element with padding, border, and margin.

CSS3 `background-clip` Property

The **`background-clip` property** confines the display of the background image with the following values:

- `content-box` clips off the image's display to fit the area behind the content
- `padding-box` clips off the image's display to fit the area behind the content and padding
- `border-box` (default) clips off the image's display to fit the area behind the content, padding, and border

The `background-clip` property is supported by current versions of modern browsers, including Internet Explorer (version 9 and later). Figure 6.18 shows div elements configured

FIGURE 6.18 *The CSS3* `background-clip` *property.*

with different values of the `background-clip` property. Note that the dashed border is intentionally large in these examples. The sample page is located in the student files (chapter6/clip folder). The CSS for the first div follows:

```
.test { background-image: url(myislandback.jpg);
        background-clip: content-box;
        width: 400px; padding: 20px; margin-bottom: 10px;
        border: 10px dashed #000; }
```

CSS3 `background-origin` Property

The CSS3 **background-origin property** positions the background image using the following values:

- ▶ `content-box` positions relative to the content area
- ▶ `padding-box` (default) positions relative to the padding area
- ▶ `border-box` positions relative to the border area

The `background-origin` property is supported by current versions of modern browsers. Figure 6.19 shows div elements configured with different values of the `background-origin` property. The sample page is located in the student files (chapter6/origin folder). The CSS for the first div follows:

```
.test { background-image: url(trilliumsolo.jpg);
        background-origin: content-box;
        background-repeat: no-repeat; background-position: right-top;
        width: 200px; padding: 20px; margin-bottom: 10px;
        border: 1px solid #000; }
```

You may have noticed that it's common to use several CSS properties when configuring background images. These properties typically work together. However, be aware that the `background-origin` property has no effect if the `background-attachment` property is set to the value `fixed`.

FIGURE 6.19 *The CSS3* `background-origin` *property.*

CSS3 Background Resize and Scale

The CSS3 `background-size` property can be used to resize or scale the background image. The `background-size` property is supported by current versions of modern browsers. Valid values for the `background-size` property can be:

▶ a pair of percentage values (width, height)

  If only one percentage value is provided, the second value defaults to `auto` and is determined by the browser.

▶ a pair of pixel values (width, height)

  If only one numeric value is provided, the second value defaults to `auto` and is determined by the browser.

▶ `cover`

  The value `cover` will preserve the aspect ratio of the image as it scales the background image to the *smallest* size for which both the height and width of the image can completely cover the area.

▶ `contain`

  The value `contain` will preserve the aspect ratio of the image as it scales the background image to the *largest* size for which both the height and width of the image will fit within the area.

Figure 6.20 shows two div elements that are each configured with the same background image to display without repeating.

FIGURE 6.20 *The CSS3* `background-size` *property set to 100% 100%.*

The background image of the first div element is not configured with the `background-size` property and the image only partially fills the space. The CSS for the second div configures the `background-size` to be 100% 100%, so the browser scales and resizes the background image to fill the space. The sample page is located in the student files (chapter6/size/sedona.html). The CSS for the second div follows:

```
#test1 { background-image: url(sedonabackground.jpg);
         background-repeat: no-repeat;
         background-size: 100% 100%; }
```

Figure 6.21 demonstrates use of the `cover` and `contain` values to configure the display of a 500×500 background image within a 200 pixel wide area on a web page. The web page on the left uses `background-size: cover;` to scale and resize the image to completely cover the area while keeping the aspect ratio of the image intact. The web page on the right uses `background-size: contain;` to scale and resize the image so that both the height and width of the image will fit within the area. Review the sample pages in the student files (chapter6/size/cover.html and chapter6/size/contain.html).

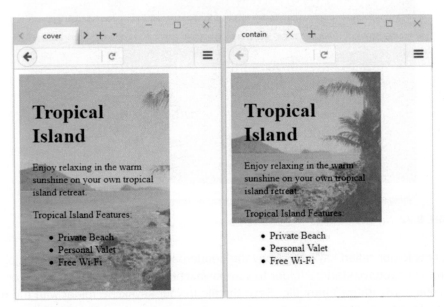

FIGURE 6.21 *Examples of* `background-size: cover;` *and* `background-size: contain;`

Practice with CSS3 Properties

 Hands-On Practice 6.6 ———————————————

In this Hands-On Practice you will configure a web page with centered content and practice configuring CSS properties. When complete, your web page will look similar to the one shown in Figure 6.22.

FIGURE 6.22 *New Home page.*

Create a new folder called kaykch6. Copy the headerbackblue.jpg and heroback2.jpg files from the chapter6/starters folder to your kayakch6 folder. Launch a text editor and open the chapter6/starter3.html file. Save the file in your kayakch6 folder with the name index.html. Modify the file as follows:

1. Center the page content by applying the coding technique from Hands-On Practice 6.4.

    a. Edit the embedded CSS, and configure a new selector, an id named `container` with style declarations for the `width`, `margin-left`, and `margin-right` properties as follows:

    ```
    #container { margin-left: auto; margin-right: auto;
                 width: 80%; }
    ```

    b. Edit the HTML. Configure a div element assigned to the id `container` that "wraps" or contains the code within the body section. Code an opening div tag on a new line after the opening body tag. Assign the div to the id named `container`.

2. Edit the embedded CSS.

    a. The container id selector. Add declarations to configure a white background color, 650px minimum width, 1280px maximum width, a box shadow with a 10px offset and blur in the color #333333, and a 1px solid dark blue (#000033) border.

```
#container { margin-left: auto; margin-right: auto;
             width: 80%;
             background-color: #FFFFFF;
             min-width: 650px; max-width: 1280px;
             box-shadow: 10px 10px 10px #333333;
             border: 1px solid #000033; }
```

    b. The body element selector. Edit the styles to change the background color to #FFFFDD.

    c. The header element selector. Add declarations to configure 80px height, 5px top padding, 2em left padding, and a text shadow in the color #FFF with a 1px offset.

```
header { background-color: #000033; color: #FFFFDD;
         background-image: url(headerbackblue.jpg);
         background-position: right;
         background-repeat: no-repeat;
         height: 80px;
         padding-top: 5px; padding-left: 2em;
         text-shadow: 1px 1px 1px #FFF; }
```

    d. The h1 element selector. Code styles to configure a zero bottom margin.

```
h1 { margin-bottom: 0; }
```

    e. The nav element selector. Add a declaration to configure centered text with the text-align property.

```
nav { font-weight: bold; font-size: 1.25em;
      background-color: #FFFFDD;
      text-align: center; }
```

    f. The main element selector. Add declarations to configure heroback2.jpg as the background image and configure `background-size: 100% 100%;`. Also configure white text (use #FFFFFF) and 2em of padding.

```
main { background-color: #004D99;
       background-image: url(heroback2.jpg);
       background-size: 100% 100%;
       color: #FFFFFF; padding: 2em; }
```

    g. The footer element selector. Add a declaration for 0.5em of padding.

```
footer { font-style: italic; background-color: #FFFFDD;
         font-size: .80em; text-align: center; padding: 0.5em;}
```

3. Save the file. When you test your index.html file in a modern browser such as Firefox or Chrome, it should look similar to the one shown in Figure 6.22. Compare your work with the solution in the student files (chapter6/6.6/index.html). Note that if you display the page in a browser (such as Internet Explorer 11) that does not support the new HTML5 main element, the display will not look as you expect. At the time this text was written, Internet Explorer did not support default styles for the HTML5 main element. You may need to nudge this browser to comply by adding the `display: block;` declaration (see Chapter 7) to the styles for the main element selector. An example solution is in the student files (chapter6/6.6/iefix.html).

CSS3 Opacity

The CSS3 **opacity property** configures the transparency of an element. The opacity property is supported by current versions of major browsers. Opacity values range from 0 (which is completely transparent) to 1 (which is completely opaque and has no transparency). An important consideration when using the opacity property is that this property applies to both the text and the background. If you configure a semitransparent opacity value for an element with the opacity property, both the background and the text displayed will be semitransparent. See Figure 6.23 for an example of using the opacity property to configure an h1 element that is 60% opaque.

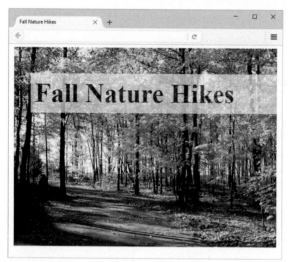

FIGURE 6.23 *The background and text of the h1 area is transparent.*

If you look very closely at Figure 6.23 or view the actual web page (student files chapter6/6.7/index.html), you'll see that both the white background and the black text in the h1 element are semi-transparent. The opacity property was applied to both the background color and to the text color.

Hands-On Practice 6.7

In this Hands-On Practice you'll work with the opacity property as you configure the web page shown in Figure 6.23.

1. Create a new folder called opacitych6. Copy fall.jpg file from the chapter6/starters folder to your opacitych6 folder. Open the chapter1/template.html file in a text editor. Save it in your opacitych6 folder with the name index.html. Change the page title to "Fall Nature Hikes".

2. Let's create the structure of the web page with a div that contains an h1 element. Add the following code to your web page in the body section:

```
<div id="content">
<h1> Fall Nature Hikes</h1>
</div>
```

3. Now, add style tags to the head section and configure the embedded CSS. You'll create an id named content to display the fall.jpg as a background image that does not repeat. The content id also has a width of 640 pixels, a height of 480 pixels,

auto margins (which will center the object horizontally in the browser viewport), and 20 pixels of top padding. The code is

```
#content { background-image: url(fall.jpg);
           background-repeat: no-repeat;
           margin: auto;
           width: 640px;
           height: 480px;
           padding-top: 20px; }
```

4. Now configure the h1 selector to have a white background color, opacity set to 0.6, font size set to 4em, 10 pixels of padding, and a 40-pixel left margin. Sample code is

```
h1 { background-color: #FFFFFF;
     opacity: 0.6;
     font-size: 4em;
     padding: 10px;
     margin-left: 40px; }
```

5. Save the file. When you test your index.html file in a browser that supports opacity such as Chrome, Firefox, Safari, or Internet Explorer (version 9 or later) it should look similar to the page shown in Figure 6.23. See the student files for a solution (chapter6/6.7/index.html).

6. Figure 6.24 shows the web page displayed in Internet Explorer 8, which does not support the `opacity` property. Notice that the visual aesthetic is not exactly the same, but the page is still usable. While Internet Explorer began to support opacity in version 9, earlier versions support the proprietary `filter` property with an opacity level configured between 1 (transparent) and 100 (opaque). A sample is found in the student files (chapter6/6.7/opacityie.html). The CSS for the IE-proprietary `filter` property is

```
filter: alpha(opacity=60);
```

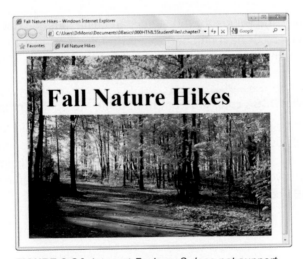

FIGURE 6.24 *Internet Explorer 8 does not support the* opacity *property and displays an opaque background color.*

CSS3 RGBA Color

CSS3 supports new syntax for the color property that configures transparent color, called **RGBA color**. RGBA color is supported by current versions of major browsers. Four values are required: red, green, blue, and alpha (transparency). RGBA color does not use hexadecimal color values. Instead, decimal color values are configured—see the partial color chart in Figure 6.25 and the Web Safe Color Palette at the end of the book for examples.

#FFFFFF
rgb (255, 255, 255)
	#FFFFCC
	rgb(255, 255, 204)
		#FFFF99
		rgb(255,255,153)
			#FFFF66
			rgb(255,255,102)

#FFFF33
rgb(255,255,51)
	#FFFF00
	rgb(255,255,0)
		#FFCCFF
		rgb(255, 204, 255)
			#FFCCCC
			rgb(255,204,204)

#FFCC99
rgb(255,204,153)
	#FFCC66
	rgb(255,204,102)
		#FFCC33
		rgb(255,204,51)
			#FFCC00
			rgb(255,204,0)

#FF99FF
rgb(255,153,255)
	#FF99CC
	rgb(255,153,204)
		#FF9999
		rgb(255,153,153)
			#FF9966
			rgb(255,153,102)

FIGURE 6.25 *Hexadecimal and RGB decimal color values.*

To configure RGBA color, the values for red, green, and blue must be decimal values from 0 to 255. The alpha value must be a number from 0 (transparent) to 1 (opaque). Figure 6.26 shows a web page with the text configured to be slightly transparent with RGBA color syntax.

? FAQ How is using RGBA color different from using the opacity property?

The `opacity` property applies to both the background and the text within an element. If you'd like to specifically configure a semitransparent background color, code the `background-color` property with RGBA color or HSLA color (described in the next section) values. If you'd like to specifically configure semitransparent text, code the `color` property with RGBA color or HSLA color values.

In this Hands-On Practice you'll configure white text with transparency as you configure the web page shown in Figure 6.26.

1. Launch a text editor and open the file you created in the previous Hands-On Practice (also located in the student files, chapter6/6.7/index.html). Save the file with the name rgba.html.

2. Delete the current style declarations for the h1 selector. You will create new style rules for the h1 selector to configure 10 pixels of right padding and right-aligned sans-serif white text that is 80% opaque with a font size of 5em. Since not all browsers support RBGA color, you'll configure the color property twice. The first instance will be the standard color value that is supported by all modern browsers; the second instance will configure the RGBA color. Older browsers will not understand the RGBA color and will ignore it. Newer browsers will "see" both of the color style declarations and will apply them in the order they are coded, so the result will be transparent color. The CSS for the h1 selector is

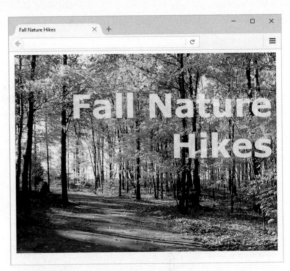

FIGURE 6.26 *CSS3 RGBA color configures the transparent text.*

```
h1 { color: #ffffff;
     color: rgba(255, 255, 255, 0.8);
     font-family: Verdana, Helvetica, sans-serif;
     font-size: 5em;
     padding-right: 10px;
     text-align: right; }
```

3. Save the file. When you test your rgba.html file in a browser that supports RGBA color such as Chrome, Firefox, Safari, or Internet Explorer version 9 or later, it should look similar to the page shown in Figure 6.26. See the student files for a solution (chapter6/6.8/rgba.html). If you are using a nonsupporting browser such as Internet Explorer 8 (or earlier), you'll see white text instead of transparent text. While Internet Explorer began to support RGBA color in version 9, earlier versions support the proprietary `filter` property; an example is in the student files (chapter6/6.8/rbgaie.html).

CSS3 HSLA Color

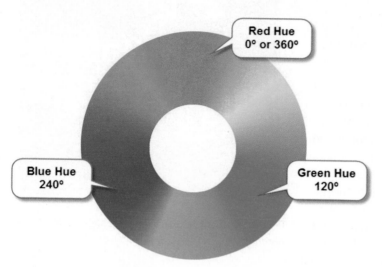

Red Hue
0° or 360°

Blue Hue
240°

Green Hue
120°

FIGURE 6.27 *A color wheel.*

For many years web designers have configured RGB color using either hexadecimal or decimal values on web pages. Recall that RGB color is based on hardware—the red, green, and blue light that is emitted by computer monitors. CSS3 introduced a new color notation system called HSLA color, based on a color wheel model, which stands for hue, saturation, lightness, and alpha. HSLA color is supported in the most recent versions of all major browsers.

Hue, Saturation, Lightness, and Alpha

When you work with HSLA color, think of a color wheel—a circle of color—with the color red at the top of the wheel as shown in Figure 6.27. **Hue** is the actual color which is represented by numeric values ranging from 0 to 360 (like the 360 degrees in a circle). For example, red is represented by both the values 0 and 360, green is represented by 120, and blue is represented by 240. Set hue to 0 when configuring black, gray, and white. **Saturation** configures the intensity of the color and is indicated by a percentage value (full color saturation= 100%, gray=0%). **Lightness** determines the brightness or darkness of the color and is indicated by a percentage value (normal color=50%, white=100%, black=0%). **Alpha** represents the transparency of the color and has a value from 0 (transparent) to 1 (opaque). Note that you can omit the alpha value and use the `hsl` keyword instead of the `hsla` keyword.

Red hsla(360, 100%, 50%, 1.0);
Green hsla(120, 100%, 50%, 1.0);
Blue hsla(240, 100%, 50%, 1.0);
Black hsla(0, 0%, 0%, 1.0);
Gray hsla(0, 0%, 50%, 1.0);
White hsla(0, 0%, 100%, 1.0);

HSLA Color Examples

Configure HSLA color as shown in Figure 6.28. with the following syntax:

hsla (*hue value, saturation value, lightness value, alpha value*);

- Red: `hsla(360, 100%, 50%, 1.0);`
- Green: `hsla(120, 100%, 50%, 1.0);`
- Blue: `hsla(240, 100%, 50%, 1.0);`
- Black: `hsla(0, 0%, 0%, 1.0);`
- Gray: `hsla(0, 0%, 50%, 1.0);`
- White: `hsla(0, 0%, 100%, 1.0);`

FIGURE 6.28 *HSLA color examples.*

According to the W3C, an advantage to using HSLA color is that it is more intuitive to work with than the hardware-oriented RGB color. You can use a color wheel model (remember your art classes in grade school) to choose colors and generate the hue value from the degree placement on the circle. If you'd like to use a tone of a color, which is a color with gray added, vary the saturation value. If you'd like to use a shade or tint of a color, use the same hue value, but vary the lightness value to meet your needs. Figure 6.29 shows three shades of cyan blue configured using three different values for lightness: 25% (dark cyan blue), 50% (cyan blue), and 75% (light cyan blue).

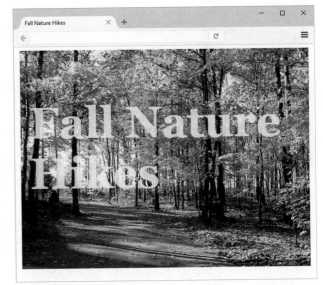

FIGURE 6.29 *Shades of cyan blue.*

▶ Dark Cyan Blue:

```
hsla(210, 100%, 25%, 1.0);
```

▶ Cyan Blue:

```
hsla(210, 100%, 50%, 1.0);
```

▶ Light Cyan Blue:

```
hsla(210, 100%, 75%, 1.0);
```

 Hands-On Practice 6.9

In this Hands-On Practice you'll configure light yellow transparent text as you configure the web page shown in Figure 6.30.

1. Launch a text editor and open the file you created in the previous Hands-On Practice (see chapter6/6.8/rgba.html in the student files). Save the file with the name hsla.html.

2. Delete the style declarations for the h1 selector. You will create new style rules for the h1 selector to configure 20 pixels of padding and serif light yellow text with a 0.8 alpha value and a font size of 6em. Since not all browsers support HSLA color, you'll configure the color property twice. The first instance will be the standard color value that is supported by all modern browsers; the second instance will configure the HSLA color. Older browsers will not understand the HSLA color and will ignore it. Newer browsers will "see" both of the color style declarations and will apply them in the order they are coded, so the result will be transparent color. The CSS for the h1 selector is

FIGURE 6.30 *HSLA color.*

```
h1 { color: #ffcccc;
     color: hsla(60, 100%, 90%, 0.8);
     font-family: Georgia, "Times New Roman", serif;
     font-size: 6em;
     padding: 20px; }
```

3. Save the file. When you test your hsla.html file in a browser that supports HSLA color, it should look similar to the page shown in Figure 6.30. See the student files for a solution (chapter6/6.9/hsla.html). If you are using a nonsupporting browser such as Internet Explorer 8 (or earlier), you'll see solid text instead of transparent text.

CSS3 Gradients

CSS3 provides a method to configure color as a **gradient**, which is a smooth blending of shades from one color to another color. A CSS3 gradient background color is defined purely with CSS—no image file is needed! This provides flexibility for web designers along with a savings in the bandwidth required to transfer gradient background image files.

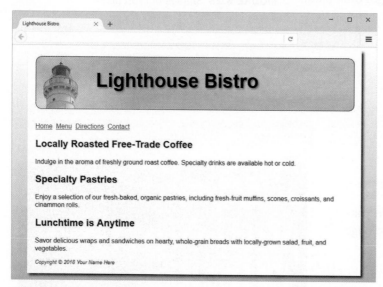

FIGURE 6.31 *The gradient in the background was configured with CSS3 without an image file.*

Figure 6.17 displays a web page with a JPG gradient background image that was configured in a graphics application. The web page shown in Figure 6.31 (available at chapter6/lighthouse/gradient.html in the student files) does not use a JPG for the background—CSS3 gradient properties recreated the look of the linear gradient image.

The syntax for CSS3 gradients changed extensively while it was in draft status and you may find conflicting information about coding CSS3 gradients on the Web. The W3C CSS3 Image Values and Replaced Content Module was moved to Candidate Recommendation status in 2012. The W3C syntax described in this section is supported by modern browsers.

Linear Gradient Syntax

A **linear gradient** is a smooth blending of color in a single direction such as from top to bottom or from left to right. To configure a basic linear gradient, code the `linear-gradient` function as the value of the `background-image` property. Indicate the direction of the gradient by coding the keyword phrase "to bottom", "to top", "to left", or "to right". Next, list the starting color and the ending color. The basic format for a two-color linear gradient that blends from white to green follows:

```
background-image: linear-gradient(to bottom, #FFFFFF, #00FF00);
```

Radial Gradient Syntax

A **radial gradient** is a smooth blending of color emanating outward from a single point. Code the radial gradient function as the value of the `background-image` property to configure a radial gradient. List two colors as the values of the function. The first color will be displayed by default in the center of the element and gradually blend outward until the second color is displayed. The basic format for a two-color radial gradient that blends from white to blue follows:

```
background-image: radial-gradient(#FFFFFF, #0000FF);
```

CSS3 Gradients and Progressive Enhancement

It's very important to keep progressive enhancement in mind when using CSS3 gradients. Configure a "fallback" `background-color` property or `background-image` property, which will be rendered by browsers that do not support CSS3 gradients. The background color in Figure 6.31 was configured to be the same value as the ending gradient color.

 ## Hands-On Practice 6.10

You'll work with CSS gradient backgrounds in this Hands-On Practice as Create a new folder called gradientch6. Copy the chapter6/starter4.html file into your gradientch6 folder. Rename the file index.html. Launch a text editor and open the file

1. First, you will configure a linear gradient. Code embedded CSS in the head section. Configure the body of the web page to display a fallback orchid background color of #DA70D6 and a linear gradient background that blends white to orchid from top to bottom without repeating:

```
body { background-color: #DA70D6;
       background-image: linear-gradient(to
       bottom, #FFFFFF, #DA70D6);
       background-repeat: no-repeat; }
```

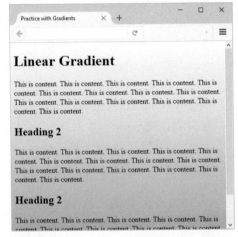

FIGURE 6.32 *Linear gradient background.*

2. Save your file and test it in a modern browser. The display should be similar to the results shown in Figure 6.32. The background gradient displays behind the page content, so scroll down the page to see the full gradient. Compare your work with the solution in the student files (chapter6/6.10/linear.html).

3. Next, you will configure a radial gradient. Edit the body section of the web page and code change the text within the h1 element to: Radial Gradient.

4. Edit the CSS and modify the value of the `background-image` property to configure a radial gradient linear gradient that blends white to orchid from center outward without repeating:

```
body { background-color: #DA70D6;
       background-image:
       radial-gradient(#FFFFFF, #DA70D6);
       background-repeat: no-repeat; }
```

FIGURE 6.33 *Radial gradient background.*

5. Save your file and test in in a modern browser. The display should be similar to the results shown in Figure 6.33. Scroll down the page to see the full gradient. Compare your work with the solution in the student files (chapter6/6.10/radial.html).

 Visit http://css-tricks.com/css3-gradients to delve deeper into CSS3 gradients. Experiment with generating CSS3 gradient code at http://www.colorzilla.com/gradient-editor and http://www.css3factory.com/linear-gradients.

CHAPTER 6

Review and Apply

Review Questions

1. Which of the following is the CSS property that configures a drop shadow effect on text?

   a. box-shadow
   b. text-shadow
   c. drop-shadow
   d. shadow

2. Which CSS property configures the area between the content and the margin?

   a. white-space
   b. box-shadow
   c. padding
   d. opacity

3. Which CSS property will configure rounded corners?

   a. border
   b. border-radius
   c. radial
   d. margin

4. Which CSS property can be used to resize or scale a background image?

   a. background-repeat
   b. background-size
   c. background-clip
   d. background-origin

5. Which of the following, from outermost to innermost, are components of the box model?

   a. margin, border, padding, content
   b. content, padding, border, margin
   c. content, margin, padding, border
   d. margin, padding, border, content

6. Which CSS property configures the empty space between adjacent elements?

   a. padding
   b. border
   c. margin
   d. letter-spacing

7. Which of the following will configure padding that is 15 pixels on the top, 0 pixels on the left and right, and 5 pixels on the bottom?

   a. padding: 0px 5px 0px 15px;
   b. padding: top-15, left-0, right-0, bottom-5;
   c. padding: 15px 0 5px 0;
   d. padding: 0 0 15px 5px;

8. Which of the following is used along with the width property to configure centered page content?

   a. margin-left: auto;
   margin-right: auto;
   b. margin: top-15, left-0, right-0, bottom-5;
   c. margin: 15px 0 5px 0;
   d. margin: 20px;

9. Which CSS property will configure a gradient background?

   a. background-gradient
   b. background-image
   c. background-clip
   d. linear-gradient

10. Which of the following will configure a border that is 5 pixels wide, the color #330000, and a solid line?

   a. border: 5px solid #330000;
   b. border-style: solid 5px;
   c. border: 5px, solid, #330000;
   d. border: 5px line #330000;

Hands-On Exercises

1. Write the CSS for a class named footer with the following characteristics: a light-blue background color, Arial or sans-serif font, dark-blue text color, 10 pixels of padding, and a narrow, dashed border in a dark-blue color.

2. Write the CSS for an id named notice that is configured with width set to 80% and centered.

3. Write the CSS to configure a class that will produce a headline with a dotted line underneath it. Choose a color that you like for the text and dotted line.

4. Write the CSS to configure an h1 selector with drop shadow text, a 50% transparent background color, and sans-serif font that is 4em in size.

5. Write the CSS to configure an id named blurb with small, red, Arial font, a white background, a width of 80%, and a drop shadow.

6. Write the CSS to configure the body element with a linear gradient background that blends from black to medium blue.

7. Write the CSS to configure an id named content with 70% opacity.

Focus on Web Design

This chapter expanded your capabilities to use CSS to configure web pages. Use a search engine to search for CSS resources. The following resources can help you get started:

- https://www.w3.org/Style/CSS/learning
- http://www.noupe.com/design/40-css-reference-websites-and-resources.html
- http://www.simplilearn.com/css3-resources-ultimate-list-article

Create a web page that provides a list of at least five CSS resources on the Web. For each CSS resource provide the URL, website name, and a brief description. Your web page content should take up 80% of the browser viewport and be centered. Use at least five CSS properties from this chapter to configure the color and text. Place your name in the e-mail address at the bottom of the web page elements.

Pacific Trails Resort Case Study

In this chapter's case study you will use the existing Pacific Trails (Chapter 5) website as a starting point to create a new version of the website. The new design is a centered page layout that takes up 80% of the browser viewport with a featured hero image on each page. You'll use CSS to configure the new page layout, a background gradient, hero image, and other styles, including margin and padding. Figure 6.34 displays a wireframe with the wrapper div, which contains the other web page elements.

You have five tasks in this case study:

1. Create a new folder for the Pacific Trails Resort website.
2. Edit the pacific.css external style sheet.
3. Update the Home page: index.html.

FIGURE 6.34 *New wireframe.*

4. Update the Activities page: activities.html.

5. Update the Yurts page: yurts.html.

Task 1: Create a folder called ch6pacific to contain your Pacific Trails Resort website files. Copy the files from the Chapter 5 Case Study ch5pacific folder.

Task 2: The External Stylesheet. Launch a text editor and open the pacific.css external style sheet file.

- **The body element Selector.** Change the background color to a light blue (#90C7E3). Add style declarations to display a linear gradient that blends from white (#FFFFFF) to light blue (#90C7E3) and does not repeat.

- **The wrapper id Selector.** Add a new selector for an id named `wrapper`. Configure the `wrapper` id to be centered (see Hands-On Practice 6.4) with a width of 80%, white background color (#FFFFFF), a minimum width of 960 pixels, a maximum width of 2048px, and a 3px offset dark (#333333) box shadow.

- **The header element Selector.** Remove declarations for line height and indented text. Add declarations to configure 60px height, centered text, and 15px top padding.

- **The h1 element Selector.** Add a style declaration to configure zero top margin.

- **The nav element Selector.** Change the background color to white (#FFFFFF). Add declarations to configure centered text and 10px padding.

- **The main element Selector.** Add a new selector for the main element. Code declarations to configure 1px top padding, 20px right padding, 20px bottom padding, and 20px left padding. At the time this was written, Internet Explorer did not support default styles the HTML5 main element, so add the following style declaration using the display property (see Chapter 7) to nudge this browser to display as expected: `display: block;`

- **The h2 element Selector.** Add a style declaration to configure 1px offset gray (#CCCCCC) text shadow.

- **The footer element Selector.** Add a declaration to configure 20px of padding.

- **The homehero id Selector.** Add a new selector for an id named `homehero`. Code declarations to configure 300px height and to display the coast.jpg background image to fill the space (use `background-size: 100% 100%;`) without repeating.

- **The yurthero id Selector.** Add a new selector for an id named `yurthero`. Code declarations to configure 300px height and to display the yurt.jpg background image to fill the space (use `background-size: 100% 100%;`) without repeating.

- **The trailhero id Selector.** Add a new selector for an id named `trailhero`. Code declarations to configure 300px height and to display the trail.jpg background image to fill the space (use `background-size: 100% 100%;`) without repeating.

Save the pacific.css file. Use the CSS validator (http://jigsaw.w3.org/css-validator) to check your syntax. Correct and retest if necessary.

Task 3: The Home Page. Launch a text editor and open the index.html file.

- Code div tags to add a `wrapper` div that contains the content of the web page. Use Hands-On Practice 6.4 as a guide.

- Configure a div element to contain the coast.jpg image. Code an opening div tag assigned to the id named `homehero` after the closing nav tag. Next, code a closing div tag. As shown in the wireframe in Figure 6.34, this div is located between the nav element and the main element. There is no HTML or text content for this div. The purpose of this div is to be a placeholder for the CSS that will display the hero image.

  Remove the img tag for the coast.jpg photo.

Save and test your page in a browser. It should look similar to Figure 6.35.

FIGURE 6.35 *Pacific Trails Home Page.*

Task 4: The Yurts Page. Launch a text editor and open the yurts.html file.

- Code div tags to add a `wrapper` div that contains the content of the web page. Use Hands-On Practice 6.4 as a guide.

- Configure a div to contain the yurt.jpg image. Code an opening div tag assigned to the id named `yurthero` after the closing nav tag. Next, code a closing div tag. As shown in the wireframe in Figure 6.34, this div is located between the nav element and the main element. There is no HTML or text content for this div.

- Remove the img tag for the yurt.jpg photo.

Save and test your page in a browser. It should look similar to Figure 6.36.

FIGURE 6.36 *Pacific Trails Yurts Page.*

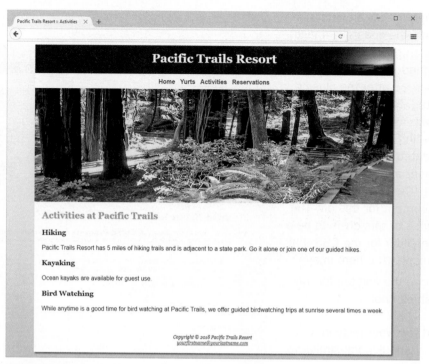

FIGURE 6.37 *Pacific Trails Activities Page.*

Task 5: The Activities Page. Launch a text editor and open the activities.html file.

- Code div tags to add a `wrapper` div that contains the content of the web page. Use Hands-On Practice 6.4 as a guide.

- Configure a div to contain the trail.jpg image. Code an opening div tag assigned to the id named `trailhero` after the closing nav tag. Next, code a closing div tag. As shown in the wireframe in Figure 6.37, this div is located between the nav element and the main element. There is no HTML or text content for this div.

- Remove the img tag for the trail.jpg photo.

Save and test your page in a browser. It should look similar to Figure 6.37.

Path of Light Yoga Studio Case Study

In this chapter's case study you will use the existing Path of Light Yoga Studio (Chapter 5) website as a starting point to create a new version of the website. The new design is a centered page layout that takes up 80% of the browser viewport. You'll use CSS to configure the new page layout, a background image, hero image on the content pages, and other styles, including margin and padding. Figure 6.38 displays a wireframe with the wrapper div, which contains the other web page elements.

You have five tasks in this case study:

1. Create a new folder for Path of Light Yoga Studio website.
2. Edit the yoga.css external style sheet.

FIGURE 6.38 *New wireframe.*

3. Update the Home page: index.html.
4. Update the Classes page: classes.html.
5. Update the Schedule page: schedule.html.

Task 1: Create a folder called ch6yoga to contain your Path of Light Yoga Studio website files. Copy the files from the Chapter 5 Case Study ch5yoga folder.

Task 2: **The External Stylesheet.** Launch a text editor and open the yoga.css external style sheet file.

- **The body element Selector.** Change the value of the background-color property to #3F2860. Remove the style declaration for the text color.

- **The wrapper id Selector.** Add a new selector for an id named `wrapper`. Configure the `wrapper` id to be centered (see Hands-On Practice 6.4) with a width of 80%, dark text color (#3F2860), light background color (#F5F5F5), a minimum width of 420 pixels, and a maximum width of 1280px.

- **The header element Selector.** Add a declaration to configure 150px height.

- **The h1 element Selector.** Remove declarations for line height and indented text. Add declarations to configure 50px top padding and 2em left padding.

- **The nav element Selector.** Add declarations to configure #DBE8E9 background color and 1em padding.

- **The main element Selector.** Add a new selector for the main element. Code declarations to configure padding: set top padding to 0 and set left, right, and bottom padding to 3em. At the time this was written, Internet Explorer did not support default styles for the HTML5 main element, so add the following style declaration using the display property (see Chapter 7) to nudge this browser to display as expected:

  ```
  display: block;
  ```

- **The mathero id Selector.** Add a new selector for an id named `mathero`. Code declarations to configure 300px height and to display the yogamat.jpg background image to fill the space (use background-size: 100% 100%;) without repeating.

- **The loungehero id Selector.** Add a new selector for an id named `loungehero`. Code declarations to configure 300px height and to display the yogalounge.jpg background image to fill the space (use background-size: 100% 100%;) without repeating.

- **The img element Selector.** Code styles to configure 2em padding.

- **The footer element Selector.** Add a declaration to configure 1em of padding.

Save the yoga.css file. Use the CSS validator (http://jigsaw.w3.org/css-validator) to check your syntax. Correct and retest if necessary.

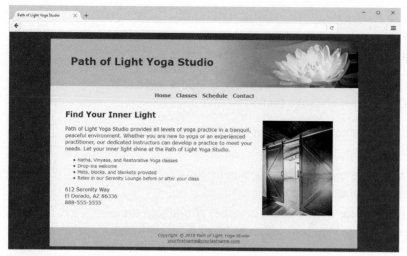

FIGURE 6.39 *Path of Light Yoga Studio Home Page.*

Task 3: The Home Page. Launch a text editor and open the index.html file.

- Configure a `wrapper` div that contains the content of the web page. Use Hands-On Practice 6.4 as a guide.

Save and test your page in a browser. It should look similar to Figure 6.39.

Task 4: The Classes Page. Launch a text editor and open the classes.html file.

- Code div tags to add a `wrapper` div that contains the content of the web page. Use Hands-On Practice 6.4 as a guide.
- Remove the img tag for the yogamat.jpg photo.
- Configure a div element to contain the yogamat.jpg image. As shown in the wireframe in Figure 6.40, this div is located within the main element. Code an opening div tag assigned to the id named `mathero` after the h2 element. Next, code a closing div tag. There is no HTML or text content for this div. The purpose of this div is to be a placeholder for the CSS that will display the yogamat.jpg hero image.

Save and test your page in a browser. It should look similar to Figure 6.41.

```
wrapper
┌─────────────────────────────┐
│ ┌─────────────────────────┐ │
│ │ header                  │ │
│ └─────────────────────────┘ │
│ ┌─────────────────────────┐ │
│ │ nav                     │ │
│ └─────────────────────────┘ │
│ ┌─────────────────────────┐ │
│ │ main                    │ │
│ │ ┌─────────────────────┐ │ │
│ │ │ div with large image│ │ │
│ │ └─────────────────────┘ │ │
│ │                         │ │
│ │                         │ │
│ └─────────────────────────┘ │
│ ┌─────────────────────────┐ │
│ │ footer                  │ │
│ └─────────────────────────┘ │
└─────────────────────────────┘
```

FIGURE 6.40 *Wireframe for content pages.*

FIGURE 6.41 *Path of Light Yoga Studio Classes Page.*

Task 5: The Classes Page.

Launch a text editor and open the classes.html file.

- Code div tags to add a `wrapper` div that contains the content of the web page. Use Hands-On Practice 6.4 as a guide.

  Remove the img tag for the yogalounge.jpg photo.

- Configure a div element to contain the yogalounge.jpg image. As shown in the wireframe in Figure 6.40, this div is located within the main element. Code an opening div tag assigned to the id named `loungehero` after the h2 element. Next, code a closing div tag. There is no HTML or text content for this div. The purpose of this div is to be a placeholder for the CSS that will display the yogalounge.jpg hero image.

FIGURE 6.42 *Path of Light Yoga Studio Classes Page.*

Save and test your page in a browser. It should look similar to Figure 6.42.

Page Layout Basics

You've already configured centered page layout with CSS; we'll add to your toolbox of CSS page layout techniques in this chapter. You'll explore floating and positioning elements with CSS. You'll be introduced to a technique for configuring images called CSS sprites. You will also learn to use CSS to add interactivity to hyperlinks with pseudo-classes.

You'll learn how to...

- Configure float with CSS
- Configure fixed positioning with CSS
- Configure relative positioning with CSS
- Configure absolute positioning with CSS
- Create two-column page layouts with CSS

- Configure navigation in unordered lists and style with CSS
- Add interactivity to hyperlinks with CSS pseudo-classes
- Configure CSS sprites

Normal Flow

Browsers render your web page code line by line in the order it appears in the .html document. This processing is called normal flow. **Normal flow** displays the elements on the page in the order they appear in the web page source code.

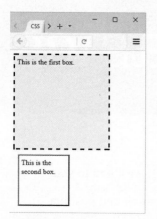

FIGURE 7.1 *The div elements.*

FIGURE 7.2 *Nested elements.*

Figures 7.1 and 7.2 each display two div elements that contain text content. Let's take a closer look. Figure 7.1 shows a screenshot of two div elements placed one after another on a web page. In Figure 7.2 the boxes are nested inside each other. In both cases, the browser used normal flow (the default) and displayed the elements in the order in which they appeared in the source code. As you've worked through the exercises in the previous chapters, you created web pages that the browser rendered using normal flow.

You'll practice normal flow a bit more in the next Hands-On Practice. Then, later in the chapter, you'll experiment with CSS positioning and float to configure the flow, or placement, of elements on a web page.

 Hands-On Practice 7.1

You will explore the box model and normal flow in this Hands-On Practice as you work with the web pages shown in Figures 7.1 and 7.2.

Practice with Normal Flow

Launch a text editor and open the chapter7/starter1.html file from the student files. Save the file with the name box1.html. Add the following code in the body of the web page to configure the two div elements:

```
<div class="div1">
This is the first box.
</div>
<div class="div2">
This is the second box.
</div>
```

Now let's add embedded CSS in the head section to configure the "boxes." Add a new style rule for a class named `div1` to configure a light blue background, dashed border, width of 200 pixels, height of 200 pixels, and 5 pixels of padding. The code is

```css
.div1 { width: 200px;
        height: 200px;
        background-color: #D1ECFF;
        border: 3px dashed #000000;
        padding: 5px; }
```

Create a style rule for a class named `div2` to configure a width and height of 100 pixels, white background color, ridged border, 10 pixel margin, and 5 pixels of padding. The code is

```css
.div2 { width: 100px;
        height: 100px;
        background-color: #FFFFFF;
        border: 3px ridge #000000;
        padding: 5px;
        margin: 10px; }
```

Save the file. Launch a browser and test your page. It should look similar to the one shown in Figure 7.1. The student files contain a sample solution at chapter7/7.1/box1.html.

Practice with Normal Flow and Nested Elements

Launch a text editor and open the box1.html file from the student files (chapter7/7.1/box1.html). Save the file with the name box2.html. Delete the content from the body section of the web page. Add the following code to configure two div elements— one nested inside the other:

```html
<div class="div1">
This is the outer box.
  <div class="div2">
  This is the inner box.
  </div>
</div>
```

Save the file. Launch a browser and test your page. It should look similar to the one shown in Figure 7.2. Notice how the browser renders the nested div elements—the second box is nested within the first box because it is coded inside the first div element in the web page source code. This is an example of normal flow. The student files contain a sample solution at chapter7/7.1/box2.html.

A Look Ahead—CSS Layout Properties

You've seen how normal flow causes the browser to render the elements in the order that they appear in the HTML source code. When using CSS for page layout there are situations in which you will want to specify the location of an element on the page—either the absolute pixel location, the location relative to where the element would normally display, or floating on the page. The CSS properties that configure the placement of elements on a web page are introduced in this chapter.

Float

The `float` Property

Elements that seem to float on the right or left side of either the browser window or another element are often configured using the `float` property. The browser renders these elements using normal flow and then shifts them to either the right or left as far as possible within their container (usually either the browser viewport or a div element).

▶ Use `float: right;` to float the element on the right side of the container.

▶ Use `float: left;` to float the element on the left side of the container.

▶ Specify a width for a floated element unless the element already has an implicit width—such as an img element.

▶ Other elements and web page content will flow around the floated element, so floated elements should always be coded before the elements that will display alongside them.

FIGURE 7.3 *The image is configured to float.*

Figure 7.3 shows a web page with an image configured with `float: right;` to float on the right side of the browser viewport (see the student files, chapter7/float1.html). When floating an image, the `margin` property is useful to configure empty space between the image and text on the page.

View Figure 7.3 and notice how the image stays on the right side of the browser viewport. An id called `yls` was created that applies the `float`, `margin`, and `border` properties. The attribute `id="yls"` was placed on the image tag. The CSS is

```
h1 { background-color: #A8C682;
     padding: 5px;
     color: #000000; }
p {  font-family: Arial, sans-serif; }
#yls { float: right;
       margin: 0 0 5px 5px;
       border: 1px solid #000000; }
```

The HTML source code is

```
<h1>Wildflowers</h1>
<img  id="yls"  src="yls.jpg" alt="Yellow Lady Slipper" height="100"
width="100">
<p>The heading and paragraph follow normal flow. The Yellow Lady Slip-
per pictured on the right is a wildflower. It grows in wooded areas
and blooms in June each year. The Yellow Lady Slipper is a member of
the orchid family.</p>
```

Hands-On Practice 7.2

In this Hands-On Practice you'll practice using the CSS `float` property as ⟨...⟩
web page shown in Figure 7.4.

Create a folder named ch7float. Copy the starter2.html and yls.jpg files fr⟨...⟩
folder in the student files into your ch7float folder. Launch a text editor a⟨...⟩
starter2.html file. Notice the order of the image and paragraphs. Notice th⟨...⟩
CSS to float the image. Display starter2.html in a browser. The browser re⟨...⟩
using normal flow and displays the elements in the order they are coded. ⟨...⟩

Let's add CSS to float the image. Save the file with the name floatyls.html. With
floatyls.html open in a text editor, modify the code as follows:

1. Add a style rule for a class named `float` that configures float, margin, and border
   properties:

   ```
   .float { float: left;
            margin-right: 10px;
            border: 3px ridge #000000; }
   ```

2. Assign the image element to the class named `float` (use `class="float"`).

Save the file. Launch a browser and test your page. It should look similar to the web page
shown in Figure 7.4. The student files contain a sample solution at chapter7/7.2/float.html.

The Floated Element and Normal Flow

Take a moment to examine your file in a browser (see Figure 7.4) and consider how the
browser rendered the page. The div element is configured with a light background color to
demonstrate how floated elements
are rendered outside of normal flow.
Observe that the floated image and the
first paragraph are contained within
the div element. The h2 element follows the div. If all the elements were
rendered using normal flow, the area
with the light background color would
contain both the child elements of the
div: the image and the first paragraph.
In addition, the h2 element would be
placed on its own line under the div
element.

However, once the image is placed
vertically on the page, it is floated
outside of normal flow—that's why the
light background color only appears
behind the first paragraph and why
the h2 element's text begins immediately after the first paragraph and
appears next to the floated image.

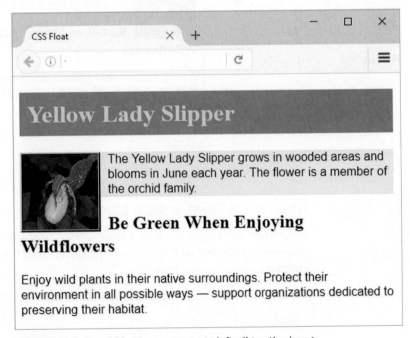

FIGURE 7.4 *The CSS* `float` *property left aligns the image.*

The `clear` Property

The `clear` property is often used to terminate, or "clear," a float. You can set the value of the `clear` property to `left`, `right`, or `both`—depending on the type of float you need to clear.

Review Figure 7.5 and the code sample in the student files at chapter7/7.2/float.html. Notice that although the div element contains both an image and the first paragraph, the light background color of the div only displays behind the screen area occupied by the first paragraph—it stops a bit earlier than expected. Clearing the float will help take care of this display issue.

FIGURE 7.5 *The float needs to be cleared to improve the display.*

Clearing a Float with a Line Break

A common technique to clear a float within a container element is to add a line break element configured with the `clear` property. See the example in the student files at chapter7/float/clear1.html.

Observe that a CSS class is configured to clear the left float:

```
.clearleft { clear: left; }
```

Also, a line break tag assigned to the `clearleft` class is coded before the closing `</div>` tag. The code snippet for the div element is

```
<div>
<img class="float" src="yls.jpg" alt="Yellow Lady Slipper"
height="100" width="100">
<p>The Yellow Lady Slipper grows in wooded areas and blooms in June
each year. The flower is a member of the orchid family.</p>
<br  class="clearleft">
</div>
```

Figure 7.6 displays a screen shot of this page. Note that the light background color of the div element extends farther down the page and the h2 element's text begins on its own line under the image.

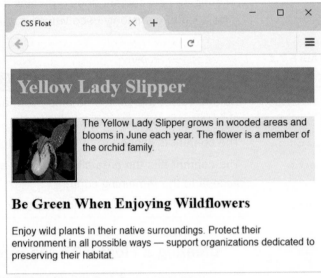

FIGURE 7.6 *The* `clear` *property is applied to a line break tag.*

If you are not concerned about the light background color display, another option is to omit the line break tag and instead apply the `clearleft` class to the h2 element. This does not change the display of the light background color, but it does force the h2 element's text to begin on its own line, as shown in Figure 7.7 (see the student files at chapter7/float/clear2.html).

FIGURE 7.7 *The* `clear` *property is applied to the h2 element.*

Overflow

The `overflow` Property

The `overflow` property is often used to clear a float, although its intended purpose is to configure how content should display if it is too large for the area allocated. See Table 7.1 for a list of commonly used values for the `overflow` property.

TABLE 7.1 *The* `overflow` *Property*

Value	Purpose
visible	Default value; the content is displayed, and if it's too large, the content will "overflow" outside the area allocated to it
hidden	The content is clipped to fit the room allocated to the element in the browser viewport
auto	The content fills the area allocated to it and, if needed, scroll bars are displayed to allow access to the remaining content
scroll	The content is rendered in the area allocated to it and scroll bars are displayed

Clearing a Float with the `overflow` Property

Review Figure 7.8 and the code sample in the student files at chapter7/7.2/float.html. Observe the div element, which contains the floated image and first paragraph on the page. Notice that although the div element contains both an image and the first paragraph, the div element's light background color does not extend as far as expected; it is only visible in the area occupied by the first paragraph. You can use the `overflow` property assigned to the container element to resolve this display issue and clear the float. In this case, we'll apply the `overflow` and `width` properties to the div element selector. The CSS to configure the div in this manner is

FIGURE 7.8 *The display can be improved by clearing the float with overflow.*

```
div { background-color: #F3F1BF;
      overflow: auto;
      width: 100%; }
```

This CSS is all that is needed to be added to the code to clear the float and cause the web page to display similar to Figure 7.9 (see the student files at chapter7/float/overflow.html).

The `clear` Property Versus the `overflow` Property

Notice that Figure 7.9 (using the `overflow` property) and Figure 7.6 (applying the `clear` property to a line break tag) result in a similar web page display. You may be wondering about which CSS property (`clear` or `overflow`) is the best to use when you need to clear a float.

Although the `clear` property is widely used, in this example it is more efficient to apply the `overflow` property to the container element (for example, a div element). This will clear the float, avoid adding an extra line break tag, and ensure that the container element expands to enclose the entire floated element. You'll get more practice with the `float`, `clear`, and `overflow` properties as you continue working through the book. Floating elements is a key technique in designing multicolumn page layouts with CSS.

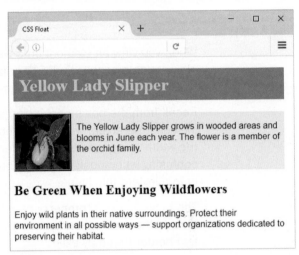

FIGURE 7.9 *The* `overflow` *property is applied to the div element selector.*

Configuring Scrollbars with the `overflow` Property

The web page in Figure 7.10 demonstrates the use of `overflow: auto;` to automatically display scroll bars if the content exceeds the space allocated to it. In this case, the div that contains the paragraph and the floated image was configured with a width of 300px and a height of 100px. See the example web page in the student files at chapter7/float/scroll.html. The CSS for the div is shown below:

```
div { background-color: #F3F1BF;
      overflow: scroll;
      width: 300px;
      height: 100px;
}
```

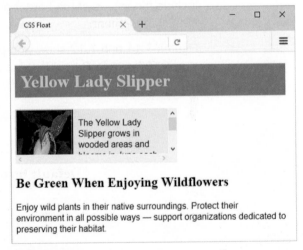

FIGURE 7.10 *The browser displays scrollbars.*

? FAQ Why aren't we using external styles?

Since we are only creating sample pages to practice new coding techniques, it is practical to work with a single file. However, if this were an actual website, you would be using an external style sheet for maximum productivity and efficiency.

CSS Box Sizing

When you view an element on a web page, it's intuitive to expect that the width of an element on a page includes the size of the element's padding and border. However, this isn't the default behavior of browsers.

Recall from the box model introduction in Chapter 6 that the `width` property by default only includes the actual width of the content itself within the element and does not also include the width of any padding or border that may exist for the element. This can sometimes be confusing when designing page layout with CSS. The purpose of the `box-sizing` property is to alleviate this issue.

The `box-sizing` **property** causes the browser calculation of the width or height to include the content's actual width or height in addition to the width or height of any padding and border that may exist.

Valid `box-sizing` property values include `content-box` (the default) and `border-box`. Use the `CSS box-sizing: border-box;` declaration to configure the browser to also include the values of the border and padding when calculating the width and height properties of an element.

Figures 7.11 and 7.12 show web pages (chapter7/boxsizing1.html and chapter7/boxsizing2.html in the student files) that each have floated elements configured

FIGURE 7.11 *Default box-sizing.*

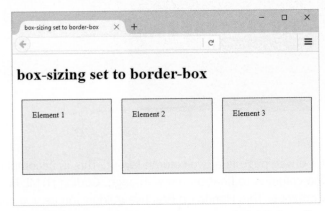

FIGURE 7.12 *The box-sizing property set to border-box.*

with 30% width, 150px height, 20px padding, and 10px margin. The page in Figure 7.11 uses default box-sizing. The page in Figure 7.12 uses box-sizing set to `border-box`. The size of the elements and the placement of the elements on the pages differ.

You may notice at first glance that the elements look larger in Figure 7.11. The larger display is because the browser sets the content to 30% width before adding the 20 pixels of padding on each side. The elements are smaller in Figure 7.12. The smaller display is because the browser applies the 30% width to the combination of the padding and the content.

Let's take a closer look at the placement of the three floated elements on the pages.

Figure 7.11 does not display all three elements side-by-side. This web page uses default `box-sizing` so the browser assigned the 30% width to each element's content only and then added 20 pixels of padding to each side of each element. Due to these calculations, the browser determined there was not enough room in the browser viewport to display all three elements next to each other and the browser dropped the third floated element to the next line.

The web page in Figure 7.12 is coded with `box-sizing` set to `border-box` which configures the three floated elements to be displayed side-by-side because the browser assigned the 30% width to the combined content and padding areas (including 20 pixels of padding on each side).

It is common practice for web developers to apply border-box box-sizing when they plan to use floated elements or multi-column layouts. It's also common practice to apply `box-sizing` by configuring the * **universal selector**, which will target all HTML elements. The CSS style rule to apply border-box box-sizing to all elements with the universal selector is

```
* { box-sizing: border-box; }
```

Feel free to experiment with the box-sizing property and the examples (chapter7/boxsizing1.html and chapter7/boxsizing2.html in the student files). You will use the box-sizing property as you explore page layout in this chapter.

Basic Two-Column Layout

A common design for a web page is a two-column layout. This is accomplished with CSS by configuring one of the columns to float on the web page. Coding HTML is a skill and skills are best learned by practice. This Hands-On Practice guides you as you convert a single-column page layout (Figure 7.13) into your first two-column layout (Figure 7.14).

FIGURE 7.13 *Single-column layout.*

FIGURE 7.14 *Two-column layout.*

 Hands-On Practice 7.3

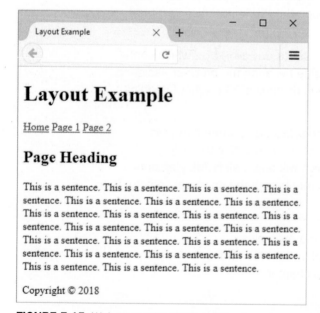

FIGURE 7.15 *Web page with single-column layout.*

A. Review single-column layout. Launch a text editor, and open the singlecol.html file from the chapter7 folder in the student files. Take a moment to look over the code. Notice the structure of the HTML tags correspond to wireframe in Figure 7.13.

```
<body>
<div id="wrapper">

  <header> </header>

  <nav> </nav>

  <main> </main>

  <footer> </footer>

</div>
</body>
```

Save the file with the name index.html. When you display index.html in a browser, your display should be similar to Figure 7.15.

B. **Configure a two-column layout.** Launch a text editor and open the index.html file. You will edit the HTML and CSS to configure a two-column layout as shown in Figure 7.14 wireframe.

1. **Edit the HTML.** The single-column navigation is horizontal but the two-column navigation will be displayed in a vertical orientation. Later in this chapter, you'll learn how to configure navigation hyperlinks within an unordered list but for now, a quick adjustment is to code a line break tag after each of the first two hyperlinks in the nav area.

2. **Configure the float with CSS.** Locate the style tags in the head section of the document and code the following style rule as embedded CSS to configure a nav element with a width of 150px that floats to the left.

```
nav { float: left;
      width: 150px; }
```

Save the file and test it in the Firefox or Chrome browser. Your display will be similar to Figure 7.16. Notice that the content in the main area wraps around the floated nav element.

3. **Configure two columns with CSS.** You just configured the nav element to float on the left. The main element will be in the right-side column and will be configured with a left margin (the same side as the float). To get a two-column look, the value of the margin should be greater than the width of the floated element. Open the index.html file in a text editor and code the following style rule to configure a 160px left margin for the main element.

```
main { margin-left: 160px; }
```

Save the file and test it in the Firefox or Chrome browser. Your display will be similar to Figure 7.17 with a two-column layout.

FIGURE 7.16 *The nav is floating on the left.*

FIGURE 7.17 *Two-column layout.*

FIGURE 7.18 *Final two-column layout.*

4. **Enhance the page with CSS.** Code the following style rules as embedded CSS to create a more appealing web page. When you have completed this step, your page should be similar to Figure 7.18.

   a. **The body element selector.** Configure a dark background color.

      ```
      body { background-color: #000066; }
      ```

   b. **The wrapper id selector.** Configure 80% width, centered on the page, and a light (#EAEAEA) background color. This background color will display behind child elements (such as the nav element) that do not have a background color configured.

   ```
   #wrapper { width: 80%;
              margin-left: auto;
              margin-right: auto;
              background-color: #EAEAEA; }
   ```

   c. **The header element selector.** Configure #CCCCFF background color.

   ```
   header { background-color: #CCCCFF; }
   ```

   d. **The h1 element selector.** Configure 0 margin and 10px of padding.

   ```
   h1 { margin: 0;
        padding: 10px; }
   ```

   e. **The nav element selector.** Edit the style rule and add a declaration for 10 pixels of padding.

   ```
   nav { float: left;
         width: 150px;
         padding: 10px;  }
   ```

   f. **The main element selector.** Edit the style rule and add a declaration for 10 pixels of padding and #FFFFFF background color.

   ```
   main { margin-left: 160px;
          padding: 10px;
          background-color: #FFFFFF;  }
   ```

   g. **The footer element selector.** Configure centered, italic text, and a #CCCCFF background color. Also configure the footer to clear all floats.

   ```
   footer { text-align: center;
            font-style: italic;
            background-color: #CCCCFF;
            clear: both; }
   ```

Save your file and test it in the Firefox or Chrome browser. Your display should be similar to Figure 7.18. You can compare your work to the sample in the student files (chapter7/7.3/index.html). At the time this was written, Internet Explorer did not support default styles like the HTML5 main element. You may need to nudge this browser to comply by adding the `display: block;` declaration (introduced later in this chapter) to the styles for the main element selector. An example solution is in the student files (chapter7/7.3/iefix.html).

Two-Column Layout Example

The web page you coded in Hands-On Practice 7.3 is just one example of a two-column layout design. Let's explore coding the two-column layout with a footer in the right column as shown in Figure 7.19 wireframe. The HTML template for the page layout is

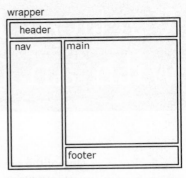

FIGURE 7.19 *Alternate wireframe.*

```
<div id="wrapper">
  <header>
  </header>
  <nav>
  </nav>
  <main>
  </main>
  <footer>
  </footer>
</div>
```

The key CSS configures a floating nav element, a main element with a left margin, and a footer with a left margin.

```
nav { float: left; width: 150px; }
main { margin-left: 165px; }
footer { margin-left: 165px; }
```

The web page shown in Figure 7.20 implements this layout. An example is in the student files, chapter7/float/twocolumn.html.

FIGURE 7.20 *Page with alternate layout.*

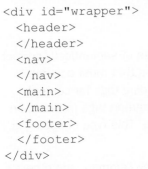 **FAQ**

Do I have to use a wrapper?

No, you are not required to use a wrapper or container for a web page layout. However, it does make it easier to get the two-column look because the background color of the wrapper div will display behind any of its child elements that do not have their own background color configured.

 Quick TIP

A key to coding successful layouts with float is in the HTML—place the element that needs to float BEFORE its companion elements. The browser will shift the floated element over to the side of the browser viewport and display the elements that follow alongside the floated element.

Vertical Navigation with an Unordered List

One of the advantages of using CSS for page layout involves the use of semantically correct code. Writing semantically correct code means using the markup tag that most accurately reflects the purpose of the content. Using the various levels of heading tags for content headings and subheadings or placing paragraphs of text within paragraph tags (rather than using line breaks) are examples of writing semantically correct code. This type of coding is a step in the direction to support the Semantic Web.

Leading Web developers such as Eric Meyer, Mark Newhouse, Jeffrey Zeldman, and others have promoted the idea of using unordered lists to configure navigation menus. After all, a navigation menu is a list of hyperlinks. Recall from Chapter 5 that you can configure an unordered list to omit the display of the list markers, or even display an image instead of a standard list marker.

Configuring navigation with a list also helps to provide for accessibility. Screen reader applications offer easy keyboard access and verbal cues for information organized in lists, such as the number of items in the list.

Figure 7.21 shows the navigation area of a web page (found in the student files chapter7/twocolumn3.html) that uses an unordered list to organize the navigation links. The HTML is

```
<ul>
<li><a href="index.html">Home</a></li>
<li><a href="menu.html">Menu</a></li>
<li><a href="directions.html">Directions</a></li>
<li><a href="contact.html">Contact</a></li>
</ul>
```

- Home
- Menu
- Directions
- Contact

FIGURE 7.21 *Navigation in an unordered list.*

Configure an Unordered List with CSS

OK, so now that we're semantically correct, how about improving the visual aesthetic? Let's use CSS to eliminate the list marker (refer back to Chapter 5). We also need to make sure that our special styles only apply to the unordered lists in the navigation area (within the nav element) so we'll use a descendant selector. The CSS to configure the list in Figure 7.22 is

```
nav ul { list-style-type: none; }
```

Home
Menu
Directions
Contact

FIGURE 7.22 *The list markers have been eliminated with CSS.*

Remove the Underline with the CSS `text-decoration` Property

The **text-decoration property** modifies the display of text in the browser and is most often used to eliminate the underline from the hyperlinks. As shown in Figure 7.23, the navigation hyperlinks are configured without an underline by coding:

```
text-decoration: none;
```

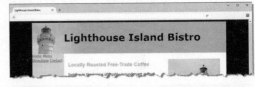

Home
Menu
Directions
Contact

FIGURE 7.23 *The CSS* `text-decoration` *property has been applied.*

 Hands-On Practice 7.4

You will configure vertical navigation with an unordered list in this Hands-On Practice. Create a folder named ch7vert. Copy the files lighthouseisland.jpg, lighthouselogo.jpg, and starter3.html from the chapter7 folder in the student files into your ch7vert folder. Display the web page in a browser. It should look similar to Figure 7.24—notice that the navigation area needs to be configured.

Launch a text editor and open the starter3.html file. Save the file as index.html in your ch7vert folder.

FIGURE 7.24 *Notice that the navigation area needs to be configured.*

1. Review the code for this page, which uses a two-column layout. Examine the nav element and modify the code surrounding the hyperlinks to configure the navigation in an unordered list.

```
<nav>
  <ul>
    <li><a href="index.html">Home</a></li>
    <li><a href="menu.html">Menu</a></li>
    <li><a href="directions.html">Directions</a></li>
    <li><a href="contact.html">Contact</a></li>
  </ul>
</nav>
```

2. Let's add CSS to the embedded styles to configure the unordered list elements only within the nav element: eliminate the list marker and set the padding to 10 pixels.

```
nav ul { list-style-type: none;
         padding: 10px; }
```

3. Next, configure the anchor tags within the nav element to have 10 pixels of padding, use bold font, and display no underline.

```
nav a { text-decoration: none;
        padding: 10px;
        font-weight: bold; }
```

Save your page and test it in a browser. Your page should look similar to Figure 7.25. A sample is found in the student files (chapter7/7.4/index.html).

FIGURE 7.25 *Two-column layout with vertical navigation.*

Horizontal Navigation with an Unordered List

You may be wondering how to use an unordered list for a horizontal navigation menu. The answer is CSS! List item elements are block display elements. They need to be configured as inline display to appear in a horizontal line. The CSS `display` property makes this possible.

CSS `display` Property

The CSS **display property** configures the way that browsers render elements. See Table 7.2 for a list of commonly used values.

TABLE 7.2   *The* `display` *Property*

Value	Purpose
`none`	The element will not display
`inline`	The element will display as an inline display element without whitespace above and below
`inline-block`	The element will display as an inline display element adjacent to other inline display elements but also can be configured with properties of block display elements including width and height
`block`	The element will display as a block display element with whitespace above and below

Home   Menu   Directions   Contact

FIGURE 7.26 *Navigation in an unordered list.*

Figure 7.26 shows the navigation area of a web page (found in the student files chapter7/navigation.html) with a horizontal navigation area organized by an unordered list. The HTML is

```
<nav>
  <ul>
    <li><a href="index.html">Home</a></li>
    <li><a href="menu.html">Menu</a></li>
    <li><a href="directions.html">Directions</a></li>
    <li><a href="contact.html">Contact</a></li>
  </ul>
</nav>
```

Configure with CSS

The following CSS was applied in this example:

▶ To eliminate the list marker from unordered lists within the nav element, apply
`list-style-type: none;` to the ul element selector:

`nav ul { list-style-type: none; }`

▶ To render the list items within the nav element horizontally instead of vertically, apply `display: inline;` to the nav `li` selector:

```
nav li { display: inline; }
```

▶ To eliminate the underline from the hyperlinks within the nav element, apply `text-decoration: none;` to the `nav a` selector. Also, configure right padding to add some space between the hyperlinks:

```
nav a { text-decoration: none; padding-right: 10px; }
```

 Hands-On Practice 7.5

You will configure horizontal navigation with an unordered list in this Hands-On Practice. Create a folder named ch7hort. Copy the files lighthouseisland.jpg, lighthouselogo.jpg, and starter4.html from the chapter7 folder in the student files into your ch7hort folder. Display the web page in a browser. It should look similar to Figure 7.27—notice that the navigation area needs to be configured to display in a single line. Launch a text editor and open the starter4.html file. Save the file as index.html in your ch7hort folder.

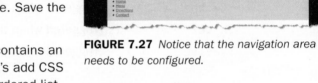

FIGURE 7.27 *Notice that the navigation area needs to be configured.*

1. Examine the nav element and notice that it contains an unordered list with navigation hyperlinks. Let's add CSS to the embedded styles to configure the unordered list element within the nav element: eliminate the list marker, center the text, set the font size to 1.5em, and set the margin to 5 pixels.

```
nav ul { list-style-type: none;
         text-align: center;
         font-size: 1.5em;
         margin: 5px; }
```

2. Configure the list item elements within the nav element to display as inline elements.

```
nav li { display: inline; }
```

3. Configure the anchor elements within the nav element to display no underline. Also set the left and right padding to 10 pixels.

```
nav a { text-decoration: none;
        padding-left: 10px;
        padding-right: 10px; }
```

Save your page and test it in a browser. Your page should look similar to Figure 7.28. A sample is found in the student files (chapter7/7.5/index.html).

FIGURE 7.28 *Horizontal navigation within an unordered list.*

CSS Interactivity with Pseudo-Classes

VideoNote
Interactivity
with CSS
Pseudo-Classes

Have you ever visited a website and found that the text hyperlinks changed color when you moved the mouse pointer over them? Often, this is accomplished using a CSS **pseudo-class**, which can be used to apply a special effect to a selector. The five pseudo-classes that can be applied to the anchor element are shown in Table 7.3.

TABLE 7.3 *Commonly Used CSS Pseudo-Classes*

Pseudo-Class	When Applied
:link	Default state for a hyperlink that has not been clicked (visited)
:visited	Default state for a visited hyperlink
:focus	Triggered when the hyperlink has keyboard focus
:hover	Triggered when the mouse moves over the hyperlink
:active	Triggered when the hyperlink is actually clicked

Notice the order in which the pseudo-classes are listed in Table 7.3. Anchor element pseudo-classes *must be coded in this order* (although it's OK to omit one or more of those listed). If you code the pseudo-classes in a different order, the styles will not be reliably applied. It's common practice to configure the :focus and :active pseudo-classes with the same styles.

To apply a pseudo-class, write it after the selector. The following code sample will configure text hyperlinks to be red initially. The sample also uses the :hover pseudo-class to configure the hyperlinks to change their appearance when the visitor places the mouse pointer over them so that the underline disappears and the color changes.

```
a:link { color: #ff0000; }
a:hover { text-decoration: none;
          color: #000066; }
```

1. Text hyperlinks are underlined by default.

🖶 Print This Page

2. The hover pseudo-class is triggered by the mouse. The browser no longer displays the underline below the hyperlink.

🖶 Print This Page

FIGURE 7.29 *Using the hover pseudo-class.*

Figure 7.29 shows part of a web page that uses a similar technique. Note the position of the mouse pointer over the "Print This Page" hyperlink—the text color has changed and has no underline. Most modern browsers support CSS pseudo-classes.

You will use pseudo-classes to create interactive hyperlinks in this Hands-On Practice. Create a folder named ch7hover. Copy the lighthouseisland.jpg, lighthouselogo.jpg, and starter3.html files from the chapter7 folder in the student files into your ch7hover folder. Display the web page in a browser. It should look similar to Figure 7.30—notice that the navigation area needs to be configured. Launch a text editor and open the starter3.html file. Save the file as index.html in your ch7hover folder.

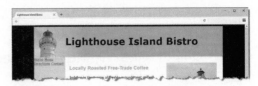

FIGURE 7.30 *The navigation area needs to be styled in this two-column page layout.*

1. Review the code for this page, which uses a two-column layout. Examine the nav element and modify the code surrounding the hyperlinks to configure the navigation in an unordered list.

```
<nav>
  <ul>
    <li><a href="index.html">Home</a></li>
    <li><a href="menu.html">Menu</a></li>
    <li><a href="directions.html">Directions</a></li>
    <li><a href="contact.html">Contact</a></li>
  </ul>
</nav>
```

2. Let's add CSS to the embedded styles to configure the unordered list element within the nav element: eliminate the list marker and set the padding to 10 pixels.

```
nav ul { list-style-type: none; padding: 10px; }
```

3. Next, configure basic interactivity with pseudo-classes.

▶ Configure the anchor elements within the nav element to have 10 pixels of padding, use bold font, and display no underline.

```
nav a { text-decoration: none; padding: 10px;
        font-weight: bold; }
```

▶ Use pseudo-classes to configure anchor tags within the nav element to display white (#FFFFFF) text for unvisited hyperlinks, light-gray (#EAEAEA) text for visited hyperlinks, and dark blue (#000066) text when the mouse hovers over hyperlinks:

```
nav a:link { color: #FFFFFF; }
nav a:visited { color: #EAEAEA; }
nav a:hover { color: #000066; }
```

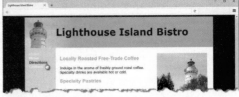

FIGURE 7.31 *CSS pseudo-classes add interactivity to the navigation.*

Save your page and test it in a browser. Move your mouse over the navigation area and notice the text color change. Your page should look similar to Figure 7.31. A sample is found in the student files (chapter7/7.6/index.html).

Practice with CSS Two-Column Layout

 Hands-On Practice 7.7

In this Hands-On Practice you'll create a new version of the Lighthouse Island Bistro home page with a top header section spanning two columns, content in the left column, navigation in the right column, and a footer section below the two columns. See Figure 7.32 for the wireframe. You will configure the CSS in an external style sheet. Create a new folder named ch7bistro. Copy the starter5.html, lighthouseisland.jpg, and lighthouselogo.jpg files from the chapter7 folder in the student files into your ch7bistro folder.

FIGURE 7.32 *The wireframe for a two-column layout with a top logo area.*

1. Launch a text editor and open the starter5.html file. Add a link element to the head section of the web page that associates this file with an external style sheet named bistro.css. A code sample is

   ```
   <link href="bistro.css" rel="stylesheet">
   ```

   Save the file with the name index.html.

2. Launch a text editor and create a new file named bistro.css in your ch7bistro folder. Configure the CSS as follows:

   ▶ **The universal selector:** set the box-sizing property to border-box.

   ```
   *{ box-sizing: border-box; }
   ```

   ▶ **The body element selector:** very dark blue background (#00005D) and Verdana, Arial, or the default sans-serif font typeface

   ```
   body { background-color: #00005D;
          font-family: Verdana, Arial, sans-serif; }
   ```

   ▶ **The wrapper id:** centered, take up 80% of the browser viewport, a minimum width of 940px, dark blue text (#000066), and medium-blue (#B3C7E6) background (*this color will display behind the nav section*)

   ```
   #wrapper { margin: 0 auto; width: 80%; min-width: 940px;
              background-color: #B3C7E6; color: #000066; }
   ```

   ▶ **The header element selector:** slate blue (#869DC7) background, very dark blue text (#00005D), 150% font size, 10px top, right, and bottom padding, 155px left padding, height set to 150 pixels, and the lighthouselogo.jpg background image

   ```
   header { background-color: #869DC7; color: #00005D;
            font-size: 150%; padding: 10px 10px 10px 155px;
            height: 150px;
            background-repeat: no-repeat;
            background-image: url(lighthouselogo.jpg); }
   ```

▶ **The nav element selector:** float on the right, 150px width, bold text, 0.1em letter spacing

```
nav { float: right; width: 150px; font-weight: bold;
      letter-spacing: 0.1em; }
```

▶ **The main element selector:** white background (#FFFFFF), black text (#000000), 10 pixels top and bottom padding, and 20 pixels left and right padding, auto overflow, and block display (fixes an Internet Explorer 11 rendering issue).

```
main { background-color: #FFFFFF; color: #000000;
       padding: 10px 20px; overflow: auto; display: block; }
```

▶ **The footer element selector:** 70% font size, centered text, 10 pixels of padding, a slate blue background color (#869DC7), and `clear` set to `both`.

```
footer { font-size: 70%; text-align: center; padding: 10px;
         background-color: #869DC7; clear: both; }
```

Save the bistro.css file. Display index.html in a browser. Your page should look similar to Figure 7.33.

3. Continue editing the bistro.css file to style the h2 element selector and floating image. Configure the h2 element selector with slate blue text color (#869DC7) and Arial or sans-serif font typeface. Configure the `floatright` id to float on the right side with 10 pixels of margin.

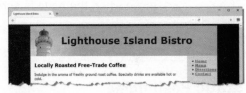

FIGURE 7.33 *The home page with major page sections configured using CSS.*

```
h2 { color: #869DC7;
     font-family: Arial, sans-serif; }
#floatright { float: right; margin: 10px; }
```

4. Continue editing the bistro.css file and configure the vertical navigation bar.

▶ Configure the unordered list: eliminate list markers, set zero margin and zero padding:

```
nav ul { list-style-type: none; margin: 0; padding: 0; }
```

▶ Configure hyperlinks: no underline, 20 pixels padding, medium-blue background color (#B3C7E6), and 1 pixel solid white bottom border. Use `display: block;` to allow the web page visitor to click anywhere in the anchor "button" to activate the hyperlink.

```
nav a { text-decoration: none; padding: 20px; display: block;
        background-color: #B3C7E6;
        border-bottom: 1px solid #FFFFFF; }
```

▶ Configure the `:link`, `:visited`, and `:hover` pseudo-classes as follows:

```
nav a:link { color: #FFFFFF; }
nav a:visited { color: #EAEAEA; }
nav a:hover { color: #869DC7;
              background-color: #EAEAEA; }
```

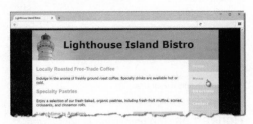

FIGURE 7.34 *CSS pseudo-classes add interactivity to the page.*

Save your file. Display your index.html page in a browser. Move your mouse over the navigation area and notice the interactivity, as shown in Figure 7.34. A sample solution is in the chapter7/7.7/index.html file.

Positioning with CSS

You've seen how normal flow causes the browser to render the elements in the order that they appear in the HTML source code. When using CSS for page layout there are situations when you may want more control over the position of an element. The **position property** configures the type of positioning used when the browser renders an element. Table 7.4 lists `position` property values and their purpose.

TABLE 7.4 *The* `position` *Property*

Value	Purpose
static	Default value; the element is rendered in normal flow
fixed	Configures the location of an element within the browser viewport; the element does not move when the page is scrolled
relative	Configures the location of an element relative to where it would otherwise render in normal flow
absolute	Precisely configures the location of an element outside of normal flow

Static Positioning

Static positioning is the default and causes the browser to render an element in normal flow. As you've worked through the exercises in this book, you have created web pages that the browser rendered using normal flow.

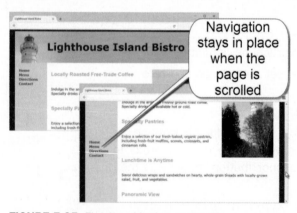

FIGURE 7.35 *Fixed positioning navigation.*

FIGURE 7.36 *The paragraph is configured using relative positioning.*

Fixed Positioning

Use **fixed positioning** to cause an element to be removed from normal flow and to remain stationary, or "fixed in place," when the web page is scrolled in the browser viewport. Figure 7.35 shows a web page (found in the student files chapter7/fixed.html) with a navigation area configured with fixed position. The navigation stays in place even though the user has scrolled down the page. The CSS follows:

```
nav { position: fixed; }
```

Relative Positioning

Use **relative positioning** to change the location of an element slightly, relative to where it would otherwise appear in normal flow. However, the area in normal flow is still reserved for the element and other elements will flow around that reserved space. Configure relative positioning with the `position: relative;` property along with one or more of the following offset properties: `left`, `right`, `top`, `bottom`. Table 7.5 lists the offset properties.

Figure 7.36 shows a web page (see the student files chapter7/relative.html) that uses relative positioning along with the `left` property to configure the placement of an element in relation to the normal flow. In this case, the container element is the body of the web page. The result is that the content of the element

TABLE 7.5 *The Position Offset Properties*

Property	Value	Purpose
left	Numeric value or percentage	The position of the element offset from the left side of the container element
right	Numeric value or percentage	The position of the element offset from the right side of the container element
top	Numeric value or percentage	The position of the element offset from the top of the container element
bottom	Numeric value or percentage	The position of the element offset from the bottom of the container element

is rendered as being offset or shifted by 30 pixels from the left where it would normally be placed at the browser's left margin. Notice also how the padding and background-color properties configure the heading element. The CSS is

```
p {  position: relative;
     left: 30px;
     font-family: Arial, sans-serif; }
h1 { background-color: #cccccc;
     padding: 5px;
     color: #000000; }
```

The HTML source code follows:

```
<h1>Relative Positioning</h1>
<p>This paragraph uses CSS relative positioning to be placed 30 pixels in from the
left side.</p>
```

Absolute Positioning

Use **absolute positioning** to precisely specify the location of an element outside of normal flow in relation to its first non-static parent element. If there is no non-static parent element, the absolute position is specified in relation to the browser viewport. Configure absolute positioning with the position: absolute; property along with one or more of the offset properties (left, right, top, bottom) listed in Table 7.5.

Figure 7.37 depicts a web page that configures an element with absolute positioning to display the content 200 pixels in from the left margin and 100 pixels down from the top of the web page document. An example is in the student files, chapter7/absolute.html).

The CSS is

```
p {  position: absolute;
     left: 200px;
     top: 100px;
     font-family: Arial, sans-serif;
     width: 300px; }
```

The HTML source code is

```
<h1> Absolute Positioning</h1>
<p>This paragraph is 300 pixels wide and uses
CSS absolute positioning to be placed 200 pixels
in from the left and 100 pixels down from the top of the browser window.</p>
```

FIGURE 7.37 *The paragraph is configured with absolute positioning.*

Practice with Positioning

Recall that the CSS `:hover` pseudo-class provides a way to configure styles to display when the web page visitor moves the mouse over an element. You'll use this basic interactivity along with CSS positioning and display properties to configure an interactive image gallery with CSS and HTML. Figure 7.38 shows the interactive image gallery in action (see chapter7/7.8/gallery.html in the student files). When you place the mouse over a thumbnail image, the larger version of the image is displayed along with a caption. If you click on the thumbnail, the larger version of the image displays in its own browser window.

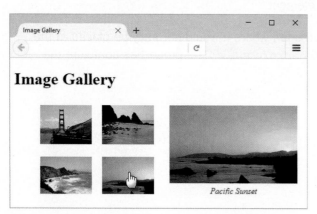

FIGURE 7.38 *An interactive image gallery with CSS.*

 Hands-On Practice 7.8

In this Hands-On Practice, you will create the interactive image gallery web page shown in Figure 7.38. Copy the following images located in the student files chapter7/starters folder into a folder named gallery: photo1.jpg, photo2.jpg, photo3.jpg, photo4.jpg, thumb1.jpg, thumb2.jpg, thumb3.jpg, and thumb4.jpg. Launch a text editor and modify the chapter1/template.html file to configure a web page as indicated:

1. Configure the text, Image Gallery, within an h1 element, and within the title element.

2. Code a div assigned to the id named `gallery`. This div will contain the thumbnail images, which will be configured within an unordered list.

3. Configure an unordered list within the div. Code four li elements, one for each thumbnail image. The thumbnail images will function as image links with a `:hover` pseudo-class that causes the larger image to display on the page. We'll make this all happen by configuring an anchor element containing both the thumbnail image and a span element that comprises the larger image along with descriptive text. An example of the first li element is

```
<li><a href="photo1.jpg"><img src="thumb1.jpg" width="100"
    height="75" alt="Golden Gate Bridge">
    <span><img src="photo1.jpg" width="250" height="150"
    alt="Golden Gate Bridge"><br>Golden Gate Bridge</span></a>
</li>
```

4. Configure all four li elements in a similar manner. Substitute the actual name of each image file for the href and src values in the code. Write your own descriptive text for

each image. Use photo2.jpg and thumb2.jpg in the second li element. Use photo3.jpg and thumb3.jpg in the third li element. Use photo4.jpg and thumb4.jpg for the fourth li element. Save the file as index.html in the gallery folder. Display your page in a browser. You'll see an unordered list with the thumbnail images, the larger images, and the descriptive text. Figure 7.39 shows a partial screen capture.

FIGURE 7.39 *The web page display before CSS.*

5. Now, let's add embedded CSS. Open your index.html file in a text editor and code a style element in the head section. Code embedded CSS as follows:

a. Configure the universal selector with box-sizing set to border-box

```
* { box-sizing: border-box; }
```

b. The `gallery` id will use relative positioning instead of the default static positioning. This does not change the location of the gallery but sets the stage to use absolute positioning on the span element in relation to its container (`#gallery`) instead of in relation to the entire web page document. This won't matter too much for our example, but it would be very helpful if the gallery were part of a more complex web page. Set the gallery id to use relative positioning.

```
#gallery { position: relative; }
```

c. The gallery unordered list should be 280px wide with no list marker.

```
#gallery ul { width: 280px; list-style-type: none; }
```

d. Configure the gallery list item elements with inline display, left float, and 10px padding.

```
#gallery li { display: inline; float: left; padding: 10px; }
```

e. The images in the gallery should not display a border.

```
#gallery img { border-style: none; }
```

f. Configure gallery anchor elements to have no underline with italic #333 text.

```
#gallery a { text-decoration: none; color: #333; font-style: italic; }
```

g. Configure span elements in the gallery not to display initially.

```
#gallery span { display: none; }
```

h. Configure the span elements in the gallery to display *only* when the web visitor hovers the mouse over the thumbnail image link. Set the location of the span to use absolute positioning. Locate the span 10 pixels down from the top and 300 pixels in from the left. Center the text within the span:

```
#gallery a:hover span { display: block; position: absolute;
        top: 10px; left: 300px; text-align: center; }
```

Save your page and display it in a browser. Your interactive image gallery should work well in modern browsers. Compare your work to Figure 7.38 and the sample in the student files (chapter7/7.8/gallery.html).

CSS Sprites

When browsers display web pages, they must make a separate http request for every file used by the page, including .css files and image files such as .gif, .jpg, and .png files. Each http request takes time and resources. A **sprite** is an image file that contains multiple small graphics. The single graphics file saves download time because the browser only needs to make one http request for the combined image instead of many requests for the individual smaller images. Using CSS to configure the small graphics combined in the sprite as background images for various web page elements is called **CSS sprites**, a technique made popular by David Shea (http://www.alistapart.com/articles/sprites).

The CSS sprites technique uses the CSS `background-image`, `background-repeat`, and `background-position` properties to manipulate the placement of the background image.

Figure 7.40 shows a sprite with two lighthouse images on a transparent background. These images are configured as background images for the navigation hyperlinks with CSS as shown in Figure 7.41. You'll see this in action as you complete the next Hands-On Practice.

FIGURE 7.40 *The sprite consists of two images.*

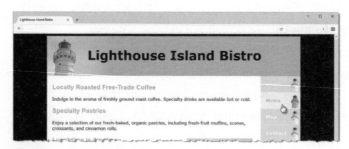

FIGURE 7.41 *Sprites in action.*

 Hands-On Practice 7.9

You will work with CSS sprites in this Hands-On Practice as you create the web page shown in Figure 7.41. Create a new folder named sprites. Copy the following files from the chapter 7 folder into your sprites folder: starter6.html, lighthouseisland.jpg, lighthouselogo.jpg, and sprites.gif. The sprites.gif, shown in Figure 7.40, contains two lighthouse images. The first lighthouse image starts at the top of the graphics file. The second lighthouse image begins 100 pixels down from the top of the graphics file. We'll use this information about the location of the second image within the graphics file when we configure the display of the second image. Launch a text editor and open starter6.html. Save the file as index.html. You will edit the embedded styles to configure background images for the navigation hyperlinks.

1. Configure the background image for navigation hyperlinks. Add the following styles to the `nav a` selector to set the background image to the sprites.gif with no repeat. The value `right` in the `background-position` property configures the lighthouse image to display at the right of the navigation element. The value 0 in the `background-position` property configures the display at offset 0 from the top (at the very top) so the first lighthouse image displays.

```
nav a {  text-decoration: none;
         display: block;
         padding: 20px;
         background-color: #B3C7E6;
         border-bottom: 1px solid #FFFFFF;
         background-image: url(sprites.gif);
         background-repeat: no-repeat;
         background-position: right 0;  }
```

2. Configure the second lighthouse image to display when the mouse pointer passes over the hyperlink. Add the following styles to the `nav a:hover` selector to display the second lighthouse image. The value `right` in the `background-position` property configures the lighthouse image to display at the right of the navigation element. The value `-100px` in the `background-position` property configures the display at an offset of 100 pixels down from the top so the second lighthouse image appears.

```
nav a:hover {  background-color: #EAEAEA;
               color: #869DC7;
               background-position: right -100px;  }
```

Save the file and test it in a browser. Your page should look similar to Figure 7.41. Move your mouse pointer over the navigation hyperlinks to see the background images change. Compare your work with the sample found in the student files (chapter7/7.9/index.html).

? FAQ **How can I create my own sprite graphics file?**

Most web developers use a graphics application such as Adobe Photoshop, Adobe Fireworks, or GIMP to edit images and save them in a single graphics file for use as a sprite. Or, you could use a web-based sprite generator such as the ones listed below:

▶ CSS Sprites Generator: http://csssprites.com
▶ CSS Sprite Generator: http://spritegen.website-performance.org
▶ SpritePad: http://wearekiss.com/spritepad

If you already have a sprite graphic, check out the online tool at Sprite Cow (http://www.spritecow.com) that can generate pixel-perfect `background-position` property values for a sprite.

Review and Apply

Review Questions

1. Which of the following pseudo-classes is the default state for a hyperlink that has already been clicked?

   a. `:hover`

   b. `:link`

   c. `:onclick`

   d. `:visited`

2. Which of the following is used to change the location of an element slightly in relation to where it would otherwise appear on the page?

   a. relative positioning

   b. static positioning

   c. absolute positioning

   d. fixed positioning

3. Which of the following properties can be used to clear a float?

   a. `float` or `clear`

   b. `clear` or `overflow`

   c. `position` or `clear`

   d. `overflow` or `float`

4. Which of the following causes an element not to display?

   a. `display: block;`

   b. `display: 0px;`

   c. `display: none;`

   d. `display: inline;`

5. Which of the following causes an element to display without empty space above and below?

   a. `display: block;`

   b. `display: static;`

   c. `display: none;`

   d. `display: inline;`

6. Which of the following is an image file that contains multiple small graphics?

   a. thumbnail

   b. snap

   c. sprite

   d. float

7. Which of the following configures a class called notes to float to the left?

   a. `.notes { left: float; }`

   b. `.notes { float: left; }`

   c. `.notes { float-left: 200px; }`

   d. `.notes { position: float; }`

8. Which of the following is the rendering flow used by a browser by default?

   a. HTML flow

   b. normal display

   c. browser flow

   d. normal flow

9. Which of the following is an example of using a descendant selector to configure the anchor tags within the nav element?

   a. `nav. a`   **b.** `a nav`

   c. `nav a`   **d.** `#nav a`

10. Which of the following is used along with the `left`, `right`, and/or `top` property to precisely configure the position of an element outside of normal flow?

    a. `position: relative;`

    b. `position: absolute;`

    c. `position: float;`

    d. `absolute: position;`

Hands-On Exercises

1. Write the CSS for an id with the following characteristics: fixed position, light gray background color, bold font weight, and 10 pixels of padding.

2. Write the CSS for an id with the following characteristics: float to the left of the page, light-beige background, Verdana or sans-serif large font, and 20 pixels of padding.

3. Write the CSS for an id that will be absolutely positioned on a page 20 pixels from the top and 40 pixels from the right. This area should have a light-gray background and a solid border.

4. Write the CSS for a class that is relatively positioned. This class should appear 15 pixels in from the left. Configure the class to have a light-green background.

5. Create a web page about your favorite hobby, movie, or music group. Configure the text, color, and a two-column layout with CSS.

Focus on Web Design

There is still much for you to learn about CSS. A great place to learn about web technology is on the Web itself. Use a search engine to search for CSS page layout tutorials. Choose a tutorial that is easy to read. Select a section that discusses a CSS technique that was not covered in this chapter. Create a web page that uses this new technique. Consider how the suggested page layout follows (or does not follow) principles of design such as contrast, repetition, alignment, and proximity (refer back to Chapter 3). The web page should provide the URL of your tutorial, the name of the website, a description of the new technique you discovered, and a discussion of how the technique follows (or does not follow) principles of design.

Pacific Trails Resort Case Study

In this chapter's case study, you will use the Pacific Trails existing website (Chapter 6) as a starting point to create a new version of the website that uses a two-column page layout. Figure 7.42 displays a wireframe with the new layout. The new Home page is shown in Figure 7.43.

You have three tasks in this case study:

1. Create a new folder for the Pacific Trails Resort website.

2. Edit the pacific.css external style sheet.

3. Edit the Home page (index.html), Yurts page (yurts.html), and Activities page (activities.html) to configure the navigation hyperlinks within an unordered list.

FIGURE 7.42 *Pacific Trails two-column page layout.*

Task 1: Create a folder called ch7pacific to contain your Pacific Trails Resort website files. Copy the files from the Chapter 6 Case Study ch6pacific folder. Copy the coast2.jpg image from the chapter7/starters folder.

Task 2: Configure the CSS. Launch a text editor and open the pacific.css external style sheet file. Edit the CSS as follows:

- **The universal selector.** Set the box-sizing property to border-box.

  ```
  * { box-sizing: border-box; }
  ```

- **The wrapper id selector.** Change the background color from white (#FFFFFF) to blue (#90C7E3). Configure a 1px solid dark blue (#000033) border. Copy the background image style declaration for the linear gradient from the body selector. This will display behind the navigation area.

- **The body element selector.** Change the background color to #B8DBED. Remove the background-image and background-repeat style declarations.

- **The header element selector.** Remove the style declarations that configure the background image. Configure text color to #FFFFFF, height to 120px, top padding to 30px, and left padding to 3em.

FIGURE 7.43 *The new Pacific Trails Home page with a two-column layout.*

- **The h1 element selector.** Configure 3em font size and 0.25em of letter spacing.

- **The nav element selector.** This is the area that will float on the page. Remove the background-color declaration—the nav area will pick up the background color of the `wrapper` id. Remove the text-align declaration. Change the padding to 1.5em. Set 120% font size. Configure left float and a width of 160 pixels.

- **The homehero id selector.** Configure a 190px left margin. Change the background image to coast2.jpg.

- **The yurthero id selector.** Configure a 190px left margin.

- **The trailhero id selector.** Configure a 190px left margin.

- **The main element selector.** Configure style declarations to set a white (#FFFFFF) background, 190 pixels of left margin, and change the left padding to 30px.

- **Configure the unordered list in the main content area.** Replace the ul element selector with a descendant selector (`main ul`) to specify only ul elements within the main content.

- **The footer element selector.** Configure styles to set a 190 pixel left margin and white (#FFFFFF) background color.

- **Configure the navigation area.** Use descendant selectors to configure the unordered list and anchor elements *within the nav element*.

  - **Style the unordered list.** Configure the `ul` element selector with no list markers, zero margin, zero left padding, and 1.2em font size.

  - **Style unvisited navigation hyperlinks.** Configure the `:link` pseudo-class with medium blue text color (#5C7FA3).

  - **Style visited navigation hyperlinks.** Configure the `:visited` pseudo-class with dark blue text color (#344873).

  - **Style interactive hyperlinks.** Configure the `:hover` pseudo-class with dark red text color (#A52A2A).

Save the pacific.css file. Check your syntax with the CSS validator (http://jigsaw.w3.org/css-validator). Correct and retest if necessary.

Task 3: Edit the web pages. Launch a text editor and open the index.html file. Configure the navigation hyperlinks using an unordered list. Remove the   special characters. Save the file. Modify the yurts.html and activities.html files in a similar manner.

Test your web pages in a browser. Your home page should be similar to the example in Figure 7.43 with a two-column page layout!

Path of Light Yoga Studio Case Study

In this chapter's case study, you will use the existing Path of Light Yoga Studio (Chapter 6) website as a starting point to create a new version of the website that uses a two-column layout. Figure 7.44 displays a wireframe with the new layout.

You have four tasks in this case study:

1. Create a new folder for the Path of Light Yoga Studio website.
2. Edit the yoga.css external style sheet.
3. Edit the Home page (index.html) to float an image on the left side of the content area.
4. Edit the Home page (index.html), Classes page (classes.html), and Schedule page (schedule.html) to configure the navigation hyperlinks within an unordered list.

FIGURE 7.44 *Path of Light Yoga Studio two-column page layout.*

Task 1: Create a folder called ch7yoga to contain your Path of Light Yoga Studio website files. Copy the files from the Chapter 6 Case Study ch6yoga folder. Copy the yogadoor2.jpg image from the chapter7/starters folder.

Task 2: Configure the CSS. Launch a text editor and open the yoga.css external style sheet file. Edit the CSS as follows:

- **The universal selector.** Set the box-sizing property to border-box.

  `* { box-sizing: border-box; }`
- **The body element selector.** Add a declaration to configure #3F2860 text color.
- **The wrapper id selector.** Change the minimum width to 550px.
- **The nav element selector.** This is the area that will float on the page. Configure left float and a width of 190 pixels. Remove the background-color declaration.
- **The nav a element selector.** Keep the text-decoration style declaration. Also configure styles to use block display, centered text, bold font, a 3 pixel gray (#CCCCCC) outset border, 1em padding, and a 1em bottom margin.
- **Configure the navigation area.** Use descendant selectors to configure the unordered list and anchor elements *within the nav element.*
  - **Style the unordered list.** Configure the `ul` element selector with no list markers, zero left padding, and 1.2em font size.
  - **Style unvisited navigation hyperlinks.** Configure the `:link` pseudo-class with #3F2860 text color.
  - **Style visited navigation hyperlinks.** Configure the `:visited` pseudo-class with #497777 text color.

- **Style interactive hyperlinks.** Configure the `:hover` pseudo-class with #A26100 text color. Also configure a 3 pixel inset #333333 border.
- **The main element selector.** Add a style declaration to configure a 170 pixel left margin.
- **The img element selector.** Remove the selector and style declaration.
- Configure a new class named `floatleft` that floats to the left with right margin set to 4em.
- Configure styles for a new class named `clear` with a `clear: both;` style declaration.

Save your yoga.css file. Use the CSS validator (http://jigsaw.w3.org/css-validator) to check your syntax. Correct and retest if necessary.

Task 3: Modify the Home page. Launch a text editor and open the index.html file. Remove the align="right" attribute. Assign the img tag to the class named `floatleft`. Change the value of the src attribute to yogadoor2.jpg. Edit the div element that contains the address information. Assign the div to the class named `clear`. Save the index.html file.

FIGURE 7.45 *The new Path of Light Yoga Studio Home page with a two-column layout.*

Task 4: Edit the navigation on the web pages. Launch a text editor and open the index.html file. Configure the navigation hyperlinks using an unordered list. Remove the ` ` special characters. Save the file. Test your web page in a browser. Your home page should be similar to the example in Figure 7.45 with a two-column page layout. Modify the classes.html and schedule.html files in a similar manner. Test your web pages in a browser. The Classes page is shown in Figure 7.46.

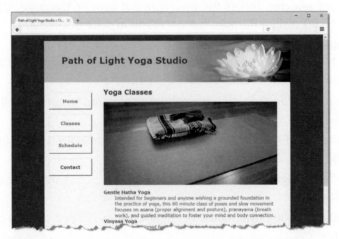

FIGURE 7.46 *The new Path of Light Yoga Studio Classes page with a two-column layout.*

CHAPTER 8

More on Links, Layout, and Mobile

Now that you've had some experience coding HTML and CSS you're ready to explore the topics in this chapter, including relative hyperlinks and named fragment hyperlinks, captioning a figure, more new HTML5 structural elements, ensuring compatibility with older browsers, styling for print, styling for mobile browsers, and responsive web design techniques as you configure CSS3 media queries to target mobile devices.

You'll learn how to...

- Code relative hyperlinks to web pages in folders within a website
- Configure a hyperlink to a named fragment internal to a web page
- Configure images with captions using the HTML5 figure and figcaption elements
- Configure a collection of images to float across a web page
- Configure web pages with HTML5 section, article, and time elements

- Apply techniques to ensure backward compatibility with older browsers
- Configure web pages for printing with CSS
- Describe mobile web design best practices
- Configure web pages for mobile display using the viewport meta tag
- Apply responsive web design techniques with CSS3 media queries
- Apply responsive image techniques including the new HTML5 picture element

More on Relative Linking

As discussed in Chapter 2, a relative hyperlink is used to link to web pages within your site. You've been coding relative links to display web pages that are all inside the same folder. There are times when you need to link to files that are located in other folders on your website. Let's consider a website for a bed and breakfast that features rooms and events. The folder and file listing is shown in Figure 8.1. The main folder for this website is called casita, and the web developer has created separate subfolders—named images, rooms, and events—to organize the site.

 casita
index.html
contact.html
casita.css

 images
logo.gif
scenery.jpg

 rooms
canyon.html
javelina.html

 events
weekend.html
festival.html

FIGURE 8.1 *The web page files are organized in folders.*

Relative Link Examples

Recall that when linking to a file located in the same folder or directory, the value of the `href` attribute is the name of the file. For example, to link from the home page (index.html) to the contact.html page, code the anchor element as follows:

```
<a href="contact.html">Contact</a>
```

When linking to a file that is inside a folder within the current directory, use both the folder name and the file name in the relative link. For example, to link from the home page (index.html) to the canyon.html page (located in the rooms folder), code the anchor element as follows:

```
<a href="rooms/canyon.html">Canyon</a>
```

As shown in Figure 8.1, the canyon.html page is located in the rooms subfolder of the casita folder. The home page for the site (index.html) is located in the casita folder. When linking to a file that is up one directory level from the current page, use the ". ./" notation. To link to the home page for the site from the canyon.html page, code the anchor element as follows:

```
<a href="../index.html">Home</a>
```

When linking to a file that is in a folder on the same level as the current folder, the href value will use the ". ./" notation to indicate moving up one level; then specify the desired folder. For example, to link to the weekend.html page in the events folder from the canyon.html page in the rooms folder, code the anchor element as follows:

```
<a href="../events/weekend.html">Weekend Events</a>
```

Don't worry if the use of ". ./" notation and linking to files in different folders seems new and different. In most of the exercises in this book, you will code either absolute links to other websites or relative links to files in the same folder. You can explore the example of the bed and breakfast website located in the student files (see chapter8/CasitaExample) to become more familiar with coding references to files in different folders.

Hands-On Practice 8.1

This hands-on practice provides an opportunity to practice coding hyperlinks to files in different folders. The website you'll be working with has pages in prototype form—the navigation and layout of the pages are configured, but the specific content has not yet been added. You'll focus on the navigation area in this Hands-On Practice. Figure 8.2 shows a partial screen shot of the bed and breakfast's prototype home page with a navigation area on the left side of the page.

Examine Figure 8.3 and notice the new juniper.html file listed within the rooms folder. You will create a new web page (Juniper Room) named juniper.html and save it in the rooms folder. Then, you will update the navigation area on each existing web page to link to the new Juniper Room page.

Let's get started.

1. Copy the CasitaExample folder (chapter8/CasitaExample) from the student files. Rename the folder casita.

2. Display the index.html file in a browser and click through the navigation links. View the source code of the pages and notice how the `href` values of the anchor tags are configured to link to and from files within different folders.

3. Launch a text editor and open the canyon.html file. You'll use this file as a starting point for your new Juniper Room page. Save the file as juniper.html in the rooms folder.

   a. Edit the page title and h2 text: change "Canyon" to "Juniper"

   b. Add a new li element in the navigation area that contains a hyperlink to the juniper.html file.

   ```
   <li><a href="juniper.html">Juniper Room</a></li>
   ```

   Place this hyperlink between the Javelina Room and Weekend Events navigation hyperlinks as shown in Figure 8.4. Save the file.

4. Use the coding for the Canyon and Javelina hyperlinks as a guide as you add the Juniper Room link to the navigation area on each of the following pages:

   index.html
   contact.html
   rooms/canyon.html
   rooms/javelina.html
   events/weekend.html
   events/festival.html

Save all the .html files and test your pages in a browser. The navigation hyperlink to the new Juniper Room page should work from every other page. The hyperlinks on the new Juniper Room page should function well and open other pages as expected. A solution is in the student files (chapter8/8.1 folder).

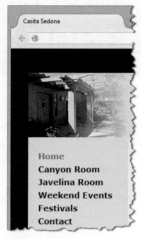

FIGURE 8.2 *The navigation area.*

FIGURE 8.3 *New juniper.html file is in the rooms folder.*

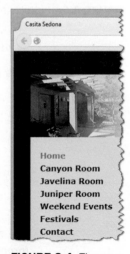

FIGURE 8.4 *The new navigation area.*

Fragment Identifiers

Browsers begin the display of a web page at the top of the document. However, there are times when you need to provide the capability to link to a specific portion of a web page instead of the top. You can accomplish this by coding a hyperlink to a **fragment identifier** (sometimes called a named fragment or fragment id), which is simply an HTML element with an `id` attribute.

There are two components to your coding when using fragment identifiers:

1. The tag that identifies the **named fragment** of a web page. This tag must be assigned to an id. For example: `<div id="content">`
2. The anchor tag that links to the named fragment on a web page.

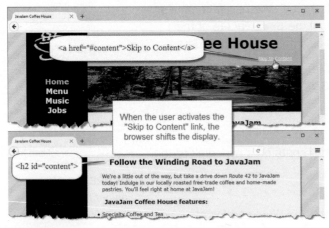

FIGURE 8.5 *The "skip to content" link in action.*

Lists of frequently asked questions (FAQs) often use fragment identifiers to jump to a specific part of the page and display the answer to a question. Linking to a named fragment is often seen on long web pages. You might see a "Back to top" hyperlink that a visitor can click to cause the browser to quickly scroll the page up to the top for easy site navigation. Another use of fragment identifiers helps to provide for accessibility. Web pages may have a fragment identifier to indicate the beginning of the actual page content. When the visitor clicks on the "Skip to content" hyperlink, the browser links to the named fragment and shifts focus to the content area of the page. This "Skip to content" or "Skip navigation" link provides a way for screen reader users to skip repetitive navigation links (see Figure 8.5).

This is accomplished in two steps:

1. **Establish the Target.** Create the "skip to content" fragment identifier by configuring an element that begins the page content with an id, for example, `<h2 id="content">`.
2. **Reference the Target.** At the point of the page where you want to place a hyperlink to the content, code an anchor element. Use the `href` attribute and place a # symbol (called a hash mark) before the name of the fragment identifier. The code for a hyperlink to the named fragment "content" is

   `<a href="#content">Skip to Content</a>`.

The hash mark indicates that the browser should search for an id on the same page. If you forget to type the hash mark, the browser will not look on the same web page; it will look for an external file.

Hands-On Practice 8.2

You will work with fragment identifiers in this Hands-On Practice. Laun editor and open the chapter8/starter1.html file from the student files file as favorites.html. Figure 8.6 shows a screenshot of this web page. Examine the source code and notice that the top portion of the page contains an unordered list with categories of interest (such as Hobbies, HTML5, and CSS) that correspond to the text displayed in the h2 elements below. Each h2 element is followed by a description list of topics and URLs related to that category. It might be helpful to web page visitors if they can click a category item and immediately jump to the page area that has information related to that item. This could be a useful application of linking to fragment identifiers!

Modify the page as follows:

1. Code a named fragment for each h2 element. For example,

   ```
   <h2 id="hobbies">Hobbies</h2>
   ```

2. Add hyperlinks to the items in the unordered list so that each entry will link to its corresponding heading.

3. Add a named fragment near the top of the page.

4. Near the bottom of the favorites.html page, add a hyperlink to scroll to the top of the page.

FIGURE 8.6 *You will add hyperlinks to fragment identifiers.*

Save the file and test it in a browser. The student files contain a sample solution in the chapter8/8.2 folder.

There may be times when you need to link to a named fragment on another web page. To accomplish this, place a "#" followed by the fragment identifier id value after the file name in the anchor tag. So, to link to the "Hobbies" (given that it is a named fragment called "hobbies") from any other page on the same website, you could use the following HTML:

```
<a href="favorites.html#hobbies">Hobbies</a>
```

Why don't some of my hyperlinks to fragment identifiers work?

The web browser fills the browser viewport with the web page and will scroll to display the named fragment at the top of the viewport. However, if there is not enough "page" left below the named fragment, the content where the named fragment is located will not be displayed at the top of the browser viewport. The browser tries to do the best it can while still filling the viewport with the web page content. Try adding some blank lines (use the `<br>` tag) or padding to the lower portion of the web page. Save your work and retest your hyperlinks.

and

aption Elements

HTML5 introduces a number of elements that are useful to semantically describe the content. While you could use a generic div element to configure an area on a web page with an image and a caption, the figure and figcaption elements are more descriptive of the content. The div element is useful but very generic in nature. When the figure and figcaption elements are used, the structure of the content is well defined.

The Figure Element

The block display **figure element** comprises a unit of content that is self-contained, such as an image, along with one optional figcaption element.

The Figcaption Element

The block display **figcaption element** provides a caption for the figure content.

Captioning a Figure

The web page shown in Figure 8.7 demonstrates the use of the figure and figcaption elements. The example in the student files (chapter8/caption/caption.html) configures a text caption centered below the image. The HTML code is

```
<figure>
  <img src="lighthouseisland.jpg"
       width="250" height="355"
       alt="Lighthouse Island">
  <figcaption>
    Island Lighthouse, Built in 1870
  </figcaption>
</figure>
```

CSS is needed to configure the display. The figure element selector is set as follows: float to the right, 260 pixels in width, and a 10 pixel margin. The figcaption element selector is configured to render small, italic, and centered text. The CSS is

```
figure { float: right;
         width: 260px;
         margin: 10px; }
```

FIGURE 8.7 *The figure and figcaption elements are used on this web page.*

```
figcaption { text-align: center;
             font-size: .8em;
             font-style: italic; }
```

 Hands-On Practice 8.3

In this Hands-On Practice you will use the figure and figcaption elements to create the web page that displays an image element with a text caption, as shown in Figure 8.8. Create a new folder named mycaption. Copy the myisland.jpg file from the student files chapter8/starters folder into the mycaption folder.

1. Launch a text editor and open the template file located at chapter1/template.html in the student files. Modify the title element. Save the file as index.html in your mycaption folder.

2. With the file open in the text editor, code the following HTML to configure a figure element that contains an image with a text caption (using the figcaption element).

```
<figure>
  <img src="myisland.jpg" width="480"
       height="320" alt="Tropical Island">
  <figcaption>
   Tropical Island Getaway
  </figcaption>
</figure>
```

FIGURE 8.8 *The figure and figcaption elements in action.*

Save the file and test it in a browser. You should see the image and text caption display.

3. Next, you'll code embedded CSS to give this page a little style. Add embedded CSS to the head section that configures the figure element selector to be 480 pixels wide, with a border, and with padding set to 5px. Configure the figcaption element selector to have centered text using the Papyrus font typeface (or the default Fantasy Family font). The code follows:

```
<style>
   figure { width: 480px;
            border: 1px solid #000000;
            padding: 5px; }
   figcaption { text-align: center;
                font-family: Papyrus, fantasy; }
</style>
```

Save the file as index.html in the mycaption folder. Launch a browser to test your page. It should look similar to the page shown in Figure 8.8. The student files contain a sample solution in the chapter8/8.3 folder.

Practice with Floating Figures

 Hands-On Practice 8.4 ─────────────────────────────────

FIGURE 8.9 *The images float in this web page.*

In this Hands-On Practice you will create the web page shown in Figure 8.9, which displays a group of images with captions.

You'll configure the images and their captions to float on the web page to fill the available space in the browser viewport. The display will change based on the size of the browser viewport.

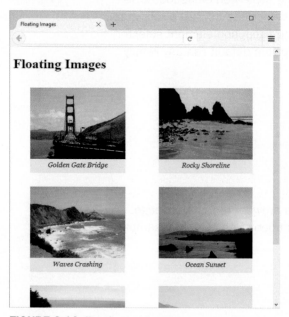

FIGURE 8.10 *The floated images move as the browser is resized.*

Figure 8.10 shows the same web page displayed in a browser that has been resized to be smaller.

Create a new folder named float8. Copy the following images from the student files chapter8/starters folder into the float8 folder: photo1.jpg, photo2.jpg, photo3.jpg, photo4.jpg, photo5.jpg, and photo6.jpg.

Launch a text editor and open the template file located at chapter1/template.html in the student files. Save the file as index.html in your float8 folder. Modify the file to configure a web page as indicated:

1. Configure the text, Floating Images, within an h1 element and the title element.

2. Code six figure elements, one for each image. Within each figure element, configure an image element and

a figcaption element with an appropriate text description of the image. An example of the first figure element follows:

```
<figure>
  <img src="photo1.jpg" alt="Golden Gate Bridge"
       width="225" height="168">
  <figcaption>Golden Gate Bridge</figcaption>
</figure>
```

3. Configure all six figure elements in a similar manner. Substitute the actual name of each image file for the `src` values in the code. Write your own descriptive text for each image. Use photo2.jpg in the second figure element, photo3.jpg in the third figure element, photo4.jpg in the fourth figure element, photo5.jpg in the fifth figure element, and photo6.jpg in the sixth figure element. Save the file. Display your page in a browser. Figure 8.11 shows a partial screen capture.

4. Now, let's add embedded CSS. Open your file in a text editor and code a style element in the head section. Configure the figure element selector to float to the left. Also set the width to 225 pixels, bottom padding to 10 pixels, and background color to light gray (#EAEAEA). Configure the figcaption element selector to display centered, italic text in the Georgia (or other serif) font. The CSS follows:

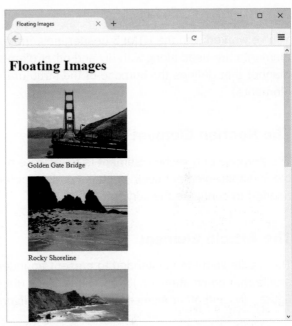

FIGURE 8.11 *The web page before CSS.*

```
figure { float: left;
         width: 225px;
         padding-bottom: 10px;
         background-color: #EAEAEA; }
figcaption { text-align: center;
             font-style: italic;
             font-family: Georgia, serif; }
```

Save your page and display it in a browser. Experiment with resizing the browser window to see the display change. Compare your work with Figures 8.9 and 8.10. A sample solution is in the student files (chapter8/8.4/index.html).

5. Next, let's explore an alternate approach to "floating" elements. Instead of using the float property, you'll set the display property to inline block. Launch a text editor and open the index.html file. Save the file with a new name, index2.html. Modify the embedded CSS by replacing the float: left; property with `display: inline-block;`. Save your page and display it in a browser. Experiment and see the display change. Compare your work with Figures 8.9 and 8.10. A sample solution is in the student files (chapter8/8.4/index2.html).

More HTML5 Elements

You've worked with the HTML5 header, nav, main, and footer elements throughout this book. These HTML5 elements are used along with div and other elements to structure web page documents in a meaningful manner that defines the purpose of the structural areas. In this section, you'll explore four more HTML5 elements.

The Section Element

The purpose of a **section element** is to indicate a "section" of a document, such as a chapter or topic. This block display element could contain header, footer, section, article, aside, figure, div, and other elements needed to configure the content.

The Article Element

The **article element** is intended to present an independent entry, such as a blog posting, comment, or e-zine article that could stand on its own. This block display element could contain header, footer, section, aside, figure, div, and other elements needed to configure the content.

The Aside Element

The **aside element** indicates a sidebar or other tangential content. This block display element could contain header, footer, section, aside, figure, div, and other elements needed to configure the content.

The Time Element

The **time element** represents a date or a time. An optional `datetime` attribute can be used to specify a calendar date and/or time in machine-readable format. Use YYYY-MM-DD for a date. Use a 24-hour clock and HH:MM for time. See http://www.w3.org/TR/html-markup/time.html.

 Hands-On Practice 8.5

In this Hands-On Practice you'll begin with the two-column Lighthouse Island Bistro home page (shown in Figure 8.7) and apply the section, article, aside, and time elements to create the page with blog postings shown in Figure 8.12.

Create a new folder named blog8. Copy the following files from the student files chapter8/caption folder into the blog8 folder: caption.html, lighthouseisland.jpg, and lighthouselogo.jpg.

Launch a text editor and open the caption.html file. Save the file as index.html. Examine the source code.

1. Locate the header element. Add the tagline "the best coffee on the coast" with a span element within the header element. Your code should look similar to the following

```
<header>
  <h1>Lighthouse Island
  Bistro</h1>
  <span>the best coffee on
  the coast</span>
</header>
```

2. Replace the contents of the main element with the following code:

```
<section>
<h2>Bistro Blog</h2>
<aside>Watch for the
March Madness Wrap next
month!</aside>
  <article>
    <header><h3>Valentine Wrap</h3></header>
    <time datetime="2018-02-01">February 1, 2018</time>
    <p>The February special sandwich is the Valentine Wrap &mdash;
    heart-healthy organic chicken with roasted red peppers on a
    whole wheat wrap.</p>
  </article>
  <article>
    <header><h3>New Coffee of the Day Promotion</h3></header>
    <time datetime="2018-01-12">January 12, 2018</time>
    <p>Enjoy the best coffee on the coast in the comfort of your
    home. We will feature a different flavor of our gourmet,
    locally roasted coffee each day with free bistro tastings and a
    discount on one-pound bags.</p>
  </article>
</section>
```

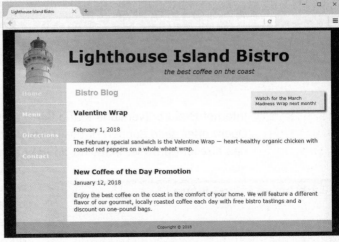

FIGURE 8.12 *This page utilizes the new elements.*

3. Configure CSS for the h1 and span elements within the header element at the top of the page. Use descendant HTML selectors. Set the h1 bottom margin to 0. Set the span with size .80em italic #00005D color text and 15em of left padding.

4. Configure CSS for the header element contained within each article element. Use a descendant HTML selector. Set background color to #FFFFFF, no background image, 100% font size, 0 left padding, and auto height (use `height: auto;`).

5. The aside element contains content that is tangential to the main content. Configure CSS to display the aside element on the right (use float) with width set to 15em, padding set to 1em, light gray background color, 80% font size, and a 5px box shadow. Configure a relative position 20 pixels from the top (use `position: relative;` `top: -20px;`).

Save your file. Display your index.html page in a browser. It should look similar to the page shown in Figure 8.12. A sample solution is in the student files (chapter8/8.5).

HTML5 Compatibility with Older Browsers

Internet Explorer (versions 9 and later) and current versions of Safari, Chrome, Firefox, and Opera offer good support of the HTML5 elements you've been using. However, not everyone has a recent browser installed on their computer. Some people still use earlier versions of browsers for a variety of reasons. Although this issue will decrease in importance over time as people update their computers, your clients will most likely insist that their web pages are usable to as broad of an audience as possible.

FIGURE 8.13 *Outdated browsers do not support HTML5.*

Figure 8.13 shows the web page you created in Hands-On Practice 8.5 displayed in the outdated Internet Explorer 7—it's quite different from the modern display shown in Figure 8.14. The most basic way to provide for backward compatibility of HTML5 with older, outdated browsers is to configure block display with CSS.

Configure CSS Block Display

Add one style rule to your CSS to inform older browsers to display HTML5 elements such as header, main, nav, footer, section, article, figure, figcaption, and aside as block display (with empty space above and below). Example CSS follows:

```
header, main, nav, footer, section, article, figure, figcaption, aside
{ display: block; }
```

This technique will work well in browsers including Internet Explorer 9 and later versions.

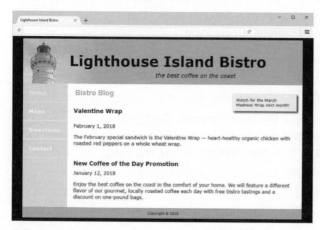

FIGURE 8.14 *Modern browsers support HTML5.*

 ### Hands-On Practice 8.6

In this Hands-On Practice you'll modify the two-column Lighthouse Island Bistro home page (shown in Figure 8.14) to provide backward compatibility with older browsers. Create a new folder named bistro8. Copy the index.html and lighthouselogo.jpg files from the student files chapter8/8.5 folder into the bistro8 folder.

1. Launch a text editor and open the index.html file. Examine the source code, and locate the head element and style element.

2. Add the following style declaration to the embedded styles:

```
header, main, nav, footer, section, article, figure, figcaption,
aside { display: block; }
```

Save your file. Display your index.html page in a modern browser. It should look similar to the page shown in Figure 8.14 in a modern browser. The solution is in the student files chapter8/8.6 folder.

The CSS technique you practiced in this section is just one basic solution to the problem of providing HTML5 backward compatibility in older browsers. Explore two other methods:

▶ The HTML5 Shiv (also referred to as the HTML5 Shim) was developed by Remy Sharp (http://remysharp.com/2009/01/07/html5-enabling-script) to enable HTML5 support by Internet Explorer 8 and earlier versions. The technique uses conditional comments that are only recognized by Internet Explorer and are ignored by other browsers. The conditional comments cause Internet Explorer to interpret JavaScript statements (see Chapter 11) that configure the browser to recognize and process CSS for the new HTML5 element selectors.

Sharp initially uploaded the HTML5 Shiv script to Google's code project but it was moved to GitHub at https://github.com/aFarkas/html5shiv, where it is maintained by Alexander Farkas. The script is freely available for download and use. No knowledge of JavaScript coding is needed to use the HTML5 Shiv. To apply the HTML5 Shiv you need to download the html5shiv.js file from GitHub into the same folder as your web pages and then include the following code in the head section of each web page:

```
<!--[if lt IE 9]>
    <script src="html5shiv.js"></script>
<![endif]-->
```

Visit the textbook's companion website at http://webdevbasics.net/4e/chapter8.html for more information about this technique.

▶ Modernizr (http://www.modernizr.com) is a free JavaScript library that includes the HTML5 Shiv and enables backward compatibility for HTML5 and CSS3 in older browsers by allowing you to check for specific HTML5 and CSS features. Modernizr is a detection tool. It's up to you whether you provide alternate CSS or even your own scripting when an HTML5 or CSS feature is detected. For this reason, it's a good idea to have some experience with JavaScript to fully utilize the power of Modernizr. You can find out more about Modernizr at the following resources:

* https://modernizr.com/docs
* http://www.hongkiat.com/blog/modernizr/
* https://www.youtube.com/watch?v=Vq3Hbf53cI0
* https://www.youtube.com/watch?v=D5UYPFDvryM

CSS for Print

Even though the "paperless society" has been talked about for decades, the fact is that many people still love paper, and you can expect your web pages to be printed. CSS offers you some control over what gets printed and how the printouts are configured. This is easy to do using external style sheets. Create one external style sheet with the configurations for browser display and a second external style sheet with the special printing configurations. Associate both of the external style sheets to the web page using two link elements. Configure a **media attribute** on each link element. Table 8.1 describes the values of the media attribute.

TABLE 8.1 *The* media *Attribute*

Value	Purpose
screen	The default value; indicates the style sheet that configures typical browser viewport display on a color computer screen
print	Indicates the style sheet that configures the printed formatting
handheld	Although this value is intended by the W3C to indicate the style sheet that configures display on handheld mobile devices, in practice, the attribute value is not reliably applied (see Return of the Mobile Stylesheet at http://www.alistapart.com/articles/return-of-the-mobile-stylesheet for more information). Methods for configuring the design of mobile web pages will be introduced later in this chapter

Modern browsers will use the correct style sheet depending on whether they are rendering a screen display or preparing to print a document. Use media="screen" to configure the link element for your browser display. Use media="print" to configure the link element for your printout. An example of the HTML is

```
<link rel="stylesheet" href="lighthouse.css" media="screen">
<link rel="stylesheet" href="lighthouseprint.css" media="print">
```

Print Styling Best Practices

You might be wondering how a print style sheet should differ from the CSS used to display the web page in a browser. Let's explore some commonly used techniques for styling printed web pages.

▶ **Hide Nonessential Content.**   It's common practice to prevent banner ads, navigation, or other extraneous areas from appearing on the printout. Use the display: none; style declaration to hide content that is not needed on a printout of the web page.

▶ **Configure Font Size and Color for Printing.**   Another common practice is to configure the font sizes on the print style sheet to use pt units. This will better control the text on the printout. You might also consider configuring the text color to black (#000000) if you envision the need for visitors to print your pages often. The default setting on most browsers prevent background colors and background images from printing, but you can also prevent background image and background color display in your print style sheet.

▶ **Control Page Breaks.**   Use the CSS `page-break-before` or `page-break-after` properties to control page breaks when printing the web page. Well-supported values for these properties are `always` (the page break will always occur as designated), `avoid` (if possible, the page break will not occur before or after, as designated), and `auto` (default). For example, to configure a page break at a specific point in the document (in this case, right before an element assigned to the class named `newpage`), configure the CSS as shown below:

```
.newpage { page-break-before: always; }
```

Hands-On Practice 8.7

In this Hands-On Practice you'll rework the Lighthouse Island Bistro home page (Figure 8.12) to use external style sheets and be configured for optimal screen display and printing. Create a new folder named print8. Copy the following files from the student files chapter8/8.5 folder into the print8 folder: index.html, lighthouseisland.jpg, and lighthouselogo.jpg.

1. Launch a text editor and open the index.html file. Examine the source code and locate the style element. Copy the CSS contained between the style tags and paste into a new text document named bistro.css. Save the bistro.css file in the print8 folder.

2. Edit the index.html file, delete the style tags and CSS, and code a link tag in the head section that associates the web page with the bistro.css file for screen display (use `media="screen"`).

3. Edit the index.html file and add another link tag that associates the web page with a file named bistroprint.css for printing (use `media="print"`). Save the index.html file.

4. Launch a text editor and open bistro.css. Since you want to keep most of the styles for printing, you will start by creating a new version of the external style sheet. Save bistro.css with the name of bistroprint.css in the ch8print folder. You will modify three areas on this style sheet: the header selector, the main selector, and the nav selector.

   ▶ Modify the header styles to print using black text in 20 point font size:
   ```
   header { color: #000000; font-size: 20pt; }
   ```

   ▶ Modify the main element area to print using a serif typeface in a 12 point font size:
   ```
   main { font-family: "Times New Roman", serif; font-size: 12pt; }
   ```

   ▶ Modify the navigation area to not display:
   ```
   nav { display: none; }
   ```
   Save your file in the print8 folder.

5. Test your work. Display your index.html file in a browser. Select Print > Preview. Your display should look similar to the page shown in Figure 8.15. The header and content font sizes have been configured. The navigation does not display. The student files contain a sample solution in the chapter8/8.7 folder.

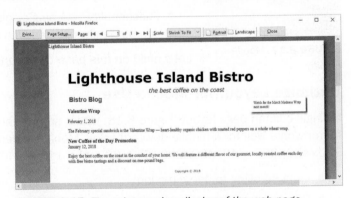

FIGURE 8.15 *The print preview display of the web page.*

Mobile Web Design

Chapter 3 introduced you to three methods that can be used to provide access for website visitors who use mobile devices. One option is to design and publish a second website with a .mobi TLD. Another option is to design and publish a separate website within your own domain that is optimized for mobile use. This technique is utilized by the White House website at http://www.whitehouse.gov and http://m.whitehouse.gov. The third option is to configure one website with separate styles for desktop browser (Figure 8.16) and mobile (Figure 8.17) display. Before we focus on coding, let's consider design techniques for the mobile web.

FIGURE 8.16 *Desktop browser display.*

Mobile Web Design Considerations

Mobile web users are typically on-the-go, need information quickly, and may be easily distracted. A web page that is optimized for mobile access should try to serve these needs. Take a moment to review Figures 8.15 and 8.16 and observe how the design of the mobile website addresses the design considerations discussed in Chapter 3:

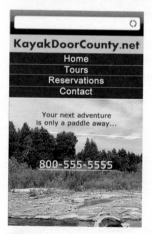

FIGURE 8.17 *Mobile display.*

▌ **Small screen size.**   The size of the header area is reduced to accommodate a small screen display.

▌ **Low bandwidth (slow connection speed).**   Note that a smaller image is displayed on the mobile version of the web page.

▌ **Font, color, and media issues.**   Common font typefaces are utilized. There is also good contrast between text and background color.

▌ **Awkward controls, and limited processor and memory.**   The mobile website uses a single-column page layout that facilitates keyboard tabbing and will be easy to control by touch. The page is mostly text, which will be quickly rendered by a mobile browser.

▌ **Functionality.**   A single-column layout is utilized with navigation areas that can be easily selected with a fingertip.

Let's build on this base of design considerations and expand them.

Optimize Layout for Mobile Use

A single-column page layout (Figure 8.18) with a small header, key navigation links, content, and page footer works well for a mobile device display. Mobile screen resolutions vary greatly (for example, 320×240, 320×480, 360×640, 480×800, 640×690, and 1136×640). W3C recommendations include the following:

▌ Limit scrolling to one direction.

▌ Use heading elements.

▌ Use lists to organize information (such as unordered lists, ordered lists, and description lists).

- Avoid using tables (see Chapter 9) because they typically force both horizontal and vertical scrolling on mobile devices.
- Provide labels for form controls (see Chapter 10).
- Avoid using pixel units in style sheets.
- Avoid absolute positioning in style sheets.
- Hide content that is not essential for mobile use.

FIGURE 8.18
Wireframe for a typical single-column page layout.

Optimize Navigation for Mobile Use

Easy-to-use navigation is crucial on a mobile device. The W3C recommends the following:

- Provide minimal navigation near the top of the page.
- Provide consistent navigation.
- Avoid hyperlinks that open files in new windows or pop-up windows.
- Try to balance both the number of hyperlinks on a page and the number of levels of links needed to access information.

Optimize Graphics for Mobile Use

Graphics can help to engage visitors, but be aware of the following W3C recommendations for mobile use:

- Avoid displaying images that are wider than the screen width (assume a 320 pixel screen width on a smartphone display).
- Configure alternate small, optimized background images.
- Some mobile browsers will downsize all images, so images with text can be difficult to read.
- Avoid the use of large graphic images.
- Specify the size of images.
- Provide alternate text for graphics and other nontext elements.

Optimize Text for Mobile Use

It can be difficult to read text on a small mobile device. The following W3C recommendations will aid your mobile visitors:

- Configure good contrast between text and background colors.
- Use common font typefaces.
- Configure font size with em units or percentages.
- Use a short, descriptive page title.

The W3C has published Mobile Web Best Practices 1.0, a list of 60 mobile web design best practices, at http://www.w3.org/TR/mobile-bp. Flipcards that summarize the Mobile Web Best Practices 1.0 document are available at http://www.w3.org/2007/02/mwbp_flip_cards.html.

Design for One Web

The W3C mission of building "**One Web**" refers to the concept of providing a single resource that is configured for optimal display on multiple types of devices. This is more efficient than creating multiple versions of a web document. With "One Web" in mind, the next sections introduce using the viewport meta tag and CSS media queries to target and deliver style sheets that are optimized for mobile display.

Viewport Meta Tag

There are multiple uses for meta tags. You've used the meta tag since Chapter 1 to configure the character encoding on a web page. In this section we'll explore the new **viewport meta tag**, which was created as an Apple extension that helps with displays on mobile devices such as iPhones and Android smartphones by setting the width and scale of the viewport. Figure 8.19 shows the display of a web page in a desktop browser.

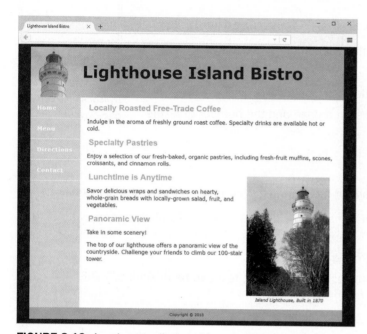

FIGURE 8.19 *A web page displayed in a desktop browser.*

Figure 8.20 displays a screen shot of the same web page displayed on an Android device. Examine Figure 8.20 and notice that the mobile device zoomed out to display the entire web page on the tiny screen. The text on the web page is difficult to read.

Figure 8.21 shows the same web page after the viewport meta tag was added to the head section of the document. Setting the `initial-scale` directive to the value 1 caused the mobile browser to avoid zooming out on the web page and to display it in a more usable manner. The code is shown below:

```
<meta name="viewport"
content="width=device-width,
initial-scale=1.0">
```

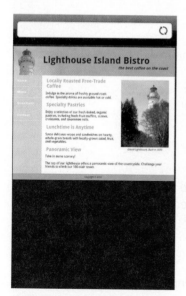

FIGURE 8.20 *Mobile display of a web page without the viewport meta tag.*

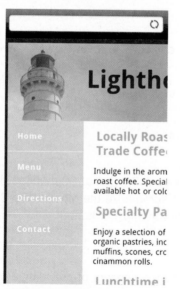

FIGURE 8.21 *The viewport meta tag helps with mobile display.*

Code the viewport meta tag with the HTML `name="viewport"` and `content` attributes. The value of the HTML `content` attribute can be one or more **directives** (also referred to as properties by Apple), such as the `device-width` directive and directives that control zooming and scale. Table 8.2 lists viewport meta tag directives and their values.

Now that you've scaled the page to be readable, what about styling it for optimal mobile use? That's where CSS comes into play. You'll explore CSS Media Queries in the next section.

TABLE 8.2 *Viewport Meta Tag Directives*

Directive	Values	Purpose
width	Numeric value or `device-width` which indicates actual width of the device screen	The width of the viewport in pixels
height	Numeric value or `device-height` which indicates actual height of the device screen	The height of the viewport in pixels
initial-scale	Numeric multiplier; Set to 1 for 100% initial scale	Initial scale of the viewport
minimum-scale	Numeric multiplier; Mobile Safari default is 0.25	Minimum scale of the viewport
maximum-scale	Numeric multiplier; Mobile Safari default is 1.6	Maximum scale of the viewport
user-scalable	`yes` allows scaling, `no` disables scaling	Determines whether a user can zoom in or out

If a web page displays a phone number, wouldn't it be handy for a person using a smartphone to be able to tap on the phone number and place a call or send an SMS (short message service) text message? It's very easy to configure a telephone hyperlink or SMS hyperlink for use by smartphones.

According to RFC 3966, you can configure a telephone hyperlink by using a telephone scheme: Begin the `href` value with `tel:` followed by the phone number. For example, to configure a telephone hyperlink on a web page for use by mobile browsers, code as follows:

```
<a href="tel:888-555-5555">Call 888-555-5555</a>
```

RFC 5724 indicates that an SMS scheme hyperlink intended to send a text message can be configured by beginning the `href` value with `sms:` followed by the phone number, as shown in the following code:

```
<a href="sms:888-555-5555">Text 888-555-5555</a>
```

Not all mobile browsers and devices support telephone and text hyperlinks, but expect increased use of this technology in the future. You'll get a chance to practice using the `tel:` scheme in Chapter 8 case study.

CSS3 Media Queries

Recall from Chapter 3 that the term **responsive web design** refers to progressively enhancing a web page for different viewing contexts (such as smartphones and tablets) through the use of coding techniques including fluid layouts, flexible images, and media queries.

For examples of the power of responsive web design techniques, review Figures 3.44, 3.45, 3.46, and 3.47, which are actually the same .html web page file that was configured with CSS to display differently, depending on the viewport size detected by media queries. Also visit the Media Queries website at http://mediaqueri.es to view a gallery of sites that demonstrate responsive web design. The screen captures in the gallery show web pages displayed with the following browser viewport widths: 320px (smartphone display), 768px (tablet portrait display), 1024px (netbook display and tablet landscape display), and 1600px (large desktop display).

What's a Media Query?

According to the W3C (http://www.w3.org/TR/css3-mediaqueries) a **media query** is made up of a media type (such as screen) and a logical expression that determines the capability of the device that the browser is running on, such as screen resolution and orientation (portrait or landscape). When the media query evaluates as true, the media query directs browsers to CSS you have coded and configured specifically for those capabilities. Media queries are supported by current versions of major browsers, including Internet Explorer (version 9 and later).

FIGURE 8.22 *CSS media queries help to configure the page for mobile display.*

Media Query Example Using a Link Element

Figure 8.22 shows the same web page as Figure 8.21, but it looks quite different because of a link element that includes a media query and is associated with a style sheet configured for optimal mobile display on a popular smartphone. The HTML is shown below:

```
<link href="lighthousemobile.css" rel="stylesheet"
      media="only screen and (max-width: 480px)">
```

The code sample above will direct browsers to an external stylesheet that has been configured for optimal display on the most popular smartphones. The media type value `only` is a keyword that will hide the media query from outdated browsers. The media type value `screen` targets devices with screens. Commonly used media types and keywords are listed in Table 8.3.

The `max-width` media feature is set to 480px. While there are many different screen sizes for smartphones these days, a maximum width of 480px will target the display size of many popular models. A media query may test for both minimum and maximum values. For example,

```
<link href="lighthousetablet.css" rel="stylesheet"
      media="only screen and (min-width: 768px) and (max-width: 1024px)">
```

TABLE 8.3 *Media Types*

Media Type	Value Purpose
all	All devices
screen	Screen display of web page
only	Causes older nonsupporting browsers to ignore the media query
print	Printout of web page

Media Query Example Using an `@media` Rule

A second method of using media queries is to code them directly in your CSS using an **@media rule**. Begin by coding `@media` followed by the media type and logical expression. Then enclose the desired CSS selector(s) and declaration(s) within a pair of braces. The sample code below configures a different background image specifically for smartphone display.

```
@media only screen and (max-width: 480px) {
  header { background-image: url(mobile.gif);
  }
}
```

Table 8.4 lists commonly used media query features.

TABLE 8.4 *Commonly Used Media Query Features*

Features	Values	Criteria
max-device-height	Numeric value	The height of the screen size of the output device in pixels is smaller or equal to the value
max-device-width	Numeric value	The width of the screen size of the output device in pixels is smaller or equal to the value
min-device-height	Numeric value	The height of the screen size of the output device in pixels is greater than or equal to the value
min-device-width	Numeric value	The width of the screen size of the output device in pixels is greater than or equal to the value
max-height	Numeric value	The height of the viewport in pixels is smaller than or equal to the value; (reevaluated when screen is resized)
min-height	Numeric value	The height of the viewport in pixels is greater than or equal to the value; (reevaluated when screen is resized)
max-width	Numeric value	The width of the viewport in pixels is smaller than or equal to the value; (reevaluated when screen is resized)
min-width	Numeric value	The width of the viewport in pixels is greater than or equal to the value; (reevaluated when screen is resized)
orientation	portrait or landscape	The orientation of the device

Practice with Media Queries

Hands-On Practice 8.8

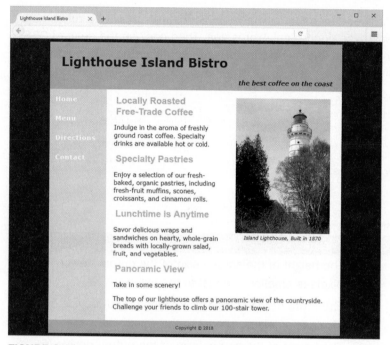

FIGURE 8.23 *The two-column desktop display.*

In this Hands-On Practice, you'll rework a version of the two-column Lighthouse Island Bistro home page (Figure 8.23) to display a single-column page when the viewport size is a maximum of 1024 pixels (a typical tablet display) and display a page further optimized for smartphone display when the viewport size is 768 pixels or smaller.

Create a folder named query8. Copy the starter2.html file from the chapter8 folder into the query8 folder and rename it as index.html. Copy the lighthouseisland.jpg file from the student files chapter8/starters folder into the query8 folder.

Launch a browser and view index.html as shown in Figure 8.23. Open index.html in a text editor. Review the embedded CSS and note that the two-column layout is fluid with an 80% width. The two-column look is accomplished by configuring a nav element that floats to the left.

1. Edit the embedded CSS to configure styles for a typical tablet display. Add the following `@media` rule after the existing style rules but before the ending style tag. The `@media` rule will configure styles that take effect when the viewport size is 1024 pixels or smaller: eliminate the left margin on the main element and change the float and width properties configured for the nav element selector. The CSS follows:

```
@media only screen and (max-width: 1024px) {
      main { margin-left: 0; }
      nav { float: none;
            width: auto; }
}
```

Save the index.html file. Test your index.html file in a desktop browser.

When the browser is maximized, the page should look similar to Figure 8.23.

When you resize the browser to be smaller (with less than or equal to 1024 pixels), the page should look similar to Figure 8.24 with a single-column layout. As you can see, we still have some work to do.

2. Continue editing the embedded CSS to configure display for a typical tablet. To allocate the entire viewport to the webpage, add style rules within the media query that remove the margin on the body element selector, and expand the wrapper id.

Create a horizontal navigation area by configuring the nav area li elements with `inline-block` display and padding, the nav area ul elements with centered text, and the nav area anchor elements with no border.

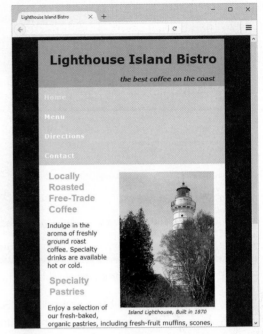

FIGURE 8.24 *The media query has been applied.*

Also set h1 elements with 120% font size, h2 elements with 120% font size, and p elements with 90% font size. The CSS follows:

```
@media only screen and (max-width: 1024px) {
  body { margin: 0; }
  #wrapper { width: auto; }
  main { margin-left: 0; }
  nav { float: none;
        width: auto; }
  nav li { display: inline-block;
           padding: 0.5em; }
  nav ul { text-align: center; }
  nav a { border-style: none;}
  h1, h2 { font-size: 120%; }
  p { font-size: 90%; }
}
```

Save the index.html file. Test your index.html file in a desktop browser.

When the browser is maximized, the page should look similar to Figure 8.23.

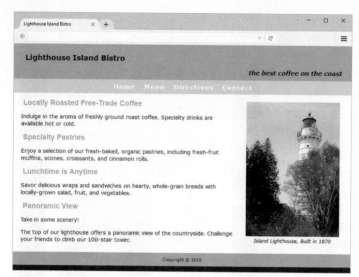

FIGURE 8.25 *Configured for a typical tablet.*

When you resize the browser to be smaller (a width less than or equal to 1024 pixels), the page should look similar to Figure 8.25.

Continue to resize the web page and notice that the navigation hyperlinks will shift and are not well aligned. We still have more work to do to optimize the page for display on small mobile devices.

3. Edit the embedded CSS to configure styles for a typical smartphone device. Note that the styles you have already coded in Step 2 will be rendered by the browser for any device with a `max-width` less than or equal to 1024 pixels (this includes tablets and smartphones). Next, you need to configure additional styles to configure the display needed for smaller devices with a `max-width` less than or equal to 768 pixels.

To optimize the display on typical smartphone devices: configure styles to prevent the figure element from displaying, decrease the font size for h1, h2, and span elements, and configure vertical navigation that is easy to select by touch (eliminate padding in the navigation area, configure li and anchor elements with block display, configure anchor elements with top padding, bottom padding, and a border). The CSS follows:

```
@media only screen and (max-width: 768px) {
    h1, h2 { font-size: 100%; }
    span { font-size: 80%; }
    figure { display: none;}
    nav, nav ul, nav li { padding: 0; }
    nav li { display: block; }
    nav a { display: block;
            padding: 0.5em 0;
            border-bottom: 2px ridge #00005D; }
}
```

Save the index.html file. Test your index.html file in a desktop browser.

When the browser is maximized, the page should look similar to Figure 8.23.

When you resize the browser to be smaller (width equal to or less than 1024 pixels and greater than 768 pixels), the page should look similar to Figure 8.25 with a single-column layout.

FIGURE 8.26 *Typical smartphone display.*

When you resize the browser to be even smaller (width equal to or less than 768 pixels) the page should look similar to Figure 8.26. The web page you've created is an example of applying responsive web design techniques. The student files contain a suggested solution in the chapter8/8.8 folder.

What values should I use in my media queries?

There is no single correct way to configure a media query. When web developers first began writing media queries there were very few mobile devices and they could be targeted with pixel-perfect precision. While this is no longer the case, web developers often use the `max-width` and/ or `min-width` features to determine the size of the viewport being used. Here is a typical media query to target a typical smartphone display which checks for a `max-width` value of 480 pixels:.

```
@media only screen and (max-width: 480px) {
}
```

If you'd like to specifically target the size of a common tablet display, check for width between 768 pixels and 1024 pixels. Example:

```
@media only screen and (min-width: 768px) and (max-width: 1024px) {
}
```

Today there are hundreds of mobile devices with varied screen resolutions, so a modern approach is to focus on the responsive display of your content and then configure media queries with em units as needed for your content to reflow on a variety of screen sizes. You will need to test your responsive web pages to find the best choices for your specific content.

Michael Barrett (http://abouthalf.com/development/ems-in-css-media-queries/) suggests targeting smartphone display with `max-width: 37.5em`, tablet display with `min-width: 37.5em` and `max-width: 64em`, and desktop display with `min-width: 64em`. Using this approach, a media query to target a typical smartphone would check for a `max-width` feature value of 37.5em units. Example:

```
@media only screen and (max-width: 37.5em) {
}
```

Testing on a variety of screen sizes is very useful when configuring media queries. Smartphones with large screens may satisfy the typical tablet media query—that's OK—you've optimized the display for some type of mobile touch device. Be flexible and prepared to adjust media query pixel and em values to best display the content of your website on smartphones, tablets, and desktops.

Visit the following resources for more information about media query breakpoints and viewport sizes:

- http://css-tricks.com/snippets/css/media-queries-for-standard-devices
- http://viewportsizes.com/
- https://css-tricks.com/snippets/css/retina-display-media-query/
- https://developers.google.com/web/fundamentals/layouts/rwd-fundamentals/how-to-choose-breakpoints

Flexible Images with CSS

In his book, *Responsive Web Design*, Ethan Marcotte described a **flexible image** as a fluid image that will not break the page layout as the browser viewport is resized. Flexible images (often referred to as **responsive images**), along with fluid layouts and media queries, are the components of responsive web design. You will be introduced to several different coding techniques to configure responsive images in this chapter.

The most widely supported technique to configure an image as flexible requires a change to the HTML and additional CSS to style the flexible image.

1. Edit the img elements in the HTML. Remove the `height` and `width` attributes.
2. Configure the `max-width: 100%;` style declaration in the CSS. If the width of the image is less than the width of the container element, the image will display with its actual dimensions. If the width of the image is greater than the width of the container element, the image will be resized by the browser to fit in the container (instead of hanging out over the margin).
3. To keep the dimensions of the image in proportion and maintain the aspect ratio of the image, Bruce Lawson suggests to also set the `height: auto;` style declaration in the CSS (see http://brucelawson.co.uk/2012/responsive-web-design-preserving-images-aspect-ratio).

Background images can also be configured for a more fluid display at various viewport sizes. Although it's common to code a `height` property when configuring a background image with CSS, the result is a somewhat nonresponsive background image. Explore configuring other CSS properties for the container such as `font-size`, `line-height`, and `padding` in percentage values. The `background-size: cover;` property can also be useful. You'll typically see a more pleasing display of the background image in various-sized viewports. Another option is to configure different image files to use for backgrounds and use media queries to determine which background image is displayed. A disadvantage to this option is that multiple files are downloaded although only one file is displayed. You'll apply flexible image techniques in the next Hands-On Practice.

Hands-On Practice 8.9

In this Hands-On Practice you'll work with a web page that demonstrates responsive web design. Figure 8.27 depicts the three-column desktop browser display and demonstrates the effects of media queries which are configured to display a two-column page when the viewport size is 1024 pixels or smaller (a tablet portrait display) and display a single-column page optimized for smartphone display when the viewport size is 480 pixels or smaller. You will edit the CSS to configure flexible images.

Create a folder named flexible8. Copy the starter3.html file from the chapter8 folder into the flexible8 folder and rename it index.html. Copy the following images from the student files chapter8/starters folder into the flexible8 folder: header.jpg and pools.jpg. Launch a browser and view index.html as shown in Figure 8.28. View the code in a text editor and notice that the `height` and `width` attributes have already been removed from the HTML.

View the CSS and notice that the web page uses a fluid layout with percentage values for widths. Edit the embedded CSS.

FIGURE 8.27 *The web page demonstrates responsive web design techniques.*

1. Locate the h1 element selector. Remove the height style declaration. Add declarations to set the font size to 300%, top padding 5%, bottom padding 5%, 0 left padding, and 0 right padding. The CSS follows:

```
h1 { text-align: center;
     font-size: 300%;
     padding: 5% 0;
     text-shadow: 3px 3px
     3px #F4E8BC; }
```

2. Locate the header element selector. Add the `background-size: cover;` declaration to cause the browser to scale the background image to fill the container. The CSS follows:

```
header { background-image: url(header.jpg);
         background-repeat: no-repeat;
         background-size: cover; }
```

3. Add a style rule for the img element selector that sets maximum width to 100% and height to the value auto. The CSS follows:

```
img { max-width: 100%;
      height: auto; }
```

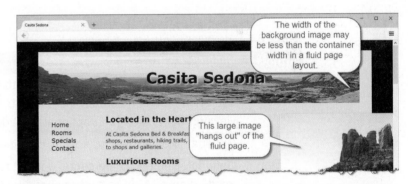

FIGURE 8.28 *The web page before the images are configured to be flexible.*

4. Save the index.html file. Test your index.html file in a desktop browser. As you resize the browser window, you'll see your page respond and look similar to the screen captures in Figure 8.27. The web page demonstrates responsive web design with the following techniques: fluid layout, media queries, and flexible images. A suggested solution is in the student files chapter8/8.9 folder.

Picture Element

New to HTML5.1 (http://www.w3.org/TR/html51) and in Candidate Recommendation status at the time this text was written, the purpose of the **picture element** is to provide a method for a browser to display different images depending on specific criteria indicated by the web developer. At the current time the picture element is supported by recent versions of Firefox, Chrome, Safari, Opera, and Edge. Check http://caniuse.com/picture for the current level of browser support. The picture element begins with the `<picture>` tag and ends with the `</picture>` tag. The picture element is a container element that is coded along with source elements and a fallback img element to provide multiple image files that can be chosen for display by the browser.

Source Element

The **source element** is a self-contained, or void, tag that is used together with a container element. The picture element is one of several elements (see the video and audio elements in Chapter 11) that can contain one or more source elements. When used with a picture element, multiple source elements are typically configured to specify different images. Code the source elements between the opening and closing picture tags. Table 8.5 lists attributes of the source element when coded within a picture element container.

TABLE 8.5 *Attributes of the Source Element*

Attribute	Value
srcset	Required. Provides image choices for the browser in a comma-separated list. Each item can contain the image URL (required), optional maximum viewport dimension, and optional pixel density for high resolution devices.
media	Optional. Media query to specify conditions for browser display.
sizes	Optional. Numeric or percentage value to specify the dimensions of the image display. May be further configured with a media query.

There are many potential ways to configure responsive images with the picture and source elements. We will focus on a basic technique that uses the media attribute to specify conditions for display.

 Hands-On Practice 8.10 ———————————————————

In this Hands-On Practice you will configure responsive images with the picture, source, and img elements as you create the page shown in Figure 8.29.

FIGURE 8.29 *Responsive image with the picture element.*

Create a new folder named ch8picture. Copy the large.jpg, medium.jpg, small.jpg, and fallback.jpg files from the chapter 8/starters folder into your ch8picture folder. Launch a text editor and open the template file located at chapter1/template.html in the student files. Save the file as index.html in your ch8picture folder. Modify the file to configure a web page as indicated:

1. Configure the text, Picture Element, within an h1 element and within the title element.

2. Code the following in the body of the web page:

```
<picture>
    <source media="(min-width: 1200px)" srcset="large.jpg">
    <source media="(min-width: 800px)" srcset="medium.jpg">
    <source media="(min-width: 320px)" srcset="small.jpg">
    <img src="fallback.jpg" alt="waterwheel">
</picture>
```

Save your file and test your page in a current version of Firefox or Chrome. Notice how a different image is displayed depending on the width of the browser viewport. If the viewport's minimum width is 1200px or greater, the large.jpg image is shown. If the viewport's minimum width is 800px or greater but less than 1200px, the medium.jpg image is displayed. If the viewport's minimum width is 320px greater but less than 800px, the small.jpg image is shown. If none of these criteria are met, the fallback.jpg image should be displayed.

As you test, try resizing and refreshing the browser display. You may need to resize the browser, close it, and launch it again to test for display of the different images. Browsers that do not support the new picture element will process the img tag and display the fallback.jpg image. A suggested solution is in the student files chapter8/8.10 folder.

This Hands-On Practice provided a very basic example of responsive images with the picture element. The picture and element responsive image technique is intended to eliminate multiple image downloads that can occur with CSS flexible image techniques. The browser downloads only the image it chose to display based on the criteria provided.

Responsive Img Element Attributes

New to HTML5.1 (http://www.w3.org/TR/html51) and in Candidate Recommendation status at the time this text was written, the new srcset and sizes attributes have been created for the img element. At the current time the new attributes are supported by recent versions of Firefox, Chrome, Opera, Safari, and Edge. Check http://caniuse.com/srcset for the current level of browser support.

The sizes Attribute

The purpose of the img element's **sizes attribute** is to inform the browser as it processes the srcset attribute about how much of the viewport should be used to display the image. The default value of the sizes attribute is 100vw, which indicates 100% of the viewport width is available to display the image. The value of the sizes attribute can be a percentage of the viewport width or a specific pixel width (such as 400px). The sizes attribute can also contain one or more media queries along with the width for each condition.

The srcset Attribute

The purpose of the img element's **srcset attribute** is to provide a method for a browser to display different images depending on specific criteria indicated by the web developer. The value of the srcset attribute provides image choices for the browser in a comma-separated list. Each list item can contain the image URL (required), optional maximum viewport dimension, and optional pixel density for high resolution devices.

There are many potential ways to configure responsive images with the img element, sizes, attribute, and srcset attribute. We will focus on a basic technique that uses the browser viewport dimension to specify conditions for display.

 Hands-On Practice 8.11

In this Hands-On Practice you will configure responsive images with the picture, source, and img elements as you create the page shown in Figure 8.30.

Create a new folder named ch7image. Copy the large.jpg, medium.jpg, small.jpg, and fallback.jpg files from the chapter7/starters folder into your ch7image folder. Launch a text editor and open the template file located at chapter1/template.html in the student files. Save the file as index.html in your ch7image folder. Modify the file to configure a web page as indicated:

1. Configure the text, Img Element, within an h1 element and within the title element.

FIGURE 8.30 *Responsive image with the image element's srcset attribute.*

2. Code the following in the body of the web page:

```
<img src="fallback.jpg"
   sizes="100vw"
   srcset="large.jpg 1200w, medium.jpg 800w, small.jpg 320w"
   alt="waterwheel">
```

Save your file and test your page in a current version of Firefox or Chrome. Notice how a different image is displayed depending on the width of the browser viewport. If the viewport's minimum width is 1200px or greater, the large.jpg image is shown. If the viewport's minimum width is 800px or greater but less than 1200px, the medium.jpg image is displayed. If the viewport's minimum width is 320px greater but less than 800px, the small.jpg image is shown. If none of these criteria are met, the fallback.jpg image should be displayed.

As you test, try resizing and refreshing the browser display. You may need to resize the browser, close it, and launch it again to test for display of the different images. Browsers that do not support the image element's new sizes and srcset attributes will ignore these attributes and display the fallback.jpg image. A suggested solution is in the student files chapter8/8.11 folder.

This Hands-On Practice provided a very basic example of responsive images with the img element and new sizes and srcset attributes which (like the picture element responsive image technique) is intended to eliminate multiple image downloads that can occur with CSS flexible image techniques. The browser downloads only the image it chose to display based on the criteria provided.

There is so much to learn about responsive image techniques! Visit the following resources to explore the topic of responsive images:

▶ http://responsiveimages.org

▶ http://html5hub.com/html5-picture-element

▶ http://www.sitepoint.com/improving-responsive-images-picture-element

▶ https://longhandpixels.net/blog/2014/02/complete-guide-picture-element

▶ http://blog.cloudfour.com/responsive-images-101-part-5-sizes

▶ http://blog.cloudfour.com/responsive-images-101-part-4-srcset-width-descriptors

Testing Mobile Display

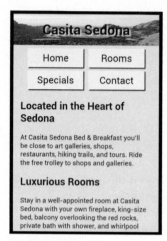

FIGURE 8.31 *Testing the web page with a smartphone.*

The best way to test the mobile display of a web page is to publish it to the Web and access it from a mobile device, as shown in Figure 8.31. (See Chapter 12 for an introduction to publishing a website with FTP.)

However, not everyone has access to a smartphone. Several options for emulating a mobile display are listed below:

▶ **Opera Mobile Classic Emulator** (shown in Figure 8.32)

Windows, Mac, and Linux download; supports media queries

http://www.opera.com/developer/mobile-emulator

▶ **iPhone Emulator**

Runs in a browser window; supports media queries

http://www.testiphone.com

▶ **iPadPeek**

Runs in a browser window; supports media queries

http://ipadpeek.com

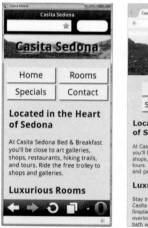

FIGURE 8.32

Testing a web page with the Opera Mobile Emulator.

FIGURE 8.33

Approximating the mobile display with a desktop browser.

Testing with a Desktop Browser

If you don't have a smartphone and/or are unable to publish your files to the Web—no worries—as you've seen in this chapter (also see Figure 8.33) you can approximate the mobile display of your web page using a desktop browser. Verify the placement of your media queries.

▶ If you have coded media queries within your CSS, display your page in a desktop browser and then reduce the width and height of the viewport until it approximates a mobile screen size (such as 320×480).

▶ If you have coded media queries within a link tag, edit the web page and temporarily modify the link tag to point to your mobile CSS style sheet. Then, display your page in a desktop browser and reduce the width and height of the viewport until it approximates a mobile screen size (such as 320×480).

Determining the Browser Viewport Size

It can be helpful to know the size of your browser viewport as you are testing a responsive web page. The following tools can help you determine your browser viewport size:

▶ **Chris Pederick's Web Developer Extension**

 Available for Firefox and Chrome

 http://chrispederick.com/work/web-developer

 Select Resize > Display Window Size

▶ **Viewport Dimensions Extension**

 Available for Chrome at https://github.com/CSWilson/Viewport-Dimensions

Responsive Testing Tools

How about an instant view of your web page in a variety of screen sizes and devices? Check out the following free online tools:

▶ Am I Responsive: http://ami.responsivedesign.is

▶ DevicePonsive: http://deviceponsive.com

▶ Responsive Test: http://responsivetest.net

▶ Screenfly: http://quirktools.com/screenfly

▶ Responsive Design Checker: http://responsivedesignchecker.com

For Serious Developers Only

If you are a software developer or information systems major, you may want to explore the SDKs (Software Development Kits) for the iOS and Android platforms. Each SDK includes a mobile device emulator.

▶ **Xcode** (Mac only)

 https://itunes.apple.com/us/app/xcode/id497799835

▶ **Android Studio**

 http://developer.android.com/sdk/index.html

This section provided an introduction to mobile web design. The styles for desktop browser viewing were coded and the media queries were constructed to adapt the layout for mobile devices. This is a typical workflow when you need to rework an existing website for mobile device display.

However, if you are designing a new website, there is an alternate approach that was first proposed by Luke Wroblewski. Design the mobile style sheet first and then develop alternate styles for tablet and/or desktop browsers that progressively enhance the design with multiple columns and larger images. You can find out more about this "Mobile First" approach at the following resources:

▶ http://www.lukew.com/ff/entry.asp?933

▶ http://www.lukew.com/ff/entry.asp?1137

▶ http://www.techradar.com/news/internet/mobile-web-design-tips-mobile-should-come-first-719677

Review and Apply

Review Questions

Multiple Choice. Choose the best answer for each item.

1. Which meta tag is used to configure display for mobile devices?

   a. viewport

   b. handheld

   c. mobile

   d. screen

2. Which of the following is the attribute used to indicate whether the style sheet is for printing or for screen display?

   a. `rel`   **b.** `type`

   c. `media`   **d.** `content`

3. How would you link to the named fragment `#jobs` on the page employ.html from the home page of the site?

   a. `<a name="employ.html#jobs">Jobs</a>`

   b. `<a href="employ.html#jobs">Jobs</a>`

   c. `<a link="employ.html#jobs">Jobs</a>`

   d. `<a href="#jobs">Jobs</a>`

4. Which of the following is a container element that is coded along with source elements and a fallback img element to provide multiple image files that can be chosen for display by the browser?

   a. photo   **b.** picture

   c. figure   **d.** sourceset

5. Which of the following attributes define a fragment identifier on a page?

   a. `bookmark`

   b. `fragment`

   c. `href`

   d. `id`

6. Which of the following is an HTML5 element that contains tangential content?

   a. header

   b. sidebar

   c. nav

   d. aside

7. Which of the following is a mobile web design best practice?

   a. Embed text in images wherever possible.

   b. Configure a single-column page layout.

   c. Configure a multiple-column page layout.

   d. Avoid using lists to organize information.

8. Which of the following font units is recommended for mobile display?

   a. pt unit

   b. px unit

   c. cm unit

   d. em unit

9. When using CSS media queries, code the _____ keyword to hide the query from older nonsupporting browsers.

   a. `modern`

   b. `screen`

   c. `only`

   d. `print`

10. Which of the following is an HTML5 element used to present an independent entry, such as a blog posting or comment that could stand on its own?

    a. section

    b. article

    c. aside

    d. content

Hands-On Exercises

1. Write the HTML to create a fragment identifier designated by `"main"` to indicate the main content area of a web page document.

2. Write the HTML to create a hyperlink to the named fragment designated by `main`.

3. Write the HTML to associate a web page with an external style sheet named myprint.css to configure a printout.

4. Write the CSS to configure a media query that triggers when the screen size is 1024 pixels or less.

5. Create a web page about your favorite hobby, movie, or music group. Include the following HTML5 elements: header, nav, main, figure, figcaption, article, and footer. Configure the text, color, and layout with CSS.

6. Modify the web page you created in Hands-On Exercise 5 to apply components of responsive web design to display well on both desktop and smartphone browsers. *Hint*: Add the viewport meta tag, configure flexible images, and edit the CSS to configure a media query with appropriate style rules for typical smartphone device display.

Focus on Web Design

As you read about mobile web design best practices in this chapter, you may have noticed some overlap with techniques that provide for accessibility, such as alternate text and use of headings. Explore the Web Content Accessibility and Mobile Web document at http://www.w3.org/WAI/mobile. Explore related links that interest you. Write a one-page, double-spaced summary that describes areas of overlap and how web developers can support both accessibility and mobile devices.

Pacific Trails Resort Case Study

In this chapter's case study you will use the existing Pacific Trails (Chapter 7) website as a starting point to create a new version of the website that utilizes media queries to configure display for mobile devices. Figure 8.34 displays wireframes for desktop browser, typical tablet screen, and typical smartphone screen display. When you have finished, the website will look the same in desktop browsers (see Figures 7.43 and 8.35). The mobile displays should be similar to the screen captures in Figure 8.35.

You have five tasks in this case study:

1. Create a new folder for the Pacific Trails Resort website.

2. Edit the pacific.css external style sheet to include media queries and styles needed for appropriate desktop, tablet, and smartphone display.

FIGURE 8.34 *Pacific Trails wireframes.*

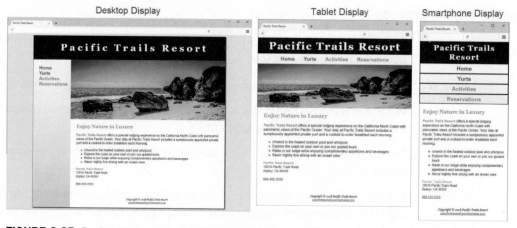

FIGURE 8.35 *Resize the browser window to approximate the new tablet and smartphone display.*

3. Edit the Home page (index.html).

4. Edit the Yurts page (yurts.html).

5. Edit the Activities page (activities.html).

Task 1: Create a folder called ch8pacific to contain your Pacific Trails Resort website files. Copy the files from the Chapter 7 Case Study ch7pacific folder into the ch8pacific folder.

Task 2: Configure the CSS. Launch a text editor and open the pacific.css external style sheet file.

   a. **Configure Support of HTML5.** Add the following style rule to configure most older browsers to render HTML5 block display elements as expected.

```
header, main, nav, footer, figure, figcaption, aside, section,
article { display: block; }
```

   b. **Configure Desktop Display.** Code the following new styles

      1. **The mobile id.** Set display to none. You'll apply this id when you edit the home page (index.html).

      2. **The desktop id.** Set display to inline. You'll apply this id later when you edit the home page (index.html).

   c. **Configure Tablet Display.**

      1. Code a media query below the existing styles to select for typical tablet device viewport size.

```
@media only screen and (max-width: 64em) {
}
```

      2. Configure the following new styles within the media query:

         a. **The body element selector.** Set margin to 0 and the background color to #FFFFFF;.

         b. **The wrapper id selector.** Set minimum width to 0, width to auto, box-shadow to none, and border to none.

         c. **The header element selector.** Set top padding to 0.5em, bottom padding to 0.5em, and left padding to 0. Set height to auto.

         d. **The h1 element selector.** Set letter-spacing to 0.1em.

e. **The main element selector.** Set left margin to 0.

f. **The nav element selector.** Eliminate float (*Hint*: Use `float: none;`), set the width to auto, centered text, and configure 0.5em padding.

g. **Navigation list items.** Use a descendant selector to configure li elements within the navigation area with inline display, 0.25em top and bottom padding, and 0.75em left and right padding.

h. **The homehero, yurthero, and trailhero id selectors.** Set left margin to 0. Set height to 200 pixels.

i. **The footer element selector.** Set left margin to 0.

d. **Configure Smartphone Display.**

1. Code a media query below the existing styles to select for typical smartphone device viewport size.

```
@media only screen and (max-width: 37.5em) {
}
```

2. Configure the following new styles within the media query:

a. **The main element selector.** Set top and bottom padding to 0.1em, left and right padding to 1em, and font size to 90%.

b. **The h1 element selector.** Set font size to 2em.

c. **The nav element selector.** Set padding to 0.

d. **Navigation list items.** Use a descendant selector to configure li elements within the navigation area with block display, 0 margin, and a 2 pixel solid dark (#330000) bottom border.

e. **Navigation hyperlinks.** Use a descendant selector to configure elements within the navigation area with block display. This will provide the user a larger area to tap when selecting a hyperlink.

f. **The homehero, yurthero, and trailhero id selectors.** Do not display the image. Set the background-image property to none and the height to 0.

g. **The mobile id selector.** Set display to inline.

h. **The desktop id selector.** Set display to none.

Save your pacific.css file. Use the CSS validator (http://jigsaw.w3.org/css-validator) to check your syntax. Correct and retest if necessary.

Task 3: **Edit the Home Page.** Launch a text editor and open the index.html file. Edit the code as follows:

a. Configure a viewport meta tag in the head section that configures the `width` to the `device-width` and sets the `initial-scale` to `1.0`.

b. The home page displays a phone number in the contact information area. Wouldn't it be handy if a person using a smartphone could click on the phone number to call the resort? You can make that happen by using `tel:` in a hyperlink. Configure a hyperlink assigned to an id named `mobile` that contains the phone number as shown below:

```
<a id="mobile" href="tel:888-555-5555">888-555-5555</a>
```

c. But wait a minute, a telephone link could confuse those visiting the site with a desktop browser. Code another phone number directly after the hyperlink. Code a span element assigned to an id named `desktop` around the phone number as shown here:

```
<span id="desktop">888-555-5555</span>
```

Save the index.html file. Remember that validating your HTML can help you find syntax errors. Validate and correct this page before you continue. Display your page in a browser. While your home page will look unchanged in maximized desktop browsers (see Figure 7.43), as you resize and reduce the browser viewport dimensions, the displays should be similar to the screen captures in Figure 8.35.

Task 4: Edit the Yurts Page. When you are finished, the Yurts page will look similar to Figure 8.36.

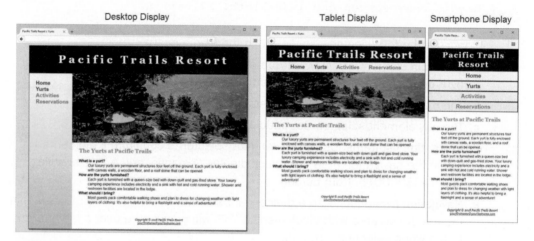

FIGURE 8.36 *Browser approximation of the yurts.html page mobile display.*

Launch a text editor and open the yurts.html file. Configure a viewport meta tag in the head section that configures the `width` to the `device-width` and sets the `initial-scale` to 1.0.

Save the yurts.html file. Remember that validating your HTML can help you find syntax errors. Validate and correct this page before you continue. Display your page in a browser. Resize the browser window to test the media queries. Compare your work with Figure 8.36, which shows screen captures of the yurts page.

Task 5: Edit the Activities Page. When you are finished, the Activities page will look similar to Figure 8.37.

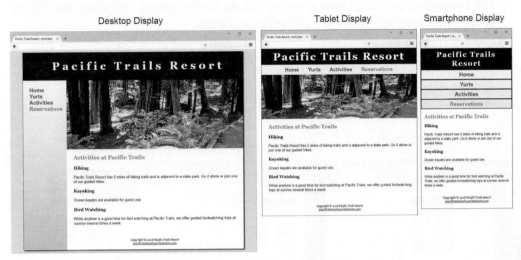

FIGURE 8.37 *Browser approximation of the activities.html page mobile display.*

Launch a text editor and open the activities.html file. Configure a viewport meta tag in the head section that configures the `width` to the `device-width` and sets the `initial-scale` to 1.0.

Save the activities.html file. Remember that validating your HTML can help you find syntax errors. Validate and correct this page before you continue. Display your page in a browser. Resize the browser window to test the media queries. Compare your work with Figure 8.37, which shows screen captures of the activities page. Pacific Trails Resort is mobile!

Path of Light Yoga Studio Case Study

In this chapter's case study you will use the existing Path of Light Yoga Studio (Chapter 7) website as a starting point to create a new version of the website that utilizes media queries to configure display for mobile devices. Figure 8.38 displays wireframes for desktop browser, typical tablet screen, and typical smartphone screen display. When you have finished, the website will look the same in desktop browsers (see Figures 7.45 and 8.39). The mobile displays should be similar to the screen captures in Figure 8.39.

FIGURE 8.38 *Path of Light Yoga Studio wireframes.*

You have five tasks in this case study:

1. Create a new folder for the Path of Light Yoga Studio website.
2. Edit the yoga.css external style sheet to include media queries and styles needed for appropriate desktop, tablet, and smartphone display.
3. Edit the Home page (index.html).
4. Edit the Classes page (classes.html).
5. Edit the Schedule page (schedule.html).

FIGURE 8.39 *Resize the browser window to approximate the new tablet and smartphone display.*

Task 1: Create a folder called ch8yoga to contain your Path of Light Yoga Studio website files. Copy the files from the Chapter 7 Case Study ch7yoga folder.

Task 2: **Configure the CSS.** Launch a text editor and open the yoga.css external style sheet file.

a. **Configure Support of HTML5.** Add the following style rule to configure most older browsers to render HTML5 block display elements as expected.

```
header, main, nav, footer, figure, figcaption, aside, section,
article { display: block; }
```

b. **Configure Phone Number Desktop Display.** Code the following new styles.
   1. **The mobile id.** Set display to none. You'll apply this id when you edit the home page (index.html).
   2. **The desktop id.** Set display to inline. You'll apply this id later when you edit the home page (index.html).

c. **Configure Tablet Display.**
   1. Code a media query below the existing styles to select for typical tablet device viewport size.
   ```
   @media only screen and (max-width: 64em) {
   }
   ```

2. Configure the following new styles within the media query:

   a. **The body element selector.** Set margin and padding to 0.

   b. **The wrapper id selector.** Set minimum width to 0, width to auto, margin to 0, and padding to 0.

   c. **The header element selector.** Set top padding to 1px.

   d. **The main element selector.** Set top padding to 0, bottom padding to 2.5em, left padding to 1em, right padding to 1em, margin to 0, 90% font size, and clear all floats.

   e. **The nav element selector.** Eliminate float (*Hint*: Use `float: none;`), set the width to auto, and configure 2em left padding.

   f. **Navigation hyperlinks.** Use a descendant selector to configure anchor elements within the navigation area. Set padding to 0.2em, left margin to 0.3em, float to left, and width to 23%.

   g. **The h2, h3, p, and dl element selectors.** Set the left and right padding to 2em.

   h. **Unordered lists within the main element.** Use a descendant selector to configure ul elements within the main element. Set left margin to 2em.

   i. **The floatleft class selector.** Set left margin to 2em and bottom margin to 1em.

   j. **The clear class selector.** Set 2em left padding.

   k. **The mathero and loungehero id selectors.** Set height to 150px, width to 80%. Center each area by setting left margin to auto and right margin to auto.

d. **Configure Smartphone Display.**

   1. Code a media query below the existing styles to select for typical smartphone device viewport size.

      ```
      @media only screen and (max-width: 37.5em) {
      }
      ```

   2. Configure the following new styles within the media query:

      a. **The h1 element selector.** Set the font size to 2em, top padding to 0.25em, left padding to 1.5em, and width to 85%. Also configure centered text.

      b. **Navigation hyperlinks.** Use a descendant selector to configure anchor elements within the navigation area. Set padding to 0.5em, width to 45%, float to left, minimum width to 6em, and left margin to 0.5em.

      c. **The li element selector.** Configure 100% font-size.

      d. **The floatleft class selector.** Set the float property to none. Set display to none.

      e. **The mathero and loungehero id selectors.** Do not display the background image. Set the background-image property to none and the height to 0.

      f. **The footer element selector.** Set padding to 0.5em and margin to 0.

      g. **The mobile id.** Set display to inline. You'll apply this id when you edit the home page (index.html).

      h. **The desktop id.** Set display to none. You'll apply this id later when you edit the home page (index.html).

Save your yoga.css file. Use the CSS validator (http://jigsaw.w3.org/css-validator) to check your syntax. Correct and retest if necessary.

Task 3: **Edit the Home Page.** Launch a text editor and open the index.html file. Edit the code as follows:

   a. Configure a viewport meta tag in the head section that configures the `width` to the `device-width` and sets the `initial-scale` to 1.0.

   b. The home page displays a phone number in the contact information area. Wouldn't it be handy if a person using a smartphone could click on the phone number to call the yoga studio? You can make that happen by using `tel:` in a hyperlink. Configure a hyperlink assigned to an id named `mobile` that contains the phone number as shown below:

      `<a id="mobile" href="tel:888-555-5555">888-555-5555</a>`

   c. But wait a minute, a telephone link could confuse those visiting the site with a desktop browser. Code another phone number directly after the hyperlink. Code a span element assigned to an id named `desktop` around the phone number as shown here:

      `<span id="desktop">888-555-5555</span>`

Save the index.html file. Remember that validating your HTML can help you find syntax errors. Validate and correct this page before you continue. Display your page in a browser. While your home page will look unchanged in maximized desktop browsers (see Figure 7.45), as you resize and reduce the browser viewport dimensions, the displays should be similar to the screen captures in Figure 8.39.

Task 4: **Edit the Classes Page.** Launch a text editor and open the classes.html file. Configure a viewport meta tag in the head section that configures the `width` to the `device-width` and sets the `initial-scale` to 1.0.

Save the classes.html file. Remember that validating your HTML can help you find syntax errors. Validate and correct this page before you continue. Display your page in a browser. Resize the browser window to test the media queries. Compare your work with Figure 8.40, which shows screen captures of the classes page.

FIGURE 8.40 *Browser approximation of the classes.html page display*

Task 5: Edit the Schedule Page. Launch a text editor and open the schedule.html file. Configure a viewport meta tag in the head section that configures the `width` to the `device-width` and sets the `initial-scale` to 1.0.

Save the schedule.html file. Remember that validating your HTML can help you find syntax errors. Validate and correct this page before you continue. Display your page in a browser. Resize the browser window to test the media queries. Compare your work with Figure 8.41, which shows screen captures of the schedule page. Path of Light Yoga Studio is mobile!

FIGURE 8.41 *Browser approximation of the schedule.html page display.*

Table Basics

Back in the day, tables were often used to format the layout of a web page. However, CSS is the page layout tool of choice for modern web designers. In this chapter, you'll become familiar with coding HTML tables to organize information on a web page.

You'll learn how to...

▶ Describe the recommended use of a table on a web page

▶ Configure a basic table with the table, table row, table header, and table cell elements

▶ Configure table sections with the thead, tbody, and tfoot elements

▶ Increase the accessibility of a table

▶ Style an HTML table with CSS

▶ Describe the purpose of CSS structural pseudo-classes

Table Overview

The purpose of a table is to organize information. In the past, before CSS was well supported by browsers, tables were also used to format web page layouts. An HTML table is composed of rows and columns, like a spreadsheet. Each individual table cell is at the intersection of a specific row and column.

- Each table begins with a `<table>` tag and ends with a `</table>` tag.
- Each table row begins with a `<tr>` tag and ends with a `</tr>` tag.
- Each cell (table data) begins with a `<td>` tag and ends with a `</td>` tag.
- Table cells can contain text, graphics, and other HTML elements.

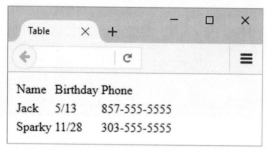

FIGURE 9.1 *Table with three rows and three columns.*

Figure 9.1 shows a sample table with three rows and three columns. The sample HTML for the table shown in Figure 9.1 is

```
<table>
  <tr>
    <td>Name</td>
    <td>Birthday</td>
    <td>Phone</td>
  </tr>
  <tr>
    <td>Jack</td>
    <td>5/13</td>
    <td>857-555-5555</td>
  </tr>
  <tr>
    <td>Sparky</td>
    <td>11/28</td>
    <td>303-555-5555</td>
  </tr>
</table>
```

Notice how the table is coded row by row. Also, each row is coded cell by cell. This attention to detail is crucial to the successful use of tables. An example can be found in the student files (chapter9/table1.html).

The Table Element

Table elements are block display elements that contain tabular information. The table begins with a `<table>` tag and ends with a `</table>` tag.

The `border` Attribute

In HTML 4 and XHTML, the purpose of the `border` attribute was to indicate the presence and the width of a visible table border. The `border` attribute is used differently in HTML5.

When following HTML5 syntax, code `border="1"` to cause the browser to render default borders around the table and table cells. The web page in Figure 9.2 (student files chapter9/table1a.html) depicts a table with `border="1"`. If the `border` attribute is omitted, most browsers will not display a default border around the table and table cells (as shown in Figure 9.1). CSS is used to style the border of a table. You'll get practice styling a table with CSS later in the chapter.

FIGURE 9.2 *A table rendered by the browser with a visible border.*

Table Captions

The **caption element** is often used with a data table to describe its contents. The table shown in Figure 9.3 uses `<caption>` tags to set "Bird Sightings" as the caption. The caption element is coded on the line immediately after the opening `<table>` tag. An example can be found in the student files (chapter9/table2.html). The HTML for the table is

```
<table border="1">
  <caption>Bird Sightings</caption>
  <tr>
    <td>Name</td>
    <td>Date</td>
  </tr>
  <tr>
    <td>Bobolink</td>
    <td>5/25/10</td>
  </tr>
  <tr>
    <td>Upland Sandpiper</td>
    <td>6/03/10</td>
  </tr>
</table>
```

FIGURE 9.3 *The caption for this table is Bird Sightings.*

FAQ

What about other attributes that I've seen coded on table tags, like `cellpadding`, `cellspacing`, and `summary` attributes?

Earlier versions of HTML (such as HTML4 and XHTML) provided a variety of attributes for configuring the table element, including `cellpadding`, `cellspacing`, `bgcolor`, `align`, `width`, and `summary`. These attributes are considered invalid and obsolete in HTML5. It is preferred to configure presentational display characteristics (such as alignment, width, cell padding, cell spacing, and background color) within CSS instead of with HTML attributes. Although the `summary` attribute supported accessibility and served to describe the table, the W3C suggests using one of the following techniques to replace the `summary` attribute and provide context for a table: configure descriptive text in the caption element, provide an explanatory paragraph directly on the web page, or simplify the table. You'll get practice configuring tables with CSS later in this chapter.

Rows, Cells, and Headers

VideoNote

Configure a Table

The **table row element** configures a row within a table on a web page. The table row begins with a `<tr>` tag and ends with a `</tr>` tag.

The **table data element** configures a cell within a row in a table on a web page. The table cell begins with a `<td>` tag and ends with a `</td>` tag. See Table 9.1 for common attributes of the table data cell element.

TABLE 9.1 *Commonly Used Attributes of the Table Data and Table Header Cell Elements*

Attribute	Value	Purpose
colspan	Numeric	The number of columns spanned by a cell
headers	The id value(s) of a column or row heading cell	Associates the table data cells with table header cells; may be accessed by screen readers
rowspan	Numeric	The number of rows spanned by a cell
scope	row or column	The scope of the table header cell contents (row or column); may be accessed by screen readers

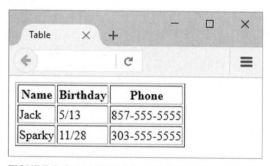

FIGURE 9.4 *Using `<th>` tags to indicate column headings.*

The **table header element** is similar to a table data element and configures a cell within a row in a table on a web page. Its special purpose is to configure column and row headings. Text displayed within a table header element is centered and bold. The table header element begins with a `<th>` tag and ends with a `</th>` tag. See Table 9.1 for common attributes of the table header element. Figure 9.4 shows a table with column headings configured by `<th>` tags. The HTML for the table shown in Figure 9.4 is as follows (also see chapter9/table3.html in the student files). Notice that the first row uses `<th>` instead of `<td>` tags:

```
<table border="1">
  <tr>
    <th>Name</th>
    <th>Birthday</th>
    <th>Phone</th>
  </tr>
  <tr>
    <td>Jack</td>
    <td>5/13</td>
    <td>857-555-5555</td>
  </tr>
  <tr>
    <td>Sparky</td>
    <td>11/28</td>
    <td>303-555-5555</td>
  </tr>
</table>
```

 Hands-On Practice 9.1

Create a web page similar to Figure 9.5 that describes two schools you have attended. Use "School History" as the caption. The table has three rows and three columns. The first row will have table header elements with the headings School Attended, Years, and Degree Awarded. You will complete the second and third rows with your own information within table data elements.

To get started, launch a text editor and open the template.html file from the chapter1 folder in the student files. Modify the title element. Use table, table row, table header, table data, and caption elements to configure a table similar to Figure 9.5.

Hints: The table has three rows and three columns. To configure a border, use `border="1"` on the `<table>` tag. Use the table header element for the cells in the first row.

School History

School Attended	Years	Degree Awarded
Schaumburg High School	2012—2016	High School Diploma
Harper College	2016—2017	Web Developer Certificate

FIGURE 9.5 *School History Table.*

Save your file and display it in a browser. It should look similar to Figure 9.5. A sample solution is found in the student files (chapter9/9.1).

Span Rows and Columns

You can alter the gridlike look of a table by applying the `colspan` and `rowspan` attributes to table data or table header elements. As you get into more complex table configurations like these, be sure to sketch the table on paper before you start typing the HTML.

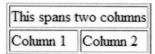

FIGURE 9.6 *Table with a row that spans two columns.*

The **colspan attribute** specifies the number of columns that a cell will occupy. Figure 9.6 shows a table cell that spans two columns.

The HTML for the table is

```
<table border="1">
  <tr>
    <td  colspan="2">This spans two columns</td>
  </tr>
  <tr>
    <td>Column 1</td>
    <td>Column 2</td>
  </tr>
</table>
```

FIGURE 9.7 *Table with a column that spans two rows.*

The `rowspan` **attribute** specifies the number of rows that a cell will occupy. An example of a table cell that spans two rows is shown in Figure 9.7.

The HTML for the table is

```
<table border="1">
  <tr>
    <td  rowspan="2">This spans two rows</td>
    <td>Row 1 Column 2</td>
  </tr>
  <tr>
    <td>Row 2 Column 2</td>
  </tr>
</table>
```

An example of the tables in Figures 9.6 and 9.7 can be found in the student files (chapter9/table4.html).

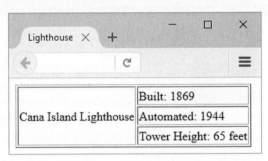

Hands-On Practice 9.2

Launch a text editor and open the template.html file from the chapter1 folder in the student files. You will create the web page shown in Figure 9.8. Modify the title element. Use table, table row, table head, and table data elements to configure the table.

1. Code the opening `<table>` tag. Configure a border with `border="1"`.

2. Begin the first row with a `<tr>` tag.

3. The table data cell with "Cana Island Lighthouse" spans three rows. Code a table data element. Use the `rowspan="3"` attribute.

4. Code a table data element that contains the text "Built: 1869".

5. End the first row with a `</tr>` tag.

6. Begin the second row with a `<tr>` tag. This row will only have one table data element because the cell in the first column is already reserved for "Cana Island Lighthouse".

7. Code a table data element that contains the text "Automated: 1944".

8. End the second row with a `</tr>` tag.

9. Begin the third row with a `<tr>` tag. This row will only have one table data element because the cell in the first column is already reserved for "Cana Island Lighthouse".

10. Code a table data element that contains the text "Tower Height: 65 feet".

11. End the third row with a `</tr>` tag.

12. Code the closing `</table>` tag.

FIGURE 9.8 *Practice with the rowspan attribute.*

Save the file and view it in a browser. A sample solution is found in the student files (chapter9/9.2). Notice how the "Cana Island Lighthouse" text is vertically aligned in the middle of the cell—this is the default vertical alignment. You can modify the vertical alignment using CSS—see the section "Style a Table with CSS" later in this chapter.

? **FAQ** **Is there a way to create a table-like page layout with CSS?**

Not exactly, but there are new CSS page layout techniques in the works, including the Flexible Box Layout Module and the CSS Grid Layout Module. The Flexible Box Layout Module (https://www.w3.org/TR/css-flexbox-1), referred to as Flexbox, is intended to provide for a flexible layout; elements contained within a flex container can be configured either horizontally or vertically in a flexible manner. Flexbox is in candidate recommendation status with growing browser support. The Appendix of this book contains an introduction to Flexbox. CSS Grid Layout (http://www.w3.org/TR/css-grid-1) provides a way for web designers to define a two-dimensional grid with rows and columns. CSS Grid Layout is currently in working draft status with only experimental browser support. For the current level of browser support, check http://caniuse.com/#feat=css-grid.

Configure an Accessible Table

 Tables can be useful to organize information on a web page, but what if you couldn't see the table and were relying on assistive technology like a screen reader to read the table to you? You'd hear the contents of the table just the way it is coded—row by row, cell by cell. This might be difficult to understand. This section discusses coding techniques to improve the accessibility of tables.

FIGURE 9.9 *This simple data table uses* <th> *tags and the caption element to provide for accessibility.*

For a simple informational data table like the one shown in Figure 9.9, the W3C recommends the following:

▶ Use table header elements (<th> tags) to indicate column or row headings.

▶ Use the caption element to provide a text title or caption for the table.

An example web page is in the student files (chapter9/table5.html). The HTML follows:

```
<table border="1">
<caption>Bird Sightings</caption>
  <tr>
    <th>Name</th>
    <th>Date</th>
  </tr>
  <tr>
    <td>Bobolink</td>
    <td>5/25/10</td>
  </tr>
  <tr>
    <td>Upland Sandpiper</td>
    <td>6/03/10</td>
  </tr>
</table>
```

However, for more complex tables the W3C recommends specifically associating the table data cell values with their corresponding headers. The technique that is recommended uses the `id` attribute (usually in a `<th>` tag) to identify a specific header cell and the **headers attribute** in a `<td>` tag. The code to configure the table in Figure 9.9 using `headers` and `id` attributes is as follows (also found in the student files chapter9/table6.html):

```
<table border="1">
<caption>Bird Sightings</caption>
  <tr>
    <th id="name">Name</th>
    <th id="date">Date</th>
  </tr>
  <tr>
    <td headers="name">Bobolink</td>
    <td headers="date">5/25/10</td>
  </tr>
  <tr>
    <td headers="name">Upland Sandpiper</td>
    <td headers="date">6/03/10</td>
  </tr>
</table>
```

?FAQ **What about the `scope` attribute?**

The `scope` attribute specifies the association of table cells and table row or column headers. It is used to indicate whether a table cell is a header for a column (`scope="col"`) or row (`scope="row"`). An example of the code for the table in Figure 9.8 that uses this attribute is as follows (also see the student files chapter9/table7.html):

```
<table border="1">
<caption>Bird Sightings</caption>
  <tr>
    <th scope="col">Name</th>
    <th scope="col">Date</th>
  </tr>
  <tr>
    <td>Bobolink</td>
    <td>5/25/10</td>
  </tr>
  <tr>
    <td>Upland Sandpiper</td>
    <td>6/03/10</td>
  </tr>
</table>
```

As you review the code sample above, you may notice that using the `scope` attribute to provide for accessibility requires less coding than implementing the `headers` and `id` attributes. However, due to inconsistent screen reader support of the `scope` attribute, the WCAG 2.0 recommendations for coding techniques encourage the use of `headers` and `id` attributes rather than the `scope` attribute.

Style a Table with CSS

Before CSS was well supported by browsers, it was common practice to configure the visual esthetic of a table with HTML attributes. The modern approach is to use CSS to style a table. Table 9.2 lists corresponding CSS properties with HTML attributes used to style tables.

TABLE 9.2 *Configuring Tables with HTML Attributes and CSS Properties*

HTML Attribute	CSS Property
align	To align a table, configure the `width` and `margin` properties for the table element selector. To center a table, use `table { width: 75%; margin: auto; }` To align content within table cells, use `text-align`
width	width
height	height
cellpadding	padding
cellspacing	`border-spacing` configures space between cell borders with a numeric value (px or em) or percentage. If you set a value to 0, omit the unit. One value configures both horizontal and vertical spacing. When two values are used, the first value configures the horizontal spacing and the second value configures the vertical spacing. `border-collapse` configures the border area. The values are `separate` (default) and `collapse` (removes extra space between table and cell borders).
bgcolor	background-color
valign	vertical-align
border	border, border-style, border-spacing
none	background-image
none	`caption-side` specifies caption placement. Values are `top` (default) and `bottom`

 Hands-On Practice 9.3

Lighthouse Island Bistro Specialty Coffee Menu

Specialty Coffee	Description	Price
Lite Latte	Indulge in a shot of espresso with steamed, skim milk.	$3.50
Mocha Latte	Choose dark or milk chocolate with steamed milk.	$4.00
MCP Latte	A luscious mocha latte with caramel and pecan syrup.	$4.50

FIGURE 9.10 *The table before CSS.*

In this Hands-On Practice you will code CSS style rules to configure an informational table on a web page. Create a folder named ch9table. Copy the starter.html file from the chapter9 folder in the student files to your ch9table folder. Display the file in a browser. The page should look similar to Figure 9.10.

Launch a text editor and open the starter.html file from your ch9table folder. Locate the style tags in the head section. You will code embedded CSS in this Hands-On Practice. Position your cursor on the blank line between the style tags.

1. Configure the table element selector to be centered, have a dark blue, 5 pixel border, and have a width of 600px:

   ```
   table { margin: auto; border: 5px solid #000066; width: 600px; }
   ```

   Save the file as menu.html and display your page in a browser. Notice that there is a dark blue border surrounding the entire table.

2. Configure the td and th element selectors with a border, padding, and Arial or the default sans-serif font typeface:

   ```
   td, th { border: 1px solid #000066; padding: 5px;
            font-family: Arial, sans-serif; }
   ```

Save the file as menu.html and display your page in a browser. Each table cell should now be outlined with a dark blue border and should display text in a sans-serif font.

3. Eliminate the empty space between the borders of the table cells with the **border-spacing property**. Add a `border-spacing: 0;` declaration to the table element selector. Save the file and display your page in a browser.

4. Configure the caption to be displayed with Verdana or the default sans-serif font typeface, bold font weight, font size 1.2em, and 5 pixels of bottom padding:

   ```
   caption { font-family: Verdana, sans-serif; font-weight: bold;
             font-size: 1.2em; padding-bottom: 5px; }
   ```

5. Let's experiment and configure background colors for the rows instead of cell borders. Modify the style rule for the td and th element selectors, remove the border declaration, and set `border-style` to none:

   ```
   td, th { padding: 5px; font-family: Arial, sans-serif;
            border-style: none; }
   ```

6. Create a new class called `altrow` that sets a background color:

   ```
   .altrow { background-color: #EAEAEA; }
   ```

7. Modify the `<tr>` tags in the HTML: assign the second and fourth `<tr>` tags to the `altrow` class. Save the file. Display it in a browser. The table area should look similar to Figure 9.11.

Notice how the background color of the alternate rows adds subtle interest to the web page. Compare your work with the sample located in the student files (chapter9/9.3).

Lighthouse Island Bistro Specialty Coffee Menu

Specialty Coffee	Description	Price
Lite Latte	Indulge in a shot of espresso with steamed, skim milk.	$3.50
Mocha Latte	Choose dark or milk chocolate with steamed milk.	$4.00
MCP Latte	A luscious mocha latte with caramel and pecan syrup.	$4.50

FIGURE 9.11 *Rows are configured with alternating background colors.*

CSS3 Structural Pseudo-classes

In the previous section you configured CSS and applied a class to every other table row to configure alternating background colors, often referred to as "zebra striping." You may have found this to be a bit inconvenient and wondered if there was a more efficient method. Well, there is! CSS3 **structural pseudo-class selectors** allow you to select and apply classes to elements based on their position in the structure of the document, such as every other row. CSS3 pseudo-classes are supported by current versions of popular browsers. Internet Explorer (version 8 and below) does not support CSS3 pseudo-classes. Table 9.3 lists common CSS3 structural pseudo-class selectors and their purpose.

To apply a pseudo-class, write it after the selector. The following code sample will configure the first item in an unordered list to display with red text.

```
li:first-of-type { color: #FF0000; }
```

TABLE 9.3 *Common CSS3 Structural Pseudo-classes*

Pseudo-class	Purpose
`:first-of-type`	Applies to the first element of the specified type
`:first-child`	Applies to the first child of an element (CSS2 selector)
`:last-of-type`	Applies to the last element of the specified type
`:last-child`	Applies to the last child of an element
`:nth-of-type(n)`	Applies to the "nth" element of the specified type
	Value: an integer, `odd`, or `even`

 Hands-On Practice 9.4

In this Hands-On Practice you will rework the table you configured in Hands-On Practice 9.3 to use CSS3 structural pseudo-class selectors to configure color.

1. Launch a text editor and open the menu.html file in your ch9table folder (also found in the student files chapter9/9.3). Save the file as menu2.html.

2. View the source code, and notice that the second and fourth tr elements are assigned to the `altrow` class. You won't need this class assignment when using CSS3 structural pseudo-class selectors. Delete `class="altrow"` from the tr elements.

3. Examine the embedded CSS and locate the `altrow` class. Change the selector to use a structural pseudo-class that will apply the style to the even-numbered table rows. Replace `.altrow` with `tr:nth-of-type (even)` as shown in the following CSS declaration:

```
tr:nth-of-type(even) { background-color: #EAEAEA; }
```

4. Save the file. Display your page in a browser. The table area should look similar to the one shown in Figure 9.11.

5. Let's configure the first row to have a dark blue background (#006) and light gray text (#EAEAEA) with the `:first-of-type` structural pseudo-class. Add the following to the embedded CSS:

```
tr:first-of-type { background-color: #006;
                   color: #EAEAEA; }
```

6. Save the file. Display your page in a browser. The table area should look similar to the one shown in Figure 9.12. A sample solution is available in the student files (chapter9/9.4).

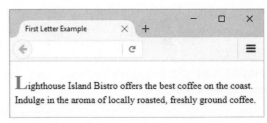

Lighthouse Island Bistro Specialty Coffee Menu

Specialty Coffee	Description	Price
Lite Latte	Indulge in a shot of espresso with steamed, skim milk.	$3.50
Mocha Latte	Choose dark or milk chocolate with steamed milk.	$4.00
MCP Latte	A luscious mocha latte with caramel and pecan syrup.	$4.50

FIGURE 9.12 *CSS3 pseudo-class selectors style the table rows.*

Configuring the First Letter

Ever wonder how to easily style the first letter of a paragraph to be different from the rest? It's easy using the CSS2 **:first-letter pseudo-element**. Use the following code to configure the text as shown in Figure 9.13:

```
p:first-letter { font-size: 3em;
                 font-weight: bold; color: #F00; }
```

See chapter9/letter.html in the student files for an example.

FIGURE 9.13 *Configure the first letter with CSS.*

Explore the topic of pseudo-elements further. Find out about the `:before`, `:after`, and `:first-line` pseudo-elements at the following resources:

▶ http://css-tricks.com/pseudo-element-roundup
▶ http://www.hongkiat.com/blog/pseudo-element-before-after

Configure Table Sections

There are many configuration options when coding tables. Table rows can be put together into three types of table row groups: table head with `<thead>`, table body with `<tbody>`, and table footer with `<tfoot>`.

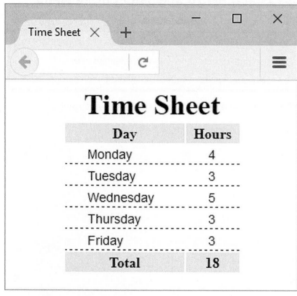

FIGURE 9.14 *CSS configures the thead, tbody, and tfoot element selectors.*

These groups can be useful when you need to configure the areas in the table in different ways, using either attributes or CSS. The `<tbody>` tag is required if you configure a `<thead>` or `<tfoot>` area, although you can omit either the table head or table footer if you like.

The following code sample (see chapter9/tfoot.html in the student files) configures the table shown in Figure 9.14 and demonstrates the use of CSS to configure a table head, table body, and table footer with different styles.

The CSS styles a centered 200-pixel-wide table with a caption that is rendered in a large, bold font; a table head section with a light gray (#EAEAEA) background color; and a table body section styled with slightly smaller text (.90em) using a sans-serif font; table body td element selectors set to display with some left padding and a dashed bottom border; and a table footer section that has centered, bolded text and a light gray background color (#EAEAEA). The CSS code follows:

```
table { width: 200px;
        margin: auto; }
table, th, td { border-style: none; }
caption { font-size: 2em;
          font-weight: bold; }
thead { background-color: #EAEAEA; }
tbody { font-family: Arial, sans-serif;
        font-size: .90em; }
tbody td { border-bottom: 1px #000033 dashed;
           padding-left: 25px; }
tfoot { background-color: #EAEAEA;
        font-weight: bold;
        text-align: center; }
```

The HTML for the table follows:

```html
<table border="1">
<caption>Time Sheet</caption>
<thead>
  <tr>
    <th id="day">Day</th>
    <th id="hours">Hours</th>
  </tr>
</thead>
<tbody>
  <tr>
    <td headers="day">Monday</td>
    <td headers="hours">4</td>
  </tr>
  <tr>
    <td headers="day">Tuesday</td>
    <td headers="hours">3</td>
  </tr>
  <tr>
    <td headers="day">Wednesday</td>
    <td headers="hours">5</td>
  </tr>
  <tr>
    <td headers="day">Thursday</td>
    <td headers="hours">3</td>
  </tr>
  <tr>
    <td headers="day">Friday</td>
    <td headers="hours">3</td>
  </tr>
</tbody>
<tfoot>
  <tr>
    <td headers="day">Total</td>
    <td headers="hours">18</td>
  </tr>
</tfoot>
</table>
```

This example demonstrates the power of CSS in styling documents. The `<td>` tags within each table row group element selector (`thead`, `tbody`, and `tfoot`) inherited the font styles configured for their parent group element selector. Notice how a descendant selector configures padding and border only for `<td>` tags that are contained within the `<tbody>` element. Sample code is located in the student files (chapter9/tfoot.html). Take a few moments to explore the web page code and display the page in a browser.

CHAPTER 9

Review and Apply

Review Questions

Multiple Choice. Choose the best answer for each item.

1. Which HTML tag pair is used to begin and end a table row?
   - **a.** `<td> </td>`
   - **b.** `<tr> </tr>`
   - **c.** `<table> </table>`
   - **d.** `<th> </th>`

2. Which CSS declaration removes extra space between table and cell borders?
   - **a.** `display: none;`
   - **b.** `border-style: none;`
   - **c.** `border-spacing: 0`
   - **d.** `border-collapse: 0;`

3. Which HTML tag pair is used to group rows in the footer of a table?
   - **a.** `<footer> </footer>`
   - **b.** `<tr> </tr>`
   - **c.** `<tfoot> </tfoot>`
   - **d.** `<trfoot> </trfoot>`

4. Which HTML element uses a border attribute to indicate a table has a border?
   - **a.** `<td>`
   - **b.** `<tr>`
   - **c.** `<table>`
   - **d.** `<tableborder>`

5. Which HTML tag pair is used to specify table headings?
   - **a.** `<td> </td>`
   - **b.** `<th> </th>`
   - **c.** `<head> </head>`
   - **d.** `<tr> </tr>`

6. Which CSS property replaces the use of the HTML cellpadding attribute?
   - **a.** `cell-padding`
   - **b.** `border-spacing`
   - **c.** `padding`
   - **d.** `border`

7. Which HTML element describes the contents of a table?
   - **a.** `<table>`
   - **b.** `<caption>`
   - **c.** `<summary>`
   - **d.** `<thead>`

8. Which of the following is the recommended use of tables on web pages?
   - **a.** configuring the layout of an entire page
   - **b.** organizing information
   - **c.** forming hyperlinks
   - **d.** configuring a resume

9. Which CSS property specifies the background color of a table?
   - **a.** `background`
   - **b.** `bgcolor`
   - **c.** `background-color`
   - **d.** `border-spacing`

10. Which HTML attribute associates a table data cell with a table header cell?
    - **a.** `head`
    - **b.** `headers`
    - **c.** `align`
    - **d.** `rowspan`

Hands-On Exercises

1. Write the HTML for a two-column table that contains the names of your friends and their birthdays. The first row of the table should span two columns and contain the following heading: "Birthday List". Include at least two people in your table.

2. Write the HTML for a three-column table to describe the courses you are taking this semester. The columns should contain the course number, course name, and instructor name. The first row of the table should use `th` tags and contain descriptive headings for the columns. Use the table row grouping tags `<thead>` and `<tbody>` in your table.

3. Use CSS to configure a table that has a red border around both the entire table and the table cells. Write the HTML to create a table with four rows and two columns. The cell in the first column of each row will contain one of the following terms: contrast, repetition, alignment, and proximity. The corresponding cell in the second column of each row will contain a description of the term as it applies to web design (see Chapter 3).

4. Create a web page about your favorite sports team with a two-column table that lists the positions and starting players. Use embedded CSS to style the table border, background color, and center the table on the web page. Place an e-mail link to yourself in the footer area. Save the file as sport9.html.

5. Create a web page about your favorite movie that uses a two-column table containing details about the movie. Use embedded CSS to style the table border and background color. Include the following in the table:

   - Title of the movie
   - Director or producer
   - Leading actor
   - Leading actress
   - Rating (R, PG-13, PG, G, NR)
   - A brief description of the movie
   - An absolute link to a review about the movie

   Place an e-mail link to yourself on the web page. Save the page as movie9.html.

Focus on Web Design

Good artists view and analyze many paintings. Good writers read and evaluate many books. Similarly, good web designers view and scrutinize many web pages. Surf the Web and find two web pages—one that is appealing to you and one that is unappealing to you. Print out each page. Create a web page that answers the following questions for each of your examples:

   a. What is the URL of the website?
   b. Does this page use tables? If so, for what purpose—page layout, organization of information, or another reason?
   c. Does this page use CSS? If so, for what purpose—page layout, text and color configuration, or another reason?
   d. Is this page appealing or unappealing? Describe three aspects of the page that you find appealing or unappealing.
   e. If this page is unappealing, what would you do to improve it?

Pacific Trails Resort Case Study

In this chapter's case study you will use the Pacific Trails existing website (Chapter 8) as a starting point and add an informational table to the Yurts page on the Pacific Trails website. Your new page will be similar to Figure 9.15 when you have completed this case study.

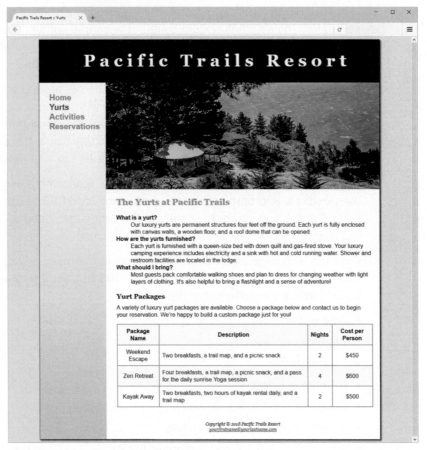

FIGURE 9.15 *Yurts page with a table.*

You have three tasks in this case study:

1. Create a new folder for this Pacific Trails case study.
2. Modify the style sheet (pacific.css) to configure style rules for the new table.
3. Modify the Yurts page to use a table to display information, as shown in Figure 9.15.

Task 1: Create a folder called ch9pacific to contain your Pacific Trails Resort website files. Copy the files from the Chapter 8 Case Study ch8pacific folder into the new ch9pacific folder.

Task 2: Configure the CSS. You will add styles to configure the table on the Yurts page. Launch a text editor and open the pacific.css external style sheet file. You will add new style rules above the media queries.

- **Configure the table.** Code a new style rule for the table element selector that configures a table with a 2 pixel solid blue border (#3399CC) and no cellspacing (use `border-collapse: collapse;`).
- **Configure the table cells.** Code a new style rule for the td and th element selectors that sets padding to 0.5em and configures a 2 pixel solid blue border (#3399CC).
- **Center the td content.** Code a new style rule for the `td` element selector that centers text.
- **Configure the text class.** Notice that the content in the table data cells that contain the text description is not centered. Code a new style rule for a class named `text` that will override the td style rule and left-align the text.

- **Configure alternate-row background color.** The table looks more appealing if the rows have alternate background colors but is still readable without them. Apply the `:nth-of-type` CSS3 pseudo-class to configure the odd table rows with a light blue background color (#F5FAFC).

Save the pacific.css file.

Task 3: Update the Yurts Page. Open the yurts.html page for the Pacific Trails Resort website in a text editor.

- Add a blank line above the closing main tag. Configure the text "Yurt Packages" within an h3 element.
- Below the new h3 element, configure a paragraph with the following text:

  A variety of luxury yurt packages are available. Choose a package below and contact us to begin your reservation. We're happy to build a custom package just for you!

- You are ready to configure the table. Position your cursor on a blank line under the paragraph and code a table with four rows, four columns, and a visible border. Use the table, th, and td elements. Assign the td elements that contain the detailed descriptions to the class named `text`. The content for the table is as follows:

Package Name	Description	Nights	Cost per Person
Weekend Escape	Two breakfasts, a trail map, and a picnic snack	2	$450
Zen Retreat	Four breakfasts, a trail map, a picnic snack, and a pass for the daily sunrise Yoga session	4	$600
Kayak Away	Two breakfasts, two hours of kayak rental daily, and a trail map	2	$500

Save your yurts.html file. Launch a browser and test your new page. It should look similar to Figure 9.15. If the page does not display as you intended, review your work, validate the CSS, validate the HTML, modify as needed, and test again.

Path of Light Yoga Studio Case Study

In this chapter's case study you will use the Path of Light Yoga Studio existing website (Chapter 8) as a starting point and modify the Schedule page to use two HTML tables to display information. Your new page will be similar to Figure 9.16 when you have completed this case study. You have three tasks in this case study:

1. Create a new folder for this Path of Light Yoga Studio case study.
2. Modify the style sheet (yoga.css) to configure style rules for the new tables.
3. Modify the Schedule page to use tables to display information as shown in Figure 9.16.

Task 1: Create a folder called ch9yoga to contain your Path of Light Yoga Studio website files. Copy the files from the Chapter 8 Case Study ch8yoga folder into the new ch9yoga folder.

Task 2: Configure the CSS. You will add styles to configure the tables on the Schedule page. Launch a text editor and open the yoga.css external style sheet file. You will add the new style rules above the media queries.

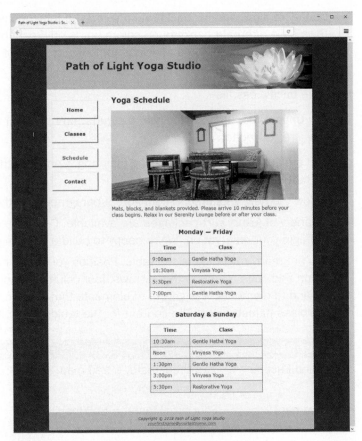

FIGURE 9.16 *Schedule page with HTML tables.*

- **Configure the tables.** Code a new style rule for the table element selector that configures a centered table (use `margin-left: auto; margin-right: auto;`) with a 60% width, a 1 pixel purple (#3F2860) border, a 1em bottom margin, and no cellspacing (use `border-collapse: collapse;`).

- **Configure the table cells.** Code a new style rule for the td and th element selectors that configures 0.5em of padding and 1 pixel purple border (#3F2860).

- **Configure alternate-row background color.** The table looks more appealing if the rows have alternate background colors but is still readable without them. Apply the `:nth-of-type` CSS3 pseudo-class to configure the even table rows with a #D7E8E9 background color.

- **Configure table captions.** Code a new style rule that sets a 1em margin, bold text, and 120% font size.

Save the yoga.css file.

Task 3: **Update the Schedule Page.** Open the schedule.html page for the Path of Light Yoga Studio website in a text editor. The schedule information currently uses the <h3>, <ul>, and <li> elements. You will rework the page to use two tables to display the schedule information instead of the h3, ul, and li tags. Use a caption element within each table. Note that the table rows have two columns. Configure "Time" and "Class" table headings within each table. Refer to Figure 9.16. Save your page and test it in a browser. If the page does not display as you intended, review your work, validate the CSS, validate the HTML, modify as needed, and test again.

Form Basics

Forms are used for many purposes all over the Web. They are used by search engines to accept keywords and by online stores to process e-commerce shopping carts. Websites use forms to help with a variety of functions—accepting visitor feedback, encouraging visitors to send a news story to a friend or colleague, collecting e-mail addresses for a newsletter, and accepting order information. This chapter introduces a very powerful tool for web developers—forms that accept information from web page visitors.

You'll learn how to...

- Describe common uses of forms on web pages
- Create forms on web pages using the form, input, textarea, and select elements
- Associate form controls and groups using label, fieldset, and legend elements
- Use CSS to style a form

- Describe the features and common uses of server-side processing
- Invoke server-side processing to handle form data
- Configure HTML5 form controls including the e-mail, URL, datalist, range, spinner, calendar, and color-well controls

Form Overview

Every time you use a search engine, place an order, or join an online mailing list, you use a form. A **form** is an HTML element that contains and organizes objects called **form controls**—such as text boxes, check boxes, and buttons—that can accept information from website visitors.

For example, you may have used Google's search form (http://www.google.com) many times but never thought about how it works. The form is quite simple; it contains just three form controls—the text box that accepts the keywords used in the search and two buttons. The "Google Search" button submits the form and invokes a process to search the Google databases and display a results page. The whimsical "I'm Feeling Lucky" button submits the form and displays the top page for your keywords.

Figure 10.1 shows a form, used to enter shipping information. This form contains text boxes to accept information such as name and address. Select lists are used to capture information with a limited number of correct values, such as state and country information. When a visitor clicks the "Continue" button, the form information is submitted and the ordering process continues.

Whether a form is used to search for web pages or to place an order, the form alone cannot do all the processing. The form needs to invoke a program or script on the server in order to search a database or record an order. There are usually two components of a form:

1. The HTML form itself, which is the web page user interface.
2. The server-side processing, which works with the form data and sends e-mail, writes to a text file, updates a database, or performs some other type of processing on the server.

Shipping Address

Name:	
Address Line 1:	
Address Line 2:	
City:	
State:	Zip:
Country:	United States

[Continue]

FIGURE 10.1 *This form accepts order information.*

The Form Element

Now that you have a basic understanding of what forms do, let's focus on the HTML to create a form. The **form element** contains a form on a web page. The `<form>` tag specifies the beginning of a form area. The closing `</form>` tag specifies the end of a form area. There can be multiple forms on a web page, but they cannot be nested inside each other. The form element can be configured with attributes that specify what server-side program or file will process the form, how the form information will be sent to the server, and the name of the form. These attributes are listed in Table 10.1.

TABLE 10.1 *Common Attributes of the Form Element*

Attribute	Value	Purpose
action	URL or file name/path of server-side processing script	Required; indicates where to send the form information when the form is submitted; `mailto:youremailaddress` will launch the visitor's default e-mail application to send the form information
autocomplete	on	HTML5 attribute; default value; browser will use autocompletion to fill form fields
	off	HTML5 attribute; browser will not use autocompletion to fill form fields
id	Alphanumeric, no spaces; the value must be unique and not used for other id values on the same web page document	Optional; provides a unique identifier for the form
method	get	Default value; the value of `get` causes the form data to be appended to the URL and sent to the web server
	post	The `post` method is more private and transmits the form data in the body of the HTTP response; this method is preferred by the W3C
name	Alphanumeric, no spaces, begins with a letter; choose a form name value that is descriptive but short; for example, OrderForm is better than Form1 or WidgetsRUsOrderForm	Optional; names the form so that it can be easily accessed by client-side scripting languages, such as JavaScript, to edit and verify the form information before the server-side processing is invoked

For example, to configure a form called order, using the post method, and invoking a script called demo.php on your web server, the code is

```
<form name="order" method="post" id="order" action="demo.php">
... form controls go here ...
</form>
```

Form Controls

The purpose of a form is to gather information from a web page visitor; form controls are the objects that accept the information. Types of form controls include text boxes, scrolling text boxes, select lists, radio buttons, check boxes, and buttons. HTML5 offers new form controls including those customized for e-mail addresses, URLs, dates, times, numbers, and color selection. HTML elements that configure form controls will be introduced in the following sections.

Text Box

The **input element** is used to configure several different types of form controls. The input element is not coded as a pair of opening and closing tags. It is considered to be a stand-alone or void element. Use the `type` attribute to specify the type of form control that the browser should display. The `<input>` tag with `type="text"` configures a text box. The text box form control accepts text or numeric information such as names, e-mail addresses, phone numbers, and other text. A sample text box is shown in Figure 10.2. The code for the text box is shown below.

FIGURE 10.2 *The* `<input>` *tag with* `type="text"` *configures this form element.*

```
E-mail: <input type="text" name="email" id="email">
```

Common input element attributes for text boxes are listed in Table 10.2. Several attributes are new in HTML5. The **required attribute** is exciting because it will cause supporting browsers to perform form validation. Browsers that support the HTML5 `required` attribute will verify that information has been entered in the text box and display an error message when the condition is not met. A code sample is

```
E-mail: <input type="text" name="email" id="email"
                required="required">
```

FIGURE 10.3 *The browser displayed an error message.*

Figure 10.3 shows an error message automatically generated by Firefox that displayed after the user clicked the form's submit button without entering information in the required text. Browsers that do not support HTML5 or the `required` attribute will ignore the attribute.

> **Quick TIP**
>
> Although web designers are enthusiastic about the `required` attribute and other new form processing functions offered by HTML5, it will be some time before all browsers support these new features. In the meantime, be aware that verification and validation of form information also must be done the old-fashioned way—with client-side or server-side scripting.

TABLE 10.2 *Common Input Element Attributes*

Attribute	Value	Usage
type	text	Configures the text box
name	Alphanumeric, no spaces, begins with a letter	Names the form element so that it can be easily accessed by client-side scripting and server-side processing; the name should be unique
id	Alphanumeric, no spaces, begins with a letter	Provides a unique identifier for the form element
size	Numeric	Configures the width of the text box as displayed by the browser; if size is omitted, the browser displays the text box with its own default size
maxlength	Numeric	Configures the maximum length of data accepted by the text box
value	Text or numeric characters	Assigns an initial value to the text box that is displayed by the browser; accepts information typed in the text box; this value can be accessed by client-side scripting languages and server-side processing
disabled	disabled	Form control is disabled
readonly	readonly	Form control is for display; cannot be edited
autocomplete	on	HTML5 attribute; default; browser will use autocompletion to fill the form control
	off	HTML5 attribute; browser will not use autocompletion to fill the form control
autofocus	autofocus	HTML5 attribute; form control has cursor focus
list	Datalist element id value	HTML5 attribute; associates the form control with a datalist element
placeholder	Text or numeric characters	HTML5 attribute; tip or hint to aid the user
required	required	HTML5 attribute; browser verifies entry of information
accesskey	Keyboard character	Configures a hot key for the form control
tabindex	Numeric	Configures the tab order of the form control

? FAQ   **Why use both the `name` and `id` attributes on form controls?**

The `name` attribute names the form control so that it can be easily accessed by client-side scripting languages such as JavaScript and by server-side processing languages such as PHP. The value given to a `name` attribute for a form element should be unique for that form. The `id` attribute is included for use with CSS and client-side scripting. The value of the `id` attribute should be unique to the entire web page document that contains the form. Typically, the values assigned to the `name` and `id` attribute on a particular form element are the same.

Submit Button and Reset Button

The Submit Button

The **submit button** form control is used to submit the form. When clicked, it triggers the action method on the `<form>` tag and causes the browser to send the form data (the name and value pairs for each form control) to the web server. The web server will invoke the server-side processing program or script listed on the form's `action` attribute.

The `<input>` tag with `type="submit"` configures a submit button. For example,

```
<input type="submit">
```

The Reset Button

The **reset button** form control is used to reset the form fields to their initial values. A reset button does not submit the form.

The `<input>` tag with `type="reset"` configures a reset button. For example,

```
<input type="reset">
```

Sample Form

Sample Form

E-mail:

[Submit Query] [Reset]

FIGURE 10.4 *The form contains a text box, a submit button, and a reset button.*

A form with a text box, a submit button, and a reset button is shown in Figure 10.4. Common attributes for submit buttons and reset buttons are listed in Table 10.3.

TABLE 10.3 *Common Attributes for Submit Buttons and Reset Buttons*

Attribute	Value	Usage
type	submit	Configures a submit button
	reset	Configures a reset button
name	Alphanumeric, no spaces, begins with a letter	Names the form element so that it can be easily accessed by client-side scripting and server-side processing; the name should be unique
id	Alphanumeric, no spaces, begins with a letter	Provides a unique identifier for the form element
value	Text or numeric characters	Configures the text displayed on the button; a submit button displays text "Submit Query" by default; a reset button displays "Reset" by default
accesskey	Keyboard character	Configures a hot key for the form control
tabindex	Numeric	Configures the tab order of the form control

Hands-On Practice 10.1

You will code a form in this Hands-On Practice. To get started, launch a text editor and open the template file located at chapter1/template.html in the student files. Save the file with the name join.html. You will create a web page with a form similar to the example in Figure 10.5.

1. Modify the title element to display the text: Form Example.

2. Configure an h1 element with the text: Join Our Newsletter.

3. You are ready to configure the form area. A form begins with the form element. Place your cursor on a blank line under the heading you just added and type in a `<form>` tag as follows:

   ```
   <form method="get">
   ```

   As you read through the chapter you will find that a number of attributes can be used with the `<form>` element. In your first form, we are using the minimal HTML needed to create the form.

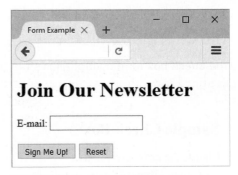

FIGURE 10.5 *Example form.*

4. To create the form control for the visitor's e-mail address to be entered, type the following code on a blank line below the form element:

   ```
   E-mail: <input type="text" name="email" id="email"><br><br>
   ```

   This places the text "E-mail:" in front of the text box used to enter the visitor's e-mail address. The input element has a `type` attribute with the value of text that causes the browser to display a text box. The `name` attribute assigns the name `email` to the information entered into the text box (the `value`) and could be used by server-side processing. The `id` attribute uniquely identifies the element on the page. The `<br>` elements configure line breaks.

5. Now you are ready to add the submit button to the form on the next line. Add a `value` attribute set to "Sign Me Up!":

   ```
   <input type="submit" value="Sign Me Up!">
   ```

   This causes the browser to display a button with "Sign Me Up!" instead of the default value of Submit Query.

6. Add a blank space after the submit button and code a reset button:

   ```
   <input type="reset">
   ```

7. Next, code the closing form tag:

   ```
   </form>
   ```

Save your file. Test your page in a browser. It should look similar to Figure 10.5.

You can compare your work with the solution found in the student files (chapter10/10.1) folder. Try entering some information into your form. Try clicking the submit button. Don't worry if the form redisplays but nothing seems to happen when you click the button—you haven't configured this form to work with any server-side processing. Connecting forms to server-side processing is demonstrated later in this chapter. The next sections will introduce you to more form controls.

Check Box and Radio Button

The Check Box

The **check box** form control allows the user to select one or more of a group of predetermined items. The `<input>` tag with `type="checkbox"` configures a check box. Figure 10.6 shows an example with several check boxes—note that more than one check box can be selected by the user. Common check box attributes are listed in Table 10.4. The HTML is

Sample Check Box

Choose the browsers you use:
- ☐ Google Chrome
- ☐ Firefox
- ☐ Microsoft Edge

FIGURE 10.6 *Check box.*

```
Choose the browsers you use: <br>
<input type="checkbox" name="Chrome" id="Chrome"
       value="yes"> Google Chrome<br>
<input type="checkbox" name="Firefox" id="Firefox"
       value="yes"> Firefox<br>
<input type="checkbox" name="Edge" id="Edge"
       value="yes"> Microsoft Edge<br>
```

TABLE 10.4 *Common Check Box Attributes*

Attribute	Value	Usage
type	checkbox	Configures the check box
name	Alphanumeric, no spaces, begins with a letter	Names the form element so that it can be easily accessed by client-side scripting and server-side processing; the name of each check box should be unique
id	Alphanumeric, no spaces, begins with a letter	Provides a unique identifier for the form element
checked	checked	Configures the check box to be checked by default when displayed by the browser
value	Text or numeric characters	Assigns a value to the check box that is triggered when the check box is checked; this value can be accessed by client-side and server-side processing
disabled	disabled	Form control is disabled and will not accept information
autofocus	autofocus	HTML5 attribute; form control has cursor focus
required	required	HTML5 attribute; browser verifies entry of information
accesskey	Keyboard character	Configures a hot key for the form control
tabindex	Numeric	Configures the tab order of the form control

The Radio Button

The **radio button** form control allows the user to select exactly one (and only one) choice from a group of predetermined items. Each radio button in a group is given the same `name` attribute and a unique `value` attribute. Because the `name` attribute is the same, the elements are identified as part of a group by the browsers and only one may be selected.

The `<input>` tag with `type="radio"` configures a radio button. Figure 10.7 shows an example with a radio button group—note that only one radio button can be selected at a time by the user. Common radio button attributes are listed in Table 10.5. The HTML is

Sample Radio Button

Select your favorite browser:
- ◉ Google Chrome
- ◉ Firefox
- ◉ Microsoft Edge

FIGURE 10.7 *Use radio buttons when only one choice is an appropriate response.*

```
Select your favorite browser:<br>
<input type="radio" name="fav" id="favCH" value="CH"> Google Chrome<br>
<input type="radio" name="fav" id="favFF" value="FF"> Firefox<br>
<input type="radio" name="fav" id="favME" value="ME"> Microsoft Edge<br>
```

Notice that all the `name` attributes have the same value: `fav`. Radio buttons with the same name attribute are treated as a group by the browser. Each radio button in the same group is typically configured with a unique `value` attribute.

TABLE 10.5 *Common Radio Button Attributes*

Attribute	Value	Usage
type	radio	Configures the radio button
name	Alphanumeric, no spaces, begins with a letter	Required; all radio buttons in a group must have the same `name`; names the form element so that it can be easily accessed by client-side scripting and server-side processing
id	Alphanumeric, no spaces, begins with a letter	Provides a unique identifier for the form element
checked	checked	Configures the radio button to be selected by default when displayed by the browser
value	Text or numeric characters	Assigns a value to the radio button that is triggered when the radio button is selected; this should be a unique value for each radio button in a group; this value can be accessed by client-side and server-side processing
disabled	disabled	Form control is disabled and will not accept information
autofocus	autofocus	HTML5 attribute; form control has cursor focus
required	required	HTML5 attribute; browser verifies entry of information
accesskey	Keyboard character	Configures a hot key for the form control
tabindex	Numeric	Configures the tab order of the form control

Hidden Field and Password Box

The Hidden Field

The **hidden field** form control stores text or numeric information, but it is not visible in the browser viewport. Hidden fields can be accessed by both client-side and server-side scripting.

The `<input>` tag with `type="hidden"` configures a hidden field. Common hidden field attributes are listed in Table 10.6.

The HTML to create a hidden form control with the `name` attribute set to "sendto" and the `value` attribute set to an e-mail address as follows:

```
<input type="hidden" name="sendto" id="sendto" value="order@site.com">
```

TABLE 10.6 *Common Hidden Field Attributes*

Attribute	Value	Usage
type	hidden	Configures the hidden form element
name	Alphanumeric, no spaces, begins with a letter	Names the form element so that it can be easily accessed by client-side scripting and server-side processing; the name should be unique
id	Alphanumeric, no spaces, begins with a letter	Provides a unique identifier for the form element
value	Text or numeric characters	Assigns a value to the hidden control; this value can be accessed by client-side scripting languages and server-side processing
disabled	disabled	Form control is disabled

The Password Box

The **password box** form control is similar to the text box, but it is used to accept information that must be hidden as it is entered, such as a password. The `<input>` tag with `type="password"` configures a password box. Common password box attributes are listed in Table 10.7.

When the user types information in a password box, asterisks (or another symbol, depending on the browser) are displayed instead of the characters that have been typed, as shown in Figure 10.8. This hides the information from someone looking over the shoulder of the person typing. The actual characters typed are sent to the server and the information is not really secret or hidden. The HTML is

```
Password: <input type="password" name="pword" id="pword">
```

Sample Password Box

Password: ●●●●●●●

FIGURE 10.8 *The characters secret9 were typed, but the browser does not display them.*

TABLE 10.7 *Common Password Box Attributes*

Attribute	Value	Usage
type	password	Configures the password box
name	Alphanumeric, no spaces, begins with a letter	Names the form element so that it can be easily accessed by client-side scripting and server-side processing; the name should be unique
id	Alphanumeric, no spaces, begins with a letter	Provides a unique identifier for the form element
size	Numeric	Configures the width of the password box as displayed by the browser; if size is omitted, the browser displays the password box with its own default size
maxlength	Numeric	Optional; configures the maximum length of data accepted by the password box
value	Text or numeric characters	Assigns an initial value to the password box that is displayed by the browser; accepts the information typed in the password box; this value can be accessed by client-side and server-side processing
disabled	disabled	Form control is disabled
readonly	readonly	Form control is for display; cannot be edited
autocomplete	on	HTML5 attribute; default; browser will use autocompletion to fill the form control
	off	HTML5 attribute; autocompletion is not used
autofocus	autofocus	HTML5 attribute; form control has cursor focus
placeholder	Text or numeric characters	HTML5 attribute; tip or hint to aid the user
required	required	HTML5 attribute; browser verifies entry of information
accesskey	Keyboard character	Configures a hot key for the form control
tabindex	Numeric	Configures the tab order of the form control

Textarea Element

Sample Scrolling Text Box

Comments:

Enter comments

FIGURE 10.9 *Scrolling text box.*

The **scrolling text box** form control accepts free-form comments, questions, or descriptions. The **textarea** **element** configures a scrolling text box. The `<textarea>` tag denotes the beginning of the scrolling text box. The closing `</textarea>` tag denotes the end of the scrolling text box. Text contained between the tags will display in the scrolling text box area. A sample scrolling text box is shown in Figure 10.9. Common attributes are listed in Table 10.8. The HTML is

```
Comments:<br>
<textarea name="cm" id="cm" cols="40" rows="2">Enter comments</textarea>
```

TABLE 10.8 *Common Scrolling Text Box Attributes*

Attribute	Value	Usage
name	Alphanumeric, no spaces, begins with a letter	Names the form element so that it can be easily accessed by client-side scripting and server-side processing; the name should be unique
id	Alphanumeric, no spaces, begins with a letter	Provides a unique identifier for the form element
cols	Numeric	Required; configures the width in character columns of the scrolling text box; if `cols` is omitted, the browser displays the scrolling text box with its own default width
rows	Numeric	Required; configures the height in rows of the scrolling text box; if `rows` is omitted, the browser displays the scrolling text box with its own default height
maxlength	Numeric	Maximum number of characters accepted
disabled	disabled	Form control is disabled
readonly	readonly	Form control is for display; cannot be edited
autofocus	autofocus	HTML5 attribute; form control has cursor focus
placeholder	Text or numeric characters	HTML5 attribute; tip or hint to aid the user
required	required	HTML5 attribute; browser verifies entry of information
wrap	hard or soft	HTML5 attribute; configures line breaks within the information entered
accesskey	Keyboard character	Configures a hot key for the form control
tabindex	Numeric	Configures the tab order of the form control

Hands-On Practice 10.2

In this Hands-On Practice you will create a contact form with the following form controls: a First Name text box, a Last Name text box, an E-mail text box, and a Comments scrolling text box. You'll use the form you created in Hands-On Practice 10.1 (see Figure 10.5) as a starting point. Launch a text editor and open the file located at chapter10/10.1/join.html in the student files. Save the file with the name contact.html. The new contact form is shown in Figure 10.10.

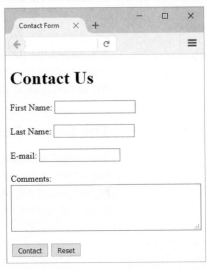
FIGURE 10.10 *A typical contact form.*

1. Modify the title element to display the text: Contact Form.

2. Configure the h1 element with the text: Contact Us.

3. A form control for the e-mail address is already coded. Refer to Figure 10.10 and note that you'll need to add text box form controls for the first name and last name above the e-mail form control. Position your cursor after the opening form tag and press the enter key twice to create two blank lines. Add the following code to accept the name of your web page visitor:

```
First Name: <input type="text" name="fname"
                id="fname"><br><br>
Last Name: <input type="text" name="lname"
                id="lname"><br><br>
```

4. Now you are ready to add the scrolling text box form control to the form using a `<textarea>` tag on a new line below the e-mail form control. The code is

```
Comments:<br>
<textarea name="comments" id="comments"></textarea><br><br>
```

Save your file and display in a browser to view the default display of a scrolling text box. Note that this default display will differ by browser. At the time this text was written, Internet Explorer always rendered a vertical scroll bar, but the Firefox browser only rendered scroll bars once enough text was entered to require them. The developers of browser rendering engines determine the default display of form controls.

5. Let's configure the `rows` and `cols` attributes for the scrolling text box form control. Modify the `<textarea>` tag and set `rows="4"` and `cols="40"` as follows:

```
Comments:<br>
<textarea name="comments" id="comments" rows="4" cols="40"></textarea><br><br>
```

6. Next, modify the text displayed on the submit button (set the `value` attribute to "Contact"). Save your file. Test your page in a browser. It should look similar to Figure 10.10.

You can compare your work with the solution found in the student files (chapter10/10.2) folder. Try entering some information into your form. Try clicking the submit button. Don't worry if the form redisplays but nothing seems to happen when you click the button—you haven't configured this form to work with any server-side processing. Connecting forms to server-side processing is demonstrated later in this chapter.

Select Element and Option Element

The **select list** form control shown in Figures 10.11 and 10.12 is also known by several other names, including select box, drop-down list, drop-down box, and option box. A select list is configured with one select element and multiple option elements.

The Select Element

The **select element** contains and configures the select list form control. The `<select>` tag denotes the beginning of the select list. The closing `</select>` tag denotes the end of the select list. Attributes configure the number of options to display and whether more than one option item may be selected. Common attributes are listed in Table 10.9.

TABLE 10.9 *Common Select Element Attributes*

Attribute	Value	Usage
name	Alphanumeric, no spaces, begins with a letter	Names the form element so that it can be easily accessed by client-side scripting and server-side processing; the name should be unique
id	Alphanumeric, no spaces, begins with a letter	Provides a unique identifier for the form element
size	Numeric	Configures the number of choices the browser will display; if set to 1, element functions as a drop-down list; scroll bars are automatically added by the browser if the number of options exceeds the space allowed
multiple	multiple	Configures a select list to accept more than one choice; by default, only one choice can be made from a select list
disabled	disabled	Form control is disabled
tabindex	Numeric	Configures the tab order of the form control

The Option Element

The **option element** contains and configures an option item displayed in the select list form control. The `<option>` tag denotes the beginning of the option item. The closing `</option>` tag denotes the end of option item. Attributes configure the value of the option and whether they are preselected. Common attributes are listed in Table 10.10.

TABLE 10.10 *Common Option Element Attributes*

Attribute	Value	Usage
value	Text or numeric characters	Assigns a value to the option; this value can be accessed by client-side scripting and server-side processing
selected	selected	Configures an option to be initially selected when displayed by a browser
disabled	disabled	Form control is disabled

The HTML for the select list in Figure 10.11 follows:

```
<select size="1" name="favbrowser" id="favbrowser">
  <option>Select your favorite browser</option>
  <option value="Chrome">Chrome</option>
  <option value="Firefox">Firefox</option>
  <option value="Edge">Edge</option>
</select>
```

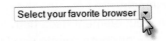

Select List: One Initial Visible Item

FIGURE 10.11 *A select list with size set to 1 functions as a drop-down box when the arrow is clicked.*

The HTML for the select list in Figure 10.12 follows:

```
<select size="4" name="jumpmenu" id="jumpmenu">
  <option value="index.html">Home</option>
  <option value="products.html">Products</option>
  <option value="services.html">Services</option>
  <option value="about.html">About</option>
  <option value="contact.html">Contact</option>
</select>
```

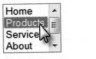

Select List: Four Items Visible

FIGURE 10.12 *Since there are more than four choices, the browser displays a scroll bar.*

Label Element

The **label element** is a container tag that associates a text description with a form control. This is helpful to visually challenged individuals using assistive technology such as a screen reader to match up the text descriptions on forms with their corresponding form controls. The label element also benefits individuals without fine motor control. Clicking anywhere on either a form control or its associated text label will set the cursor focus to the form control.

There are two different methods to associate a label with a form control.

1. The first method places the label element as a container around both the text description and the HTML form element. Notice that both the text label and the form control must be adjacent elements. The code is

   ```
   <label>E-mail: <input type="text" name="email" id="email"></label>
   ```

2. The second method uses the `for` attribute to associate the label with a particular HTML form element. This is more flexible and it does not require the text label and the form control to be adjacent. The code is

   ```
   <label for="email">E-mail: </label>
   <input type="text" name="email" id="email">
   ```

   Notice that the value of the **for attribute** on the label element is the same as the value of the `id` attribute on the input element. This creates the association between the text label and the form control. The input element uses both the `name` and `id` attributes for different purposes. The `name` attribute can be used by client-side scripting and server-side processing. The `id` attribute creates an identifier that can be used by the label element, anchor element, and CSS selectors.

The label element does not display on the web page—it works behind the scenes to provide for accessibility.

Hands-On Practice 10.3

In this Hands-On Practice you will add the label element to the text box and scrolling text area form controls on the form you created in Hands-On Practice 10.2 (see Figure 10.10) as a starting point. Launch a text editor and open the file located at chapter10/10.2/contact.html in the student files. Save the file with the name label.html.

1. Locate the text box for the first name. Add a label element to wrap around the input tag as follows:

```
<label>First Name: <input type="text" name="fname" id="fname">
</label>
```

2. Using the method shown previously, add a label element for the last name and e-mail form controls.

3. Configure the text "Comments:" within a label element. Associate the label with the scrolling text box form control. Sample code is

```
<label for="comments">Comments:</label><br>
<textarea name="comments" id="comments" rows="4" cols="40"></textarea>
```

4. Save your file. Test your page in a browser. It should look similar to the page shown in Figure 10.10—the label elements do not change the way the page displays, but a web visitor with physical challenges should find the form easier to use.

You can compare your work with the solution found in the student files (chapter10/10.3) folder. Try entering some information into your form. Try clicking the submit button. Don't worry if the form redisplays but nothing seems to happen when you click the button—you haven't configured this form to work with any server-side processing. Connecting a form to server-side processing is demonstrated later in this chapter.

Fieldset Element and Legend Element

Fieldset and legend elements work together to visually group form controls together and increase the usability of the form.

The Fieldset Element

A technique that can be used to create a more visually pleasing form is to group elements of a similar purpose together using the **fieldset element**, which will cause the browser to render a visual cue, such as an outline or a border, around form elements grouped together within the fieldset. The `<fieldset>` tag denotes the beginning of the grouping. The closing `</fieldset>` tag denotes the end of the grouping.

The Legend Element

The **legend element** provides a text description for the fieldset grouping. The `<legend>` tag denotes the beginning of the text description. The closing `</legend>` tag denotes the end of the text description.

The HTML to create the grouping shown in Figure 10.13 follows:

```
<fieldset>
<legend>Billing Address</legend>
<label>Street: <input type="text" name="street" id="street"
                  size="54"></label><br><br>
<label>City: <input type="text" name="city" id="city"></label>
<label>State: <input type="text" name="state" id="state" maxlength="2"
                  size="5"></label>
<label>Zip: <input type="text" name="zip" id="zip" maxlength="5"
                  size="5"></label>
</fieldset>
```

FIGURE 10.13 *Form controls that are all related to a mailing address.*

The grouping and visual effect of the fieldset element creates an organized and appealing web page containing a form. Using the fieldset and legend elements to group form controls enhances accessibility by organizing the controls both visually and semantically.

The fieldset and legend elements can be accessed by screen readers and are useful tools to configure groups of radio buttons and check boxes on web pages.

A Look Ahead—Styling a Fieldset Group with CSS

The next section focuses on styling a form with CSS. But how about a quick preview?

Figures 10.13 and 10.14 show the same form elements, but the form in Figure 10.14 is styled with CSS—the same functionality with increased visual appeal. Access the example page at chapter10/fieldset.html in the student files. The style rules follow:

```
fieldset { width: 500px; border: 2px ridge #ff0000;
          font-family: Arial, sans-serif; padding: 10px; }
legend { font-family: Georgia, "Times New Roman", serif;
         font-weight: bold; }
label { padding-left: 10px; }
```

Fieldset and Legend Styled with CSS

Billing Address

Street:

City: State: Zip:

FIGURE 10.14 *The fieldset, legend, and label elements are configured with CSS.*

Accessibility and Forms

Using the HTML elements label, fieldset, and legend will increase the accessibility of your web forms. This makes it easier for individuals with vision and mobility challenges to use your form pages. An added benefit is that the use of label, fieldset, and legend elements may increase the readability and usability of the web form for all visitors. Be sure to include contact information (e-mail address and/or phone number) just in case a visitor is unable to submit your form successfully and requires additional assistance.

Some of your website visitors may have difficulty using the mouse and will access your form with a keyboard. The Tab key can be used to move from one form control to another. The default action for the Tab key within a form is to move to the next form control in the order in which the form controls are coded in the web page document. This is usually appropriate. However, if the tab order needs to be changed for a form, use the **tabindex** attribute on each form control.

Another technique that can make your form keyboard-friendly is the use of the **accesskey attribute** on form controls. Assigning accesskey a value of one of the characters (letter or number) on the keyboard will create a hot key that your website visitor can press to move the cursor immediately to a form control. Windows users will press the Alt key and the character key. Mac users will press the Ctrl key and the character key. When choosing accesskey values, avoid combinations that are already used by the operating system (such as Alt+F to display the File menu). Testing hot keys is crucial.

Style a Form with CSS

FIGURE 10.15 *The alignment needs improvement.*

The form in Figure 10.15 looks a little "messy" and you might be wondering how the alignment could be improved. Before CSS was well supported by browsers web designers typically used a table to configure the display of form elements, often placing the text labels and form field elements in separate table data cells. However, the table approach is outdated, does not provide support for accessibility, and can be difficult to maintain over time. The modern approach is to style the form with CSS.

FIGURE 10.16 *Form wireframe.*

When styling a form with CSS, the box model is used to create a series of boxes, as shown in Figure 10.16. The outermost box defines the form area. Other boxes indicate label elements and form controls. CSS is used to configure these components.

 Hands-On Practice 10.4

You will style a form with CSS in this Hands-On Practice. To get started, launch a text editor and open the starter.html file from the chapter10 folder in the student files. Save the file with the name contactus.html. When you have completed, your form will be similar to the example in Figure 10.17.

The HTML for the form is shown below for your reference:

```
<form>
  <label for="myName">Name:</label>
  <input type="text" name="myName" id="myName">
  <label for="myEmail">E-mail:</label>
  <input type="text" name="myEmail" id="myEmail">
  <label for="myComments">Comments:</label>
  <textarea name="myComments" id="myComments"
    rows="2" cols="2 0"></textarea>
  <input type="submit" value="Submit">
</form>
```

FIGURE 10.17 *The form is styled with CSS.*

Configure embedded CSS within the style element as follows:

1. **The form element selector.** Configure form elements with a #EAEAEA background color, Arial or sans serif font, 350px width, and 10 pixels of padding:

```
form { background-color: #EAEAEA;
       font-family: Arial, sans-serif;
       width: 350px; padding: 10px; }
```

2. **The label element selector.** Configure label elements to float to the left, clear left floats, and use block display. Also set width to 100px, 10 pixels of right padding, a 10px top margin, and right-aligned text:

```
label { float: left; clear: left; display: block;
        width: 100px; padding-right: 10px;
        margin-top: 10px; text-align: right; }
```

3. **The input element selector.** Configure input elements with block display and a 10px top margin:

```
input { display: block; margin-top: 10px; }
```

4. **The textarea element selector.** Configure textarea elements with block display and a 10px top margin:

```
textarea { display: block; margin-top: 10px; }
```

5. **The submit button.** The submit button needs to display under the other form controls, with a 110 pixel margin on the left. You could configure a new id or class and then edit the HTML, but there is a more efficient method. You will configure a new type of selector, an **attribute selector**, which allows you to select using both the element name and attribute value as the criteria. In this case we need to style input tags that have a type attribute with the value submit in a different manner than the other input tags, so we'll configure an attribute selector for this purpose. The CSS follows:

```
input[type="submit"] { margin-left: 110px; }
```

Save your file and test your page in a browser. It should look similar to Figure 10.17. You can compare your work with the sample in the student files (chapter10/10.4).

The Attribute Selector

Use an **attribute selector** when you need to configure an element that has a specific attribute value and you would like to avoid creating a new id or class. When you code the selector, type the element name first followed by a set of braces that contain the name and value of the attribute you chose to use for the criteria. For example, the input[type="radio"] selector will configure styles for the radio button form controls but will not configure styles for other input elements. Find out more about attribute selectors at the following resources: http://css-tricks.com/attribute-selectors and https://www.w3.org/TR/CSS22/selector.html#attribute-selectors.

Server-Side Processing

VideoNote
Connect a Form to Server-side Processing

As you've coded and tested the forms in this chapter, you may have noticed that when you click the submit button, the form just redisplays—the form doesn't "do" anything. This is because the forms haven't been configured to invoke server-side processing.

Your web browser requests web pages and their related files from a web server. The web server locates the files and sends them to your web browser. Then the web browser renders the returned files and displays the requested web pages. Figure 10.18 illustrates the communication between the web browser and the web server.

FIGURE 10.18 *The web browser (client) communicates with the web server.*

Sometimes a website needs more functionality than static web pages—possibly a site search, order form, e-mail list, database display, or other type of interactive, dynamic processing. This is when server-side processing is needed. Early web servers used a protocol called **Common Gateway Interface** (CGI) to provide this functionality. CGI is a protocol, or standard method, for a web server to pass a web page user's request (which is typically initiated through the use of a form) to an application program and to accept information to send to the user. The web server typically passes the form information to a small application program that is run by the operating system and processes the data, and it usually sends back a confirmation web page or message. Perl and C are popular programming languages for CGI applications.

Server-side scripting is a technology in which a server-side script is run on a web server to dynamically generate web pages. Examples of server-side scripting technologies include PHP, Ruby on Rails, Adobe ColdFusion, Sun JavaServer Pages, and Microsoft.NET. Server-side scripting differs from CGI in that it uses **direct execution**—the script is run either by the web server itself or by an extension module to the web server.

A web page invokes server-side processing by either an attribute on a form or by a hyperlink—the URL of the script is used. Any form data that exists is passed to the script. The script completes its processing and may generate a confirmation or response web page with the requested information. When invoking a server-side script, the web developer and the server-side programmer must communicate about the form **method attribute** (`get` or `post`), form **action attribute** (URL of the server-side script), and any special form element control(s) expected by the server-side script.

The `method` attribute is used on the form tag to indicate the way in which the name and value pairs should be passed to the server. The `method` attribute value of `get` causes the form data to be appended to the URL, which is easily visible and not secure. The `method` attribute value of `post` does not pass the form information in the URL; it passes it in the entity body of the HTTP request, which makes it more private. The W3C recommends the `method="post"` method.

The `action` attribute is used on the `<form>` tag to invoke a server-side script. The `name` attribute and the `value` attribute associated with each form control are passed to the server-side script. The `name` attribute may be used as a variable name in the server-side processing.

Privacy and Forms

A **privacy policy** lists the guidelines that you develop to protect the privacy of your visitors' information. Websites either indicate this policy on the form page itself or create a separate page that describes the privacy policy (and other company policies).

If you browse popular sites such as Amazon.com or eBay.com, you'll find links to their privacy policies (sometimes called a privacy notice) in the page footer area. The privacy policy of the Better Business Bureau can be found at http://www.bbb.org/us/privacy-policy. Include a privacy notice in your site to inform your visitors how you plan to use the information they share with you. The Better Business Bureau (https://www.bbb.org/dallas/for-businesses/bbb-sample-privacy-policy1) recommends that a privacy policy describes the type of information collected, the methods used to collect the information, the way that the information is used, the methods used to protect the information, and provisions for customers or visitors to control their personal information.

Sources of Free Remote-Hosted Form Processing

If your web host provider does not support server-side processing, free remotely hosted scripts may be an option. Try out the free form processing offered by http://formbuddy.com, http://www.expressdb.com, or http://www.formmail.com.

Sources of Free Server-Side Scripts

To use free scripts, you need to have access to a web server that supports the language used by the script. Contact your web host provider to determine what is supported. Be aware that many free web host providers do not support server-side processing (you get what you pay for!). Visit http://scriptarchive.com and http://php.resourceindex.com for free scripts and related resources.

Practice with a Form

  Hands-On Practice 10.5

In this Hands-On Practice you will modify the form page that you created earlier in this chapter, configuring the form so that it uses the post method to invoke a server-side script. Your computer must be connected to the Internet when you test your work. The post method is more secure than the get method because the post method does not pass the form information in the URL; it passes it in the entity-body of the HTTP Request, which makes it more private.

When using a server-side script you will need to obtain some information, or documentation, from the person or organization providing the script. You will need to know the location of the script, whether it requires the get or post method, whether it requires any specific names for the form controls, and whether it requires any hidden form elements. The `action` attribute is used on the `<form>` tag to invoke a server-side script. A server-side script has been created at http://webdevbasics.net/scripts/demo.php for students to use for this exercise. The documentation for the server-side script is listed in Table 10.11.

TABLE 10.11   *Server-Side Script Documentation*

Script URL	http://webdevbasics.net/scripts/demo.php
Form method	`post`
Script purpose	This script will accept form input and display the form control names and values in a web page. This is a sample script for student assignments. It demonstrates that server-side processing has been invoked. A script used by an actual website would perform a function such as sending an e-mail message or updating a database.

Launch a text editor and open the file you created in Hands-On Practice 10.4, also found in the student files (chapter10/10.4/contactus.html).

Modify the `<form>` tag by adding a `method` attribute with a value of post and an `action` attribute with a value of http://webdevbasics.net/scripts/demo.php. The HTML for the revised `<form>` tag is

```
<form method="post" action="http://webdevbasics.net/scripts/demo.php">
```

Save your page and test it in a browser. Your screen should look similar to Figure 10.17. Compare your work with the solution in the student files (chapter10/10.5/contactus.html).

Now you are ready to test your form. You must be connected to the Internet to test your form successfully. Enter information in the form controls and click the submit button. You should see a confirmation page similar to the one shown in Figure 10.19.

The demo.php script creates a web page that displays a message and the form information you entered. This confirmation page was created by the server-side script on the `action` attribute in the `<form>` tag. Writing scripts for server-side processing is beyond the scope of this textbook. However, if you are curious, visit http://webdevbasics.net/4e/chapter10.html to see the source code for the demo.php script.

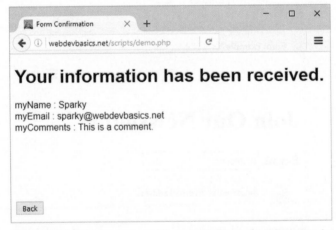

FIGURE 10.19 *The server-side script has created this page in response to the form.*

 What should I do if nothing happened when I tested my form?

Try these troubleshooting hints:

▶ Verify that your computer is connected to the Internet.

▶ Verify the spelling of the script location in the `action` attribute.

▶ Recall that attention to detail is crucial!

HTML5 Text Form Controls

The E-mail Address Input Form Control

The **e-mail address** form control is similar to the text box. Its purpose is to accept information that must be in e-mail format, such as DrMorris2010@gmail.com. The `<input>` element with `type="email"` configures an e-mail address form control. Only browsers that support the HTML5 `email` attribute value will verify the format of the information. Other browsers will treat this form control as a text box. Figure 10.20 (see chapter10/email.html in the student files) shows an error message displayed by Firefox when text other than an e-mail address is entered. Note that the browser does not verify that the e-mail address actually exists—just that the text entered is in the correct format. The HTML is

```
<label for="myEmail">E-mail:</label>
<input type="email" name="myEmail" id="myEmail">
```

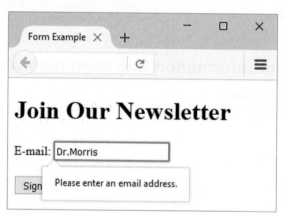

FIGURE 10.20 *The browser displays an error message.*

The URL Form Input Control

The **URL** form control is similar to the text box. It is intended to accept any type of URL or URI, such as http://webdevbasics.net. The `<input>` element with `type="url"` configures a URL form control. Only browsers that support the HTML5 `url` attribute value will verify the format of the information. Other browsers render this form control as a text box. Figure 10.21 (see chapter10/url.html in the student files) shows an error message displayed by Firefox when text other than a URL is entered. Note that the browser does not verify that the URL actually exists—just that the text entered is in the correct format. The HTML is

```
<label for="myWebsite">Suggest a Website:</label>
<input type="url" name="myWebsite" id="myWebsite">
```

FIGURE 10.21 *The browser displays an error message.*

The Telephone Number Input Form Control

The **telephone number** form control is similar to the text box. Its purpose is to accept a telephone number. The `<input>` element with `type="tel"` configures a telephone number form control. An example is in the student files (chapter10/tel.html). Browsers that do not support `type="tel"` will render this form control as a text box. Some mobile devices display a numeric keypad for entry into telephone number input form controls. The HTML is

```
<label for="mobile">Mobile Number:</label>
<input type="tel" name="mobile" id="mobile">
```

The Search Input Form Control

The **search** form control is similar to the text box and is used to accept a search term. The `<input>` element with `type="search"` configures a search input form control. An example is in the student files (chapter10/search.html). Browsers that do not support `type="search"` will render this form control as a text box. The HTML is

```
<label for="keyword">Search:</label>
<input type="search" name="keyword" id="keyword">
```

Valid Attributes for HTML5 Text Form Controls

Attributes supported by the HTML5 text form controls are listed in Table 10.2.

How can I tell which browsers support the new HTML5 form elements?

There's no substitute for testing. With that in mind, several resources are listed below that provide information about browser support for new HTML5 elements:

▶ http://caniuse.com (also CSS3 browser support information)
▶ http://findmebyip.com/litmus (also CSS3 browser support information)
▶ http://html5readiness.com
▶ http://html5test.com

HTML5 Datalist Element

Figure 10.22 shows the **datalist** form control in action. Notice how a selection of choices is offered to the user along with a text box for entry. A datalist can be used to suggest predefined input values to the web page visitor. Configure a datalist using three components: an input element, the datalist element, and one or more option elements. Only browsers that support the HTML5 datalist element will display and process the datalist items. Other browsers ignore the datalist element and render the form control as a text box.

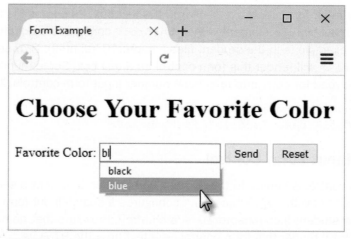

FIGURE 10.22 *Firefox displays the datalist form control.*

The source code for the datalist is available in the student files (chapter10/list.html). The HTML follows:

```
<label for="color">Favorite Color:</label>
<input type="text" name="color" id="color" list="colors">
  <datalist id="colors">
  <option>black</option>
  <option>red</option>
  <option>green</option>
  <option>blue</option>
  <option>yellow</option>
  <option>pink</option>
  <option>cyan</option>
</datalist>
```

Notice that the value of the **list attribute** on the input element is the same as the value of the id attribute on the datalist element. This creates the association between the text box and the datalist form control. One or more option elements can be used to offer predefined choices to your web page visitor. The text contained within the option element configures the text displayed in each list entry. The list can be used to suggest input values to the user corresponding to the characters they type in the text box. When a web page visitor types characters in the text box, the option elements with text that match the characters typed are displayed. The web page visitor can choose an option from the displayed list (see Figure 10.22) or type directly in the text box, as shown in Figure 10.23.

The datalist form control offers a convenient way to offer choices yet provide for flexibility on a form. At the time this text was written, current versions of Internet Explorer, Edge, Firefox, Chrome, and Opera browsers supported this new HTML5 element.

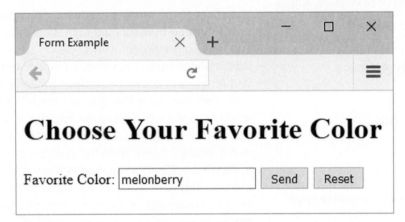

FIGURE 10.23 *The user can choose to type a value not on the list in the text box.*

What happens in browsers that do not support the new HTML5 form controls?

Browsers that do not support the new input types will display them as text boxes and ignore unsupported attributes or elements. Figure 10.24 depicts the display of a datalist in the Internet Explorer 9 browser. Notice that, unlike Firefox, the browser does not render the list—it only renders a text box.

FIGURE 10.24 *Browsers that do not support the datalist form control display a text box.*

HTML5 Slider and Spinner Controls

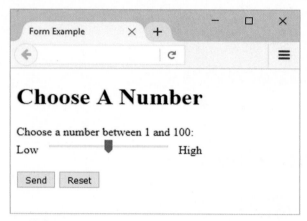

FIGURE 10.25 *The Firefox browser displays the range form control.*

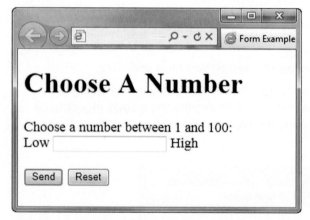

FIGURE 10.26 *Internet Explorer 9 renders the range form control as a text box.*

The Slider Input Form Control

The **slider** form control provides a visual, interactive user interface that accepts numerical information. The `<input>` element with `type="range"` configures a slider control in which a number within a specified range is chosen. The default range is from 0 to 100. Only browsers that support the HTML5 `range` attribute value will display the interactive slider control, shown in Figure 10.25 (chapter10/range.html in the student files). Note the position of the slider in Figure 10.25; this resulted in the value 80 being chosen. The nondisplay of the value to the user may be a disadvantage of the slider control. Nonsupporting browsers render this form control as a text box, as shown in Figure 10.26.

The slider control accepts attributes listed in Tables 10.2 and 10.12. The `min`, `max`, and `step` attributes are new. Use the **min attribute** to configure the minimum range value. Use the **max attribute** to configure the maximum range value. Use the **step attribute** to configure a value for the step between values to be other than 1.

The HTML for the slider control rendered in Figures 10.25 and 10.26 is shown below.

```
<label for="myChoice">Choose a number between 1 and 100:</label><br>
Low <input type="range" min="1" and max="100" name="myChoice" id="myChoice"> High
```

The Spinner Input Form Control

The **spinner** form control displays an interface that accepts numerical information and provides feedback to the user. The `<input>` element with `type="number"` configures a spinner control in which the user can either type a number into the text box or select a number from a specified range. Only browsers that support the HTML5 `number` attribute value will display the interactive spinner control, shown in Figure 10.27 (chapter10/spinner.html in the student files). Other browsers render this form control as a text box. Expect increased support in the future.

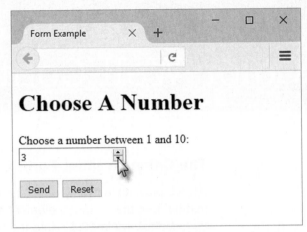

FIGURE 10.27 *A spinner control displayed in the Firefox browser.*

The spinner control accepts attributes listed in Tables 10.2 and 10.12. Use the `min` attribute to configure the minimum value. Use the `max` attribute to configure the maximum value. Use the `step` attribute to configure a value for the step between values to be other than 1. The HTML for the spinner control displayed in Figure 10.27 is

```
<label for="myChoice">Choose a number between 1 and 10:</label>
<input type="number" name="myChoice" id="myChoice" min="1" max="10">
```

TABLE 10.12 *Additional Attributes for Slider, Spinner, and Date/Time Form Controls*

Attribute	Value	Usage
max	Maximum value	HTML5 attribute for range, number, and date/time input controls; specifies a maximum value
min	Minimum value	HTML5 attribute for range, number, and date/time input controls; specifies a minimum value
step	Incremental step value	HTML5 attribute for range, number, and date/time input controls; specifies a value for incremental steps

HTML5 and Progressive Enhancement

Use HTML5 form elements with the concept of progressive enhancement in mind. Nonsupporting browsers will display text boxes in place of form elements that are not recognized. Supporting browsers will display and process the new form controls. This is progressive enhancement in action—everyone sees a usable form, and those using modern browsers benefit from enhanced features.

HTML5 Calendar and Color-Well Controls

The Calendar Input Form Control

HTML5 provides a variety of calendar form controls to accept date- and time-related information. Use the `<input>` element and configure the `type` attribute to specify a date or time control. Table 10.13 lists the HTML5 date and time controls.

TABLE 10.13 *Date and Time Controls*

Type Attribute	Value	Purpose Format
`date`	A date	YYYY-MM-DD Example: January 2, 2018, is represented by "20180102"
`datetime`	A date and time with time zone information; note that the time zone is indicated by the offset from UTC time	YYYY-MM-DDTHH:MM:SS-##:##Z Example: January 2, 2018, at exactly 9:58 AM Chicago time (CST) is represented by "2018-01-02T09:58:00-06:00Z"
`datetime-local`	A date and time without time zone information	YYYY-MM-DDTHH:MM:SS Example: January 2, 2018, at exactly 9:58 AM is represented by "2018-01-02T09:58:00"
`time`	A time without time zone information	HH:MM:SS Example: 1:34 PM is represented by "13:34"
`month`	A year and month	YYYY-MM Example: January, 2018, is represented by "2018-01"
`week`	A year and week	YYYY-W##, where ## represents the week in the year Example: The third week in 2018 is represented by "2018-W03"

The form in Figure 10.28 (see chapter10/date.html in the student files) uses the `<input>` element with `type="date"` to configure a calendar control with which the user can select a date.

The HTML for the date control displayed in Figure 10.28 is

```
<label for="myDate">Choose a
Date</label>
<input type="date" name="myDate"
id="myDate">
```

The date and time controls accept attributes listed in Tables 10.2 and 10.12. The implementation of the date control is determined by the browser. Google Chrome and Opera display a calendar interface. However, Microsoft Edge displays a spinner interface for date selection. Non-supporting browsers currently render the date and time form controls as a text box, but you should expect increased support in the future.

FIGURE 10.28 *A date form control displayed in the Google Chrome browser.*

The Color-Well Form Control

The **color-well** form control displays an interface that offers a color-picker interface to the user. The input element with `type="color"` configures a control with which the user can choose a color. At the time this text was written, only the Firefox, Google Chrome, Safari, and Opera browsers supported the color-picker interface, as shown in Figure 10.29 (see chapter10/color.html in the student files). Other browsers render this form control as a text box.

The HTML for the color-well form control rendered in Figure 10.29 is

```
<label for="myColor">Choose
a color:</label>
<input type="color"
name="myColor" id="myColor">
```

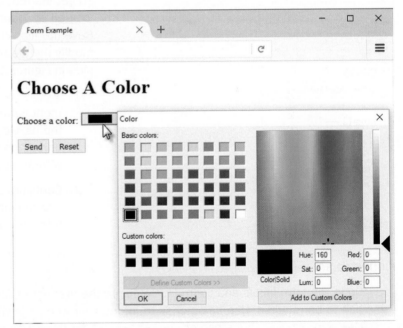

FIGURE 10.29 *The Google Chrome browser supports the color-well form control.*

In the next section, you'll get some experience with the new HTML5 form controls.

Practice with an HTML5 Form

FIGURE 10.30 *The form displayed in Firefox.*

In this Hands-On Practice you will code HTML5 form controls as you configure a form that accepts a first name, a last name, an e-mail address, a rating value, and comments from a website visitor. Figure 10.30 displays the form in the Firefox browser, which supports the HTML5 features used in the Hands-On Practice. Figure 10.31 displays the form in Internet Explorer 9, which does not support the HTML5 features. Notice that the form is enhanced in Firefox but is still usable in both browsers—demonstrating the concept of progressive enhancement.

To get started, launch a text editor and open the file located at chapter1/template.html in the student files. Save the file with the name comment.html. You will modify the file to create a web page similar to the examples in Figures 10.30 and 10.31.

1. Modify the title element to display the text: Comment Form. Configure the text contained within the h1 element to be: Comment Form. Add a paragraph to indicate: Required fields are marked with an asterisk *.

2. Configure the form element to submit the form information to the textbook's form processor at http://webdevbasics.net/scripts/demo.php.

```
<form method="post" action="http://
webdevbasics.net/scripts/demo.php">
```

3. Code the form labels and controls. Configure the first name, last name, e-mail, and comment information to be required. Use an asterisk to inform your web page visitor about the required fields. Use `type="email"` instead of `type="input"` for the e-mail address. Use the `placeholder` attribute to provide hints to the user in the name and e-mail form controls. Add a slider control (use `type="range"`) to generate a value from 1 to 10 for the rating. The HTML follows:

```
<form method="post" action="http://webdevbasics.net/scripts/demo.php">
  <label for="myFirstName">* First Name</label>
  <input type="text" name="myFirstName" id="myFirstName"
      required="required" placeholder="your first name">
  <label for="myLastName">* Last Name</label>
```

```
    <input type="text" name="myLastName"
           id="myLastName" required="required"
           placeholder="your last name">
    <label for="myEmail">* E-mail</label>
    <input type="email" name="myEmail" id="myEmail"
           required="required"
           placeholder="you@yourdomain.com">
    <label for="myRating">Rating (1 &mdash; 10)
           </label>
    <input type="range" name="myRating"
           id="myRating" min="1" max="10">
    <label for="myComments">* Comments</label>
    <textarea name="myComments" id="myComments"
              rows="2" cols="40"
              required="required"
              placeholder="your comments here">
    </textarea>
    <input type="submit" value="Submit">
</form>
```

FIGURE 10.31 *The form displayed in Internet Explorer 9.*

4. Code embedded CSS. Configure the label element selector to use block display with a 20px top margin. Configure the input element selector to use block display with a 20 pixel bottom margin. The CSS follows:

```
label { display: block;
        margin-top: 20px; }
input { display: block;
        margin-bottom: 20px; }
```

5. Save your file. Test your page in a browser. If you use a browser that supports the HTML5 features used in the form, your page should look similar to Figure 10.30. If you use a browser that does not offer support of the form's HTML5 attributes (such as Internet Explorer 9), your form should look similar to Figure 10.31. The display in other browsers will depend on the level of HTML5 support.

6. Try submitting the form without entering any information. Figure 10.32 shows the error message displayed by Firefox.

Compare your work with the solution in the student files (chapter10/10.6). As this Hands-On Practice demonstrated, support of the new HTML5 form control attributes and values is not uniform. It will be some time before all browsers support these new features. Design forms with progressive enhancement in mind and be aware of both the benefits and the limitations of using new HTML5 features.

FIGURE 10.32 *The Firefox browser displays an error message.*

CHAPTER 10

Review and Apply

Review Questions

Multiple Choice. Choose the best answer for each item.

1. What will happen when a browser encounters a new HTML5 form control that it does not support?

   a. The computer will shut down.

   b. The browser will display an error message.

   c. The browser will crash.

   d. The browser will display an input text box.

2. Which attribute of the `<form>` tag is used to specify the name and location of the script that will process the form field values?

   a. `action`   b. `process`

   c. `method`   d. `id`

3. Forms contain various types of _____, such as text boxes and buttons, that accept information from a web page visitor.

   a. hidden elements   b. labels

   c. form controls   d. legends

4. Choose the tag that would configure a text box with the name "city" and a width of 35 characters.

   a. `<input type="text" id="city" width="35">`

   b. `<input type="text" name="city" size="35">`

   c. `<input type="text" name="city" space="35">`

   d. `<input type="text" name="city" width="35">`

5. You would like to accept a number that is in a range from 1 to 50. The user needs visual verification of the number selected. Which of the following form controls is best to use for this purpose?

   a. spinner   b. radio button

   c. check box   d. slider

6. Which of the following form controls would be appropriate for an area that your visitors can use to type in their e-mail address?

   a. check box   b. select list

   c. text box   d. scrolling text box

7. You would like to conduct a survey and ask your web page visitors to vote for their favorite search engine. Which of the following form controls is best to use for this purpose?

   a. radio button   b. text box

   c. scrolling text box   d. check box

8. Which of the following form controls would be appropriate for an area that your visitors can use to type in comments about your website?

   a. textbox   b. select list

   c. radio button   d. scrolling text box

9. Which tag would configure a scrolling text box with the name comments, four rows, and thirty characters?

   a. `<textarea name="comments" width="30" rows="4"></textarea>`

   b. `<input type="textarea" name="comments" size="30" rows="4">`

   c. `<textarea name="comments" rows="4" cols="30"></textarea>`

   d. `<textarea name="comments" width="30" rows="4">`

10. Choose the item that would associate a label displaying the text E-mail: with the text box named email.

a. `E-mail: <input type="textbox" name="email" id="email">`

b. `<label>E-mail: <input type="text" name="email" id="email"></label>`

c. `<label for="email">E-mail:</label> <input type="text" name="email" id="email">`

d. both b and c

Hands-On Exercises

1. Write the code to create the following:
   a. A text box named username that will accept the user name of web page visitors. The text box should allow a maximum of 30 characters to be entered.
   b. A group of radio buttons that website visitors can check to vote for their favorite day of the week.
   c. A select list that asks website visitors to select their favorite social networking website.
   d. A fieldset and legend with the text "Billing Address" around the form controls for the following fields: AddressLine1, AddressLine2, City, State, Zip Code.
   e. A hidden form control with the name of userid.
   f. A password form control with the name of password.

2. Create a web page with a form that accepts requests for a brochure to be sent in the mail. Use the HTML5 `required` attribute to configure the browser to verify that all fields have been entered by the user. Sketch out the form on paper before you begin.

3. Create a web page with a form that accepts feedback from website visitors. Use the HTML5 input `type="email"` along with the `required` attribute to configure the browser to verify the data entered. Also configure the browser to require user comments with a maximum length of 1200 characters accepted. Sketch out the form on paper before you begin.

4. Create a web page with a form that accepts a website visitor's name, e-mail, and birthdate. Use the HTML5 `type="date"` attribute to configure a calendar control on browsers that support the attribute value.

Focus on Web Design

1. Search the Web for a web page that uses an HTML form. Print the browser view of the page. Print out the source code of the web page. Using the printout, highlight or circle the tags related to forms. On a separate sheet of paper, create some notes by listing the tags and attributes related to forms found on your sample page along with a brief description of their purpose. Place your name in an e-mail link on the web page.

2. Choose one server-side technology mentioned in this chapter: Ruby on Rails, PHP, JSP, or ASP.NET. Use the resources listed in the chapter as a starting point, but also search the Web for additional resources on the server-side technology you have chosen. Create a web page that lists at least five useful resources along with information about each that provides the name of the site, the URL, a brief description of what is offered, and a recommended page (such as a tutorial, free script, and so on). Place your name in an e-mail link on the web page.

Pacific Trails Resort Case Study

In this chapter's case study you will use the existing Pacific Trails website (Chapter 9) as a starting point. You will add a new page to the Pacific Trails website—the Reservations page. Refer back to the site map for the Pacific Trails website in Chapter 2, Figure 2.27. The Reservations page will use the same two-column layout as the other Pacific Trails web pages. You'll apply your new skills from this chapter and code a form in the content area of the Reservations page.

You have four tasks in this case study:

1. Create a folder for the Pacific Trails website.
2. Modify the CSS to configure style rules needed for the Reservations page.
3. Create the Reservations page: reservations.html. Your new page will be similar to Figure 10.33 when you have completed this step.
4. Configure HTML5 form control features on the Reservations page.

Task 1: Create a folder called ch10pacific to contain your Pacific Trails Resort website files. Copy the files from the Chapter 9 Case Study ch9pacific folder to your new ch10pacific folder.

Task 2: Configure the CSS. Review Figure 10.33 and the wireframe in Figure 10.34. Notice how the text labels for the form controls are on the left side of the content area but contain right-aligned text. Notice the empty vertical space between each form control. Open pacific.css in a text editor. You will code the following styles above the media queries.

FIGURE 10.33 *The new Pacific Trails Reservations page.*

a. Configure a label element selector. Set left float, block display, right alignment for text, a width of 120 pixels, and an appropriate amount of right padding.

b. Configure the input element and textarea element selectors. Set block display and 20 pixels of bottom margin.

c. Configure the submit button with a 130px left margin.

d. Configure style rules to optimize the display on smartphone-sized mobile devices by rendering the label text above each form control and eliminating the submit button's left margin. Add the following style rules to the media query that targets a maximum width 37.5em:

```
label { float: none;
        text-align: left; }
input[type="submit"]
        { margin-left: 0; }
```

Save the pacific.css file.

Task 3: **Create the Reservations Page.** A productivity technique is to create new pages based on existing pages so you can benefit from your previous work. Your new Reservations page will use the index.html page as a starting point. Open the index.html page for the Pacific Trails Resort website in a text editor. Select File > Save As and save the file with the new name of reservations.html in the ch10pacific folder.

Launch a text editor and edit the reservations.html file.

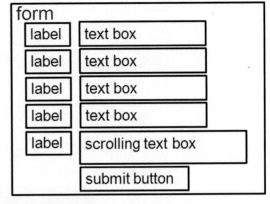

FIGURE 10.34 *The sketch of the form.*

1. Modify the page title. Change the text contained between the `<title>` and `</title>` tags to: Pacific Trails Resort :: Reservations.

2. The Reservations page will not feature a large image. Remove the div element assigned to the homehero id.

3. Replace the text contained within the `<h2>` tags with: Reservations at Pacific Trails.

4. Delete the paragraph and the unordered list. Do not delete the logo, navigation, contact information, or footer areas of the page.

5. Position your cursor on a blank line below the h2 element. Configure an h3 element with the following text: Contact Us Today!

6. Position your cursor on a blank line under the h3 element. You are ready to configure the form. Begin with a `<form>` tag that uses the post method and the `action` attribute to invoke server-side processing. Unless directed otherwise by your instructor, use http://webdevbasics.net/scripts/pacific.php as the value of the `action` attribute.

7. Configure the form control for the First Name information. Create a `<label>` element that contains the text "First Name:". Create a text box configured with "myFName" as the value of the `id` and `name` attributes. Use the `for` attribute to associate the label element with the form control.

8. In a similar way, configure form controls and label elements to collect the following information: Last Name, E-mail Address, and Phone Number. Use myLName, myEmail, and myPhone as the `id` and `name` values for the last name, e-mail, and phone form controls. Also set the `size` of the e-mail text box to 35 and the `maxlength` of the phone text box to 12.

9. Configure the Comments area on the form. Create a label element that contains the text "Comments:". Create a textarea element configured with "myComments" as the value of the id and name attributes, `rows` set to 2, and `cols` set to 30. Use the `for` attribute to associate the label element with the form control.

10. Configure the submit button on the form (code an input element with `type="submit"` and `value="Submit"`).

11. Code an ending `</form>` tag on a blank line after the submit button.

Save your reservations.html page and test it in a browser. It should look similar to the page shown in Figure 10.33. If you are connected to the Internet, submit the form. This will send your form information to the server-side script configured in the `<form>` tag. A confirmation page similar to Figure 10.35 will be displayed that lists the form control names and the values you entered.

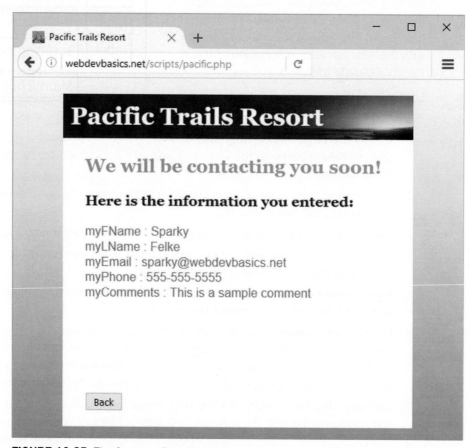

FIGURE 10.35 *The form confirmation page.*

Task 4: Configure the Form with HTML5 Attributes and Values. Get more practice with the new HTML5 elements by modifying the form on the Reservations page to use HTML5 attributes and values. You'll also improve the form by adding form controls to accept the date and number of nights. Modify the reservations.html file in a text editor.

1. Add a paragraph above the form to indicate:
   Required fields are marked with an asterisk *.

2. Use the `required` attribute to require the first name, last name, e-mail, and comments form controls to be entered. Add an asterisk at the beginning of each label text.

3. Configure the input element for the e-mail address (use `type="email"`).

4. Configure the input element for the phone number (use `type="tel"`).

5. Code a label element containing the text "Arrival Date" that is associated with a calendar form control to accept a reservation arrival date (use `type="date"`).

6. Code a label element containing the text "Nights" that is associated with a spinner form control to accept a value between 1 and 14 to indicate the number of nights for

the length of stay (use `type="number"`). Use the `min` and `max` attributes to configure the range of values.

Save your file. Display your web page in browser. Submit the form with missing information or only a partial e-mail address. Depending on the browser's level of HTML5 support, the browser may perform form validation and display an error message. Figure 10.36 shows the Reservations page rendered in the Firefox browser with an incorrectly formatted e-mail address.

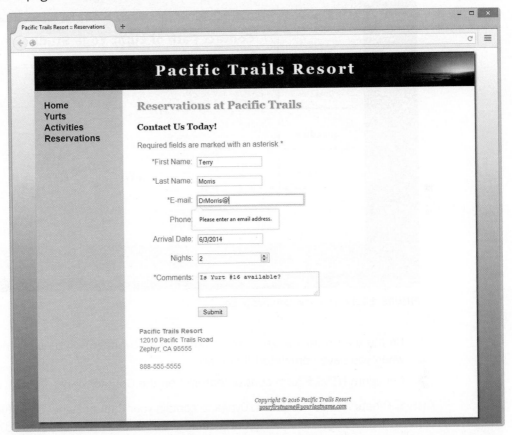

FIGURE 10.36 *HTML5 attributes and values are coded in the form.*

Task 4 in this case study provided you with additional practice using new HTML5 attributes and values. The display and functioning of browsers will depend on the level of HTML5 support. See http://caniuse.com/#feat=forms for an HTML5 browser support list.

Path of Light Yoga Studio Case Study

In this chapter's case study you will use the existing Path of Light Yoga Studio website (Chapter 9) as a starting point. You will add a new page to the Path of Light Yoga Studio website—the Contact page. Refer back to the site map for the Path of Light Yoga Studio website in Chapter 2, Figure 2.31. The Contact page will use the same page layout as the other Path of Light Yoga Studio web pages. You'll apply your new skills from this chapter and code a form in the content area of the Contact page.

You have four tasks in this case study:

1. Create a new folder for this Path of Light Yoga Studio case study.
2. Modify the style sheet (yoga.css) to configure style rules for the new Contact page.

FIGURE 10.37 *The new Contact page.*

3. Create the Contact page: contact.html. Your new page will be similar to Figure 10.37 when you have completed this step.

4. Configure HTML5 form control features on the Contact page.

Task 1: Create a folder called ch10yoga to contain your Path of Light Yoga Studio website files. Copy the files from the Chapter 9 Case Study ch9yoga folder to your new ch10yoga folder.

Task 2: Configure the CSS. Review Figure 10.37 and the wireframe in Figure 10.38. Notice how the text labels for the form controls are on the left side of the content area but contain right-aligned text. Notice the empty vertical space between each form control. Open yoga.css in a text editor. Place your cursor on a new blank line above the media queries.

FIGURE 10.38 *The sketch of the form.*

1. Configure a label element selector. Set left float, block display, right alignment for text, assign a width of 10em, and configure 1em right padding.

2. Configure the input element and textarea element selectors. Set block display and 2em of bottom margin.

3. Configure the submit button with a 12em left margin.

4. Configure the form element selector with 3em padding.

5. Configure style rules to optimize the display on smartphone-sized mobile devices by rendering the label text above each form control and eliminating the

submit button's left margin. Add the following style rules to the media query that targets a maximum width of 37.5em:

```
label { float: none; text-align: left; }
input[type="submit"] { margin-left: 0; }
```

Save the yoga.css file.

Task 3: Create the Contact Page. Use the Home page as the starting point for the Contact page. Launch a text editor and open index.html. Save the file as contact.html. Modify your contact.html file to look similar to the Contact page (shown in Figure 10.37) as follows:

1. Change the page title to an appropriate phrase.

2. The Contact page will display a form in the main element. Delete all HTML and content within the main element except for the <h2> element and its text.

3. Change the text in the <h2> element to "Contact Path of Light Yoga Studio".

4. Prepare to code the HTML for the form area. Begin with a form element that uses the post method and the `action` attribute to invoke server-side processing. Unless directed otherwise by your instructor, configure the `action` attribute to send the form data to http://webdevbasics.net/scripts/yoga.php.

5. Configure the form control for the Name information. Create a label element that contains the text "Name:". Create a text box configured with "myName" as the value of the `id` and `name` attributes. Use the `for` attribute to associate the label element with the form control.

6. Configure the form control for the E-mail information. Create a label element that contains the text "E-mail:". Create a text box configured with "myEmail" as the value of the `id` and `name` attributes. Use the `for` attribute to associate the label element with the form control.

7. Configure the Comments area on the form. Create a label element that contains the text "Comments:". Create a textarea element configured with "myComments" as the value of the `id` and `name` attributes, `rows` set to 2, and `cols` set to 20. Use the `for` attribute to associate the label element with the form control.

8. Configure the submit button to display "Send Now".

9. Code an ending </form> tag on a blank line after the submit button.

Save your file and test your web page in a browser. It should look similar to the page shown in Figure 10.37. If you are connected to the Internet, submit the form. This will send your form information to the server-side script configured in the form tag. A confirmation page similar to Figure 10.39 will be displayed that lists the form control names and the values you entered.

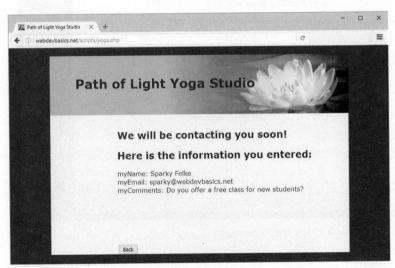

FIGURE 10.39 *The form confirmation page.*

Task 4: Configure the Form with HTML5 Attributes and Values. Get more practice with the new HTML5 elements by modifying the form on the Contact page to use HTML5 attributes and values. Modify the contact.html file in a text editor.

1. Add a paragraph above the form to indicate:
   Required information is marked with an asterisk *.

2. Use the `required` attribute to require the name, e-mail, and comments form controls to be entered. Add an asterisk at the beginning of each label text.

3. Configure the input element for the e-mail address (use `type="email"`).

4. Add a new label and form control between the e-mail and comments area. Code a label element containing the text "How did you hear about us?" that is associated with a textbox and datalist form control with the following options configured: Google, Bing, Facebook, Friend, Radio Ad.

Save your file and display your web page in a browser. Submit the form with missing information or only a partial e-mail address. Depending on the browser's level of HTML5 support, the browser may perform form validation and display an error message. Figure 10.40 shows the Contact page rendered in the Firefox browser with an incorrectly formatted e-mail address and missing comments.

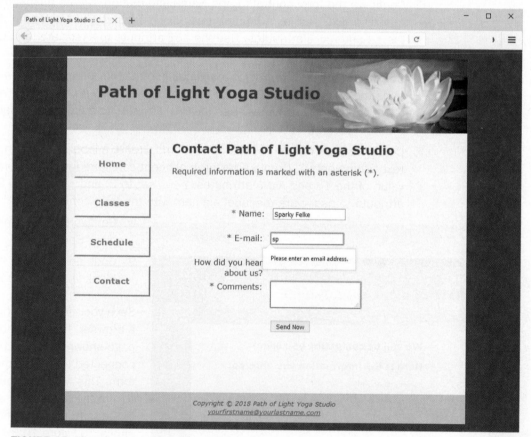

FIGURE 10.40 *The Contact page with HTML5 form controls.*

Task 4 in this case study provided you with additional practice using the new HTML5 attributes and values. The display and functioning of browsers will depend on the level of HTML5 support. See http://caniuse.com/#feat=forms for an HTML5 browser support list.

Media and Interactivity Basics

Videos and sounds on your web pages can make them more interesting and informative. This chapter introduces you to working with multimedia and interactive elements on web pages. Methods to add audio, video, and Flash to your web pages are introduced. Sources of these media types, the HTML code needed to place the media on a web page, and suggested uses of the media are discussed. You'll also create an interactive image gallery with CSS, a drop down menu with CSS, and explore new CSS3 properties. Adding the right touch of multimedia and interactivity to a web page can make it engaging and compelling for your visitors.

You'll learn how to...

- Describe types of multimedia files used on the Web
- Configure hyperlinks to multimedia files
- Configure audio and video on a web page with HTML5 elements
- Configure a Flash animation on a web page
- Use the CSS3 transform and transition properties

- Configure an interactive drop-down menu
- Configure an interactive widget with the HTML5 details and summary elements
- Describe features and common uses of JavaScript and jQuery
- Describe the purpose of HTML5 APIs such as geolocation, web storage, offline web applications, and canvas

Plug-ins, Containers, and Codecs

Helper Applications and Plug-ins

Web browsers are designed to display certain file types such as .html, .htm, .gif, .jpg, and .png, among others. When the media is not one of these file types, the browser searches for a **plug-in** or **helper application** configured to display the file type. If it cannot find a plug-in or helper application (which runs in a separate window from the browser) on the visitor's computer, the web browser offers the visitors the option of saving the file to their computer. Several commonly used plug-ins are as follows:

▶ **Adobe Flash Player** (http://www.adobe.com/products/flashplayer). The Flash Player displays **.swf** format files. These can contain audio, video, and animation along with interactivity.

▶ **Adobe Shockwave Player** (http://www.adobe.com/products/shockwaveplayer). The Shockwave Player displays high-performance multimedia created using the Adobe Director application.

▶ **Adobe Reader** (http://get.adobe.com/reader). Adobe Reader is commonly used to exchange information stored in .pdf format.

▶ **Java Runtime Environment** (http://www.java.com/en/download/manual.jsp). The Java Runtime Environment (JRE) is used to run applications and applets using Java technology.

▶ **Windows Media Player** (http://windows.microsoft.com/en-us/windows/download-windows-media-player). The Windows Media plug-in plays streaming audio, video, animations, and multimedia presentations.

▶ **Apple QuickTime** (http://www.apple.com/quicktime/download). The Apple QuickTime plug-in displays QuickTime animation, music, audio, and video directly within the web page.

The plug-ins and helper applications listed above have been used on the Web for many years. What is new about HTML5 video and audio is that it is native to the browser—with no plug-in needed. When working with native HTML5 video and audio, you need to be aware of the **container** (which is designated by the file extension) and the **codec** (which is the algorithm used to compress the media). There is no single codec that is supported by all popular browsers. For example, the H.264 codec requires licensing fees and is not supported by the Firefox and Opera web browsers, which support royalty-free Vorbis and Theora codecs. Explore Tables 11.1 and 11.2, which list common media file extensions, the container file type, and a description with codec information (if applicable for HTML5).

TABLE 11.1 *Common Audio File Types*

Extension	Container	Description
.wav	Wave	This format was originally created by Microsoft. It is a standard on the PC platform but is also supported by the Mac platform
.aiff or .aif	Audio Interchange	A popular audio file format on the Mac platform. It is also supported on the PC platform
.mid	Musical Instrument Digital Interface	Contain instructions to recreate a musical sound rather than a digital recording of the sound itself. However, a limited number of types of sounds can be reproduced
.au	Sun UNIX Sound File	This is an older type of sound file that generally has poorer sound quality than the newer audio file formats
.mp3	MPEG-1 Audio Layer-3	This sound file format is popular for music files due to the MP3 codec, which supports two channels and advanced compression
.ogg	Ogg	An open-source audio file format (see http://www.vorbis.com) that uses the Vorbis codec
.m4a	MPEG 4 Audio	This audio-only MPEG-4 format uses the Advanced Audio Coding (AAC) codec; supported by QuickTime, iTunes, and mobile devices such as the iPod and iPad

TABLE 11.2 *Common Video File Types*

Extension	Container	Description
.mov	QuickTime	Created by Apple and initially used on the Macintosh platform; also supported by Windows
.avi	Audio Video Interleaved	Microsoft's original standard video format for PC platforms
.flv	Flash Video	A Flash-compatible video file container; supports H.264 codec
.wmv	Windows Media Video	A streaming video technology developed by Microsoft. The Windows Media Player supports this file format
.mpg	MPEG	Developed under the sponsorship of the Moving Picture Experts Group (MPEG), http://mpeg.chiariglione.org/; supported on both Windows and Mac platforms
.m4v and .mp4	MPEG-4	MPEG4 (MP4) codec; H.264 codec; played by QuickTime, iTunes, and mobile devices such as the iPod and iPad
.3gp	3GPP Multimedia	H.264 codec; a standard for delivery of multimedia over third-generation, high-speed wireless networks
.ogv or .ogg	Ogg	This open-source video file format uses the Theora codec (see http://www.theora.org)
.webm	WebM	This open media file format sponsored by Google, uses the VP8 video codec and Vorbis audio codec (see http://www.webmproject.org)

Configure Audio and Video

Accessing an Audio or Video File

The easiest way to give your website visitors access to an audio or a video file is to create a simple hyperlink to the file. For example, the code to hyperlink to a sound file named WDFpodcast.mp3 is

```
<a href="WDFpodcast.mp3">Podcast Episode 1</a> (MP3)
```

When your website visitor clicks the link, the plug-in for .mp3 files that is installed on the computer (such as QuickTime) will typically display embedded in a new browser window or tab. Your web page visitor can then use the plug-in to play the sound.

 Hands-On Practice 11.1

In this Hands-On Practice you will create a web page similar to Figure 11.1 that contains an h1 element and a hyperlink to an MP3 file. The web page will also provide a hyperlink to a text transcript of that file to provide for accessibility. It can also be useful to your web page visitors if you indicate the type of file (such as an MP3) and, optionally, the size of the file to be accessed.

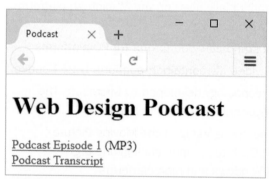

FIGURE 11.1 *The default MP3 player will launch in the browser when the visitor clicks on Podcast Episode 1.*

Copy the podcast.mp3 and podcast.txt files from the chapter11/starters folder in the student files and save them to a folder named podcast. Use the chapter1/template.html file as a starting point and create a web page containing a page title of Podcast, an h1 element with the text Web Design Podcast, a hyperlink to the MP3 file, and a hyperlink to the text transcript. Save your page as podcast.html. Display the file in a browser. Try to test your page in different browsers and browser versions. When you click on the MP3 hyperlink, an audio player (whichever player or plug-in is configured for the browser) will launch to play the file. When you click on the hyperlink for the text transcript, the text will display in the browser. Compare your work to the sample in the student files (chapter11/11.1/podcast.html).

Multimedia and Accessibility

Provide alternate content for the media files you use on your website in transcript, caption, or printable PDF format.

▶ Provide a text transcript for audio files such as podcasts. Often you can use the podcast script as the basis of the text transcript file that you create as a PDF and upload to your website.

▶ Provide captions for video files. Apple QuickTime Pro includes a captioning function—view an example in the student files at chapter11/starters/sparkycaptioned.mov. Captions can be added to your YouTube Videos. When you upload a video to YouTube (http://www.youtube.com), captions can be automatically generated (although you'll probably want to make some corrections). You can also create a transcript or text captions for an existing YouTube video (see https://support.google.com/youtube/topic/3014331?rd=1).

Multimedia and Browser Compatibility Issues

Providing your website visitor a hyperlink to download and save a multimedia file is the most basic method to provide access to your media, although your visitor will need an application installed on their computer (such as Adobe Quicktime, Apple iTunes, or Windows Media Player) to play the file after download. You are dependent on whether your website visitors have installed the corresponding player. For this reason, many websites began to use the Adobe Flash file format to share video and audio files.

In response to these browser plug-in compatibility issues and in an effort to reduce reliance on a proprietary technology like Adobe Flash, HTML5 introduces new audio and video elements that are native to the browser and do not require browser plug-ins or players. However, because HTML5 is not supported by older browsers, web designers still need to provide for a fallback option, such as providing a hyperlink to the media file or displaying a Flash version of the multimedia. You'll work with Flash, HTML5 video, and HTML5 audio later in this chapter.

FAQ

Why doesn't my audio or video file play?

Playing audio and video files on the Web depends on the plug-ins installed in your visitor's web browsers. A page that works perfectly on your home computer may not work for all visitors—depending on the configuration of their computer. Some visitors will not have the plug-ins properly installed. Some visitors may have file types associated with incorrect plug-ins or incorrectly installed plug-ins. Some visitors may be using low bandwidth and have to wait an overly long time for your media file to download. Are you detecting a pattern here? Sometimes multimedia on the Web can be problematic.

Flash and the HTML5 Embed Element

Flash multimedia content can add visual interest and interactivity to web pages with slide-shows, animations, and other multimedia effects. The Adobe Flash and Adobe Animate CC applications can be used to create Flash multimedia content. Flash animation may be interactive—it can be scripted, with a language called ActionScript, to respond to mouse clicks, accept information in text boxes, and invoke server-side scripting. Flash can also be used to play audio and video files. Flash multimedia files are stored in a **.swf** file extension and require the Flash Player browser plug-in. Although the Flash player is installed on most desktop web browsers, be aware that users of mobile devices will not be able to view your Flash multimedia. The lack of mobile support has contributed to a decrease in the use of use of Flash (.swf) media on web pages.

FIGURE 11.2 *The embed element was used to configure the Flash media.*

The Embed Element

The **embed element** is a self-contained, or void, element whose purpose is to provide a container for external content (such as Flash) that requires a plug-in or player. Although used for many years to display Flash on web pages, the embed element was never an official W3C element until HTML5. One of the design principles of HTML5 is to "pave the cowpaths"—to smooth the way for valid use of techniques that, although supported by browsers, were not part of the official W3C standard. Figure 11.2 (also in the student files at chapter11/flashembed.html) shows a web page using an embed element to display a Flash .swf file. The attributes of the embed element commonly used with Flash media are listed in Table 11.3.

TABLE 11.3 *Embed Element Attributes*

Attribute	Description and Value
src	File name of the Flash media (.swf file)
height	Specifies the height of the object area in pixels
type	The MIME type of the object; use `type="application/x-shockwave-flash"`
width	Specifies the width of the object area in pixels
bgcolor	Optional; background color of the Flash media, using a hexadecimal color value
quality	Optional; describes the quality of the media, usually set to "high"
title	Optional; specifies a brief text description
wmode	Optional; set to "transparent" to configure transparent background

In this Hands-On Practice you will launch a text editor and create a web page that displays a Flash slideshow of photographs. Your page will look like the one shown in Figure 11.3.

Create a folder called embed. Copy the lighthouse.swf file from the student files chapter11/starters folder and save it in your embed folder.

Use the chapter1/template.html file as a starting point, and create a web page containing a page title and an h1 element with the text "Door County Lighthouse Cruise" and an `<embed>` tag to display a Flash file named lighthouse.swf that is 320 pixels wide and 240 pixels high. A sample embed tag follows:

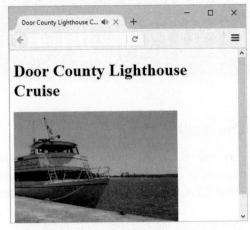

FIGURE 11.3 *Flash slideshow of images configured with the embed element.*

```
<embed type="application/x-shockwave-flash"
    src="lighthouse.swf" quality="high"
    width="320" height="240"
    title="Door County Lighthouse Cruise">
```

Notice the value of the `title` attribute in the code sample. The descriptive text could be accessed by assistive technologies such as a screen reader application.

Save your page as index.html in the embed folder. Test it in a browser. Compare your work to the sample in the student files (chapter11/11.2/embed.html).

 FAQ **What will happen if my web page visitor uses a browser that does not support Flash?**

If you used the code in this section to display Flash media on a web page and your visitor's browser does not support Flash, the browser will typically display a message about a missing plug-in. The code in this section passes W3C HTML5 conformance checks and is the minimum code needed to display Flash media on a web page.

FAQ **Can Adobe Animate CC do more than create Flash media?**

Yes! Adobe Animate CC, the newest version of the Adobe Flash Professional application, can export animations and interactions in a variety of formats including Flash .swf files, HTML5 Canvas, and Scalable Vector Graphics (SVG).

Explore FURTHER Scalable Vector Graphics (SVG) is a language that describes vector-based two-dimensional graphics in XML. Vector graphic shapes, images, and text objects can be included in an SVG, which can scale to increase or decrease in size without losing clarity. SVG content is stored in the .svg file extension and can be interactive and animated. Adobe Illustrator and Adobe Animate CC can be used to generate SVG. You can try out an online SVG editor at http://editor.method.ac. To learn more about SVG visit https://www.w3.org/TR/SVG/intro.htm and http://alistapart.com/article/practical-svg.

HTML5 Audio and Source Elements

The Audio Element

The new HTML5 **audio element** supports native play of audio files in the browser—without the need for plug-ins or players. The audio element begins with the `<audio>` tag and ends with the `</audio>` tag. Table 11.4 lists the attributes of the audio element.

TABLE 11.4 *Audio Element Attributes*

Attribute	Value	Description
src	file name	Optional; audio file name
type	MIME Type	Optional; the MIME type of the audio file, such as audio/mpeg or audio/ogg
autoplay	autoplay	Optional; indicates whether audio should start playing automatically; use with caution
controls	controls	Optional; indicates whether controls should be displayed; recommended
loop	loop	Optional; indicates whether audio should be played over and over
preload	none, auto, metadata	Optional; values: `none` (no preload), `metadata` (only download media file metadata), and `auto` (download the media file)
title		Optional; specifies a brief text description that may be displayed by browsers or assistive technologies

You'll need to supply multiple versions of the audio due to browser support of different codecs. Plan to supply audio files in at least two different containers, including ogg and mp3. It is typical to omit the `src` and `type` attributes from the audio tag and, instead, configure multiple versions of the audio file with the source element.

The Source Element

The **source element** is a self-contained, or void, tag that specifies a multimedia file and a MIME type. The `src` attribute identifies the file name of the media file. The `type` attribute indicates the MIME type of the file. Code `type="audio/mpeg"` for an MP3 file. Code `type="audio/ogg"` for audio files using the Vorbis codec. Configure a source element for each version of the audio file. Place the source elements before the closing audio tag.

FIGURE 11.4 *The Firefox browser supports the HTML5 audio element.*

The following code sample configures the web page shown in Figure 11.4 (also in the student files chapter11/audio.html) to display a controller for an audio file:

```
<audio controls="controls">
  <source src="soundloop.mp3" type="audio/mpeg">
  <source src="soundloop.ogg" type="audio/ogg">
  <a href="soundloop.mp3">Download the Audio File</a> (MP3)
</audio>
```

Current versions of modern browsers support the HTML5 audio element. The controls displayed by each browser are different. Review the code sample just given and note the hyperlink placed between the second source element and the closing audio tag. Any HTML elements or text placed in this area is rendered by browsers that do not support the HTML5 audio element. This is referred to as fallback content—if the audio element is not supported, the MP3 version of the file is made available for download. Internet Explorer began support of the audio element with Version 9. Figure 11.5 shows a screen shot of Internet Explorer 8 displaying "fallback content."

FIGURE 11.5 *Internet Explorer 8 does not recognize the audio element.*

 Hands-On Practice 11.3

In this Hands-On Practice you will launch a text editor and create a web page (see Figure 11.6) that displays an audio control to play a podcast.

Copy the podcast.mp3, podcast.ogg, and podcast.txt files from the chapter11/starters folder in the student files and save them to a folder named audio. Use the chapter1/template.html file as a starting point and create a web page containing a page title and an h1 element with the text Web Design Podcast, an audio control (use the audio element and two source elements), and a hyperlink to the text transcript. Configure a hyperlink to the MP3 file as the fallback content. The code for the audio element is

```
<audio controls="controls">
  <source src="podcast.mp3" type="audio/mpeg">
  <source src="podcast.ogg" type="audio/ogg"><br>
  <a href="podcast.mp3">Download the Podcast</a> (MP3)
</audio>
```

FIGURE 11.6 *Using the audio element to provide access to a podcast.*

Save your page as index.html in the audio folder. Display the file in a browser. Try to test your page in different browsers and browser versions. Recall that Internet Explorer versions prior to Version 9 do not support the audio element but will display the fallback content. When you click on the hyperlink for the text transcript, the text will display in the browser. Compare your work to the sample in the student files (chapter11/11.3/audio.html).

HTML5 Video and Source Elements

The Video Element

VideoNote
HTML5 Video

The new HTML5 **video element** supports native play of video files in the browser—without the need for plug-ins or players. The video element begins with the `<video>` tag and ends with the `</video>` tag. Table 11.5 lists the attributes of the video element.

TABLE 11.5   *Video Element Attributes*

Attribute	Value	Description
src	file name	Optional; video file name
type	MIME Type	Optional; the MIME type of the video file, such as video/mp4 or video/ogg
autoplay	autoplay	Optional; indicates whether video should start playing automatically; use with caution
controls	controls	Optional; indicates whether controls should be displayed
height	number	Optional; video height in pixels
loop	loop	Optional; indicates whether video plays continuously
poster	file name	Optional; specifies an image to display if the browser cannot play the video
preload	none, metadata, auto	Optional; values: none (no preload), metadata (only download media file metadata), and auto (download the media file)
title		Optional; specifies a brief text description that may be displayed by browsers or assistive technologies
width	number	Optional; video width in pixels

Due to browser support of different codecs, plan to supply video files in at least two different containers, including mp4 and ogg (or ogv). See http://caniuse.com/video for browser compatibility charts. It is typical to omit the `src` and `type` attributes from the video tag and, instead, configure multiple versions of the audio file with the source element.

The Source Element

The **source element** is a self-contained, or void, tag that specifies a multimedia file and a MIME type. The `src` attribute identifies the file name of the media file. The `type` attribute indicates the MIME type of the file. Code `type="video/mp4"` for video files using the MP4 codec. Code `type="video/ogg"` for video files using the Theora codec. Configure a source element for each version of the video file. Place the source elements before the closing video tag.

FIGURE 11.7 *The video element.*

The following code sample configures the web page shown in Figure 11.7 (see the student files chapter11/sparky.html) with the native HTML5 browser controls to display and play a video.

```
<video controls="controls" poster="sparky.jpg"
width="160" height="150">
  <source src="sparky.m4v" type="video/mp4">
  <source src="sparky.ogv" type="video/ogg">
  <a href="sparky.mov">Sparky the Dog</a> (.mov)
</video>
```

Current versions of modern browsers support the HTML5 video element. The controls displayed by each browser are different. Internet Explorer 9 supports the video element, but earlier versions do not. Review the code sample just given and note the anchor element placed between the second source element and the closing video tag. Any HTML elements or text placed in this area is rendered by browsers that do not support the HTML5 video element. This is referred to as fallback content. In this case, a hyperlink to a QuickTime (.mov) version of the file is supplied for the user to download. Another fallback option is to configure an embed element to play a Flash .swf version of the video. Internet Explorer began support of the video element with Version 9. Figure 11.8 shows Internet Explorer 8 displaying the web page.

FIGURE 11.8 *Internet Explorer 8 displays the hyperlink.*

Practice with HTML5 Video

 Hands-On Practice 11.4

In this Hands-On Practice you will launch a text editor and create the web page in Figure 11.9, which displays a video control to play a movie. Copy the lighthouse.m4v, lighthouse.ogv, lighthouse.swf, and lighthouse.jpg files from the chapter11/starters folder in the student files and save them to a new folder named video.

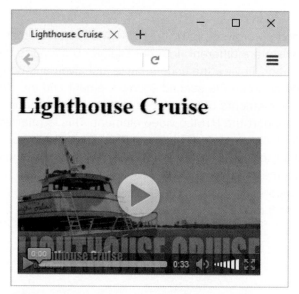

FIGURE 11.9 *HTML5 video element.*

Open the chapter1/template.html file in a text editor. Save the file with the name index.html in the video folder.

Edit the index.html file:

1. Modify the title element to display the text Lighthouse Cruise.

2. Configure the h1 element with the text Lighthouse Cruise.

3. Configure a video control (use the video element and two source elements) to display the lighthouse video.

   a. Configure an embed element to display the Flash content, lighthouse.swf, as fallback content.

b. Configure the lighthouse.jpg file as a poster image, which will display if the browser supports the video element but cannot play any of the video files.

c. The code for the video element follows:

```
<video controls="controls" poster="lighthouse.jpg">
  <source src="lighthouse.m4v" type="video/mp4">
  <source src="lighthouse.ogv" type="video/ogg">
  <embed type="application/x-shockwave-flash"
    src="lighthouse.swf" quality="high"
    width="320" height="240"
    title="Door County Lighthouse Cruise">
</video>
```

4. Notice that the video element does not contain `height` and `width` attributes. Recall the method to configure flexible images in Chapter 8 and configure the HTML5 video to be flexible with CSS. Place your cursor in the head section and code a style element. Configure the following style rule to set 100% width, auto height, and a maximum width of 320 pixels (which is the actual width of the video).

```
video { width: 100%; height: auto; max-width: 320px; }
```

Save your page as index.html in the video folder. Display the index.html page in a browser. Try to test your page in different browsers and browser versions. Compare your work with Figure 11.9 and the sample in the student files (chapter11/11.4/video.html).

How can I convert a video file to the new codecs?

You can use Firefogg (http://firefogg.org) to convert your video file to the Ogg Theora codec. Online-Convert (http://video.online-convert.com/convert-to-webm) offers free conversion to WebM.

Iframe Element

Inline frames are widely used on the Web for a variety of marketing and promotional purposes, including displaying banner ads, playing multimedia that may be hosted on an external web server, and serving content for associate and partner sites to display.

The iframe Element

The **iframe element** configures an **inline frame** that displays the contents of another web page within your web page document, referred to as *nested browsing*. The iframe element begins with the `<iframe>` tag and ends with the `</iframe>` tag. Fallback content that should be displayed if the browser does not support inline frames (such as a text description or hyperlink to the actual web page) should be placed between the tags. Figure 11.10 shows a web page that displays a YouTube video within an iframe element. See Table 11.6 for a list of iframe element attributes.

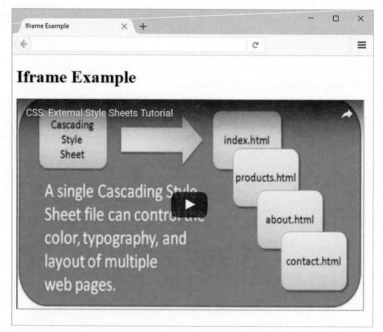

FIGURE 11.10 *The iframe element in action.*

TABLE 11.6 *iframe Element Attributes*

Attribute	Description and Value
src	URL of the web page to display in the inline frame
height	Inline frame height in pixels
width	Inline frame width in pixels
id	Optional; text name, alphanumeric, beginning with a letter, no spaces—the value must be unique and not used for other id values on the same web page document
name	Optional; text name, alphanumeric, beginning with a letter, no spaces
sandbox	Optional; disallow/disable features such as plug-ins, scripts, forms (HTML5)
title	Optional; specifies a brief text description

 Hands-On Practice 11.5

VideoNote
Configure an Inline Frame

In this Hands-On Practice you will launch a text editor and create a web page that displays a YouTube video within an iframe element. This example embeds the video found at https://www.youtube.com/watch?v=2CuOug8KDWI. You can choose to embed this video or select a different video. The process is to display the YouTube page for the video and copy the video identifier which is the text after the "=" in the URL. In this example, the video identifier is 2CuOug8KDWI.

Use the chapter1/template.html file as a starting point and configure a web page containing a page title and an h1 element with the text "YouTube Video" and an iframe element. Code the src attribute with http://www.youtube.com/embed/ followed by the video identifier. In this example, set the src attribute to the value http://www.youtube.com/embed/2CuOug8KDWI. Configure a hyperlink to the YouTube video page as fallback content. The code to display the video shown in Figure 11.10 is

```
<iframe src="http://www.youtube.com/embed/2CuOug8KDWI"
  width="640" height="385">
  <a href="http://www.youtube.com/embed/2CuOug8KDWI">YouTube Video</a>
</iframe>
```

Save your page as youtubevideo.html and display it in a browser. Compare your work with Figure 11.10 and the sample in the student files (chapter11/11.5.html).

In Hands-On Practice 11.5 you configured a web page to play multimedia that was hosted on another web server. You can view an example of using an iframe to display an ad banner hosted by Google at http://webdevfoundations.net (scroll down the page and look in the right-hand column). The advantage of inline frames is separation of control. The dynamic content—such as the ad banner or multimedia clip—can be modified by the partner site at any time, just as YouTube dynamically configures the format of the video display in this section.

CSS3 Transform Property

CSS transforms allow you to change the display of an element and provide functions to rotate, scale, skew, and reposition an element.

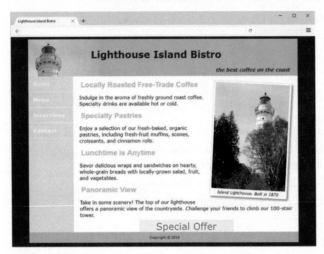

FIGURE 11.11 *The transform property in action.*

The transform property is supported by current versions of modern browsers, including Internet Explorer (version 10 and later). Both two-dimensional (2D) and three-dimensional (3D) transforms are possible. Table 11.7 lists commonly used 2D transform property function values and their purpose. See http://www.w3.org/TR/css3-transforms/#transform-property for a complete list. We'll focus on the rotate and scale transforms in this section.

CSS3 Rotate Transform

The `rotate()` **transform** function takes a value in degrees (like an angle in geometry). Rotate to the right with a positive value. Rotate to the left with a negative value. The rotation is around the origin, which, by default, is the middle of the element. The web page in Figure 11.11 demonstrates the use of the CSS3 transform property to slightly rotate the figure.

TABLE 11.7 *Values of the Transform Property*

Value	Purpose
rotate (*degree*)	Rotates the element by the angle
scale (*number, number*)	Scales or resizes the element along the X- and Y-axes (X,Y); if only one value is provided it configures the horizontal and vertical scale amount
scaleX (*number*)	Scales or resizes the element along the X-axis
scaleY (*number*)	Scales or resizes the element along the Y-axis
skewX (*number*)	Distorts the display of the element along the X-axis
skewY (*number*)	Distorts the display of the element along the Y-axis
translate (*number, number*)	Repositions the element along the X- and Y-axes (X,Y)
translateX (*number*)	Repositions the element along the X-axis
translateY (*number*)	Repositions the element along the Y-axis

CSS3 Scale Transform

The `scale()` **transform** function resizes an element in three different ways: along the X-axis, along the Y-axis, and along both the X- and Y-axes. Specify the amount of resizing using a number without units. For example, `scale(1)` does not change the element's size, `scale(2)` indicates the element should render two times as large, `scale(3)` indicates the element should render three times as large, and `scale(0)` indicates the element should not display.

 Hands-On Practice 11.6

In this Hands-On Practice you will configure the rotate and scale transforms shown in Figure 11.11. Create a new folder named transform. Copy the lighthouseisland.jpg, lighthousemini.jpg, and lighthouselogo.jpg images from the chapter11/starters folder in the student files to your transform folder. Launch a text editor and open the starter.html file in the chapter11 folder. Save the file as index.html in your transform folder. Launch the file in a browser and it will look similar to Figure 11.12.

Open index.html in a text editor and view the embedded CSS.

FIGURE 11.12 *Before the transform property.*

1. Locate the figure element selector. You will add a style declaration to the figure element selector that will configure a three-degree rotation transform. The new CSS is shown in blue.

```
figure {  float: right; margin: 10px; background-color: #FFF;
          padding: 5px; border: 1px solid #CCC;
          box-shadow: 5px 5px 5px #828282;
          transform: rotate(3deg);   }
```

2. Locate the #offer selector. This configures the "Special Offer" div displayed above the page footer. You will add a style declaration to the #offer selector that configures the browser to display the element two times larger. The new CSS is shown in blue.

```
#offer {  background-color: #EAEAEA;
          width: 10em;
          margin: auto;
          text-align: center;
          transform: scale(2);   }
```

Save the file and display it in a browser. You should see two changes: the figure displayed on a slight angle and larger "Special Offer" text. Compare your work to Figure 11.11 and the sample in the student files (chapter11/11.6/index.html).

 This section provided a brief introduction to the transform property, but there is much more to explore. Visit http://www.westciv.com/tools/transforms/index.html to generate the CSS for rotate, scale, translate, and skew transforms. Find out more about transforms at http://www.css3files.com/transform and http://developer.mozilla.org/en/CSS/Using_CSS_transforms.

CSS Transition Property

CSS3 **transitions** provide for changes in property values to display in a smoother manner over a specified time. Transitions are supported by current versions of most modern browsers, including Internet Explorer (version 10 and later). You can apply a transition to a variety of CSS properties including `color`, `background-color`, `border`, `font-size`, `font-weight`, `margin`, `padding`, `opacity`, and `text-shadow`. A full list of applicable properties is available at http://www.w3.org/TR/css3-transitions. When you configure a transition for a property, you need to configure values for the `transition-property`, `transition-duration`, `transition-timing-function`, and `transition-delay` properties. These can be combined in a single transition shorthand property. Table 11.8 lists the transition properties and their purpose. Table 11.9 lists commonly used `transition-timing-function` values and their purpose.

TABLE 11.8 *CSS Transition Properties*

Property	Description
`transition-property`	Indicates the CSS property to which the transition applies
`transition-duration`	Indicates the length of time to apply the transition; default value 0 configures an immediate transition; a numeric value specifies time (usually in seconds)
`transition-timing-function`	Configures changes in the speed of the transition by describing how intermediate property values are calculated; common values include `ease` (default), `linear`, `ease-in`, `ease-out`, `ease-in-out`
`transition-delay`	Indicates the beginning of the transition; default value 0 configures no delay; a numeric value specifies time (usually in seconds)
`transition`	Shorthand property; list the value for `transition-property`, `transition-duration`, `transition-timing-function`, and `transition-delay` separated by spaces; default values can be omitted, but the first time unit applies to `transition-duration`

TABLE 11.9 *Commonly Used* `transition-timing-function` *Values*

Value	Purpose
`ease`	Default; transition effect begins slowly, speeds up, and ends slowly
`linear`	Transition effect has a constant speed
`ease-in`	Transition effect begins slowly and speeds up to a constant speed
`ease-out`	Transition effect begins at a constant speed and slows down
`ease-in-out`	Transition effect is slightly slower; Begins slowly, speeds up, and slows down

Recall that the CSS `:hover` pseudo-class provides a way to configure styles to display when the web page visitor moves the mouse over an element. The change in display happens somewhat abruptly. Web designers can use a CSS transition to create a more gradual change to the hover state. You'll try this out in this Hands-On Practice when you configure a transition for the navigation hyperlinks on a web page.

Create a new folder named transition. Copy the lighthouseisland.jpg, lighthousemini.jpg, and lighthouselogo.jpg images from the chapter11/ starters folder in the student files to your transition folder. Launch a text editor and open the starter.html file in the chapter11 folder. Save the file as index.html in your transition folder. Open

FIGURE 11.13 *The transition causes the hyperlink background color to change in a more gradual manner.*

index.html in a browser and it will look similar to Figure 11.12. Place your mouse over one of the navigation hyperlinks and notice that the background color and text color change immediately.

Open index.html in a text editor and view the embedded CSS. Locate the `nav a:hover` selector and notice that the color and background-color properties are configured. You will add a style declaration to the `nav a` selector to cause a more gradual change in the background color when the user places the mouse over the hyperlink. The new CSS is shown in blue.

```
nav a { text-decoration: none;
        display: block;
        padding: 15px;
        transition: background-color 2s linear;  }
```

Save the file and display it in a browser. Place your mouse over one of the navigation hyperlinks and notice that while the text color changes immediately, the background color changes in a more gradual manner—the transition is working! Compare your work to Figure 11.13 and the student files (chapter11/11.7/index.html).

If you'd like more control over the transition than what is provided by the values listed in Table 11.9, explore using the cubic-bezier value for the transition-timing-function. A Bezier curve is a mathematically defined curve often used in graphic applications to describe motion. Explore the following resources:

▶ http://www.the-art-of-web.com/css/timing-function

▶ http://roblaplaca.com/blog/2011/03/11/understanding-css-cubic-bezier

▶ http://cubic-bezier.com

Practice with Transitions

Hands-On Practice 11.8

In this Hands-On Practice you will use CSS `positioning`, `opacity,` and `transition` properties to config-ure an interactive image gallery with CSS and HTML. This is a slightly different version of the image gallery than the web page you created in Hands-on Practice 7.8.

Figure 11.14 shows the initial display of the gallery (see the student files chapter11/11.8/gallery.html) with a semi-opaque placeholder image. When you place the mouse over a thumbnail image, the larger ver-sion of that image is gradually displayed along with a caption (see Figure 11.15). If you click the thumbnail, the image will display in its own browser window.

FIGURE 11.14 *Initial display of the gallery.*

Create a new folder called g11. Copy all the images from the chapter11/starters/gallery folder in the student files to the new g11 folder.

Launch a text editor and modify the chapter1/template.html file to configure a web page as indicated:

1. Configure the text Image Gallery, within an h1 ele-ment and within the title element.

2. Code a div element assigned to the id named `gallery`. This div will contain a placeholder figure element and an unordered list that contains the thumbnail images.

3. Configure a figure element within the div. The figure element will contain a placeholder img element that displays photo1.jpg.

4. Configure an unordered list within the div. Code six li elements, one for each thumbnail image. The thumbnail images will function as image links with a `:hover` pseudo-class that causes the larger image to display on the page. We'll make this all happen by configuring an anchor element containing

FIGURE 11.15 *The new photo gradually displays.*

both the thumbnail image and a span element that comprises the larger image along with descriptive text. An example of the first li element follows:

```
<li><a href="photo1.jpg"><img src="thumb1.jpg" width="100" height="75"
     alt="Golden Gate Bridge">
     <span><img src="photo1.jpg" width="400" height="300"
     alt="Golden Gate Bridge"><br>Golden Gate Bridge</span></a>
</li>
```

5. Configure all six li elements in a similar manner. Substitute the actual name of each image file for the `href` and `src` values in the code. Write your own descriptive text for each image. Use photo2.jpg and thumb2.jpg in the second li element. Use photo3.jpg and thumb3.jpg in the third li element, and so on for all six images. Save the file as index.html in the g11 folder. Display your page in a browser. You'll see the placeholder image followed by an unordered list with the thumbnail images, the larger images, and the descriptive text.

6. Now, let's add CSS. Open your file in a text editor and code a style element in the head section. Configure embedded CSS as follows:

   a. Configure the body element selector with a dark background color (#333333) and a light gray text color (#EAEAEA).

   b. Configure the `gallery` id selector. Set `position` to `relative`. This does not change the location of the gallery but sets the stage to use absolute positioning on the span element relative to its container (#gallery) instead of relative to the entire web page document.

   c. Configure the figure element selector. Set `position` to `absolute`, `left` to 280px, `text-align` to center and `opacity` to .25. This will cause the figure to initially be semi-opaque.

   d. Configure the unordered list within the #gallery with a width of 300 pixels and no list marker.

   e. Configure the list item elements within the #gallery with inline display, left float, and 10 pixels of padding.

   f. Configure the img elements within the #gallery to not display a border.

   g. Configure anchor elements within the #gallery with no underline, #EAEAEA text color, and italic text.

   h. Configure span elements within the #gallery. Set `position` to `absolute`, `left` to -1000px (which causes them not to display initially in the browser viewport), and `opacity` to 0. Also configure a three second `ease-in-out transition`.

   ```
   #gallery span { position: absolute; left: -1000px; opacity: 0;
                   transition: opacity 3s ease-in-out; }
   ```

   i. Configure the span elements within the #gallery to display when the web visitor hovers the mouse over the thumbnail image link. Set `position` to `absolute`, `top` to 15px, `left` to 320px, centered text, and `opacity` to 1.

   ```
   #gallery a:hover span { position: absolute; top: 16px; left: 320px;
                           text-align: center; opacity: 1; }
   ```

Save your file in the g11 folder and display it in a browser. Compare your work with Figures 11.14 and 11.15 and the student files (chapter11/11.8/gallery.html).

CSS Drop Down Menu

 Hands-On Practice 11.9

FIGURE 11.16 *Site map.*

In this Hands-On Practice you will configure a navigation menu that is interactive and displays a drop down menu. Figure 11.16 displays a site map for the website. Notice how the Cuisine page has three subpages: Breakfast, Lunch, and Dinner. You will configure a drop down menu that displays when a visitor hovers over the Cuisine navigation hyperlink as shown in Figure 11.17.

Create a folder named mybistro. Copy the files from the chapter11/bistro folder in the student files into your mybistro folder. Notice the main menu has hyperlinks for Home, Coffee, Cuisine, Directions, and Contact. You will edit the CSS and edit each page to configure a Cuisine submenu that provides hyperlinks to three pages (Breakfast, Lunch, and Dinner).

Task 1: Configure the HTML.

Launch a text editor and open the index.html file. You will modify the nav area to contain a new unordered list with hyperlinks to the Breakfast, Lunch, and Dinner pages. You will configure a new ul element that is contained *within* the Cuisine li element. The new ul element will contain an li element for each room. The HTML follows with the new code displayed in blue.

```
<nav>
<ul>
  <li><a href="index.html">Home</a></li>
  <li><a href="coffee.html">Coffee</a></li>
  <li><a href="cuisine.html">Cuisine</a>
    <ul>
      <li><a href="breakfast.html">Breakfast</a></li>
      <li><a href="lunch.html">Lunch</a></li>
      <li><a href="dinner.html">Dinner</a></li>
    </ul>
  </li>
  <li><a href="directions.html">Directions</a></li>
  <li><a href="contact.html">Contact</a></li>
</ul>
</nav>
```

Save the file and display it in a browser. Don't worry if the navigation area seems a bit garbled—you'll configure the submenu CSS in Step 2. Next, edit the nav area in each page (coffee.html, cuisine.html, breakfast.html, lunch.html, dinner.html, directions.html, and contact.html) as you did in the index.html file.

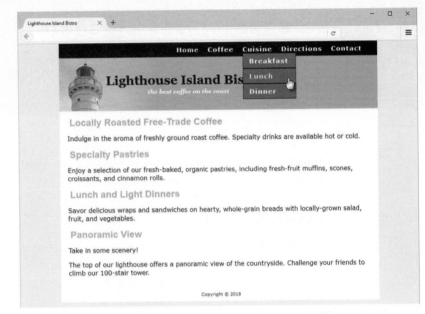

FIGURE 11.17 *The dropdown menu displays.*

Task 2: Configure the CSS.

Launch a text editor and open the bistro.css file.

a. Configure the submenu with absolute positioning. Recall from Chapter 7 that absolute positioning precisely specifies the location of an element outside of normal flow in relation to its first parent nonstatic element. The nav element's position is static by default so add the following declaration to the styles for the nav element selector: position: relative;

b. The submenu that displays the hyperlinks for the Breakfast, Lunch, and Dinner pages is configured using a new ul element that is contained within the existing ul element in the nav area. Configure a descendent nav ul ul selector and code style declarations to use absolute positioning, #5564A0 background color, 0 padding, left text alignment, and display set to none. The CSS follows:

```
nav ul ul { position: absolute; background-color: #5564A0;
            padding: 0; text-align: left; display: none; }
```

c. To style each li element within the submenu, use a descendent nav ul ul li selector and configure the li elements in the submenu with a border, block display, 8em width, 1em left padding, and 0 left margin. The CSS follows:

```
nav ul ul li { border: 1px solid #00005D;
               display: block; width: 8em;
               padding-left: 1em; margin-left: 0; }
```

d. Configure the submenu ul to display when the :hover is triggered for the li elements in the nav area. The CSS follows:

```
nav li:hover ul { display: block; }
```

Test your pages in a browser. The drop down menu should look similar to Figure 11.17. You can compare your work to the sample in the student files (chapter11/11.9/horizontal). An example of a web page with a vertical fly-out menu is available in the student files (chapter11/11.9/vertical).

HTML5 Details and Summary Elements

The details element and summary element are used together to configure an interactive widget that will hide and show information.

Details Element

The purpose of the **details element** is to configure the browser to render an interactive widget which contains one summary element and detailed information (which can be a combination of text and HTML tags). The details element begins with the `<details>` tag and ends with the `</details>` tag.

Summary Element

The **summary element** is coded within the details element. The purpose of the summary element is to contain the text summary (typically some type of term or heading) shown in the interactive widget. The summary element begins with the `<summary>` tag and ends with the `</summary>` tag.

Details and Summary Widget

Figures 11.18 and 11.19 show the details and summary elements in action using the Chrome browser. Figure 11.18 shows the initial display of the web page with each summary item (in this case the terms Repetition, Contrast, Proximity, and Alignment) visible and displayed next to a triangle rendered automatically by the Chrome browser.

In Figure 11.19, the visitor has selected the first summary item (Repetition) which caused browser to display the detailed information for that item. The visitor can select the same summary item again to hide the details or can select another summary item to also show its corresponding detailed information.

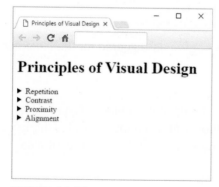

FIGURE 11.18 *Initial browser display.*

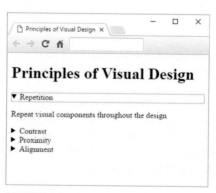

FIGURE 11.19 *Detailed information displays.*

Browsers that do not support the details and summary elements display all the information immediately and do not provide interactivity. At the time this text was written, only the Chrome and Firefox browsers supported the details and summary elements. Check http://caniuse.com/details for the current level of browser support.

Hands-On Practice 11.10

In this Hands-On Practice you will configure an interactive widget with the details and summary elements as you create the page shown in Figures 11.18 and 11.19. Create a new folder named ch11details. Launch a text editor and open the template file located at chapter1/template.html in the student files. Save the file as index.html in your ch11details folder. Modify the file to configure a web page as indicated:

1. Configure the text, Principles of Visual Design, within an h1 element and within the title element.

2. Code the following in the body of the web page:

```
<details>
  <summary>Repetition</summary>
  <p>Repeat visual components throughout the design</p>
</details>
<details>
  <summary>Contrast</summary>
  <p>Add visual excitement and draw attention</p>
</details>
<details>
  <summary>Proximity</summary>
  <p>Group related items</p>
</details>
<details>
  <summary>Alignment</summary>
  <p>Align elements to create visual unity</p>
</details>
```

Save your file and test your page in Chrome. The initial display should be similar to Figure 11.18. Try selecting or clicking on one of the terms or arrows to display the information you coded within the details element. If you select the term "Repetition", your browser should be similar to Figure 11.19.

If you are using a browser that does not support the details and summary elements, your display will be similar to Figure 11.20.

A suggested solution is in the student files chapter11/11.10 folder.

FIGURE 11.20 *Display in a nonsupporting browser.*

JavaScript & jQuery

JavaScript

Although some interactivity on web pages can be achieved with CSS, JavaScript powers much of the interactivity on the Web. **JavaScript**, developed initially by Brendan Eich at Netscape, is an object-based, client-side scripting language interpreted by a web browser. JavaScript is considered to be **object-based** because it's used to work with the objects associated with a web page document: the browser window, the document itself, and elements such as forms, images, and hyperlinks.

JavaScript statements can be placed in a separate file (with a .js extension) that is accessed by a web browser or within an HTML script element. The purpose of the **script element** is to either contain scripting statements or to indicate a file that contains scripting statements. Some JavaScript also can be coded within the HTML. In all cases, the web browser interprets the JavaScript statements. Because JavaScript is interpreted by a browser, it is considered to be a **client-side scripting** language.

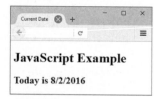

FIGURE 11.21 *JavaScript in action.*

JavaScript can be used to respond to events such as moving the mouse, clicking a button, and loading a web page. This technology is also often utilized to edit and verify information on HTML form controls such as text boxes, check boxes, and radio buttons. Other uses for JavaScript include pop-up windows, image slideshows, animation, date manipulation, and calculations. Figure 11.21 shows a web page (found in the student files at chapter11/date.html) that uses JavaScript to determine and display the current date. The JavaScript statements are enclosed within an HTML **script element** and coded directly in the .html file. The code sample is below:

```
<h2>Today is
<script>
var myDate = new Date()
var month = myDate.getMonth() + 1
var day = myDate.getDate()
var year = myDate.getFullYear()
document.write(month + "/" + day + "/" + year)
</script>
</h2>
```

JavaScript is a powerful scripting language and is a good choice to learn as you continue your studies. There are many free resources for JavaScript code and JavaScript tutorials on the Web. Here are a few sites that offer free tutorials or free scripts:

▶ JavaScript Tutorial: http://echoecho.com/javascript.htm

▶ Mozilla Developer Network JavaScript Guide: https://developer.mozilla.org/en-US/docs/Web/JavaScript/Guide

▶ JavaScript Tutorial: http://www.w3schools.com/JS

▶ JavaScript for Designers: http://rachelnabors.com/javascript-for-designers/

jQuery

Web developers often need to configure the same type of common interactive features (such as slideshows, form validation, and animation) on web pages. One approach is to write one's own JavaScript code and test it in a wide variety of browsers and operating systems. As you might guess, this can become quite time consuming. The free, open-source **jQuery** JavaScript library was developed by John Resig in 2006 to simplify client-side scripting. The jQuery Foundation is a volunteer organization that contributes to the continued development of jQuery and provides jQuery documentation at http://api.jquery.com.

An **application programming interface** (API) is a protocol that allows software components to communicate—interacting and sharing data. The jQuery API can be used to configure many interactive features, including:

- image slideshows
- animation (moving, hiding, and fading)
- event handling (mouse movements and mouse clicking)
- document manipulation

Many web developers and designers have found that jQuery is easier to learn and work with than writing their own JavaScript, although a basic understanding of JavaScript is needed to be efficient when using jQuery. An advantage of the jQuery library is its compatibility with all current browsers.

jQuery Slideshow Example

FIGURE 11.22 *jQuery plugin slideshow.*

jQuery is often used on popular websites, such as Amazon, Google, and Twitter. Because jQuery is an open-source library, anyone can extend the jQuery library by writing a new **jQuery plugin** that provides a new or enhanced interactive feature. For example, the jQuery Cycle plugin (http://jquery.malsup.com/cycle) supports a variety of transition effects. Figure 11.22 (see http://webdevfoundations.net/jQuery) shows an example of using jQuery and the Cycle plugin to create an image slideshow. There are many jQuery plugins available, providing interactions and functionality such as slideshows, tooltips, and form validation. Visit the jQuery Plugin Registry at http://plugins.jquery.com for a list. You can also find jQuery plugins by searching the Web.

There are many free tutorials and resources that can help you learn about jQuery. You may wish to do further research using some of the following resources:

- How jQuery Works: http://learn.jquery.com/about-jquery/how-jquery-works/
- jQuery Fundamentals: http://jqfundamentals.com/chapter/jquery-basics
- jQuery Tutorials for Web Designers: http://webdesignerwall.com/tutorials/jquery-tutorials-for-designers

HTML5 APIs

You've already been introduced to the term **application programming interface** (API), which is a protocol that allows software components to communicate—interacting and sharing data. A variety of APIs that are intended to work with HTML5, CSS, and JavaScript are currently under development and in the W3C approval process. We'll explore some of the new APIs in this section:

- geolocation
- web storage
- offline web applications
- two-dimensional drawing

Geolocation

The **geolocation** API (http://www.w3.org/TR/geolocation-API/) allows your web page visitors to share their geographic location. The browser will first confirm that your visitors want to share their location. Then, their location may be determined by the IP address, wireless network connection, local cell tower, or GPS hardware depending on the type of device and browser. JavaScript is used to work with the latitude and longitude coordinates provided by the browser. See http://webdevfoundations.net/geo and http://html5demos.com/geo for examples of geolocation in action.

Web Storage

Web developers have traditionally used the JavaScript cookie object to store information in key-value pairs on the client (the website visitor's computer). The **web storage** API (http://www.w3.org/TR/webstorage) provides two new ways to store information on the client side: local storage and session storage. An advantage to using web storage is the increase in the amount of data that can be stored (5MB per domain). The **localStorage** object stores data without an expiration date. The **sessionStorage** object stores data only for the duration of the current browser session. JavaScript is used to work with the values stored in the localStorage and sessionStorage objects. Visit http://webdevfoundations.net/storage and http://html5demos.com/storage for examples of web storage.

Offline Web Applications

An **offline web application** (https://www.w3.org/TR/html5/browsers.html#offline) enables website visitors to view documents and access web applications even when they are not connected to the Internet. You've heard of native applications (apps) for mobile phones. A native app must be built and distributed specifically for the platform it will be used on. If your client would like a native mobile app for both an iPhone and an Android, you'll need to create two different apps! In contrast, a web application (app) can be written with HTML, CSS, and JavaScript and can run in any browser—as long as you are online. An offline web application takes this one step further and stores the HTML, CSS, and JavaScript files on the visitor's device for use offline, even when the device is not connected to the Internet.

The key to an offline web application is the **manifest** file, which is a plain text file having the file extension .appcache. The manifest provides information about the web app in three sections:

▶ Cache—lists every resource (web pages, CSS, JavaScript, images, etc.) that is associated with the web app

▶ Fallback—lists fallback files to display when a visitor tries to access a file that is not cached

▶ Network—lists files that are only available when the visitor has an Internet connection

The web browser reads the list of URLs from the manifest file, downloads the resources, stores them locally, and automatically updates the local files when the resources change. If the visitor tries to access the app without an Internet connection, the web browser will render the local files and follow the fallback and network procedures. Try out a demonstration of an offline web application at http://html5demos.com/offlineapp and http://www.w3schools.com/html/html5_app_cache.asp.

Drawing with the Canvas Element

The HTML5 canvas element is a container for dynamic graphics. The canvas element begins with the `<canvas>` tag and ends with the `</canvas>` tag. The canvas element is configured with the Canvas 2D Context API (http://www.w3.org/TR/2dcontext2), which provides a way to dynamically draw and transform lines, shapes, images, and text on web pages. If that wasn't enough, the canvas API also provides for interaction with actions taken by the user, like moving the mouse.

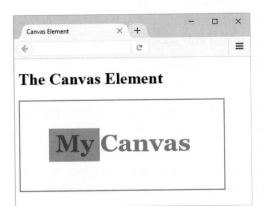

FIGURE 11.23 *The canvas element.*

The canvas API offers methods for two-dimensional (2D) bitmap drawing, including lines, strokes, arcs, fills, gradients, images, and text. However, instead of drawing visually using a graphics application, you draw programmatically by writing JavaScript statements. A very basic example of using JavaScript to draw within the canvas element is shown in Figure 11.23 (see chapter11/canvas.html in the student files).

The promise of the canvas element is that it can be used to provide interactions as sophisticated as those developed with Adobe Flash. At the time this text was written, all modern browsers (including Internet Explorer version 9 and later) support the canvas element. Experience virtuoso examples of the canvas element in action at http://www.canvasdemos.com.

This section provided a brief overview of several of new HTML5 APIs. Visit the following resources for more information, tutorials, and demos.

▶ HTML5 Demos and Examples: http://html5demos.com

▶ IBM developerWorks: http://www.ibm.com/developerworks/library/wa-html5fundamentals3

▶ The Web platform: http://platform.html5.org

▶ Mozilla Developer Network: https://developer.mozilla.org/en-US/docs/Web/Guide/HTML/Canvas_tutorial

Review and Apply

Review Questions

Multiple Choice. Choose the best answer for each item.

1. Which property provides a way for you to rotate, scale, skew, or move an element?
   a. display
   b. transition
   c. transform
   d. list-style-type

2. What type of files are .webm, .ogv, and .m4v?
   a. audio files
   b. video files
   c. Flash files
   d. none of the above

3. What happens when a browser does not support the `<video>` or `<audio>` element?
   a. The computer crashes.
   b. The web page does not display.
   c. The fallback content, if it exists, will display.
   d. None of the above.

4. Which property enables changes in property values to display in gradual manner over a specified time?
   a. transition
   b. transform
   c. display
   d. opacity

5. Which of the following is an open-source video codec?
   a. Theora
   b. MP3
   c. Vorbis
   d. Flash

6. Which of the following is an object-based, client-side scripting language?
   a. HTML
   b. CSS
   c. JavaScript
   d. API

7. Which of the following is an HTML API that stores information on the client?
   a. geolocation
   b. web storage
   c. client storage
   d. canvas

8. Which elements can be used to configure an interactive widget?
   a. hide and show
   b. details and summary
   c. display and hidden
   d. title and summary

9. Which of the following should you do to provide for usability and accessibility?
   a. Use video and sound whenever possible.
   b. Supply text descriptions of audio files and caption video files that appear in your web pages.
   c. Never use audio and video files.
   d. None of the above.

10. Which of the following elements displays the contents of another web page document?
    a. iframe
    b. div
    c. document
    d. object

Hands-On Exercises

1. Write the HTML for a hyperlink to a video called sparky.mov on a web page.

2. Write the HTML to embed an audio file called soundloop.mp3 on a web page that can be controlled by the visitor.

3. Write the HTML to display a video on a web page. The video files are named prime.m4v, prime.webm, and prime.ogv. The width is 213 pixels. The height is 163 pixels. The poster image is prime.jpg.

4. Write the HTML to display a Flash file named flashbutton.swf on a web page.

5. Write the HTML to configure an inline frame to display the home page of http://webdevbasics.net in your web page.

 Although you can configure an inline frame to display another website, it is an ethical practice to only do so when you have obtained permission or have an arrangement with the other website.

6. Create a web page about your favorite movie that contains an audio file with your review of the movie. Use an application of your choice to record your review (visit http://audacity.sourceforge.net/download for a free download of Audacity). Place an e-mail hyperlink to yourself on the web page. Save the page as review.html.

7. Create a web page about your favorite music group that contains either a brief audio file with your review or an audio clip of the group. Use an application of your choice to record your review (visit http://audacity.sourceforge.net/download for a free download of Audacity). Place an e-mail hyperlink to yourself on the web page. Save the page as music.html.

8. Visit the textbook website at http://webdevbasics.net/flashcs5 and follow the instructions to create a Flash logo banner.

9. Add new transitions to the Lighthouse Bistro home page (found in the student files at chapter11/11.7/index.html). Configure the opacity property to display the lighthouse figure initially at 50% opacity and slowly change the opacity to 100% when the visitor places their mouse over the figure area.

Focus on Web Design

This chapter mentioned "pave the cowpaths" as one of the design principles of HTML5. You may be wondering about the others. The W3C has a list of the HTML5 Design Principles at http://www.w3.org/TR/html-design-principles. Review the page and write a one-page summary and reaction to these principles and what they mean to you as a web designer.

Pacific Trails Resort Case Study

In this chapter's case study you will use the existing Pacific Trails website (Chapter 10) as a starting point to create a new version of the website that incorporates multimedia and interactivity. You have four tasks in this case study:

1. Create a new folder for this Pacific Trails case study.

2. Modify the style sheet (pacific.css) to configure a transition for the navigation hyperlink color.

3. Add a video to the home page (index.html) and update the external CSS file.

4. Configure an image gallery on the Activities page (activities.html) and update the external CSS file.

Task 1: Create a folder called ch11pacific to contain your Pacific Trails Resort website files. Copy the files from the Chapter 10 Case Study ch10pacific folder. Copy the following files from the chapter11/casestudystarters folder in the student files and save them in your ch11pacific folder: pacifictrailsresort.mp4, pacifictrailsresort.ogv, pacifictrailsresort.jpg, and pacifictrailsresort.swf. Copy the following files from the chapter11/starters/gallery folder in the student files and save them in your ch11pacific folder: photo2.jpg, photo3.jpg, photo4.jpg, photo6.jpg, thumb2.jpg, thumb3.jpg, thumb4.jpg, and thumb6.jpg.

Task 2: Configure a Navigation Transition with CSS. Open pacific.css in a text editor. Locate the `nav a` selector. Code additional style declarations to configure a three-second ease-out transition in the `color` property. Save the file. Display any of the web pages in a browser that supports transitions and place your mouse over a navigation link. You should see a gradual change in the color of the text in the navigation link.

Task 3: Configure the Video. Launch a text editor and open the home page (index.html). Code an HTML5 video control below the h2 element. Configure the video, source, and embed elements to work with the following files: pacifictrailsresort.mp4, pacifictrailsresort.ogv, pacifictrailsresort.swf, and pacifictrailsresort.jpg. The dimensions of the video are 320 pixels wide by 240 pixels high. Save the file. Check your HTML syntax using the W3C validator (http://validator.w3.org). Correct and retest if necessary.

Next, configure the CSS. Launch a text editor and open pacific.css.

Code CSS above the media queries to configure the style rule for the video element selector and embed element selector as follows:

```
video, embed { float: right; padding-left: 20px; }
```

Save the pacific.css file. Launch a browser and test your new index.html page. It should look similar to Figure 11.24.

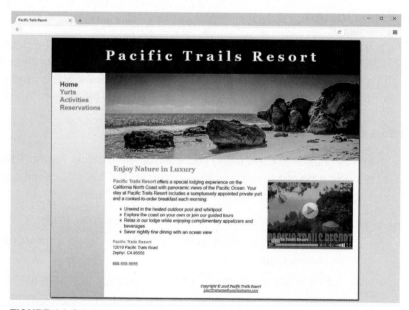

FIGURE 11.24 *Pacific Trails Resort home page.*

Task 4: Configure the Image Gallery. Launch a text editor and open activities.html. Modify the page by adding an image gallery within the main element above the footer area. You'll need to modify both the activities.html file and the pacific.css file. Use Hands-On Practice 11.8 as a guide and configure a div assigned to the `gallery` id within the main element. This gallery will initially display a placeholder image within a figure element and four thumbnail images. Code an img element that displays photo2.jpg within a figure element. Code an unordered list within the `gallery` div that has four li elements, one for each thumbnail image. The thumbnail images will function as image links with `a:hover` pseudo-class that causes the larger image to display on the page. Within each li element, configure an anchor element to contain both the thumbnail image and a span element that contains the larger image along with descriptive text. Configure the dimensions of the larger images to be 200 pixels wide by 150 pixels high. Save the activities.html file.

Open pacific.css in a text editor. Code CSS above the media queries for the gallery as shown in Hands-On Practice 11.8. Configure a height of 200px for the gallery id. Also add a style declaration to the footer element selector to clear all floats. Finally, add style declarations to the media queries to prevent mobile devices from displaying the gallery on devices with browser viewport width less than 37.5em. Save the pacific.css file.

Launch a browser and test your new Activities page (activities.html). It should look similar to Figure 11.25.

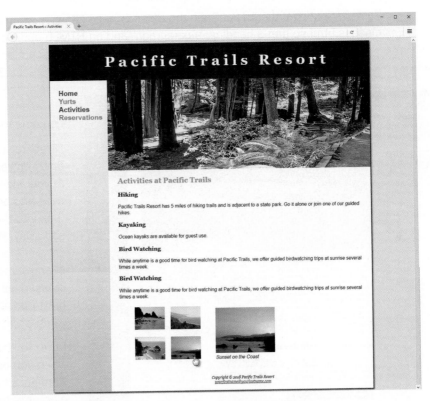

FIGURE 11.25 *New Pacific Trails Resort activities page.*

Path of Light Yoga Studio Case Study

In this chapter's case study you will use the existing Path of Light Yoga Studio website (Chapter 10) as a starting point to create a new version of the website that incorporates multimedia and interactivity. You have three tasks in this case study:

1. Create a new folder for this Path of Light Yoga Studio case study.
2. Modify the style sheet (yoga.css) to configure a transition for the navigation background color.
3. Configure the Classes page (classes.html) to display an audio control and update the external CSS file.

Task 1: Create a folder called ch11yoga to contain your Path of Light Yoga Studio website files. Copy the files from the Chapter 10 Case Study ch10yoga folder to your new ch11yoga folder. Copy the savasana.mp3 and savasana.ogg files from the chapter11/casestudystarters folder in the student files and save them in your ch11yoga folder.

Task 2: Configure a Navigation Transition with CSS. Open yoga.css in a text editor. Locate the `nav a` selector. Code additional style declarations to set the background color for `nav a:hover` to #B6D2D3 and to configure a three-second ease-out transition in the `background-color` property. Save the file. Display any of the web pages in a browser that supports transitions and place your mouse over a navigation link. You should see a gradual change in the background color of the navigation link.

Task 3: Configure the Audio. Open the Classes page (classes.html) in a text editor. Modify classes.html so that a heading, a paragraph, and an HTML5 audio control displays below the description list area on the page (see Figure 11.26). Use an h2 element to display the text "Relax Anytime with Savasana". Add a paragraph that contains the following text:

"Prepare yourself for savasana. Lie down on your yoga mat with your arms at your side with palms up. Close your eyes and breathe slowly but deeply. Sink into the mat and let your worries slip away. When you are ready, roll on your side and use your arms to push yourself to a sitting position with crossed legs. Place your hands in a prayer position. Be grateful for all that you have in life. Namaste."

Refer to Hands-On Practice 11.3 when you create the audio control. Configure the audio and source elements to work with the following files: savasana.mp3 and savasana.ogg. Configure a hyperlink to the savasana.mp3 file as a fallback if

FIGURE 11.26 *New Path of Light Yoga Studio classes page.*

the audio element is not supported. Save the file. Check your HTML syntax using the W3C validator (http://validator.w3.org). Correct and retest if necessary.

Next, configure the CSS. Launch a text editor. Open yoga.css. Configure a style above the media queries for the audio element selector that sets 1em margins.

Save the yoga.css file. Launch a browser to test your classes.html page. It should look similar to Figure 11.26.

You were briefly introduced to JavaScript in this chapter. JavaScript is often used to respond to events such as moving the mouse, clicking a button, and loading a web page. JavaScript is also the "J" in **AJAX**, which stands for Asynchronous JavaScript and XML, a technology that powers interactive web applications including Gmail (http://gmail.google.com) and Flickr (http://flickr.com). Recall the client/server model discussed in Chapters 1 and 10. The browser makes a request to the server (often triggered by clicking a hyperlink or a submit button), and the server returns an entire new web page for the browser to display. AJAX pushes more of the processing on the client (browser) with JavaScript and XML and often uses "behind the scenes" asynchronous requests to the server to refresh a portion of the browser display instead of the entire web page. The key is that when using AJAX technology, JavaScript code (which runs on the client computer within the confines of the browser) can communicate directly with the server—exchanging data and modifying parts of the web page display without reloading of the entire web page.

For example, as soon as a website visitor types a Zip Code into a form, the value could be looked up on a Zip Code database and the city/state automatically populated using AJAX—and all this takes place while the visitor is entering the form information before he or she clicks the submit button. The result is that the visitor perceives the web page as being more responsive and has a more interactive experience. Visit the following websites to explore this topic further:

- http://www.w3schools.com/ajax/ajax_intro.asp
- http://www.alistapart.com/articles/gettingstartedwithajax
- http://www.tizag.com/ajaxTutorial

Web Publishing Basics

Well, you've designed and built a website, but there is still much more to do. You need to obtain a domain name, select a web host, publish your files to the Web, and submit your site to search engines. In addition to discussing these tasks, this chapter introduces you to evaluating the accessibility and usability of your website.

You'll learn how to...

- Describe criteria to consider when you're selecting a web host
- Obtain a domain name for your website
- Publish a website using FTP
- Design web pages that are friendly to search engines
- Submit a website for inclusion in a search engine
- Determine whether a website meets accessibility requirements
- Evaluate the usability of a website

Register a Domain Name

VideoNote

Choosing a Domain Name

A crucial part of establishing an effective web presence is choosing a **domain name**; it serves to locate your website on the Internet (Figure 12.1). If your business or organization is brand new, then it's often convenient to select a domain name while you are deciding on a company name. If your organization is well established, you should choose a domain name that relates to your existing business presence. Although many domain names have already been purchased, there are still many options available.

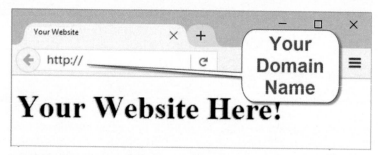

FIGURE 12.1 *Your domain name establishes your presence on the Web.*

Describe Your Business. Although there is a long-standing trend to use "fun" words as domain names (such as yahoo.com, google.com, bing.com, woofoo.com, and so on), think carefully before doing so. Domain names for traditional businesses and organizations are the foundation of the organization's web presence and should include the business name or purpose.

Be Brief, If Possible. Although most people find new websites with search engines, some of your visitors will type your domain name in a browser. A shorter domain name is preferable to a longer one—it's easier for your web visitors to remember.

Avoid Hyphens. Using the hyphen character (commonly called a dash) in a domain name makes it difficult to pronounce the name. Also, someone typing your domain name may forget the dash and end up at a competitor's site! If you can, avoid the use of dashes in a domain name.

There's More Than .com. While the .com top-level domain name (TLD) is still the most popular for commercial and personal websites, consider also registering your domain name with other TLDs, such as .biz, .net, .us, .mobi, and so on. Commercial businesses should avoid the .org TLD, which is the first choice for nonprofit organizations. You don't have to create a website for each domain name that you register. You can arrange with your domain name registrar (such as http://register.com) for the "extra" domain names to point visitors to the domain name where your website is located. This is called **domain name redirection**.

Brainstorm Potential Keywords. Think about words that a potential visitor might type into a search engine when looking for your type of business or organization. This is the starting point for your list of **keywords**. If possible, work one or more keywords into your domain name (but still keep it as short as possible).

Avoid Trademarked Words or Phrases. The U.S. Patent and Trademark Office (USPTO) defines a **trademark** as a word, phrase, symbol, or design, or a combination of words, phrases, symbols, or designs, that identifies and distinguishes the source of the goods of one party from those of others. A starting point in researching trademarks is the USPTO Trademark Electronic Search System (TESS) at http://tess2.uspto.gov.

Know the Territory. Explore the way your potential domain name and keywords are already used on the Web. It's a good idea to type your potential domain names (and related words) into a search engine to see what may already exist.

Verify Availability. Check with one of the many **domain name registrars** to determine whether your domain name choices are available. A few of the many sites that offer domain name registration services are as follows:

- ▶ http://register.com
- ▶ http://networksolutions.com
- ▶ http://godaddy.com

Each of these sites offers a WHOIS search feature that provides a way to determine whether a potential domain name is available and, if it is owned, who owns it. Often the domain name is already taken. If that's the case, the sites listed here will provide alternate suggestions that may be appropriate. Don't give up; a domain name is out there waiting for your business.

Registering a Domain Name

Once you've found your perfect domain name, don't waste any time in registering it. The cost of registering a domain name varies but is quite reasonable. The top rate for a .com one-year registration is currently $35 (and there are numerous opportunities for discounts with multiyear packages or bundled web hosting services). It's perfectly OK to register a domain name even if you are not ready to publish your website immediately. There are many companies that provide domain registration services, as listed earlier. When you register a domain name, your contact information (such as name, phone number, mailing address, and e-mail address) will be entered into the WHOIS database and available to anyone unless you choose the option for private registration. While there is usually a small annual fee for **private registration**, it shields your personal information from unwanted spam and curiosity seekers.

Obtaining a domain name is just one part of establishing a web presence—you also need to host your website somewhere. The next section introduces you to factors involved in choosing a web host.

Choose a Web Host

A **web host provider** is an organization that offers storage for your website files along with the service of making them available on the Internet. Your domain name, such as webdevbasics.net, is associated with an IP address that points to your website on the web server at the web host provider.

It is common for web host providers to charge a setup fee in addition to the monthly hosting fee. Hosting fees vary widely. The cheapest hosting company is not necessarily the one to use. Never consider using a "free" web host provider for a business website. These free sites are great for kids, college students, and hobbyists, but they are unprofessional. The last thing you or your client wants is to be perceived as unprofessional or not serious about the business at hand. As you consider different web host providers, try contacting their support phone numbers and e-mail addresses to determine just how responsive they really are. Word of mouth, web searches, and online directories such as http://www.hosting-review.com are all resources in your quest for the perfect web host provider.

Types of Web Hosting

▶ **Virtual Hosting,** or shared hosting, is a popular choice for small websites (Figure 12.2). The web host provider's physical web server is divided into a number of virtual domains, and multiple websites are setup on the same computer. You have the authority to update files in your own website space, while the web host provider maintains the web server computer and Internet connectivity.

FIGURE 12.2 *Virtual web hosting.*

▶ **Dedicated Hosting** is the rental and exclusive use of a computer and connection to the Internet that is housed on the web hosting company's premises. A dedicated server is usually needed for a website that could have a considerable amount of traffic, such as tens of millions of hits a day. The server can usually be configured and operated remotely from the client company, or you can pay the web host provider to administer it for you.

▶ **Co-Located Hosting** uses a computer that your organization has purchased and configured. Your web server is housed and connected to the Internet at the web host's physical location, but your organization administers this computer.

Choosing a Virtual Host

There are a number of factors to consider when choosing a web host. Table 12.1 provides a checklist.

TABLE 12.1   *Web Host Checklist*

Operating system	☐ UNIX ☐ Linux ☐ Windows	Some web hosts offer a choice of these platforms. If you need to integrate your web host with your business systems, choose the same operating system for both.
Web server	☐ Apache ☐ IIS	These two web server applications are the most popular. Apache usually runs on a UNIX or Linux operating system. Internet Information Services (IIS) is bundled with selected versions of Microsoft Windows.
Bandwidth	☐ ___ GB per month ☐ ___ Charge for overage	Some web hosts carefully monitor your data transfer bandwidth and charge you for overages. While unlimited bandwidth is great, it is not always available. A typical low-traffic website varies between 100GB and 200GB per month. A medium-traffic site should be OK with about 500GB of data transfer bandwidth per month.
Technical support	☐ E-mail ☐ Chat ☐ Forum ☐ Phone	Review the description of technical support on the web host's site. Is it available 24 hours a day, 7 days a week? E-mail or phone a question to test it. If the organization is not responsive to you as a prospective customer, be leery about the availability of its technical support later.
Service agreement	☐ Uptime guarantee ☐ Automatic monitoring	A web host that offers a Service Level Agreement (SLA) with an uptime guarantee shows that service and reliability are valued. The use of automatic monitoring will inform the web host technical support staff when a server is not functioning.
Disk space	☐ ___ GB	Many virtual hosts routinely offer 100GB+ disk storage space. If you have a small site that is not graphic intensive, you may never even use more than 50MB of disk storage space.
E-mail	☐ ___ Mailboxes	Most virtual hosts offer multiple e-mail mailboxes per site. These can be used to filter messages—customer service, technical support, general inquiries, and so on.
Uploading files	☐ FTP access ☐ Web-based file manager	A web host that offers FTP access will allow the most flexibility. Others only allow updates through a web-based file manager application. Some web hosts offer both options.
Canned scripts	☐ Form processing	Many web hosts supply canned, prewritten scripts to process form information.
Scripting support	☐ PHP ☐ .NET	If you plan to use server-side scripting (refer back to Chapter 10) on your site, determine which, if any, scripting is supported by your web host.
Database support	☐ MySQL ☐ SQL Server	If you plan to access a database with your scripting, determine which, if any, database is supported by your web host.
E-commerce packages	☐ _____	If you plan to enter into e-commerce, it may be easier if your web host offers a shopping cart package. Check to see if one is available.
Scalability	☐ Scripting ☐ Database ☐ E-commerce	You probably will choose a basic (low-end) plan for your first website. Note the scalability of your web host—are there other plans with scripting, database, e-commerce packages, and additional bandwidth or disk space available as your site grows?
Backups	☐ Daily ☐ Periodic ☐ No backups	Most web hosts will back up your files regularly. Check to see how often the backups are made and if they are accessible to you. Be sure to make your own site backups as well.
Site statistics	☐ Raw log file ☐ Log reports ☐ No log	The website log contains useful information about your visitors, how they find your site, and what pages they visit. Check to see if the log is available to you. Some web hosts provide reports about the log.
Domain name	☐ Included ☐ On your own	Some web hosts offer a package that includes registering your domain name. You may prefer to register your domain name yourself (see http://register.com or http://networksolutions.com) and retain control of your domain name account.
Price	☐ $___ setup fee ☐ $___ per month	Price is last in this list for a reason. Do not choose a web host based on price alone—the old adage "you get what you pay for" is definitely true here. It is not unusual to pay a one-time setup fee and then a periodic fee—monthly, quarterly, or annually.

Publish with File Transfer Protocol

Once you obtain your web hosting, you'll need to upload your files. While your web host may offer a web-based file manager application for client use, a common method of transferring files is to use **File Transfer Protocol** (FTP). A **protocol** is a convention or standard that enables computers to speak to one another. **FTP** is used to copy and manage files and folders over the Internet. FTP uses two ports to communicate over a network—one for the data (typically port 20) and one for control commands (typically port 21). See http://www.iana.org/assignments/port-numbers for a list of port numbers used on the Internet.

FTP Applications

There are many FTP applications available for download or purchase on the Web; several are listed in Table 12.2.

TABLE 12.2 *FTP Applications*

Application	Platform	URL	Cost
FileZilla	Windows, Mac, Linux	http://filezilla-project.org	Free download
SmartFTP	Windows	http://www.smartftp.com	Free download
CuteFTP	Windows, Mac	http://www.cuteftp.com	Free trial download, academic pricing available
WS_FTP	Windows	http://www.ipswitchft.com	Free trial download

Connecting with FTP

Your web host will provide you with the following information for connecting to your FTP server, along with any other specifications, such as whether the FTP server requires the use of active mode or passive mode:

FTP Host: ftp://*yourhostaddress*

Username: *your_account_username*

Password: *your_account_password*

Overview of Using an FTP Application

This section focuses on FileZilla, a free FTP application with versions for the Windows, Mac, and Linux platforms. A free download of FileZilla is available at http://filezilla-project.org. After you download an FTP application of your choice, install the program on your computer using the instructions provided.

Launch and Login. Launch Filezilla or another FTP application. Enter the information required by your web host (such as FTP host, username, and password) and initiate the connection. An example screenshot of FileZilla after a connection is shown in Figure 12.3.

As you examine Figure 12.3, notice the text boxes near the top of the application for the Host, Username, and Password information. Under this area is a display of messages from the FTP server. Review this area to confirm a successful connection and the results of file transfers. Next, notice that the applica-

FIGURE 12.3 *The FileZilla FTP application.*

tion is divided into a left panel and a right panel. The left panel is the local site—it displays information about your local computer and allows you to navigate to your drives, folders, and files. The right panel is the remote site—it displays information about your website and provides a way to navigate to its folders and files.

Uploading a File. It's really easy to transfer a file from your local computer to your remote website—just select the file with your mouse in the left panel (local site list) and drag it to the right panel (remote site list).

Downloading a File. If you need to download a file from your website to your local computer, just drag the file from the right panel (remote site list) to the left panel (local site list).

Deleting a File. To delete a file on your website, right-click (Ctrl-click if using a Mac) on the file name (in the right panel) and select Delete from the context-sensitive menu.

And There's More! Explore other functions offered by FileZilla (and most FTP applications)—right-click (Ctrl-click if using a Mac) on a file in the remote site list to display a context-sensitive menu with several options, including renaming a file, creating a new directory (also known as a folder), and viewing a file.

Search Engine Submission

Using a search engine is a popular way to navigate the Web and find websites. The PEW Internet and American Life Project (http://www.pewinternet.org/files/2014/01/Usage-Over-Time-_May-2013.xlsx) reports that the percentage of individuals who use a search engine has been steadily rising. Over 90% of American adult Internet users utilize search engines, with 59% accessing a search engine on a typical day. Search engine listings can be an excellent marketing tool for your business. To harness the power of search engines and search indexes (sometimes called search directories), it helps to know how they work.

According to NetMarketShare (http://www.netmarketshare.com/search-enginemarket-share.aspx?qprid=4&qpcustomd=0), Google (http://www.google.com) and Bing (http://www.bing.com) were the two most popular sites used to search the Web during a recent month. Google was reported to have an overwhelming desktop market share of 72.48%, while the closest competitors were Bing (10.39%), Yahoo! (7.78%), and Baidu (7.14%). Check http://marketshare.hitslink.com for the most currrent survey results.

Components of a Search Engine

The components of a search engine (robot, database, and search form) work together to obtain information about web pages, store information about web pages, and provide a graphical user interface to facilitate searching for and displaying a list of web pages relevant to given keywords.

Robot. A **robot** (sometimes called a spider or bot) is a program that automatically traverses the hypertext structure of the Web by retrieving a web page document and following the hyperlinks on the page. It moves like a robot spider on the Web, accessing and storing information about the web pages in a database. Visit The Web Robots Pages at http://www.robotstxt.org if you'd like more details about web robots.

Database. A **database** is a collection of information organized so that its contents can easily be accessed, managed, and updated. Database management systems (DBMSs) such as Oracle, Microsoft SQL Server, MySQL, or IBM DB2 are used to configure and manage the database. The web page that displays the results of your search, called the Search Engine Results Page (SERP), lists information from the database accessed by the search engine.

Search Form. The search form is the graphical user interface that allows a user to type in the word or phrase he or she is searching for. It is typically a text box and a submit button. The visitor to the search engine types words (called keywords) related to his or her search into the text box. When the form is submitted, the keywords are sent to a server-side script that searches the database for matches. The results are displayed on a SERP and formatted with a hyperlink to each page along with additional information that might include the page title, a brief description, the first few lines of text, or the size of the page. The order in which the results are displayed may depend on paid advertisements, alphabetical order, and link popularity. The link popularity of a website is a rating determined by a search engine based on the quantity and quality of incoming hyperlinks. Each search engine has its own policy for ordering the search results. Be aware that these policies can change over time.

Listing Your Site in a Search Engine

Search engines spiders routinely traverse the web and should eventually visit your website, but it can take some time. You can potentially speed up the process by submitting your website manually to a search engine. Follow these steps to submit your website to a search engine:

Step 1: Visit the search engine site (such as http://google.com or http://yahoo.com) and look for an "Add site" or "List URL" link. This is typically on the home page (or About Us page) of the search engine. Be patient—these links are sometimes not obvious. If you don't see a link to submit your site, then use the search engine to search for a phrase similar to "Submit to Google" or "Submit to Bing". To submit your website to Bing, visit http://www.bing.com/toolbox/submit-site-url. To submit your website to Google, visit http://www.google.com/submityourcontent/website-owner/ and select the "Add your URL" link.

Step 2: Follow the directions listed on the page and submit the form to request that your site be added to the search engine. Currently, there is no fee to submit a site to Bing or Google.

Step 3: The spider from the search engine will index your site. This may take several weeks.

Step 4: Several weeks after you submit your website, check the search engine or search directory to see if your site is listed. If it is not listed, review your pages and check whether they are optimized for search engines (see the next section) and display in common browsers.

? FAQ   Is advertising on a search engine worth the cost?

It depends. How much is it worth to your client to appear on the first page of the search engine results? You select the keywords that will trigger the display of your ad. You also set your monthly budget and the maximum amount to pay for each click. While costs and charges vary by search engine, at this time Google charges are based on cost per click—you'll be charged each time a visitor to Google clicks on your advertisement. Visit http://google.com/adwords for more information about their program.

Search Engine Optimization

If you have followed recommended web design practices, you've already designed your website so that the pages are appealing and compelling to your target audience. How can you also make your site work well with search engines? Here are some suggestions and hints on designing your pages for optimal ranking by search engines—a process called **Search Engine Optimization (SEO)**.

Keywords

Spend some time brainstorming about terms and phrases that people may use when searching for your site. These terms or phrases that describe your website or business are your **keywords**.

Page Titles

A descriptive page title (the text between the `<title>` tags) that includes your company and/or website name will help your site market itself. It's common for search engines to display the text in the page title in the SERP. The page title is also saved by default when a visitor bookmarks your site and is often included when a visitor prints a page of your site. Avoid using the exact same title for every page; include keywords in the page title that are appropriate for the page.

Heading Tags

Use structural tags such as `<h1>`, `<h2>`, and so on to organize your page content. If it is appropriate for the web page content, also include some keywords in the text contained within heading tags. Some search engines will give a higher list position if keywords are included in a page title or headings. Also include keywords as appropriate within the page text content. However, avoid spamming keywords—that is, do not list them over and over again. The programs behind search engines become more sophisticated all the time, and you can actually be prevented from being listed if it is perceived that you are not being honest or are trying to cheat the system.

Description

What is special about your website that would make someone want to visit? With this in mind, write a few sentences about your website or business. This description should be inviting and interesting so that a person searching the Web will choose your site from the list provided by a search engine or search directory. Some search engines will display your description on the SERP. You can configure a description for your web page by coding a meta tag in the page header area.

The Meta Tag

A **meta tag** is a self-contained tag that is placed in the header section of a web page. You've been using a meta tag to indicate character encoding. There are a number of other uses for a meta tag. We'll focus here on providing a description of a website for use by search engines. The description meta tag content is displayed on the SERP by some search engines, such as Google. The **name** attribute indicates the purpose of the meta tag. The **content** attribute provides the value needed for the specific purpose. For example, the description meta tag for a website about a web development consulting firm called Acme Design could be configured as follows:

```
<meta name="description" content="Acme Design, a web consulting group that
specializes in e-commerce, website design, development, and redesign.">
```

? FAQ **What if I don't want a search engine to index a page?**

To indicate to a search engine robot that a page should not be indexed and the links should not be followed, do not place keywords and description meta tags in the page. Instead, add a "robots" meta tag to the page as follows:

```
<meta name="robots" content="noindex,nofollow">
```

To indicate that search engines should not index your entire website, use the Robots Exclusion Protocol described at http://www.robotstxt.org. Create a small text file named robots. txt and store it in the top level folder of your website. Place the following statements in the text file:

```
User-agent: *
Disallow: /
```

Linking

Verify that all hyperlinks are working and not broken. Each page on your website should be reachable by a text hyperlink. The text should be descriptive—avoid phrases like "more info" and "click here"—and should include keywords as appropriate. Inbound links (sometimes called incoming links) are also a factor in SEO. All these linking issues can affect your website's link popularity, and its link popularity can determine its order in the search engine results page.

Images and Multimedia

Be mindful that search engine robots do not "see" the text embedded within your images and multimedia. Configure meaningful alternate text for images. Include relevant keywords in the alternate text. Although some search engine robots, such as Google's Googlebot, have recently added functionality to index text and hyperlinks contained within Flash media, be aware that a website that contains hyperlinks within Flash and Silverlight media will be less visible to search engines and may rank lower as a result.

Valid Code

Search engines do not require that your HTML and CSS code pass validation tests. However, code that is valid and well structured is likely to be more easily processed by search engine robots. This may help with your placement in the search engine results.

Content of Value

Probably the most basic, but often overlooked, component of SEO is providing content of value that follows web design best practices (see Chapter 3). Your website should contain high-quality, well-organized content that is of value to your visitors.

Accessibility Testing

Universal Design and Accessibility

The Center for Universal Design defines universal design as "the design of products and environments to be usable by all people, to the greatest extent possible, without the need for adaptation or specialized design." Web pages that follow the principle of universal design are **accessible** to all individuals, including those with visual, hearing, mobility, and cognitive challenges. As you've worked through this book, accessibility has been an integral part of your web page design and coding rather than an afterthought. You've configured headings and subheadings, navigation within unordered lists, images with alternate text, alternate text for multimedia, and associations between text and form controls. These techniques all increase the accessibility of a web page.

Web Accessibility Standards

Recall from Chapter 3 that the accessibility recommendations presented in this text are intended to satisfy Section 508 of the Rehabilitation Act and the W3C's Web Content Accessibility Guidelines.

Section 508 of the Rehabilitation Act. Section 508 (http://www.access-board.gov) requires electronic and information technology, including web pages, that are used by federal agencies to be accessible to people with disabilities. At the time this was written the Section 508 standards were undergoing revision.

Web Content Accessibility Guidelines (WCAG 2.0). WCAG 2.0 (http://www.w3.org/TR/WCAG20) considers an accessible web page to be perceivable, operable, and understandable for people with a wide range of abilities. The page should be robust to work with a variety of browsers and other user agents, such as screen readers and mobile devices. The guiding principles of WCAG 2.0 are as follows:

1. Content must be **P**erceivable.
2. Interface components in the content must be **O**perable.
3. Content and controls must be **U**nderstandable.
4. Content should be **R**obust enough to work with current and future user agents, including assistive technologies.

What is assistive technology and what is a screen reader?

Assistive technology is a term that describes any tool that a person can use to help him or her to overcome a disability and use a computer. Examples of assistive technologies include screen readers, head- and mouth-wands, and specialized keyboards, such as a single-hand keyboard. A screen reader is a software application that can be controlled by the user to read aloud what is displayed on the computer screen. Visit https://www.youtube.com/watch?v=VvWCnFjAGgo for a video introduction using a screen reader. JAWS is a popular screen reader application. A free time-restricted download of JAWS is available at http://freedomscientific.com/downloads/jaws/jaws-downloads.asp. A free download of the open-source NVDA screen reader is available at http://www.nvda-project.org.

Testing for Accessibility Compliance

No single testing tool can automatically test for all web standards. The first step in testing the accessibility of a web page is to verify that it is coded according to W3C standards with the (X)HTML syntax validator (http://validator.w3.org) and the CSS syntax validator (http://jigsaw.w3.org/css-validator).

Automated Accessibility Testing. An automated accessibility evaluation tool is no substitute for your own manual evaluation but can be useful to quickly identify potential issues with a web page. WebAim Wave (http://wave.webaim.org) and ATRC AChecker (http://www.achecker.ca/checker) are two popular free online accessibility evaluation tools. The online applications typically require the URL of a web page and reply with an accessibility report. The Web Developer Extension (http://chrispederick.com/work/web-developer) is a browser toolbar that can be used to assess accessibility. The Web Developer Extension is multifunctional, with options to validate HTML, validate CSS, disable images, view alt text, outline block-level elements, resize the browser viewport, disable styles, and more. Figure 12.4 shows the Web Developer Extension toolbar in action.

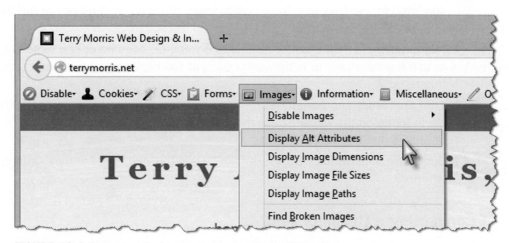

FIGURE 12.4 *Selecting the Images > Display Alt Attributes feature.*

Manual Accessibility Testing. It's important not to rely completely on automated tests—you'll want to review the pages yourself. For example, while an automated test can check for the presence of an `alt` attribute, it takes a human to critically think and decide whether the text of the `alt` attribute is an appropriate description for a person who cannot view the image.

Usability Testing

An addition to accessibility, another aspect of universal design is the usability of the website. **Usability** is the measure of the quality of a user's experience when interacting with a website. It's about making a website that is easy, efficient, and pleasant for your visitors. Usability.gov describes factors that affect the user's experience:

▶ **Intuitive Design**—How easy is it for a new visitor to understand the organization of the site? Is the navigation intuitive for a new user?

▶ **Ease of Learning**—How easy is it to learn to use the website? Does a new visitor consider it easy to learn to perform basic tasks on the website or is he or she frustrated?

▶ **Efficiency of Use**—How do experienced users perceive the website? Once they are comfortable, are they able to complete tasks efficiently and quickly or are they frustrated?

▶ **Memorability**—When a visitor returns to a website, does he or she remember enough to use it productively or is the visitor back at the beginning of the learning curve (and frustrated)?

▶ **Error Frequency and Severity**—Do website visitors make errors when navigating or filling in forms on the website? Are they serious errors? Is it easy to recover from errors or are visitors frustrated?

▶ **Subjective Satisfaction**—Do users "like" using the website? Are they satisfied? Why or why not?

Conducting a Usability Test

Testing how people use a website is called **usability testing**. Usability testing can be conducted at any phase of a website's development and is often performed more than once. A usability test is conducted by asking users to complete tasks on a website, such as placing an order, looking up the phone number of a company, or finding a product. The exact tasks will vary depending on the website being evaluated. The users are monitored while they try to perform these tasks. They are asked to think out loud about their doubts and hesitations. The results are recorded (often on video) and discussed with the web design team. Often changes are made to the navigation and page layouts based on these tests.

If usability testing is done early in the development phase of a website, it may use the printed page layouts and site map. If the web development team is struggling with a design issue, sometimes a usability test can help to determine which design idea is the better choice. When usability is done during a later phase after the pages have been built, the actual website is tested. This can lead to confirmation that the site is easy to use and well designed, to last-minute changes in the website, or to a plan for website enhancements in the near future.

Hands-On Practice 12.1

Perform a small-scale usability test with a group of other students. Decide who will be the "typical users," the tester, and the observer. You will perform a usability test on your school's website.

- The "typical users" are the test subjects.
- The tester oversees the usability test and emphasizes that the users are not being tested—the website is being tested.
- The observer takes notes on the user's reactions and comments.

Step 1: The tester welcomes the users and introduces them to the website they will be testing.

Step 2: For each of the following scenarios, the tester introduces the scenario and questions the users as they work through the task. The tester should ask the users to indicate when they are in doubt, confused, or frustrated. The observer takes notes.

- Scenario 1: Find the phone number of the contact person for the Web Development program at your school.
- Scenario 2: Determine when to register for the next semester.
- Scenario 3: Find the requirements to earn a degree or certificate in Web Development or a related area.

Step 3: The tester and observer organize the results and write a brief report. If this were a usability test for an actual website, the development team would meet to review the results and discuss necessary improvements to the site.

Step 4: Hand in a report with your group's usability test results. Complete the report using a word processor. Write no more than one page about each scenario. Write one page of recommendations for improving your school's website.

 Continue to explore the topic of usability testing at the following resources:

- Keith Instone's Classic Presentation on How to Test Usability: http://instone.org/files/KEI-Howtotest-19990721.pdf
- Advanced Common Sense—the website of usability expert Steve Krug: http://www.sensible.com
- Usability Basics: http://usability.gov/basics/index.html
- Usability Resources: http://www.infodesign.com.au/usabilityresources
- Usability Testing Materials: http://www.infodesign.com.au/usabilityresources/usabilitytestingmaterials

Review and Apply

Review Questions

Multiple Choice. Choose the best answer for each item.

1. Which of the following is a protocol commonly used to transfer files over the Internet?
   - **a.** port
   - **b.** http
   - **c.** FTP
   - **d.** SMTP

2. In which of the following sections of a web page should meta tags be placed?
   - **a.** head
   - **b.** body
   - **c.** comment
   - **d.** none of the above

3. Which of the following statements is true?
   - **a.** No single testing tool can automatically test for all web standards.
   - **b.** Include as many people as possible when you conduct usability tests.
   - **c.** Search engine listings are effective immediately after submission.
   - **d.** None of the above statements are true.

4. Which are the four principles of the Web Content Accessibility Guidelines?
   - **a.** contrast, repetition, alignment, and proximity
   - **b.** perceivable, operable, understandable, and robust
   - **c.** accessible, readable, maintainable, and reliable
   - **d.** hierarchical, linear, random, and sequential

5. What is the measure of the quality of a user's experience when interacting with a website?
   - **a.** accessibility
   - **b.** usability
   - **c.** universal design
   - **d.** assistive technology

6. Which web hosting option is appropriate for the initial web presence of an organization?
   - **a.** dedicated hosting
   - **b.** free web hosting
   - **c.** virtual hosting
   - **d.** colocated hosting

7. What is the purpose of private registration for a domain name?
   - **a.** It protects the privacy of your web host.
   - **b.** It is the cheapest form of domain name registration.
   - **c.** It protects the privacy of your contact information.
   - **d.** None of the above.

8. Which of the following is true about domain names?
   - **a.** It is recommended to register multiple domain names that are redirected to your website.
   - **b.** It is recommended to use long, descriptive domain names.
   - **c.** It is recommended to use hyphens in domain names.
   - **d.** There is no reason to check for trademarks when you are choosing a domain name.

9. Which of the following is a rating determined by a search engine based on the number and quality of hyperlinks to a website?
   - **a.** link checking
   - **b.** link rating
   - **c.** link popularity
   - **d.** search engine optimization

10. Which of the following is the design of products and environments to be usable by all people, to the greatest extent possible, without the need for adaptation or specialized design?
    - **a.** accessibility
    - **b.** usability
    - **c.** universal design
    - **d.** functionality

Hands-On Exercises

1. Run an automated accessibility test on the home page of your school website. Use both the WebAim Wave (http://wave.webaim.org) and ATRC AChecker (http://www.achecker.ca/checker) automated tests. Describe the differences in the way these tools report the results of the test. Did both tests find similar errors? Write a one-page report that describes the results of the tests. Include your recommendations for improving the website.

2. Search for web host providers and report on three that meet the following criteria:
   - Support PHP and MySQL
   - Offer e-commerce capabilities
   - Provide at least 1GB hard disk space

   Use your favorite search engine to find web host providers or visit web host directories such as http://www.hosting-review.com and http://www.hostindex.com. The web host survey results provided by http://uptime.netcraft.com/perf/reports/Hosters may also be useful. Create a web page that presents your findings. Include links to the three web host providers you selected. Your web page should include a table of information such as setup fees, monthly fees, domain name registration costs, amount of hard disk space, type of e-commerce package, and cost of e-commerce package. Use color and graphics appropriately on your web page. Place your name and e-mail address at the bottom of your web page.

Focus on Web Design

1. Explore how to design your website so that it is optimized for search engines (Search Engine Optimization or SEO). Visit the following resources as a starting point as you search for three SEO tips or hints:
   - http://www.forbes.com/sites/jaysondemers/2015/11/10/the-fundamental-guide-to-seo-in-2016/
   - http://www.seomoz.org/beginners-guide-to-seo
   - http://www.bruceclay.com/seo/search-engine-optimization.htm

   Write a one-page report that describes three tips that you found interesting or potentially useful. Cite the URLs of the resources you used.

2. Explore how to reach out to your current and potential website visitors with **Social Media Optimization** (SMO), which is described by Rohit Bhargava as optimizing a website so that it is "more easily linked to, more highly visible in social media searches on custom search engines (such as Technorati), and more frequently included in relevant posts on blogs, podcasts and vlogs." Benefits of SMO include increased awareness of your brand and/or site along with an increase in the number of inbound links (which can help with SEO). Visit the following resources as a starting point as you search for three SMO tips or hints:
   - The Beginners Guide to Social Media: https://moz.com/beginners-guide-to-social-media
   - http://www.rohitbhargava.com/2010/08/the-5-new-rules-of-social-media-optimization-smo.html
   - http://www.socialmediaexaminer.com/social-media-seo/

Write a one-page report that describes three tips that you found interesting or potentially useful. Cite the URLs of the resources you used.

Pacific Trails Resort Case Study

In this chapter's case study you will use the existing Pacific Trails website (Chapter 11) as a starting point to create a new version of the website that implements the description meta tag on each page. You have three tasks in this case study:

1. Create a new folder for this Pacific Trails case study.
2. Write a description of the Pacific Trails Resort business.
3. Code a description meta tag on each page in the website.

Task 1: Create a folder called ch12pacific to contain your Pacific Trails Resort website files. Copy the files from the Chapter 11 Case Study ch11pacific folder.

Task 2: Write a Description. Review the Pacific Trails Resort pages that you created in earlier chapters. Write a brief paragraph that describes the Pacific Trails Resort site. Edit the paragraph down to a description that is only a few sentences and less than 25 words in length.

Task 3: Update Each Page. Open each page in a text editor and add a description meta tag to the head section. Save the files and test them in a browser. They will not look different, but they are much friendlier to search engines!

Path of Light Yoga Studio Case Study

In this chapter's case study you will use the existing Path of Light Yoga Studio website (Chapter 11) as a starting point to create a new version of the website that implements the description meta tag on each page. You have three tasks in this case study:

1. Create a new folder for this Path of Light Yoga Studio case study.
2. Write a description of the Path of Light Yoga Studio business.
3. Code a description meta tag on each page in the website.

Task 1: Create a folder called ch12yoga to contain your Path of Light Yoga Studio website files. Copy the files from the Chapter 11 Case Study ch11yoga folder.

Task 2: Write a Description. Review the Path of Light Yoga Studio pages that you created in earlier chapters. Write a brief paragraph that describes the Path of Light Yoga Studio site. Edit the paragraph down to a description that is only a few sentences and less than 25 words in length.

Task 3: Update Each Page. Open each page in a text editor and add a description meta tag to the head section. Save the files and test them in a browser. They will not look different, but they are much friendlier to search engines!

Answers to Review Questions

Chapter 1

1. b	2. b	3. b
4. d	5. True	6. False
7. False	8. HTML	9. .htm, .html
10. index.htm, index.html		

Chapter 2

1. c	2. a	3. c
4. c	5. a	6. b
7. c	8. b	9. b
10. b		

Chapter 3

1. d	2. b	3. b
4. b	5. c	6. b
7. c	8. a	9. c
10. d		

Chapter 4

1. b	2. d	3. d
4. a	5. c	6. b
7. b	8. d	9. a
10. b		

Chapter 5

1. a	2. b	3. b
4. b	5. c	6. d
7. d	8. d	9. b
10. b		

Chapter 6

1. b	2. c	3. b
4. b	5. a	6. c
7. c	8. a	9. b
10. a		

Chapter 7

1. d	2. a	3. b
4. c	5. d	6. c
7. b	8. d	9. c
10. b		

Chapter 8

1. a	2. c	3. b
4. b	5. d	6. d
7. b	8. d	9. c
10. b		

Chapter 9

1. b	2. c	3. c
4. c	5. b	6. c
7. b	8. b	9. c
10. b		

Chapter 10

1. d	2. a	3. c
4. b	5. a	6. c
7. a	8. d	9. c
10. d		

Chapter 11

1. c	2. b	3. c
4. a	5. a	6. c
7. b	8. b	9. b
10. a		

Chapter 12

1. c	2. a	3. a
4. b	5. b	6. c
7. c	8. a	9. c
10. c		

HTML5 Cheat Sheet

Commonly Used HTML5 Tags

Tag	Purpose	Commonly Used Attributes
`<!-- -->`	Comment	
`<a>`	Anchor tag: configures hyperlinks	`accesskey, class, href, id, name, rel, style, tabindex, target, title`
`<abbr>`	Configures an abbreviation	`class, id, style`
`<address>`	Configures contact information	`class, id, style`
`<area>`	Configures an area in an image map	`accesskey, alt, class, href, hreflang, id, media, rel, shape, style, tabindex, target, type`
`<article>`	Configures an independent section of a document as an article	`class, id, style`
`<aside>`	Configures tangential content	`class, id, style`
`<audio>`	Configures an audio control native to the browser	`autoplay, class, controls, id, loop, preload, src, style, title`
`<b>`	Configures bold text with no implied importance	`class, id, style`
`<bdi>`	Configures text used in bi-directional text formatting (bi-directional isolation)	`class, id, style`
`<bdo>`	Specifies a bi-directional override	`class, id, style`
`<blockquote>`	Configures a long quotation	`class, id, style`
`<body>`	Configures the body section	`class, id, style`
` `	Configures a line break	`class, id, style`
`<button>`	Configures a button	`accesskey, autofocus, class, disabled, format, formaction, formenctype, mormmethod, formtarget, formnovalidate, id, name, type, style, value`
`<canvas>`	Configures dynamic graphics	`class, height, id, style, title, width`
`<caption>`	Configures a caption for a table	`class, id, style`
`<cite>`	Configures the title of a cited work	`class, height, id, style, title`

Tag	Purpose	Commonly Used Attributes
`<code>`	Configures a fragment of computer code	`class, id, style`
`<col>`	Configures a table column	`class, id, span, style`
`<colgroup>`	Configures a group of one or more columns in a table	`class, id, span, style`
`<command>`	Configures an area to represent commands	`class, id, style, type`
`<datalist>`	Configures a control that contains one or more option elements	`class, id, style`
`<dd>`	Configures a description area in a description list	`class, id, style`
`<del>`	Configures deleted text (with strikethrough)	`cite, class, datetime, id, style`
`<details>`	Configures a control to provide additional information to the user on demand	`class, id, open, style`
`<dfn>`	Configures the definition of a term	`class, id, style`
`<div>`	Configures a generic section or division in a document	`class, id, style`
`<dl>`	Configures a description list (formerly called a definition list)	`class, id, style`
`<dt>`	Configures a term in a description list	`class, id, style`
`<em>`	Configures emphasized text (usually displays in italics)	`class, id, style`
`<embed>`	Plug-in integration (such as Adobe Flash Player)	`class, id, height, src, style, type, width`
`<fieldset>`	Configures a grouping of form elements with a border	`class, id, style`
`<figcaption>`	Configures a caption for a figure	`class, id, style`
`<figure>`	Configures a figure	`class, id, style`
`<footer>`	Configures a footer area	`class, id, style`
`<form>`	Configures a form	`accept-charset, action, autocomplete, class, enctype, id, method, name, novalidate, style, target`
`<h1>...<h6>`	Configures headings	`class, id, style`
`<head>`	Configures the head section	
`<header>`	Configures a header area	`class, id, style`
`<hr>`	Configures a horizontal line; indicates a thematic break in HTML5	`class, id, style`

(*Continued*)

Tag	Purpose	Commonly Used Attributes
`<html>`	Configures the root element of a web page document	`lang`, `manifest`
`<i>`	Configures italic text	`class`, `id`, `style`
`<iframe>`	Configures an inline frame	`class`, `height`, `id`, `name`, `sandbox`, `src`, `style`, `width`
`<img>`	Configures an image	`alt`, `class`, `height`, `id`, `ismap`, `longdesc`, `name`, `sizes`, `src`, `srcset`, `style`, `usemap`, `width`
`<input>`	Configures an input control; text box, email text box, URL text box, search text box, telephone number text box, scrolling text box, submit button, reset button, password box, calendar control, slider control, spinner control, color picker control, or hidden field form control	`accesskey`, `autocomplete`, `autofocus`, `class`, `checked`, `disabled`, `form`, `id`, `list`, `max`, `maxlength`, `min`, `name`, `pattern`, `placeholder`, `readonly`, `required`, `size`, `step`, `style`, `tabindex`, `type`, `value`
`<ins>`	Configures text that has been inserted with an underline	`cite`, `class`, `datetime`, `id`, `style`
`<kbd>`	Configures a representation of user input	`class`, `id`, `style`
`<keygen>`	Configures a control that generates a public–private key pair or submits the public key	`autofocus`, `challenge`, `class`, `disabled`, `form`, `id`, `keytype`, `style`
`<label>`	Configures a label for a form control	`class`, `for`, `form`, `id`, `style`
`<legend>`	Configures a caption for a fieldset element	`class`, `id`, `style`
`<li>`	Configures a list item in an unordered or ordered list	`class`, `id`, `style`, `value`
`<link>`	Associates a web page document with an external resource	`class`, `href`, `hreflang`, `id`, `rel`, `media`, `sizes`, `style`, `type`
`<main>`	Configures the main content area of a web page	`class`, `id`, `style`
`<map>`	Configures an image map	`class`, `id`, `name`, `style`
`<mark>`	Configures text as marked (or highlighted) for easy reference	`class`, `id`, `style`
`<menu>`	Configures a list of commands	`class`, `id`, `label`, `style`, `type`
`<meta>`	Configures meta data	`charset`, `content`, `http-equiv`, `name`
`<meter>`	Configures visual gauge of a value	`class`, `id`, `high`, `low`, `max`, `min`, `optimum`, `style`, `value`
`<nav>`	Configures an area with navigation hyperlinks	`class`, `id`, `style`

Tag	Purpose	Commonly Used Attributes
`<noscript>`	Configures content for browsers that do not support client-side scripting	
`<object>`	Configures a generic embedded object	`classid, codebase, data, form, height, name, id, style, title, tabindex, type, width`
`<ol>`	Configures an ordered list	`class, id, reversed, start, style, type`
`<optgroup>`	Configures a group of related options in a select list	`class, disabled, id, label, style`
`<option>`	Configures an option in a select list	`class, disabled, id, selected, style, value`
`<output>`	Configures result of processing in a form	`class, for, form, id, style`
`<p>`	Configures a paragraph	`class, id, style`
`<param>`	Configures a parameter for plug-ins	`name, value`
`<picture>`	Configures images for responsive display with media queries	`class, id, style`
`<pre>`	Configures preformatted text	`class, id, style`
`<progress>`	Configures a visual progress indicator	`class, id, max, style, value`
`<q>`	Configures quoted text	`cite, class, id, style`
`<rp>`	Configures a ruby parentheses	`class, id, style`
`<rt>`	Configures ruby text component of a ruby annotation	`class, id, style`
`<ruby>`	Configures a ruby annotation	`class, id, style`
`<samp>`	Configures sample output from a computer program or system	`class, id, style`
`<script>`	Configures a client-side script (typically JavaScript)	`async, charset, defer, src, type`
`<section>`	Configures a section of a document	`class, id, style`
`<select>`	Configures a select list form control	`class, disabled, form, id, multiple, name, size, style, tabindex`
`<small>`	Configures a disclaimer in small text size	`class, id, style`
`<source>`	Configures a media file and MIME type	`class, id, media, sizes, src, srcset, style, type`
`<span>`	Configures a generic section of a document with inline display	`class, id, style`

(Continued)

Tag	Purpose	Commonly Used Attributes
`<strong>`	Configures text with strong importance (typically displayed as bold)	`class`, `id`, `style`
`<style>`	Configures embedded styles in a web page document	`media`, `scoped`, `type`
`<sub>`	Configures subscript text	`class`, `id`, `style`
`<summary>`	Configures text as a summary, caption, or legend for a details control	`class`, `id`, `style`
`<sup>`	Configures superscript text	`class`, `id`, `style`
`<table>`	Configures a table	`class`, `id`, `style`, `border`
`<tbody>`	Configures the body section of a table	`class`, `id`, `style`
`<td>`	Configures a table data cell in a table	`class`, `colspan`, `id`, `headers`, `rowspan`
`<textarea>`	Configures a scrolling text box form control	`accesskey`, `autofocus`, `class`, `cols`, `disabled`, `id`, `maxlength`, `name`, `placeholder`, `readonly`, `required`, `rows`, `style`, `tabindex`, `wrap`
`<tfoot>`	Configures the footer section of a table	`class`, `id`, `style`
`<th>`	Configures a table header cell in a table	`class`, `colspan`, `id`, `headers`, `rowspan`, `scope`, `style`
`<thead>`	Configures the head section of a table	`class`, `id`, `style`
`<time>`	Configures a date and/or time	`class`, `datetime`, `id`, `pubdate`, `style`
`<title>`	Configures the title of a web page document	
`<tr>`	Configures a row in a table	`class`, `id`, `style`
`<track>`	Configures a subtitle or caption track for media	`class`, `default`, `id`, `kind`, `label`, `src`, `srclang`, `style`
`<u>`	Configures text displayed with an underline	`class`, `id`, `style`
`<ul>`	Configures an unordered list	`class`, `id`, `style`
`<var>`	Configures text as a variable or placeholder text	`class`, `id`, `style`
`<video>`	Configures a video control native to the browser	`autoplay`, `class`, `controls`, `height`, `id`, `loop`, `poster`, `preload`, `src`, `style`, `width`
`<wbr>`	Configures a line-break opportunity	`class`, `id`, `style`

CSS Cheat Sheet

Commonly Used CSS Properties

Property	Description
background	Shorthand to configure all the background properties of an element Value: `background-color`, `background-image`, `background-repeat`, `background-position`
background-attachment	Configures a background image as fixed-in-place or scrolling Value: `scroll` (default) or `fixed`
background-clip	CSS3; configures the area to display the background Value: `border-box`, `padding-box`, or `content-box`
background-color	Configures the background color of an element Value: Valid color value
background-image	Configures a background image for an element Value: `url` (*file name or path to the image*), none (default) Optional new CSS3 functions: `linear-gradient()` and `radial-gradient()`
background-origin	CSS3; configures the background positioning area Value: `padding-box`, `border-box`, or `content-box`
background-position	Configures the position of a background image Value: Two percentages, pixel values, or position values (`left`, `top`, `center`, `bottom`, `right`)
background-repeat	Configures how the background image will be repeated Value: `repeat` (default), `repeat-y`, `repeat-x`, or `no-repeat`
background-size	CSS3; configures the size of the background images Value: Numeric value (px or em), percentage, `contain`, `cover`
border	Shorthand to configure the border of an element Value: `border-width`, `border-style`, `border-color`
border-bottom	Configures the bottom border of an element Value: `border-width`, `border-style`, `border-color`
border-collapse	Configures the display of borders in a table Value: `separate` (default) or `collapse`
border-color	Configures the border color of an element Value: Valid color value
border-image	CSS3; configures an image in the border of an element See http://www.w3.org/TR/css3-background/#the-border-image

(Continued)

	Description
left	Configures the left border of an element Value: `border-width`, `border-style`, `border-color`
der-radius	CSS3; configures rounded corners Value: One or two numeric values (px or em) or percentages that configure horizontal and vertical radius of the corner. If one value is provided, it applies to both horizontal and vertical radius. Related properties: `border-top-left-radius`, `border-top-right-radius`, `border-bottom-left-radius`, and `border-bottom-right-radius`
border-right	Configures the right border of an element Value: `border-width`, `border-style`, `border-color`
border-spacing	Configures the space between table cells in a table Value: Numeric value (px or em)
border-style	Configures the style of the borders around an element Value: `none` (default), `inset`, `outset`, `double`, `groove`, `ridge`, `solid`, `dashed`, or `dotted`
border-top	Configures the top border of an element Value: `border-width`, `border-style`, `border-color`
border-width	Configures the width of an element's border Value: Numeric pixel value (such as 1 px), `thin`, `medium`, or `thick`
bottom	Configures the offset position from the bottom of a containing element Value: Numeric value (px or em), percentage, or `auto` (default)
box-shadow	CSS3; configures a drop shadow on an element Value: Three or four numerical values (px or em) to indicate horizontal offset, vertical offset, blur radius, (optional) spread distance, and a valid color value. Use the `inset` keyword to configure an inner shadow.
box-sizing	CSS3; alters the default CSS box model that calculates widths and heights of elements Value: `content-box` (default), `padding-box`, or `border-box`
caption-side	Configures the placement of a table caption Value: `top` (default), or `bottom`
clear	Configures the display of an element in relation to floating elements Value: `none` (default), `left`, `right`, or `both`
color	Configures the color of text within an element Value: Valid color value
display	Configures how and if an element will display Value: `inline`, `inline-block`, `none`, `block`, `flex`, `inline-flex`, `list-item`, `table`, `table-row`, or `table-cell`

Property	Description
flex	CSS3; configures the size of each flex item proportionate to the whole Value: Numeric integer value, `auto`, `flex-grow`, `flex-shrink`, or `flex-basis`
flex-direction	CSS3; configures the direction of flex items Value: `row`, `column`, `row-reverse`, or `column-reverse`
flex-wrap	CSS3; configures whether flex items are displayed on multiple lines Value: `nowrap (default)`, `wrap`, or `wrap-reverse`
float	Configures the horizontal placement (left or right) of an element Value: `none` (default), `left`, or `right`
font	Shorthand to configure the font properties of an element Value: `font-style`, `font-variant`, `font-weight`, `font-size/line-height`, `font-family`
font-family	Configures the font typeface of text Value: List of valid font names or generic font family names
font-size	Configures the font size of text Value: Numeric value (px, pt, em), percentage value, `xx-small`, `x-small`, `small`, `medium` (default), `large`, `x-large`, `xx-large`, `smaller`, or `larger`
font-stretch	CSS3; configures a normal, condensed, or expanded face from a font family Value: `normal`, `wider`, `narrower`, `condensed`, `semi-condensed`, `expanded`, or `ultra-expanded`
font-style	Configures the font style of text Value: `normal` (default), `italic`, or `oblique`
font-variant	Configures whether text is displayed in small-caps font Value: `normal` (default) or `small-caps`
font-weight	Configures the weight (boldness) of text Value: `normal` (default), `bold`, `bolder`, `lighter`, `100`, `200`, `300`, `400`, `500`, `600`, `700`, `800`, or `900`
height	Configures the height of an element Value: Numeric value (px or em), percentage, or `auto` (default)
justify-content	CSS3; configures how the browser should display any extra space Value: `center`, `space-between`, `space-around`, `flex-start` (default), or `flex-end`
left	Configures the offset position from the left of a containing element Value: Numeric value (px or em), percentage, or `auto` (default)
letter-spacing	Configures the space between text characters Value: Numeric value (px or em) or `normal` (default)

(Continued)

Property	Description
line-height	Configures the line height of text Value: Numeric value (px or em), percentage, multiplier numeric value, or normal (default)
list-style	Shorthand to configure the properties of a list list-style-type, list-style-position, list-style-image
list-style-image	Configures an image as a list marker Value: url (*file name or path to the image*) or none (default)
list-style-position	Configures the position of the list markers Value: inside, or outside (default)
list-style-type	Configures the type of list marker displayed Value: none, circle, disc (default), square, decimal, decimal-leading-zero, Georgian, lower-alpha, lower-roman, upper-alpha, or upper-roman
margin	Shorthand to configure the margin of an element Value: One to four numeric values (px or em), percentages, auto or 0
margin-bottom	Configures the bottom margin of an element Value: Numeric value (px or em), percentage, auto or 0
margin-left	Configures the left margin of an element Value: Numeric value (px or em), percentage, auto or 0
margin-right	Configures the right margin of an element Value: Numeric value (px or em), percentage, auto or 0
margin-top	Configures the top margin of an element Value: Numeric value (px or em), percentage, auto or 0
max-height	Configures the maximum height of an element Value: Numeric value (px or em), percentage, or none (default)
max-width	Configures the maximum width of an element Value: Numeric value (px or em), percentage, or none (default)
min-height	Configures the minimum height of an element Value: Numeric value (px or em), or percentage
min-width	Configures the minimum width of an element Value: Numeric value (px or em), or percentage
opacity	CSS3; configures the transparency of an element Value: Numeric value between 1 (fully opaque) and 0 (completely transparent)
order	CSS3; configures the display of flex items in a different order than coded Value: Numeric integer
outline	Shorthand to configure an outline of an element Value: outline-width, outline-style, outline-color

Property	Description
`outline-color`	Configures the outline color of an element Value: Valid color value
`outline-style`	Configures the style of the outline around an element Value: `none` (default), `inset`, `outset`, `double`, `groove`, `ridge`, `solid`, `dashed`, or `dotted`
`outline-width`	Configures the width of an element's outline Value: Numeric pixel value (such as 1 px), `thin`, `medium`, or `thick`
`overflow`	Configures how content should display if it is too large for the area allocated Value: `visible` (default), `hidden`, `auto`, or `scroll`
`padding`	Shorthand to configure the padding of an element Value: One to four numeric values (px or em), percentages, or 0
`padding-bottom`	Configures the bottom padding of an element Value: Numeric value (px or em), percentage, or 0
`padding-left`	Configures the left padding of an element Value: Numeric value (px or em), percentage, or 0
`padding-right`	Configures the right padding of an element Value: Numeric value (px or em), percentage, or 0
`padding-top`	Configures the top padding of an element Value: Numeric value (px or em), percentage, or 0
`page-break-after`	Configures the page break after an element Value: `auto` (default), `always`, `avoid`, `left`, or `right`
`page-break-before`	Configures the page break before an element Value: `auto` (default), `always`, `avoid`, `left`, or `right`
`page-break-inside`	Configures the page break inside an element Value: `auto` (default) or `avoid`
`position`	Configures the type of positioning used to display an element Value: `static` (default), `absolute`, `fixed`, or `relative`
`right`	Configures the offset position from the right of a containing element Value: Numeric value (px or em), percentage, or `auto` (default)
`text-align`	Configures the horizontal alignment of text Value: `left (default)`, `right`, `center`, or `justify`
`text-decoration`	Configures the decoration added to text Value: `none` (default), `underline`, `overline`, `line-through`, or `blink`
`text-indent`	Configures the indentation of the first line of text Value: Numeric value (px or em), or percentage

(Continued)

Property	Description
text-outline	CSS3; configures an outline around text displayed within an element Value: One or two numerical values (px or em) to indicate thickness and (optionally) blur radius, and a valid color value
text-overflow	CSS3; configures how the browser indicates content that has overflowed the container and is not visible Value: `clip` (default), `ellipsis`, or string value
text-shadow	CSS3; configures a drop shadow on the text displayed within an element Value: Three or four numerical values (px or em) to indicate horizontal offset, vertical offset, blur radius, (optional) spread distance, and a valid color value
text-transform	Configures the capitalization of text Value: `none` (default), `capitalize`, `uppercase`, or `lowercase`
top	Configures the offset position from the top of a containing element Value: Numeric value (px or em), percentage, or `auto` (default)
transform	CSS3; configures change or transformation in the display of an element Value: A transform function such as `scale()`, `translate()`, `matrix()`, `rotate()`, `skew()`, or `perspective()`
transition	CSS3; shorthand property to configure the presentational transition of a CSS property value Value: list the value for `transition-property`, `transition-duration`, `transition-timing-function`, and `transition-delay` separated by spaces; default values can be omitted, but the first time unit applies to `transition-duration`
transition-delay	CSS3; indicates the beginning of the transition Value: default value 0 configures no delay, otherwise use a numeric value to specify time (usually in seconds)
transition-duration	CSS3; indicates the length of time to apply the transition Value: default value 0 configures an immediate transition, otherwise use a numeric value to specify time (usually in seconds)
transition-property	CSS3; indicates the CSS property that the transition applies to; a list of applicable properties is available at http://www.w3.org/TR/css3-transitions
transition-timing-function	CSS3; configures changes in the speed of the transition by describing how intermediate property values are calculated; common values include `ease` (default), `linear`, `ease-in`, `ease-out`, or `ease-in-out`
vertical-align	Configures the vertical alignment of an element Value: Numeric value (px or em), percentage, baseline (default), `sub`, `super`, `top`, `text-top`, `middle`, `bottom`, or `text-bottom`
visibility	Configures the visibility of an element Value: `visible` (default), `hidden`, or `collapse`
white-space	Configures white space inside an element Value: `normal` (default), `nowrap`, `pre`, `pre-line`, or `pre-wrap`

Property	Description
width	Configures the width of an element Value: Numeric value (px or em), percentage, or auto (default)
word-spacing	Configures the space between words within text Value: Numeric value (px or em) or auto (default)
z-index	Configures the stacking order of an element Value: A numeric value or auto (default)

Commonly Used CSS Pseudo-Classes and Pseudo-Elements

Name	Purpose
:active	Configures an element that is being clicked
:after	Inserts and configures content after an element
:before	Inserts and configures content before an element
:first-child	Configures an element that is the first child of another element
:first-letter	Configures the first character of text
:first-line	Configures the first line of text
:first-of-type	CSS3; configures the first element of the specified type
:focus	Configures an element that has keyboard focus
:hover	Configures an element that has a mouse placed over it
:last-child	CSS3; configures the last child of an element
:last-of-type	CSS3; configures the last element of the specified type
:link	Configures a hyperlink that has not been visited
:nth-of-type(n)	CSS3; configures the "nth" element of the specified type Value: a number, odd, or even
:visited	Configures a hyperlink that has been visited

Comparison of XHTML and HTML5

As you traverse the Web and view the source code of pages created by others, you may notice that the style and syntax of the coding sometimes uses XHTML syntax.

XHTML, eXtensible HyperText Markup Language, utilizes the tags and attributes of HTML along with the syntax of XML (eXtensible Markup Language). For the most part, you will use the same tags and attributes in HTML and XHTML; the major change is the syntax and additional restrictions in XHTML. The W3C has created a draft recommendation for HTML5, which is intended to be the successor to HTML4 and to replace XHTML. HTML5 incorporates features of both HTML and XHTML, adds new elements and attributes, provides new features, such as form edits and native video, and is intended to be backward compatible.

In this section we'll concentrate on the differences between XHTML and HTML5—introducing you to some specific examples of syntax differences.

XML Declaration

Since XHTML follows XML syntax, each document should begin with an XML declaration. HTML5 has no such requirement.

XHTML

```
<?xml version="1.0" encoding="UTF-8"?>
```

HTML5

Not required

Document Type Definition

XHTML 1.0, the first version of XHTML (and the version that has been most widely used on the Web), has three distinct document type definitions: strict, transitional, and frameset. HTML5 has one document type definition. The Document Type Definitions (DTDs) follow:

XHTML 1.0 Strict DTD

```
<!DOCTYPE html PUBLIC "-//W3C//DTD XHTML 1.0 Strict//EN"
"http://www.w3.org/TR/xhtml1/DTD/xhtml1-strict.dtd">
```

XHTML 1.0 Transitional DTD

```
<!DOCTYPE html PUBLIC "-//W3C//DTD XHMTL 1.0 Transitional//EN"
"http://www.w3.org/TR/xhtml1/DTD/xhmtl1-transitional.dtd">
```

XHTML 1.0 Frameset DTD

```
<!DOCTYPE html PUBLIC "-//W3C//DTD XHMTL 1.0 Frameset//EN"
"http://www.w3.org/TR/xhtml1/DTD/xhmtl1-frameset.dtd">
```

HTML5

```
<!doctype html>
```

The `<html>` Tag

XHTML requires that the root element (immediately after the DTD) is an `<html>` tag which refers to the XML namespace. HTML5 has no such namespace requirement. To assist the interpreting of page content by search engines and screen readers, use the `lang` attribute to indicate the spoken language of the web page content. See http://www.w3.org/TR/REC-html40/struct/dirlang.html\#adef-lang.

XHTML

```
<html xmlns="http://www.w3.org/1999/xhtml" lang="en" xml:lang="en">
```

HTML5

```
<html lang="en">
```

Uppercase versus Lowercase

The XHTML standard follows XML syntax, which requires lowercase. HTML5 allows both upper and lowercase letters; lowercase is preferred.

XHTML

```
<table>
```

HTML5

Either `<TABLE>` or `<table>`

Note: lowercase is preferred.

Quotation Marks with Attributes

The XHTML standard requires that the values for all attributes be enclosed in quotation marks. This is recommended (but not required) when coding HTML5.

XHTML

```
<p id="article">
```

HTML5

```
Either <p id=article> or <p id="article">
```

Start and End Tags

The XHTML standard requires both opening (start) and closing (end) tags for all elements except self-closing (void) elements (such as br, hr, img, input, link, and meta). HTML5 requires both start and end tags for all non-void elements except body, dd, dt, head, html, li, option, p, tbody, td, tfoot, th, thead, and tr. However, it is good coding practice to always code both start and end tags for nonvoid elements.

XHTML

```
<p>This is the first paragraph.</p>
<p>This is the second paragraph.</p>
```

HTML5

```
<p>This is the first paragraph.</p>
<p>This is the second paragraph.</p>
```

Self-Closing Elements

The XHTML standard requires that all self-closing elements are properly closed using " />". HTML5 does not require this and refers to self-closing elements as void elements.

XHTML

```
This is the first line.<br />
This is the second line.
```

HTML5

```
This is the first line.<br>
This is the second line.
```

Attribute Values

The XHTML standard requires that all attributes be assigned values. HTML5 allows some attributes, such as `checked`, to be minimized. Since these attributes only have a single value, HTML5 does not require that the value be provided.

XHTML 1.0

```
<input type="radio" checked="checked" name="gender" id="gender"
value="male" />
```

HTML5

Either
```
<input type="radio" checked id="gender" name="gender" value="male">
```
or
```
<input type="radio" checked="checked" id="gender" name="gender"
value="male">
```

Elements New to HTML5

The following elements are new in HTML5: article, aside, audio, bdi, canvas, command, datalist, details, embed, figcaption, figure, footer, header, keygen, main, mark, meter, nav, output, picture, progress, ruby, rt, rp, section, source, summary, time, track, video, and wbr. See the HTML5 Cheat Sheet Appendix and http://www.w3.org/TR/html5-diff/#new-elements for information about these new elements.

Attributes New to HTML5

HTML5 includes a variety of new attributes and new attribute values. The `autocomplete`, `autofocus`, `min`, `max`, `multiple`, `pattern`, `placeholder`, `required`, and `step` attributes are new for the input element. The textarea element now supports the following new attributes: `autofocus`, `maxlength`, `placeholder`, `required`, and `wrap`. The `autofocus` and `required` attributes are new for the select element. The input element supports the following new values for the type attribute: `color`, `date`, `datetime`, `datetime-local`, `email`, `month`, `number`, `range`, `search`, `tel`, `time`, `url`, and `week`. The `srcset`, `sizes`, and `longdesc` attributes are new for the img element. See http://www.w3.org/TR/html5-diff/#new-elements for more information about these new attributes and attribute values.

Elements Considered Obsolete in HTML5

The following elements are obsolete in HTML5: acronym, applet, basefont, big, center, dir, font, frame, frameset, isindex, noframes, strike, and tt. An obsolete element may be displayed by a browser. However, the code will not pass syntax validation and browsers may drop support of obsolete elements/attributes at any time. See http://www.whatwg.org/specs/web-apps/current-work/multipage/ obsolete.html#non-conforming-features for suggestions on replacing these elements.

Attributes Considered Obsolete in HTML5

A number of attributes present in XHTML and HTML4 are obsolete in HTML5, including align, alink, background, bgcolor, border, cellpadding, cellspacing, clear, frameborder, hspace, link, marginheight, marginwidth, noshade, nowrap, summary, text, valign, and vspace. See http://www.w3.org/TR/html5-diff/#obsolete-attributes for a complete list.

Elements Changed in HTML5

The purpose of the address, b, cite, dl, hr, I, label, menu, noscript, s, script, small, strong, and u elements was changed in HTML5. Visit http://www.w3.org/TR/html5-diff/#changed-elements for detailed information.

Attributes Changed in HTML5

The use of over 20 attributes was changed in HTML5. Of note is that the id value can now begin with any nonspace character. Visit http://www.w3.org/TR/html5-diff/#changedattributes for detailed information.

Video and Audio Support

XHTML required the use of the object element to provide a video or audio player on a web page and was dependent on the visitor's browser having the corresponding plug-in or helper application installed. HTML5 supports video and audio native to the browser using the video, audio, and source elements. Because all browsers do not support the same media encoding formats, multiple versions of the media file should be provided when using HTML5 video and audio elements. The following code samples configure an audio file player on a web page.

XHTML

```
<object data="soundloop.mp3" height="50" width="100" type="audio/mpeg"
title="Music Sound Loop">
  <param name="src" value="soundloop.mp3" />
  <param name="controller" value="true" />
  <param name="autoplay" value="false" />
</object>
```

HTML5

```
<audio controls="controls">
  <source src="soundloop.mp3" type="audio/mpeg">
  <source src="soundloop.ogg" type="audio/ogg">
  <a href="soundloop.mp3">Download the Soundloop</a> (MP3)
</audio>
```

Adobe Flash Support

XHTML required the use of the object element to play a Flash .swf file on a web page, although the embed element had been used and supported by browsers for many years. HTML5 still supports the use of the object element. However, the embed element is now officially supported in HTML5.

XHTML

```
<object type="application/x-shockwave-flash" data="lighthouse.swf"
width="320" height="240" title="Door County Lighthouse Cruise">
  <param name="movie" value="lighthouse.swf">
  <param name="bgcolor" value="#FFFFFF">
  <param name="quality" value="high">
</object>
```

HTML5

```
<embed type="application/x-shockwave-flash" src="lighthouse.swf"
quality="high" width="320" height="240"
title="Door County Lighthouse Cruise">
```

Document Outline

The document outline is the structure of a document indicated by the heading-level elements, such as h1, h2, and so on. XHTML coding practice is to use only one h1 element on a web page and to configure the heading-level elements in outline format. Outlining is different in HTML5. Instead of a solely heading-level outline, the HTML5 outline is also configured using sectioning elements (such as section, article, nav, and aside), each of which may contain headings. Try out an HTML5 outliner at http://gsnedders.html5.org/outliner.

JavaScript and the `<script>` Tag

XHTML considers JavaScript statements to be arbitrary character data (CDATA). The XML parser should not process them. The CDATA statement tells the XML parser to ignore the JavaScript. This is not part of HTML and not supported by many current browsers.

XHTML

```
<script type="text/javascript">

<![CDATA[

...JavaScript statements go here

]]>
</script>
```

HTML5

```
<script>

...JavaScript statements go here

</script>
```

An alternative method for using JavaScript on a web page that is supported by XHTML standards is to place JavaScript statements in a separate (.js) file. This file can be configured by the `<script>` tag. HTML5 also supports this syntax.

XHTML

```
<script src="myscript.js" type="text/javascript"></script>
```

HTML5

```
<script src="myscript.js">
```

Wrap-Up

Visit the W3C's website for the most up-to-date information about XHTML (http://www.w3.org/TR/xhtml1), HTML5 (http://www.w3.org/TR/html5), and HTML5.1 (http://www.w3.org/TR/html51).

WCAG 2.0 Quick Reference

Perceivable

▶ **1.1 Text Alternatives:** Provide text alternatives for any nontext content so that it can be changed into other forms people need, such as large print, Braille, speech, symbols, or simpler language. *You configure images (Chapter 5) and multimedia (Chapter 11) on web pages and provide for alternate text content.*

▶ **1.2 Time-Based Media:** Provide alternatives for time-based media. *We don't create time-based media in this textbook, but keep this in mind for the future if you create animation or use client-side scripting for features such as interactive slide shows.*

▶ **1.3 Adaptable:** Create content that can be presented in different ways (for example, simpler layout) without losing information or structure. *In Chapter 2, you use block elements (such as headings, paragraphs, and lists) to create single-column web pages. You create multicolumn web pages in Chapter 7.* You use media queries and apply principles of responsive web design in *Chapter 8.*

▶ **1.4 Distinguishable:** Make it easier for users to see and hear content, including separating foreground from background. *You are aware of the importance of good contrast between text and background.*

Operable

▶ **2.1 Keyboard Accessible:** Make all functionality available from a keyboard. *In Chapter 8 you configure hyperlinks to named fragment identifiers on a web page. The label element is introduced in Chapter 10.*

▶ **2.2 Enough Time:** Provide users enough time to read and use content. *We don't create time-based media in this textbook, but keep this in mind for the future if you create animation or use client-side scripting for features such as interactive slide shows.*

▶ **2.3 Seizures:** Do not design content in a way that is known to cause seizures. *Be careful when you use animation created by others; web pages should not contain elements that flash more than three times in a one-second period.*

▶ **2.4 Navigable:** Provide ways to help users navigate, find content, and determine where they are. *In Chapter 2 you use block elements (such as headings and lists) to organize web page content. In Chapter 8 you configure hyperlinks to named fragment identifiers on a web page.*

Understandable

▶ **3.1 Readable:** Make text content readable and understandable. *You explore techniques used when writing for the Web in Chapter 3.*

▶ **3.2 Predictable:** Make web pages appear and operate in predictable ways. *The websites you create in the case studies have a consistent design, with clearly labeled and functioning hyperlinks.*

▶ **3.3 Input Assistance:** Help users avoid and correct mistakes. *In Chapter 10, you used new HTML5 form controls and attributes to verify entry of information on web page forms and provide feedback to users.*

Robust

▶ **4.1 Compatible:** *Maximize compatibility with current and future user agents, including assistive technologies. You provide for future compatibility by writing code that follows W3C Recommendations (standards).*

The WCAG 2.0 Quick Reference List (https://www.w3.org/WAI/WCAG20/quickref/) entries are copyright © 2016 World Wide Web Consortium, (MIT, ERCIM, Keio, Beihang). http://www.w3.org/Consortium/Legal/2015/doc-license.

You'll find the most up-to-date information about WCAG 2.0 at the following resources:

▶ Overview of WCAG 2.0
  http://www.w3.org/TR/WCAG20

▶ Understanding WCAG 2.0
  http://www.w3.org/TR/UNDERSTANDING-WCAG20

▶ How to Meet WCAG 2.0
  http://www.w3.org/WAI/WCAG20/quickref

▶ Techniques for WCAG 2.0
  http://www.w3.org/TR/WCAG-TECHS

Landmark Roles with ARIA

The W3C's Web Accessibility Initiative (WAI) has developed a standard to provide for additional accessibility, called **Accessible Rich Internet Applications (ARIA)**. ARIA provides methods intended to increase the accessibility of web pages and web applications by identifying the role or purpose of an element on a web page (http://www.w3.org/WAI/intro/aria).

We'll focus on ARIA landmark roles in this appendix. A **landmark** on a web page is a major section such as a banner, navigation, main content, and so on. **ARIA landmark roles** allow web developers to configure semantic descriptions of HTML elements using the **role attribute** to indicate landmarks on the web page. For example, to indicate the landmark role of main on an element containing the main content of a web page document, code `role="main"` on the opening tag.

People visiting a web page with a screen reader or other assistive technology can access the landmark roles to quickly skip to specific areas on a web page (watch the video at http://www.youtube.com/watch?v=IhWMou12_Vk for a demonstration). Visit http://www.w3.org/TR/wai-aria/roles#landmark_roles for a complete list of ARIA landmark roles.

Commonly used ARIA landmark roles include:

- `banner` (a header/logo area)
- `navigation` (a collection of navigation elements)
- `main` (the main content of a document)
- `complementary` (a supporting part of the web page document, designed to be complementary to the main content)
- `contentinfo` (an area that contains information about the content such as copyright)
- `form` (an area that contains a form)
- `search` (an area of a web page that provides search functionality)

The code for the body section of sample web page with the banner, navigation, main, and contentinfo roles configured is shown below. Notice that while the role attribute will not change the way the web page displays, it offers additional information about the document that can be used by assistive technologies.

```
<body>
  <header role="banner">
    <h1>Heading Logo Banner</h1>
  </header>
  <nav role="navigation">
    <a href="index.html">Home</a> <a href="contact.html">Contact</a>
  </nav>
  <main role="main">
    This is the main content area.
  </main>
  <footer role="contentinfo">
    Copyright &copy; 2018 Your Name Here
  </footer>
</body>
```

CSS Flexible Box Layout

CSS Flexbox Layout

Since the early days of the Web, designers have striven to configure multi-column web pages. Back in the 1990s, it was common to use tables to configure a two- or three-column page layout. As browsers offered increased support for CSS, the CSS float property technique (see Chapter 6) to create the look of multi-column pages became popular and is still widely used today. However, the quest for a more robust multi-column layout has continued. There is a new emerging flexbox layout technique that uses the CSS3 Flexible Box Layout Module (https://www.w3.org/TR/css-flexbox-1) which is currently in W3C Candidate Recommendation status.

The purpose of **flexbox** is to provide for a flexible layout—elements contained within a flex container can be configured either horizontally or vertically in a flexible manner with flexible sizing. In addition to changing the horizontal or vertical organization of elements, flexbox can also be used to change the order of display of the elements. Due to its flexibility, flexbox is well suited for responsive web design!

At the time this text was written, current versions of Firefox, Chrome, Opera, Microsoft Edge, and Safari supported flexbox. Check http://caniuse.com/flexbox for the current level of browser support.

Configure a Flexible Container

To configure an area on a web page that uses flexbox layout, you need to indicate the **flex container**, which is the element that will contain the flexible area. Use the CSS `display` property to configure a flex container. The value `flex` indicates a flexible block container. The value `inline-flex` indicates a flexible inline-display container. Elements contained within a flex container are referred to as **flex items**.

The `flex-direction` Property

Configure the direction of the flex items with the **`flex-direction` property**. The value `row` configures a horizontal direction. The value `column` configures a vertical direction. For example, to configure an id named demo as a flexible block container with a horizontal flexible flow, code the following CSS:

```
#demo { display: flex;
        flex-direction: row; }
```

The `flex-wrap` Property

The **`flex-wrap` property** configures whether flex items are displayed on multiple lines. The default value is `nowrap`, which configures single-line display. The value `wrap` will allow the flex items to display on multiple lines, which could be useful for navigation or for an image gallery.

The `justify-content` Property

The **justify-content property** configures how the browser should display any extra space that may exist in the flex container. A list of values for the `justify-content` property is available at https://www.w3.org/TR/css-flexbox-1/#justify-content-property. The value `center` will center the flex items with equal amounts of empty space before and after. The value `space-between` evenly distributes the flex items and allocates empty space between them.

Configure the Flex Items

By default, all elements contained within a flex container are flexible in size, are allocated the same amount of display area in the flex container, and display in the same order they are coded in. You can modify the default display with CSS, including the new flex and order properties.

The `flex` Property

Use the **flex property** to customize the size of each flex item. The value of the flex property does not correspond to a unit of measure but is proportionate to the whole. Values for the flex property include both keywords and positive numbers. See https://www.w3.org/TR/css-flexbox-1/#flex-common for a list of values commonly used with the flex property. We'll focus on the numeric values in this section. The default value is 1. If you configure an element with `flex: 2;` then it will take up twice as much space within the container element as the others. Since the values work in proportion to the whole, use flex values for companion flex items that add up to 10. Examine the three-column page layout in Figure Flex.1 and notice how the `nav`, `main`, and `aside` elements are within another element that will serve as a flex container. The CSS to configure the proportion of the flexible area allocated to each column could be as follows:

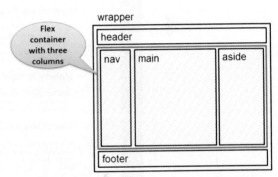

FIGURE Flex.1 *Three-column page layout with the flex container indicated.*

```
nav    { flex: 1; }
main   { flex: 7; }
aside  { flex: 2;}
```

Notice in Figure Flex.1 that we are using a flex container for the portion of the layout that we'd like to treat as one "row." Flexbox is best suited to configure a portion of a page layout in a row or in a column. In our example, we're using Flexbox to configure the "row" consisting of the nav, main, and aside elements.

The `order` Property

Use the **order property** to display the flex items in a different order than they are coded. The `order` property accepts numeric values. The default value of the order property is 0. To configure an element to display *before* the other flex items within the flex container, set its order to −1. Similarly, to configure an element to display *after* the other flex items within the flex container, set its order to 1. You'll practice using the `order` property in the next Hands-On Practice.

In this Hands-On Practice you'll use flexbox layout to configure a three-column layout (Figure Flex.1) on a web page and also apply media queries to modify the display for mobile devices. Figure Flex.2 shows the three-column desktop browser display.

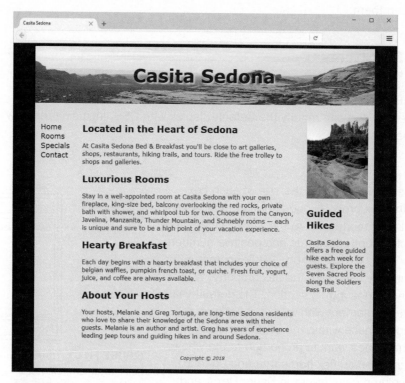

FIGURE Flex.2 *Three-column layout using flexbox.*

You'll configure the desktop browser display first and then modify the media queries to configure a single-column tablet display with horizontal navigation (Figure Flex.3) and a single-column smartphone display with navigation reordered to appear above the footer (Figure Flex.4).

Create a folder named flex. Copy the starter.html file from the student files flexbox folder into the flex folder and rename it index.html. Copy the header.jpg and pools.jpg images from the student files flexbox folder into your flex folder. When you launch a browser to view the index.html file, it will look similar to Figure Flex.5 with a single-column layout.

1. View the code in a text editor and locate the opening div tag coded above the nav element—this is the beginning of the flexible container. Edit the HTML and assign this div to an id named demo. Notice that three elements are contained within the #demo div: the nav element, the main element, and the aside element. These three elements are flex items.

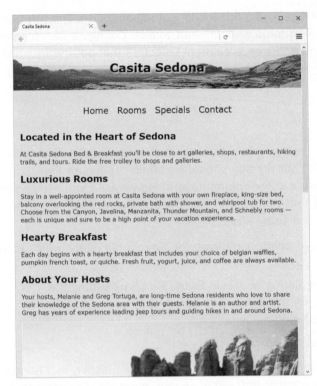

FIGURE Flex.3 *Single-column tablet display.*

FIGURE Flex.4
Smartphone display.

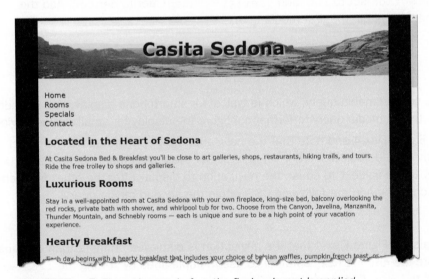

FIGURE Flex.5 *The web page before the flexbox layout is applied.*

2. Edit the embedded CSS above the media queries and add styles to configure the flexible layout:

a. To create a flexible container that displays its flex items in a row, configure an id selector named `demo` with `display` set to `flex` and `flex-direction` set to `row`.

```
#demo { display: flex;
        flex-direction: row; }
```

b. By default, the browser will display the flex items as the same size. The wireframe in Figure Flex.1 shows the flex items with different widths. Configure CSS for the nav element, main element, and aside element selectors that set the flex property as follows:

```
nav { flex: 1; }
main { flex: 7; }
aside { flex: 2; }
```

3. Save the index.html file and display it in a browser that supports flexbox, such as Firefox, Chrome or Opera. Your display should be similar to Figure Flex.2. What an easy way to configure a three-column layout! However, if you resize your browser to be smaller, you'll find that we need to make some adjustments for typical tablet and smartphone display sizes.

4. Open the index.html file in a text editor and locate the first media query, which is for typical tablet display.

   a. Configure the single-column display shown in Figure Flex.3 by setting the flex-direction property for the demo id to the value column. Add the following CSS within the first media query:

   ```
   #demo { flex-direction: column; }
   ```

   b. Review Figure Flex.3 and notice that the navigation hyperlinks display in a horizontal manner even though they are structured within an unordered list. To accomplish the horizontal display, configure a nav ul selector with display set to flex, flex-direction set to row, and justify-content set to center. Add the following CSS within the first media query:

   ```
   nav ul { display: flex;
            flex-direction: row;
            justify-content: center; }
   ```

5. Locate the second media query, which is typical for smartphone display. You will add style rules to this media query to further configure the display for small mobile devices.

   a. Review Figure Flex.4 and note that the navigation now appears above the footer. Recall that the default flex order value is 0. Set the nav element selector's order property to the value 1 to cause the navigation to display after the other flex items in the container. Add the following CSS within the second media query:

   ```
   nav { order: 1; }
   ```

   b. Notice also in Figure Flex.4 that the navigation is displayed on more than one line. Configure the nav ul flex container to use multiple lines by setting the flex-wrap property to wrap. Add the following CSS within the second media query:

   ```
   nav ul { flex-wrap: wrap; }
   ```

6. Save the index.html file and display it in a browser that supports flexbox, such as Chrome or Opera. Your desktop display should be similar to Figure Flex.2. When you resize your browser to be smaller, the display should be similar to Figure Flex.3 or Figure Flex.4. A suggested solution is in the student files flexbox/practice folder.

FAQ

What happens when browsers that don't support flexbox display the web page?

Browsers that don't support flexbox will ignore the new properties and values. So, be sure your page is still readable and usable if the new flexbox properties are not supported. Flexbox is an intriguing layout technique that promises to simplify page layout for web developers. Check http://caniuse.com/flexbox for the current level of browser support.

Explore FURTHER

You've just been introduced to several new CSS properties used with Flexible Box Layout, but there is much more to explore about this powerful new layout technique. Visit the following resources to delve deeper into flexbox:

▶ http://css-tricks.com/snippets/css/a-guide-to-flexbox

▶ http://demo.agektmr.com/flexbox

▶ https://developer.mozilla.org/en-US/docs/Web/Guide/CSS/Flexible_boxes

Index

application programming interface (API)
   geolocation API, 382
   HTML API, 382–383
   jQuery API, 381
   offline web application, 382–383
   web storage API, 382
area element (`<area>`), 164
article element (`<article>`), HTML5, 256
aside element (`<aside>`), 256, 257
assistive technology, 402
attributes
   audio element, 362
   check box form controls, 318
   date and time form controls, 342
   embed element, 360–361
   form element, 313
   hidden fields, 320
   HTML, 17
   HTML5, 410–414
   iframe element, 369
   image element, 144
   lang attribute in web pages, 19
   media attribute, 274
   new in HTML5, 425
   obsolete and changed in HTML5, 425
   option element, 325
   password box form controls, 321
   radio button form controls, 319
   scrolling text box form controls, 322
   select element, 324
   selector, 331
   `sizes` attribute, 274, 276, 277
   slider, spinner, and date/time form controls,
      340–341
   source element, 274
   `srcset` attribute, 274, 276, 277
   submit buttons and reset buttons, 316
   table attributes obsolete in HTML5, 293
   table data and table header cell elements,
      294–295
   table element, 300
   text form control, 337
   use of quotation marks in HTML5
      and XHTML, 423
   values in HTML5 and XHTML, 424
   video element, 364
Audacity application, 363
audio. *see also* multimedia

   common file types, 357
   fallback content, 363
   file accessing, 358
   file troubleshooting, 359
   HTML5 audio element, 362–363
automated accessibility testing, 403

B

`background-attachment` property, 149
`background-clip` property, 190–191
`background-color` property, 112, 113, 148
`background-image` property, 148
background images
   applying multiple, 152–153
   clipping and sizing, 190–191
   fluid display of, 272
   overview of, 148–149
   positioning, 150–151
   resizing and scaling, 192–193
   tiling with `background-repeat` property, 150
`background-origin` property, 191
`background-position` property, 150–151
`background-repeat` property, 150, 151
`background-size` property, 192–193
Berners-Lee, Tim, 3
Bezier curve, 373
`bgcolor` attribute
   configuring tables in HTML, 300
   obsolete in HTML5, 293
block anchor, 53
blockquote element (`<blockquote>`), HTML,
      34–35
body element (`<body>`), HTML, 19
body element selector, 226
`border` attribute, 292–293
`border` property, 182–183
`border-radius` property, 184–185
borders
   configuring, 182–183
   in CSS box model, 179
   rounded corners, 184–185
`border-spacing` property, 301
`border-style` property, 182–183
box model
   in action, 179
   border area, 179
   content area, 178

World Intellectual Property Organization (WIPO), 15
World Wide Web (WWW). *see also* Internet
  birth of, 3
  ethical use of, 15
  hyperlinks, 14
World Wide Web Consortium (W3C)
  CSS standard, 110
  HSL color values, 115
  HTML5 conformance checks, 361
  markup languages and, 17
  Markup Validation Service, 46–47, 132–133
  One Web initiative, 100, 263
  recommendations, 4, 262–263
  WAI, 4
  Web Content Accessibility Guidelines, 402
wrapper id selector, 226

XHTML. *see* eXtensible Hypertext Markup
    Language (XHTML)
XML. *see also* eXtensible Markup Language (XML)
  declaration in HTML5 *vs.* XHTML, 422
  overview of, 17

YouTube videos, 359, 368–369

Zeldman, Jeffrey, 228

Credits

Cover image © Warut Prathaksithorn/123RF

Figures 1.2, 1.4, 1.9, 1.10, 5.3–5.5, 5.23, 10.18, 12.2 © Terry Ann Morris, Ed.D. Reprinted with permission

Figures 1.12–1.14, 4.11, 4.16, 5.10, 8.1, 8.3, 10.26, 10.31, 11.5, 11.8 © Microsoft Corporation

Table 3.1 © Terry Ann Morris, Ed.D.

Figure 8.32 Testing a web page with Opera Mobile Emulator screenshot. Copyright © Opera Software A/S. Reprinted with permission

Figure 12.3 © FileZilla. Reprinted with permission

Figures 2.14–2.16, 4.22–4.24, WCAG 2.0 Quick Reference © W3C (World Wide Web Consortium)

Figure 10.27 A spinner control displayed in the Google Chrome browser. Copyright © Google, Inc.

Figure 10.28 A date form control displayed in the Google Chrome browser. Copyright © Google, Inc.

Figure 10.29 The Google Chrome browser supports the color-well form control. Copyright © Google, Inc.

Figures 1.11, 10.22, 10.25, 10.27, 10.30, 10.32, 11.4 and Mozilla Firefox frames that are used around the OM figures © Mozilla Foundation

TEXT:

Page 333: Reprinted with permission of the Council of Better Business Bureaus, Inc. Copyright 2014. Council of Better Business Bureaus, Inc., 3033 Wilson Blvd., 6th Floor, Arlington, VA 22201, www.bbb.org

Web Safe Color Palette

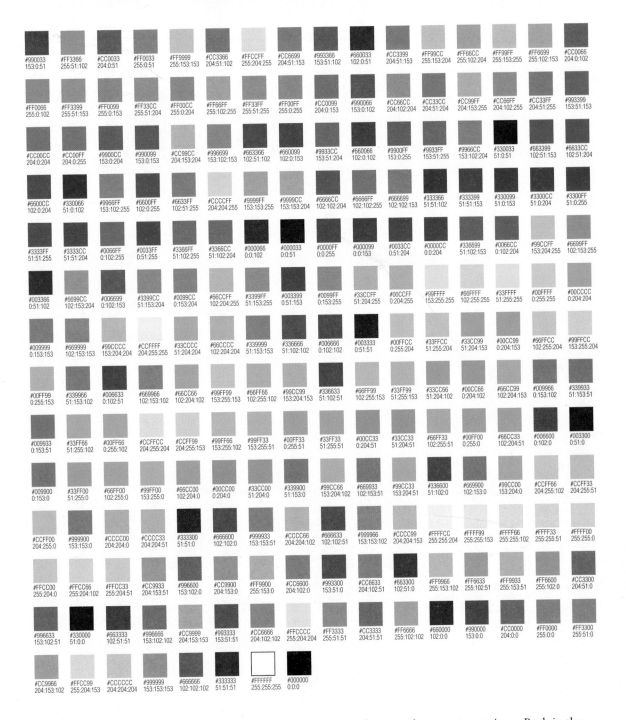

Web safe colors look the most similar on various computer platforms and computer monitors. Back in the day of eight-bit color it was crucial to use web safe colors. Since most modern video drivers support millions of colors the use of web safe colors is now optional. The hexadecimal and decimal RGB values are shown for each color in the palette above.

```
function f1(x)
{
  var y = prompt('      ')
  var z = document.getElementById('+1').value

  alert((x+y+z)/3)          var avg=    alert((parseFloat(y) + parseFloat
    3                                              (z) + x)/3)

      parseFloat !  Δ from
                       string → #
```